EIGHTEENTH-CENTURY NATURALISTS OF HUDSON BAY

MCGILL-QUEEN'S NATIVE AND NORTHERN SERIES

Bruce G. Trigger, Editor

1 *When the Whalers Were Up North*
   Inuit Memories from the Eastern Arctic
   Dorothy Harley Eber

2 *The Challenge of Arctic Shipping*
   Science, Environmental Assessment, and
   Human Values
   David L. VanderZwaag and
   Cynthia Lamson, Editors

3 *Lost Harvests*
   Prairie Indian Reserve Farmers and
   Government Policy
   Sarah Carter

4 *Native Liberty, Crown Sovereignty*
   The Existing Aboriginal Right of
   Self-Government in Canada
   Bruce Clark

4 *Unravelling the Franklin Mystery*
   Inuit Testimony
   David C. Woodman

6 *Otter Skins, Boston Ships, and China*
   Goods
   The Maritime Fur Trade of the Northwest
   Coast, 1785–1841
   James R. Gibson

7 *From Wooden Ploughs to Welfare*
   The Story of the Western Reserves
   Helen Buckley

8 *In Business for Ourselves*
   Northern Entrepreneurs
   Wanda A. Wuttunee

9 *For an Amerindian Autohistory*
   An Essay on the Foundations of a Social
   Ethic
   Georges E. Sioui

10 *Strangers Among Us*
   David Woodman

11 *When the North Was Red*
   Aboriginal Education in Soviet Siberia
   Dennis A. Bartels and Alice L.
   Bartels

12 *From Talking Chiefs to a Native Corporate*
   Elite
   The Birth of Class and Nationalism
   among Canadian Inuit
   Marybelle Mitchell

13 *Cold Comfort*
   My Love Affair with the Arctic
   Graham W. Rowley

14 *The True Spirit and Original Intent of*
   Treaty 7
   Treaty 7 Elders and Tribal Council
   with Walter Hildebrandt, Dorothy
   First Rider, and Sarah Carter

15 *This Distant and Unsurveyed Country*
A Woman's Winter at Baffin Island,
1857–1858
W. Gillies Ross

16 *Images of Justice*
Dorothy Harley Eber

17 *Capturing Women*
The Manipulation of Cultural Imagery in
Canada's Prairie West
Sarah A. Carter

18 *Social and Environmental Impacts of the*
James Bay Hydroelectric Project
Edited by James F. Hornig

19 *Saqiyuq*
Stories from the Lives of Three Inuit
Women
Nancy Wachowich in collaboration
with Apphia Agalakti Awa, Rhoda
Kaukjak Katsak, and Sandra
Pikujak Katsak

20 *Justice in Paradise*
Bruce Clark

21 *Aboriginal Rights and Self-Government*
The Canadian and Mexican Experience in
North American Perspective
Edited by Curtis Cook and Juan D.
Lindau

22 *Harvest of Souls*
The Jesuit Missions and Colonialism in
North America, 1632–1650
Carole Blackburn

23 *Bounty and Benevolence*
A History of Saskatchewan Treaties
Arthur J. Ray, Jim Miller, and Frank
Tough

24 *The People of Denendeh*
Ethnohistory of the Indians of Canada's
Northwest Territories
June Helm

25 *The Marshall Decision and Native Rights*
Ken Coates

26 *The Flying Tiger*
Women Shamans and Storytellers of the
Amur
Kira Van Deusen

27 *Alone in Silence*
European Women in the Canadian North
before 1940
Barbara E. Kelcey

28 *The Arctic Voyages of Martin Frobisher*
An Elizabethan Adventure
Robert McGhee

29 *Northern Experience and the Myths of*
Canadian Culture
Renée Hulan

30 *The White Man's Gonna Getcha*
The Colonial Challenge to the Crees in
Quebec
Toby Morantz

31 *The Heavens Are Changing*
Nineteenth-Century Protestant Missions
and Tsimshian Christianity
Susan Neylan

32 *Arctic Migrants / Arctic Villagers*
    The Transformation of Inuit Settlement in
    the Central Arctic
    David Damas

33 *Arctic Justice*
    On Trial for Murder – Pond Inlet, 1923
    Shelagh D. Grant

34 *Eighteenth-Century Naturalists of*
    Hudson Bay
    Stuart Houston, Tim Ball, and
    Mary Houston

EIGHTEENTH-CENTURY NATURALISTS
OF HUDSON BAY

Stuart Houston, Tim Ball, and Mary Houston

McGill-Queen's University Press

Montreal & Kingston · London · Ithaca

© McGill-Queen's University Press 2003
ISBN 0-7735-2285-9

Legal deposit third quarter 2003
Bibliothèque nationale du Québec

Printed in Canada on acid-free paper that is 100% ancient forest free
(100% post-consumer recycled), processed chlorine free.

This book has been published with the help of a grant from the
Canadian Federation for the Humanities and Social Sciences, through
the Aid to Scholarly Publications program using funds provided by
the Social Sciences and Humanities Research Council of Canada.

McGill-Queen's University Press acknowledges the support of the
Canada Council for the Arts for our publishing program. We also
acknowledge the financial support of the Government of Canada
through the Book Publishing Industry Development Program (BPIDP)
for our publishing activities

National Library of Canada Cataloguing in Publication

Houston, Stuart
Eighteenth-century naturalists of Hudson Bay / Stuart Houston, Tim
Ball, and Mary Houston.
Includes bibliographical references and index.
ISBN 0-7735-2285-9
1. Naturalists – Great Britain – Biography.   2. Naturalists – Hudson
Bay Region – Biography.   3. Hudson's Bay Company – Biography.
I. Ball, Tim   II. Houston, Mary   III. Title.
QH26.H68 2003   508'.092'241   C2003-904457-2

Typeset in 10.5/13 Monotype Baskerville and 10/13 Sabon and
Sabon CE. Book design and typesetting by zijn digital.

TO WILLIAM B. EWART, MD, FRCPC, 1925–1995

This book is dedicated to the memory of Bill Ewart, who graduated from the University of Manitoba with his MD and the Neil John McLean Scholarship in 1952.[1] Bill was the first to try to persuade the Hudson's Bay Company to transfer its archives from London, England, to Winnipeg, Manitoba.[2] After the transfer, Bill spent much of his spare time in the archives. There he read each of the York Factory journals and made notes on each episode of illness recorded therein. He published landmark medical-history papers in *The Beaver* and the *Canadian Medical Association Journal*, appropriately cited in this book.

William Bissett Ewart was born in Red Deer, Alberta, on 13 May 1925. After living briefly in Fort William, Ontario, the family moved to Winnipeg in 1936. Bill attended La Verendrye, Laura Secord, and Gordon Bell schools, graduating from Grade 12 at the age of sixteen.

Bill joined the Canadian Navy at eighteen and served in the Pacific. After discharge as an able seaman he returned to the University of Manitoba, graduating with a BSc in 1947. Bill was involved in a successful campaign to eliminate ethnic and sexual discrimination and to increase medical-school grants for veterans.

Bill's interest in history began with his summer employment as a medical student with the tuberculosis survey in northern Manitoba. He became fascinated by the lives of the early settlers and the battles they waged against scurvy and smallpox.

He began his medical practice in Ponteix, Saskatchewan, where he formed a lasting friendship with Dr Vince Matthews, who later became Saskatchewan's deputy minister of health. This association spawned Bill's life-long interest in the delivery of medical and health services. In subsequent

---

[1] He graduated one year behind Stuart Houston, an enthusiastic supporter of his efforts from 1947 until Bill's death.

[2] As recounted by Deidre Simmons in Appendix A.

years he contributed frequently to public debate and government policy-making in these areas in Manitoba.

After two years at Ponteix, Bill returned to the Winnipeg General Hospital for post-graduate training in internal medicine. He was chief resident 1957–58, then went to England to study gastroenterology at Middlesex Hospital. In 1959–60, as medical adviser to Care Services, Manitoba Department of Health, he helped to develop nursing-home standards. In 1960 he joined the Winnipeg Clinic.

Bill served for many years on the executive of the Manitoba Medical Association, was a member of the board of the Manitoba College of Physicians and Surgeons 1976–90, and its president in 1988–89. He also served as a member of the Manitoba Health Commission, 1977–81. He published scientific articles in *Lancet* and in the *Canadian Medical Association Journal*.

Bill also served as a member of the executive of the Manitoba Museum of Man and Nature. He was president of the University of Manitoba Alumni Association 1970–71, and president of the Citizens Committee on Public Education in Manitoba.

Bill supported his friend Dr George Johnson when George became Manitoba's minister of health. Later, when Dr Johnson became lieutenant-governor of Manitoba, December 1986 to March 1993, Bill served as civilian aide-de-camp to the lieutenant-governor. Earlier, Bill had been president of the Crescentwood Progressive Conservative constituency association.

An enthusiast, with a lilt in his voice and a twinkle in his eye, Bill's sense of humour prevailed even during the darkest days when his first wife, Signe, was ill.

Bill's medical career was best noted for the care and attention he bestowed upon his patients. His knowledge of medicine, and the empathy and consideration he showed in practice, earned him the respect and affection of all those he attended. He was, in every sense of the term, an excellent physician.

CONTENTS

Illustrations   xi

Tables   xv

Colour plates   following page xvi

Acknowledgments   xvii

Supplementary Natural History Documents   xix

Abbreviations   xxi

Foreword   xxiii
Judith Hudson Beattie

Introduction   3

1   The European Connection   15

2   Alexander Light   34

3   James Isham   41

4   Humphrey Marten   55

5   Andrew Graham   61

6   Thomas Hutchins   66

7   Moses Norton   79

8   Samuel Hearne   81

9   Peter Fidler   92

10   Natural History   98

11   Climatology   113

12   In striking contrast: Charleston   135

APPENDICES

A   Sailing Ships to York Factory, 1716–1827   145

B   Provenance of Hudson's Bay Company Journals   159
    Deidre A. Simmons

C   The Ten HBC Manuscripts of Graham and Hutchins   161
    Stuart and Mary Houston

D   Ten-Year Cycles   177
    Stuart Houston

E   How the HBC Swan Quill and Swan Skin Trade Almost Extirpated
    the Trumpeter Swan   188
    Stuart Houston, Mary Houston, and Henry M. Reeves

F   How the Canada Goose Got Its Name before There Was a
    Canada   200
    Stuart Houston

G   Cree Names for Natural History Species   203
    compiled by Stuart Houston, Mary Houston, and Arok Wolvengrey

    Notes   253

    References   293

    Index   319

ILLUSTRATIONS

I.1 Map of HBC Territory, 1670–1870, showing approximate limits of tree line and permafrost, both continuous and discontinuous   5

I.2 York Factory, sketch by Samuel Hearne, 1 March 1797. Engraved by Wise   8

I.3 Northwest view of Prince of Wales's Fort in Hudson Bay (Churchill). Sketch by Samuel Hearne, 1777, engraved by J. Saunders   9

I.4 *Ice Fayre on the Thames River, 1683.* Painting by Jan Griffier   12

1.1 Title page of Linnaeus' *Systema Naturae*, 1758   20

1.2 J.R. Forster, portrait by Anton Graff. From Hoare 1976   22

1.3 Thomas Pennant, portrait by Thomas Gainsborough, engraved by T. Shermin   25

1.4 Horned Grebe   26

1.5 John Latham, portrait   29

1.6 Samuel Wegg Esq., governor, Hudson's Bay Company, 1782–99   32

2.1 Spruce Grouse, collected by Alexander Light   36

2.2 Willow Ptarmigan in summer plumage   37

2.3 Northern Hawk-Owl   38

2.4 Golden Eagle   39

3.1 Title page of Isham's *Observations*, edited by E.E. Rich, 1949   43

3.2 Great Blue Heron   46

3.3 Blue Goose (blue morph of Snow Goose)   46

3.4 Surf Scoter. 47

3.5 Sharp-tailed Grouse 47

3.6 Whooping Crane 48

3.7 Sandhill Crane 48

3.8 Sora 49

3.9 Marbled Godwit 49

3.10 Hudsonian Godwit 50

3.11 Red Phalarope 50

3.12 Red-necked Phalarope 51

3.13 Purple Martin 51

3.14 Northern Harrier female 53

4.1 Albany Fort, 1791–92 57

4.2 Daines Barrington, 1770 portrait by Slater, engraved by C. Knight, 1795 59

5.1 Graham's map G.2/15 63

6.1 East view of Moose Factory. Watercolour by William Richards, 1804–1811 68

6.2 Compass with thirty-two directions 70

6.3 Letter from Joseph Black to Andrew Graham 71

8.1 Samuel Hearne. The *European Magazine* 1797 82

11.1 Graph: Climate change over five centuries: Little Ice Age, 1560–1830 114

11.2 Map of thirty HBC posts with weather records for more than thirty years 119

11.3 Circular diagram showing numbers of years of weather observations at HBC posts 120

11.4 Graph: Number of days with heavy or continuous rainfall, Churchill and York Factory 125

11.5 Graph: Number of days of thunder at Churchill and York Factory, 1715–1805 126

11.6 Graph: Percent Frequency of North wind at Churchill and York Factory   127

C.1 Photo of the ten volumes of *Observations*, series E.2, by Andrew Graham and Thomas Hutchins   164

C.2 Sample page from Hutchins' Royal Society journal. Account of *Tho,those,kau,seu*, the Short-eared Owl   166

C.3 Andrew Graham's handwriting: Title page of *Observations on Hudson Bay*   168

C.4 Title page of Miller Christy's proposed edition of Hutchins' observations, 1910   175

D.1 HBC lynx returns, 1820–1934. Cycle has mean length of 9.6 years   184

E.1 HBC swan skin annual totals, 1804–91   189

E.2 Directions for curing and preserving swan skins, circa 1817. HBCA A.63/22, fo. 3   191

E.3 HBC goose and swan quill annual totals, 1799–1911. Listed for sale by the HBC, London   197

TABLES

6.1 Eighteenth-century surgeons, Hudson's Bay Company, York Factory 1714–1801   67

10.1 Birds of Hudson Bay as mentioned in ten eighteenth-century HBC manuscripts   99

11.1 HBC meteorological records held in the library of the Royal Society, London   133

12.1 Catesby's new North American bird species   140

C.1 The ten manuscripts of Andrew Graham and Thomas Hutchins   162

E.1 Swan skins from Hudson Bay, listed for sale 1804–1819   193

E.2 District fur returns, swan skins, 1821–1842   194

Colour plate 1
Great Blue Heron. Edwards 1750, 3:135

Colour plate 2
Whooping Crane. Edwards 1750, 3:132

Colour plate 3
Blue Goose (blue morph of Snow Goose). Edwards 1750, 3:152

Colour plate 4
Willow Ptarmigan in summer plumage. Edwards 1747, 2:72

Colour plate 5
Northern Harrier. Edwards 1750, 3:107

The great Black Duck from Hudson's Bay 1749   G Edwards

155

Colour plate 6
Surf Scoter. Edwards 1750, 3:155

Colour plate 7
Red–necked Phalarope. Edwards 1750, 3:143

Colour plate 8
Hudsonian Godwit. Edwards 1750, 3:138

ACKNOWLEDGMENTS

We wish to thank Judith Hudson Beattie, Keeper, Hudson's Bay Company Archives, Provincial Archives of Manitoba (PAM), Winnipeg, for assistance in many biographical details, for corrections to the surgeon's list, and for the sketch of Fort Albany. Judith also provided the print of the broadside giving directions for preparation of swan skins. Anne Morton, PAM, offered additional help and particularly suggestions concerning the origin of *Pro pelle cutem*.

A great many others helped in numerous ways. We thank Dennis Chitty for comments on Appendix C; Francis R. Cook for identification of the Box and Painted Turtles; Sheila Edwards, Librarian of the Royal Society, London, England, for an electrostatic copy of Humphrey Marten's "Birds in a Box"; the late Dr William B. Ewart for additional material concerning Thomas Hutchins; Cedric Gillott for assistance with identification of insects in E.2/5; the late W. Earl Godfrey, National Museum of Natural Sciences, Ottawa, for his notes on the possible identity of the birds described by Marten; J.V. Howard, Special Collections Librarian, University of Edinburgh Library, for the excerpts from Professor John Walker's specimen-acquisition books; John H. Hudson and Anna Leighton, for settling questions concerning plants and botanists; Clinton H. Keeling of Guildford, Surrey, for information on domestication of the Canada Goose in England; Harry Lumsden of Aurora, Ontario, for unpublished information on Greater Prairie-Chicken on Manitoulin Island; Laura Macleod and one anonymous reviewer, then of University of Toronto Press, who in early 1993 provided constructive criticism that led to expansion of the background material; Allan and Jennifer Merkowsky, for assistance with identification of fish in E.2/5; James S. Pringle of the Royal Botanical Gardens, Hamilton, Ontario, for background information about Mr Lide and Dr John Smart; Heather Rollason, PhD student in history, University of Alberta, for her assessment of Samuel Hearne; Professor Charles W.J. Withers, at the Cheltenham and Gloucester College of Higher Education, for his insights into the life of Professor John Walker.

David E. Allen kindly provided permission to quote extensively from his article on eighteenth-century naturalists in Britain. Allan J.W. Catchpole kindly provided Figures 11.2 and 11.3. Judith Beattie, Keeper of the Hudson's Bay Archives, and Glyndwr Williams, professor of history at Queen Mary College, London, provided advice and assistance throughout this project. Bill Barr, Margaret Belcher, and Frank Roy offered constructive criticism. We wish to thank Geraldine Alton Harris and Deidre Simmons for permission to quote from their theses; the Royal Society for permission to publish Thomas Hutchins MS 129 and Humphrey Marten's "Birds in a Box" from their archives; Michael Hoare, for use of portraits; and the Hudson's Bay Company Archives for permission to publish Andrew Graham's 1769 manuscript E.2/5, with additional quotations from his E.2/7. Joyce Gunn Anaka generously shared her transcription of her great-great-grandfather's (Peter Fidler's) "report of district" (Fort Dauphin, 1820). Janet Hinshaw, Museum of Zoology, University of Michigan, Ann Arbor, allowed access to the Edwards volumes and paintings, and arranged for David Bay to photograph them in colour. Margaret Belcher's generous donation allowed for some of these to be reproduced in colour in this book. We are grateful to Dr Ted Cuddy and especially to the late Honourable George Johnson, OC, MD, LLD,[1] for allowing use of excerpts from their memorials to Bill Ewart. Joan McGilvray brought her creative talents and good sense to bear upon this manuscript, improving it beyond measure.

For Appendix D, Harold Burgess found two sources of information concerning the use of swan skins. Ruth E. Shea and Rod C. Drewein provided constructive criticism of an earlier draft of Appendix D. Harry Duckworth provided dates for operation of R. Causton printing in London and, on our behalf, posed a question to members of the Eighteenth-Century Interdisciplinary Discussion Group on e-mail, which brought helpful responses from Karen Lunsford at the University of Chicago and Brian Burchett at the University of North Dakota. Cam Finlay provided data on swan skins and quills from Fort Edmonton. I wish to thank Alan Brown of Toronto, who, through numerous trips to the Royal Ontario Museum of Zoology and the Thomas Fisher Rare Books Library at the University of Toronto, researched the earlier use of the name Canada Goose, by Willughby, for Appendix E.

---

[1] George Johnson died at Gimli, Manitoba, on 8 July 1995

SUPPLEMENTARY NATURAL HISTORY
DOCUMENTS

http://www.mqup.mcgill.ca/books/houston/eighteenth-century

Hard copies of the seven documents listed below would be too expensive to print and would be of interest to a minority of readers of this book. Yet we feel they should be made available as reference tools. We had two choices: inclusion of a CD-ROM, which would raise the price and bulk of *Eighteenth-Century Naturalists* or, on the date of the book launch, to make the information available, free of charge, on the world wide web. More readers will have access to the web than will own a CD-ROM. Following the precedent of Laura Cameron's attractive book *Openings: A Meditation on History, Method, and Sumas Lake* (1997), whereby Laura offered supplementary material on the web, we have chosen the inexpensive route. We encourage readers to visit the McGill-Queen's website, http://www.mqup.mcgill.ca/books/houston/eighteenth-century, and browse through the seven documents. We suggest you begin with Andrew Graham's manuscript, E.2/5, which shows the contrast between his writing style and that of Thomas Hutchins, as explained in Appendix B. Following this, Peter Fidler's Manitoba report of 1820 makes interesting reading.

1 Andrew Graham's natural history observations, 1768 (E.2/5, chiefly from Severn, with new material from E.2/7, York Factory 1770, interpolated).
2 Thomas Hutchins's Natural History Observations, 1772, submitted to the Royal Society with the 1772 collection, chiefly from York Factory.
3 Humphrey Marten's "Birds in a Box," 1772, submitted with collection from Albany.
4 Forster's paper in *Philosophical Transactions*, 1772.
5 Rev. Dr John Walker's acquisitions, from Hudson Bay, Edinburgh, 1787.
6 Peter Fidler's *General report of the Manetoba District for 1820* (HBCA B.51/e/1).
7 Outline of Miller Christy's unpublished history of the HBC.

ABBREVIATIONS

AOU   American Ornithologists' Union

CSH   C. Stuart Houston

DAB   *Dictionary of American Biography*

DCB   *Dictionary of Canadian Biography*

DNB   *Dictionary of National Biography*

E.2/5   Ms by Graham-Hutchins, PAM, HBC Archives
(other volumes – E.2/7–E.2/12 – are indicated in the same way)

HBC   Hudson's Bay Company

HBCA   Hudson's Bay Company Archives

HBRS   Hudson's Bay Record Society

MIH   Mary I. Houston

NWC   North West Company

PAM   Provincial Archives of Manitoba

TFB   Timothy F. Ball

FOREWORD

The Hudson's Bay Company had a deep interest in the natural history of its territory from its earliest activities in North America. The weather affected the success of its annual voyages, when an early winter could trap ships or cut off men from European provisions and European markets from a supply of furs. By diligent observation of weather, animal and bird habits, vegetation, and celestial phenomena, the men at the posts across the Atlantic were not only pleasing their masters in London; they were also increasing their chances of survival. The records preserved in the daily journals and ships' logs in the Hudson's Bay Company Archives provide some of the earliest and longest series of data, of particular importance when there is so much concern about climate change and the impact of humans on the environment.

Ever since the Hudson's Bay Company's archives arrived in Winnipeg in 1974, some of the most diligent researchers have been the historical geographers and those pursing research into natural history. However, there has been more attention paid to the data than to those who recorded it. In this volume that imbalance has been redressed. The men themselves take centre stage, and the importance of their role is set in the wider context of other North American initiatives at the time. Mary and Stuart Houston and Tim Ball have combined their knowledge of science and of the original sources with their appreciation of the men and their accomplishments. William B. Ewart, to whom the book is dedicated, was also a special friend of the archives. I hope the book will entice others to use the extensive resources of the Hudson's Bay Company Archives, and give those who do not conduct research a better understanding of these men and their many accomplishments.

Judith Hudson Beattie
Keeper, Hudson's Bay Company Archives

EIGHTEENTH-CENTURY NATURALISTS OF HUDSON BAY

INTRODUCTION

This book hopes to make amends for past neglect: the outstanding achievements of a small group of early weather observers and natural-history collectors around Hudson Bay have long been overlooked by most naturalists and historians. Yet the meteorologic data and weather information recorded at the Hudson's Bay Company trading posts over three centuries are the largest and longest series available anywhere in North America, and perhaps in the world.[1] Furthermore, in all North America, Hudson Bay was second only to South Carolina as a source of records and data for the revolutionary scientific endeavour led by a Swede, Carolus von Linnaeus, and supported by the paintings of an Englishman, George Edwards, to affix permanent Latin names to the type specimens of birds, thereby describing them for science for the first time.[2]

While researching the natural-history contributions of John Franklin's first Arctic exploring expedition in the 1820s, and editing the three officers' journals for publication, the two Houstons became interested in the natural-history observations at Hudson Bay in the last half of the eighteenth century. We visited Churchill and York Factory, the Orkney Islands, Charleston, and especially the Hudson's Bay Company (HBC) Archives in Winnipeg.

Timothy Ball spent four years in the HBC archives transcribing the weather observations at Churchill and York Factory, the subject of his PhD thesis. A professor of geography at the University of Winnipeg, he was also founder and director of the Rupert's Land Research Centre (RLRC, now known as the Centre for Rupert's Land Studies), created in 1984 to promote public and academic awareness and interest in the Hudson's Bay Company Archives. The RLRC and its affiliated Rupert's Land Record Society together filled in part of the gap in publications and researcher support caused by the demise of the Hudson's Bay Record Society in 1983. The RLRC's bi-annual colloquia, held at important fur-trade locations as diverse as Churchill, Manitoba, and Stromness in the Orkney Islands, helped to spur on the enthusiasm of the authors who have worked together to write this book.

In addition to the story of climate and natural history, we present biographies of eight Hudson's Bay Company men who deserve special recognition for their landmark achievements in natural history. Five were collectors: Alexander Light, James Isham, Humphrey Marten, Andrew Graham, and Thomas Hutchins. Samuel Hearne was an astute observer. Peter Fidler was the first to comprehend the ten-year cycle of the lynx and hare. Moses Norton played a lesser role.

The collections from Hudson Bay would have been lost to science without the receiving network of naturalists in Europe, who drew and named the specimens provided by the Company fur traders. The first chapter explains, in rough chronological order, the roles of six eighteenth-century Europeans who played a pivotal role. Sir Hans Sloane (whose collections later formed the basis of the British Museum of Natural History), George Edwards (who illustrated the Hudson Bay specimens), Carolus von Linnaeus (who gave a Latin genus and species name to each), Johann Reinhold Forster and Thomas Pennant (who described later Hudson Bay specimens), the Rev Dr John Walker (who catalogued Andrew Graham's Hudson Bay specimens in the Edinburgh Museum), and Samuel Wegg (the connecting link between the HBC and the Royal Society).

In studying this magnificent collaboration, we offer the first accurate assessment of the co-operation and relative contributions of Thomas Hutchins and Andrew Graham. We summarize the fascinating story of the ten-year cycle of the hare and lynx, best known from nearly two centuries of fur-trade records. We clear up confusion about the type locality of Hudson Bay and how the Canada Goose got its name, and show how the swan-skin and swan-quill trade almost extirpated the Trumpeter Swan. We correct a few omissions and misidentifications, and offer available Swampy Cree names for birds, mammals, and fish that were in use from 1770 to the 1820s. In sum, we present the Hudson Bay Company's main eighteenth-century achievements in science.

THE COMPANY

In 1668 Prince Rupert and twelve other London investors sponsored a trial fur-trading voyage by Pierre-Esprit Radisson in the *Eaglet* and Médard Chouart des Groseilliers in the *Nonsuch*. This reconnaissance gathered so many furs from the Indians at the mouth of the Rupert River that the investing group in London added five others to their number and secured the Hudson's Bay Company charter on 2 May 1670.[3] This charter gave the company an extremely successful trade monopoly; it was the earliest long-

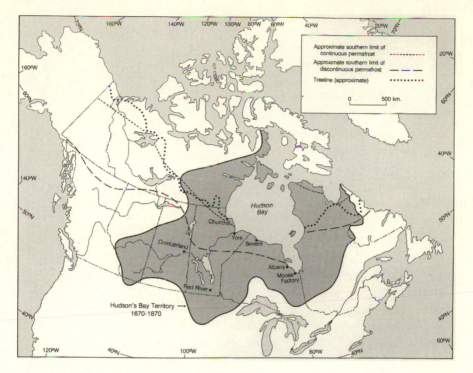

Figure I.1.
Map of HBC Territory, 1670–1870, showing approximate limits of tree line and permafrost, both continuous and discontinuous. Map by Keith Bigelow, Geography Department, University of Saskatchewan

term, successful multinational company in world history, based on a vast inland empire.

The Company was more than just the employer for its fur traders: it acted in many ways as the government, "the sovereign power,"[4] of the vast area known as Rupert's Land, encompassing all the land draining into Hudson Bay (Figure I.1). As Harold A. Innis wrote in 1956, "The northern half of North America remained British because of the importance of fur as a staple product ... It is no mere accident that the present Dominion coincides roughly with the fur-trading areas of northern North America."[5]

The HBC was a marvellous amalgam of businessmen, entrepreneurs, and ordinary working-class people. The Company's main goal was trade profit, but there was possibility of mineral riches and an underlying colonial purpose.[6] It also "had a long history of supporting scientific activities.

Five of its eighteen founding members, as well as Prince Rupert (the first governor) and several shareholders, were fellows of the Royal Society and their scientific interests meant that HBC data on North American geography, meteorology, and terrestrial magnetism were made available to the society during the seventeenth and eighteenth centuries."[7]

In assertion of its 1670 charter-derived hegemony, the Company undertook occasional forays into exploration: five of the fur traders discussed in this book made direct or indirect contributions to geographic exploration and map-making. There were three motives for fur trade exploration: geopolitical, economic, and geographical.[8]

As befits a commercial company with responsibility for governing its territory, the HBC made

a special cartographic contribution ... not the evolution of unique cartographic designs or of methodologies applied to the special purpose of the fur trade. Rather it was the continuing support the company gave to map making as an essential element of its business operations. In reaching out for new trading partners, company men were often the first Europeans to see, to explore, and to survey the northern and western lands that the company claimed as its territory. At the cost of wearisome, difficult, and often dangerous travail, whether on the open sea or the great plains, in the intricate water tangles of the northern forest or up the high passes of the Rocky Mountains, these men, mostly amateur map makers, did, all unknowingly, provide Canada with the largest collection of original, primary map documents depicting the geographical form of her emerging national territory. In truth, the Hudson's Bay Company was Canada's first national mapping agency.[9]

HBC contributions to natural history were made largely during two periods: in the 1770s, as described in this book, and again in 1857–62 when specimens were collected for the Smithsonian Institution.

THE ORKNEY CONNECTION

How did the furs and specimens reach Europe and how did the fur-traders receive their items for trade? The widely scattered HBC fur-trading posts on Hudson Bay had tenuous contact with the outside world. Only once a year, usually in August (Appendix A), did the supply ship risk the often-prevalent pack ice in Hudson Straits, sometimes in self-protection grappling a ship firmly to pack ice to avoid being crushed. This ship brought letters, books, and a year's supply of magazines and newspapers. After the Treaty of Utrecht in 1713 ended twenty years of French occupation of York Factory, at least one ship got through with supplies each year. A second ship supplied

Moose Factory, James Bay, and posts such as Eastmain on the east side of Hudson Bay.

An unusually early season at York Factory in 1740 allowed the *Mary IV* to arrive on 20 July, but in the cold decade of the 1780s, when the bay was often blocked with ice, the ship's arrival could be delayed until 14 or 15 September (in 1783 and 1780 respectively).

En route to Hudson Bay, the annual ships sailed from the Orkney Islands for a variety of reasons. Stromness offered "an excellent deep anchorage sheltered in all directions except for the southeast, which fortunately seldom produces severe weather."[10] Each ship took on fresh food and a supply of fresh drinking water from Login's well along the main street of the harbour. But the main cargo was men. The local HBC agent in Stromness recruited men for HBC service[11] because the Orcadians were "more sober and tractable than the Irish, and they engage for lower wages than either the English or the Irish."[12] Most Orcadians could read and write, were accustomed to hardship, and were also "quiet and deeply self-reliant."

The ships sailed due west from Stromness for ease of navigation; they followed "latitude sailing," travelling almost straight west at just above sixty degrees north latitude until they entered Hudson Strait. The difficult and inexact measurements of longitude were thereby rendered unnecessary. Except in cold summers such as 1816, when Hudson Strait was packed with ice, the ships were often south of most icebergs and yet avoided the full force of the North Atlantic Drift and Gulf Stream;[13] by being north, they also avoided marauding French warships that were a danger in the English Channel.[14]

THE PLACE

The HBC fur-trading posts, inhospitably cold in winter, were located on year-round permafrost, around the periphery of poor, remote, thinly populated Hudson Bay ("York Factory even today is considered remote").[15]

York Factory, the largest settlement,[16] at the mouth of the Hayes River, was a large, "handsome, well-built Fort, log on log and plastered on the outside, consisting of four bastions with sheds between them"[17] (Figure I.2). A remarkable number of furs passed through this post, averaging "16,000 made beaver[18] [a unit of exchange equivalent to the value of one prime beaver pelt][19] a year," though there was storage space for "43,000 made beaver and all provisions and stores belonging thereto."[20] The complement of men at York Fort, including officers, was from thirty-six to fifty.[21] In 1775, due to inclement weather and also to overtrapping, the fur-trade return dropped to 10,000 made beaver, "the lowest level of trade at York in over 50 years."[22]

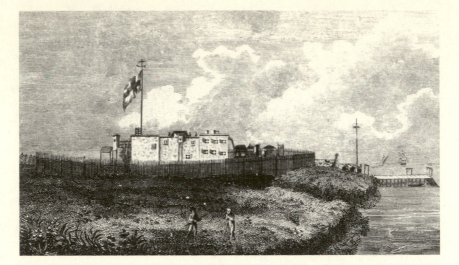

Figure I.2
York Factory, sketch by Samuel Hearne, 1 March 1797.
Engraved by Wise. HBC Archives, PAM

Churchill, the Stone Fort[23] (Figure I.3), was governed by a chief factor, "a proper number of officers ... Second, ... Surgeon, Master of the brig, Master of the sloop ... and from forty to fifty servants of different trades and callings" including "a trader, an accomptant, two vessels' mates, steward, armourer, shipwright, blacksmith, two masons, bricklayer, carpenter, cooper, tailor, three harpooners."[24] The number of men could rise to "seventy-two, according as the building and fishery is prosecuted."[25]

The average annual trade at Churchill was "about twelve thousand made-beaver in furs, pelts, castoreum, and goose feathers and quills, together with whale-bone and train-oil." The men were usually well fed: "many hogsheads of salmon, and also goose every year: ptarmigans are plentiful in winter, and they get a large supply of venison from the natives."[26] The greatest inconvenience was the lack "of fresh water, which in summer is drawn some miles by horses, or else brought by a long-boat or shallop; but in winter they melt snow making several tons of water in a day."[27]

Two other HBC forts, Severn,[28] with a year-round population of eighteen fur traders, and Albany,[29] with forty, became immortalized in the scientific literature of natural history as type localities for species. Moose Fort,[30] with twenty-five to thirty white residents, Henley House with fifteen, and Eastmain with thirteen, brought the total population of Caucasians in the Hudson's Bay Company territory to fewer than 250.[31]

Figure I.3
Northwest view of Prince of Wales's Fort in Hudson Bay (Churchill).
Sketch by Samuel Hearne, 1777, engraved by J. Saunders. HBC Archives, PAM

THE PEOPLE

Symbiosis and mutual interdependence between the First Nations and the HBC men existed from the beginning, in striking contrast to the way many aboriginals were treated south of the forty-ninth parallel. The Europeans of the HBC, as Olive Dickason writes, "quickly learned to appreciate certain aspects of Amerindian technology, such as the canoe, snowshoes, toboggan, and moccasins."[32] The native had unexcelled skills, as David Thompson observes, "in being able to guide himself through the darkest pine forests to exactly the place he intended to go, his keen, constant attention on everything: the removal of the smallest stone, the bent or broken twig; a slight mark on the ground, all spoke plain language to him."[33]

The aboriginal's nomadic existence was superbly adapted to one of the harshest environments in the world. They were brave, resourceful and hardy beyond the imagination of any white man. Their motive power was dog team in winter and canoe in summer. The larger game animals, hunted by bow-and-arrow, provided food, clothing, and shelter. Their nomadic life precluded amassing of any material possessions, other than dogs (and, after the mid-1600s, horses) that could move with them. A fixed schedule was impossible and there were no meal times; when an animal was killed, it was shared at once with both friends and strangers. Generosity and sharing were part of their way of life. Women rarely had difficulty during childbirth; they would stop by the trail in minus forty weather, give birth to a lusty infant, and move along the trail within hours.

The arrival of traders in 1670 was a mixed blessing. The traders brought diseases to which the native lacked resistance, but provided guns and ammunition, and useful knives, kettles and pots. For some Indians, these goods justified a six hundred mile annual trip to the bay. An almost insatiable European appetite for furs resulted in a reasonably happy symbiosis between native trappers and the traders who bought their furs; between them they fed the irrepressible advance of Commerce.

HBC men everywhere were "forced to subsist almost exclusively upon indigenous sources." English provisions were of limited quantity, to limit expense, and they were also often of poor quality. "Country provisions," including geese, ptarmigan, and caribou, were provided largely by the native peoples, but also fluctuated in availability. Similarly, the business venture, collecting furs, was "dependent on the skill and knowledge of indigenous peoples,"[34] who "dictated the pattern of trade."[35] Dickason has pointed out that the canoe trade routes were established by the natives, not by the company men. Initially, "no Europeans ... could make ... a journey without Amerindians acting as guides and hunters."[36] First Nations peoples and HBC employees alike had to endure, along the west coast of Hudson Bay, one of the harshest climates in the world. The bay was frozen for eight months of each year.

HBC employees, with few exceptions, were unusually loyal. The breadth and complexity of this company are evident to anyone who reads the original post journals and the Minutes of the Governor and London committee.[37] In return, the company involved itself constantly in educating and upgrading its men. Some recruits, including David Thompson, were orphans educated at either the Christ's Hospital (Blue Coat) School or the Grey Coat Hospital School in London, where students received mariner training, which included weather conditions and navigation; the mathematical master at Grey Coat School was John Robertson, author of *Robertson's Elements of Navigation*.[38] William Wales, a teacher at Christ's Hospital, was an astronomer with the Royal Society.[39]

Company employees were encouraged to advance their careers and themselves and industrious apprentices were able to work their way up through the ranks.[40] William Tomison began as a labourer without formal schooling, yet under Andrew Graham's encouragement he learned to read and write on the job and advanced to become inland master of the HBC and then chief

at York Factory. He was so grateful for this education that when he retired
to his home island of South Ronaldsay, Orkney Islands, he built a school,
which still stands, so that other youths would not begin life disadvantaged.[41]
Some HBC fur-trading posts offered reading and writing classes during long
winter evenings. Such progressive practices included, for example, providing Philip Turnor and Peter Fidler with both instruction and instruments. Turnor in turn instructed Grey Coat School graduates such as David
Thompson.[42]

THE TIME

It is more than coincidence that the Hudson's Bay Company received its
charter in 1670, during the Little Ice Age, just prior to the coldest decade,
the 1680s.[43] The cold belt extended across the northern hemisphere, making
furs valuable throughout Europe. Visual evidence of extreme cold in London
is provided by Jan Griffier's 1683 painting titled "The Great Frost," which
depicts an Ice Fair on the Thames, with ice thick enough to bear a coach
and four horses (Figure I.4). The longest period of extreme cold in modern
European history occurred between December 1739 and September 1741,
with rivers and lakes frozen solid throughout Ireland and England in January 1740.[44]

During this period the men in the remote, harsh environment of Hudson
Bay shared in a small way the energy, excitement, and optimism of the European phenomenon, "enlightenment";[45] "the unfolding of empire coincided
with the Scientific Revolution."[46]

Hudson Bay and Charles Town, South Carolina, were the pre-eminent
eighteenth-century sites in North America for observations and for specimens, and many of their observations reached publication. Printing of
books "was normally practicable only by public subscription. The collecting
of subscribers ... was an onerous and expensive process ... a list of their names
[was] included in the eventual book. The high price of books ... kept them
as desirable articles of luxury ... as status symbols for the affluent."[47] Those
fortunate enough to learn to read and write had access to a restricted list of
books, published in small printing runs of thousands or only hundreds of
copies. Peter Collinson in 1747 wrote that works on natural history sold "the
best of any books in England."[48] Later, journals of exploration, such as those
of Alexander Mackenzie and Samuel Hearne, became immensely popular.[49]

There were as yet no specialists, no "scientists," and no professionals,
except in medicine, theology, and law.[50] At the time, most scientists were amateurs, fuelled by that all-consuming virtue, curiosity.[51] But curiosity was

Figure I.4
Ice Fayre on the Thames River, 1683. Painting by Jan Griffier

unlimited, and those with it were termed ʻcurious' men,[52] meaning something very different from twentieth-century usage. The fur-trade officers of the Hudson's Bay Company lived in and contributed to one of the most exciting periods in the history of science. Yet they were unwitting, one might almost say reluctant, conscripts to the cause of science.[53] With one noteworthy exception, Dr Thomas Hutchins, they lacked training for their role. Their collection of specimens was also a response to a request from members of the Royal Society in far-away London, transmitted through their all-powerful employer, the HBC.

A few of the fur traders obviously found the diversion an interesting one, "giving them a sense of purpose that helped maintain their spirits during the long northern winters," as Victoria Dickenson has so aptly said. She continues: "Their contributions changed not only the content, but the direction of natural history at the end of the eighteenth century, leading to a new appreciation for field observation, and to a new kind of science based, not on the cabinet or the herbarium, but on nature observed."[54] The Hudson Bay naturalists made their observations in the time available after they had completed their day's work for the Company, isolated from others with similar interests.

David E. Allen, Britain's foremost historian of natural history, has placed the last four decades of the eighteenth century in perspective:

Then finally came those wonderful last 40 years, bursting with new vigour, taking us into the Romantic Movement on the one hand and into the so-called Industrial Revolution on the other. Somehow 1760 feels closer in mood to 1860 than it does to 1700 or even to 1720. In those mysterious middle years Western Man suddenly grew up ... One result was that outburst of intellectual creativity that goes by the name of the Enlightenment; the other was a responsiveness to wild scenery and the birth of that empathy that lies at the heart of latter-day natural history ...

The eighteenth century was the first great age of taxonomic description ... The drive to ransack the globe for its variety had originally been in the service of medicine; more and more now it was becoming an end in itself ... collecting and describing were the sole concerns of almost all naturalists ... In default of societies to belong to, naturalists were obliged to develop networks of correspondents.[55]

In Europe science was not restricted to nobles and elite university students. Public lectures to satisfy curiosity in science began around the turn of the century in London. From 1698 to 1707, John Harris delivered a series of mathematical lectures, which provided "solid, substantial, profitable learning," catering mainly to shipping interests and investors, centred on Birchin Lane in London. In 1705–08, James Hodgson lectured on natural philosophy and astronomy, directing his teaching to mariners. As Larry Stewart remarks: "The links between the popular science of the Newtonians and the mercantile community were to be far more deliberate than has been generally assumed." These lecturers aimed "to improve the world through knowledge of the principles of nature." John Theophilus Desaguliers was one of the most successful lecturers at outlining for a public audience the "close relation between the mathematical and mechanical in experimental courses."[56] Lectures sponsored by the Spitalfields Mathematical Society ranged from merchants' accounts to discussions of longitude and through the breadth of natural philosophy. Dr Peter Shaw gave lectures on chemistry and John Martyn on botany. The notion of public knowledge eroded the private paternalism of the client economy.[57]

Nor should one underestimate the central, motivating role of religion. A main aim of early naturalists was to catalogue God's creation. The title of John Ray's 1691 book, *The Wisdom of God Manifested in the Works of Creation*, indicated his intent.[58] As Carl Berger has observed so appropriately, "The belief that religious insight could be acquired from the study of nature equated science with an act of worship and coloured perception of its laws and facts ... Since nature stood for an overriding kindliness, its study was held to offer an unfailing source of consolation as well as pleasure." Science had a "legitimacy in a profoundly religious culture."[59]

In the eighteenth century the term "natural history" encompassed both climatology and astronomy as well as the study of animals, plants, and minerals.[60] Collectors were the only category of naturalist then known, and most of them devoted their energy to collecting plants – from every continent.[61] Field naturalists would not appear until the next century.

In chapter 12 we will draw attention to the other locality, Charles Town, South Carolina, which made significant weather and natural history contributions in the 1700s and which was coincidentally "founded" in the same year, 1670. In all North America, Hudson Bay was first in weather recording and second in the number of Linnaean natural-history specimens it provided, while Charles Town was second for weather and first for natural history specimens. Major natural-history collections were sent to England from Charles Town between 1712 and 1725, and from Hudson Bay in the 1770s.

THE EUROPEAN CONNECTION

Before we discuss the fur traders who, through the collection of specimens, took their first tentative steps into the beginnings of science, we must describe six pivotal European figures whose names recur again and again throughout the remainder of this book. These European scientists, introduced here in roughly chronological order, provided encouragement and help to the fur traders and were their connection to scientific endeavours in Europe.

SIR HANS SLOANE (1660–1753)

Hans Sloane was born in County Down, Ireland, on 16 April 1660. He studied medicine at London, Paris (where he studied botany under Joseph Pitton de Tournefort at the Royal Garden of Plants each morning from 6 to 8 a.m.), and Montpelier (where he studied plants under Pierre Magnol). He obtained his MD from the University of Orange in 1683.[1]

During a fifteen-month visit to Jamaica in 1687, Sloane collected eight hundred new species of plants.[2] He became a Fellow of the Royal Society in 1685 and was elected secretary in 1693, simultaneously taking over the *Philosophical Transactions*, which he edited for twenty years.[3] He was then vice-president and finally president, 1727–40, succeeding Sir Isaac Newton. In 1716 he was the first medical practitioner to receive a hereditary title as baronet. His unrivalled collections of natural history, some obtained by purchase – "the most comprehensive private collection ever assembled"[4] – were donated following his death at ninety-two on 11 January 1753 and formed the basis for the British Museum, which opened to the public on 15 January 1759, six years after his death.[5]

Alexander Light, the earliest HBC bird collector, sent his specimens to Sloane. Mark Catesby's second trip was partially financed by Sloane. George Edwards, who owed his appointment to Sloane, dedicated his second volume to him and cared for him during his final illness.

GEORGE EDWARDS (1694–1773)

As Sir Cyril Clarke says in his foreword to Stuart Mason's 1991 book about George Edwards: "Oh, to have been around in the 1730s – for then a third of the Fellows of the Royal College of Physicians were also Fellows of the Royal Society, all 'curious men' and interested in natural history, identifying and classifying not only diseases, but monkeys, birds, fish, butterflies, and flowers." Of all these, Clarke goes on to say, "Our hero is George Edwards."[6]

George Edwards, sometimes called the "Father of British ornithology," was born at Stratford near Westham, Essex, on 3 April 1694 and educated at Leytonstone. His good fortune was to be an apprentice to a London tradesman who provided him with living quarters that contained a substantial library. Thus Edwards had the opportunity to study books about natural history, sculpture, painting, astronomy, and the antiquities. After completing his apprenticeship he travelled in Europe from 1718 to 1720. In Holland he collected scarce books and prints, examined the original paintings of several great masters, and took up drawing and colouring.

In 1733 Edwards was chosen by Sir Hans Sloane to be library-keeper (bedell or beadle) of the College of Physicians, where he administered the college and cared for legal documents and the library of eight thousand books. He purchased items as diverse as food, candles, brooms, and chamber-pots. He designed and etched the college diplomas, each decorated with the college's coat of arms. For these services he was given living quarters at the college and thus had prime access to an even more substantial library. His own bookplate, inscribed "Librarian to the College of Physicians," indicates where his main duties lay.

Mark Catesby, who collected and painted Carolina birds, taught Edwards how to make etchings and Edwards eventually published seven volumes of natural history. *A Natural History of Birds* appeared in four volumes with a total of 210 plates in 1743, 1747, 1750, and 1751, and *Gleanings of Natural History* in three volumes with 362 plates in 1758, 1760, and 1764.[7]

Edwards became a friend and correspondent of Linnaeus, who wrote of Edwards' "indefatigable assiduity in collecting, delineating, and describing,"[8] and said in a letter to him dated 13 April 1764, "I congratulate you on the acquisition of such beautiful and innumerable rare birds, beyond what any other person has seen, or is likely to meet with; still less is any other hand likely to equal your representations in which nothing is wanting to the birds but their song."[9] Edwards also brought out another edition of Catesby's *Natural History* after the latter's death.

Edwards was deeply religious. He dedicated part 4 of his *Natural History of Birds*

to God, the One Eternal! the Incomprehensible! the Omnipresent! Omniscient, and Almighty CREATOR of all Things that exist! from Orbs immensurably great, to the minutest Points of Matter, this ATOM is Dedicated and Devoted, with all possible Gratitude, Humiliation, Worship, and the highest Adoration both of Body and Mind, By His most resigned, Low, and humble Creature, George Edwards.

Edwards' bird paintings have received appropriate recognition over two-and-a-half centuries. Thomas Bewick (1753–1828), the famous English ornithologist, wrote: "I find that Edwards and Buffon[10] are the only books that will be worth anything to us – I mean for the figures, which are generally extremely well done and indeed I think better to copy than the stuffed birds here."[11] In the bibliography compiled for Sacheverell Sitwell's *Fine Bird Books*, Handasyde Buchanan and James Fisher said, "At its date of issue the *Natural History* ... was one of the most important of all Bird Books, both as a Fine Bird Book and a work of Ornithology. It is still high on each list."[12] A more recent study by Victoria Dickenson, which begins with the Edwards painting of the bittern, gives a more balanced view. On the one hand, Dickenson correctly states that "to the modern eye Edwards' illustrations are stilted, even inept," yet on the other hand she speaks of their "truthful rendering."[13]

Mason has described Edwards as one whose "skill lay in accurate representation rather than in artistic impression ... He was a painstaking recorder of nature, not a gifted artist."[14] Mullens and Swann said he was "an unscientific but very accurate describer and painter of animal life, and his writings will always remain of paramount authority, from the faithfulness of his description of many new birds, subsequently incorporated in the Linnean System."[15] Edwards was awarded the prestigious Copley gold medal of the Royal Society in 1750, and shortly thereafter was elected a Fellow. His paintings of undescribed ("non-descript") birds,[16] which served as type specimens once Linnaeus bestowed on them a Latin binomial, made a permanent imprint on the scientific record.[17] He died at Plaistow, Essex, on 23 July 1773.

In his seven volumes Edwards illustrated "nearly six hundred subjects in natural history not before delineated."[18] These included the first depictions and descriptions of eighty-six North American birds (albino specimens of a godwit and a possible yellowlegs are not identifiable as to species). The accepted new species or subspecies include five from Alexander Light among the first fifty species illustrated in the first volume, and thirty from James Isham, the second Hudson Bay collector, in the third volume.[19]

CAROLUS VON LINNAEUS (CARL VON LINNÉ) (1707–1778)

Linnaeus was born on 23 May 1707 at Räshult in Sweden. At school he showed no interest in classical learning but spent most of his time in the fields searching for plants and insects. Just when his despairing father was ready to bind him as apprentice to a shoemaker, Dr Rothman, a physician, took Linnaeus into his home for a year. Rothman was the first of at least seven mentors or sponsors who spurred Linnaeus on whenever his future appeared bleak. Rothman prodded him to complete the gymnasium course and then to go to the University of Lund. When Linnaeus moved from Lund to Uppsala for further study, he was so poor that he was forced to repair his friends' cast-off shoes for his own use (His father, a pastor, could offer him no financial support.) Professor Olof Rudbeck hired Linnaeus to tutor his children, and Dr Anders Celsius, who invented the centigrade scale, then took him into his home so that he could continue his studies.[20]

In 1735, at age twenty-seven, Linnaeus moved from Uppsala to take a medical degree at Harderwijk in Holland and thereby gain permission to marry Sara Moraeus, daughter of a wealthy physician. The wedding, however, did not take place until 1739, after a nearly five-year engagement.[21] After his degree, Linnaeus moved to the University at Leyden, where the famous physician Hermann Boerhaave became his "fatherly friend." George Clifford, a banker, became his main Dutch patron, employing Linnaeus as superintendent of his botanical gardens.[22]

L.T. Gronovius, a wealthy naturalist and collector,[23] persuaded Linnaeus that he must publish the outline he had brought from Sweden of a new system of classification of plants based on the "basic parts of fructification (calyx, corolla, pericarp, pistil, seed, stamen, and receptacle)."[24] This simple beginning was printed "in the form of placards on just a few sheets."[25] His most recent biographer, Lisbet Koerner, speculates that Linnaeus's binomial system may have resulted from "his attempts to practice science as an auxiliary branch of economics." He built on the foundation of Aristotle, John Ray (his special hero), Joseph Tournefort, and Sébastien Vaillant, but he was the first to make "botany easy for people without schooling or wealth": the "workaday usefulness" of his binomial system "appealed to both learned men and novices."[26] The universal adoption of Linnaean classification is explained by "its orderly clear arrangement, ... precision, ... use of an international language, Latin, ... and its worldwide scope."[27]

With his best friend and fellow student Petrus Artedi, "a fanatic for method and a devil for work," Linnaeus began to categorize specimens according to genus and species.[28] The first folio seven-page edition of Linnaeus's *Systema Naturae* published in 1735 set out the hierarchy of class, order, genus, and species, with each genus roughly equivalent to the modern designation of family. Later copies of the *Systema* included a 1736 broadsheet describing Linnaeus's proposed method for preparing the descriptions of plants and animals.[29]

It would have helped the cause of science greatly had early collectors consistently followed the wise admonitions in the "Methodus" to name the specific locality where each specimen was collected, together with the latitude and longitude of that place; to explain the derivation of each new scientific name, together with a list of synonyms, including Greek names for the species, and a vernacular name; and to provide an account of the natural, the essential, and the artificial characters of each genus, with an explanation of the erroneous ideas or "hallucinations" of previous authors. Finally, the "Methodus" demanded a detailed description for each new species, listing the differences between the proposed new species and the other described species in the same genus.[30]

Linnaeus returned to Stockholm in 1738. Count Carl Gustav Tessin housed him in his town palace, introduced him to society, and secured for him the post of chief physician to the Swedish navy. In his private medical practice Linnaeus specialized in treatment of venereal disease.[31] After three years as a successful physician in Stockholm, in 1741 he was appointed to the prestigious chair of medicine at the University of Uppsala. But his interest was in plants rather than the sick, so the following year he exchanged his chair in medicine for one in botany. His publications eventually numbered over 180: as he wrote to his brother and sisters in 1763, "I have written more than anyone else now alive; 72 of my own books are at present on my desk."[32] These books included *Flora Lapponica* in 1737, *Flora Suecica* and *Fauna Suecica* in 1745, and *Species Plantarum* in 1753.[33] He continued to catalogue known species even as he prepared a generation of students to gather useful plants from around the world.[34] One student, Pehr Kalm, for whom Linnaeus named the mountain laurel, *Kalmia*, visited North America, including Quebec, Montreal, and Niagara Falls, in 1747–51.[35] Ninety of his plant species were cited in *Species Plantarum* (1753).[36]

Linnaeus's tenth edition of *Systema Naturae* in 1758 (Figure 1.1), accepted since its publication as the starting-point for zoological nomenclature, listed nearly 4,400 species of animals then known worldwide, including 554 species of birds, 133 of which were found in North America.[37] As Gavin de Beer wrote in the introduction to the 1956 reprint, *Systema Naturae* is "one of the great books in the history of science because it marked the start of an epoch in two essential fields of zoological study: systematics or taxonomy, and nomenclature."[38] Linnaeus's final edition, the twelfth, with additional species, was published in 1766.[39]

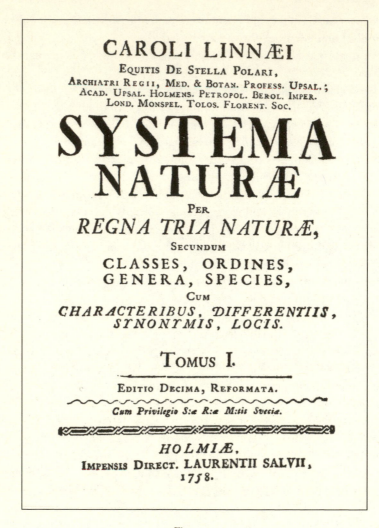

CAROLI LINNÆI

EQUITIS DE STELLA POLARI,
ARCHIATRI REGII, MED. & BOTAN. PROFESS. UPSAL.;
ACAD. UPSAL. HOLMENS. PETROPOL. BEROL. IMPER.
LOND. MONSPEL. TOLOS. FLORENT. SOC.

SYSTEMA NATURÆ

PER

REGNA TRIA NATURÆ,

SECUNDUM

CLASSES, ORDINES,
GENERA, SPECIES,

CUM

CHARACTERIBUS, DIFFERENTIIS,
SYNONYMIS, LOCIS.

TOMUS I.

EDITIO DECIMA, REFORMATA.

Cum Privilegio S:æ R:æ M:tis Sveciæ.

HOLMIÆ,
IMPENSIS DIRECT. LAURENTII SALVII,
1758.

Figure 1.1
Title page of Linnaeus' *Systema Naturae*, 1758

Linnaeus's proudest day came when he received Sweden's Order of the Polar Star, the first naturalist to be so honoured. However, a recent biography by Lisbet Koerner shows that he had feet of clay: he attempted to defraud the Uppsala Science Society by falsifying his expenses for fieldwork in Lapland,[40] and he wrote anonymous glowing reviews of his own books for Stockholm newspapers.[41]

After a decade of declining health, Linnaeus died on 10 January 1778 and was buried in the cathedral in Uppsala.

Following his death, the thirteenth edition of *Systema Naturae* was produced in 1788–89 by Johann Friedrich Gmelin in Germany. Gmelin translated the English texts of John Latham and Thomas Pennant into Latin and gave Latin names to many English birds a year before both English authors reluctantly accepted the Linnaean system. Through his translation and the law of zoological priority Gmelin thus achieved priority of recognition for new species first described by Latham and Pennant, who in turn had obtained some of their specimens from Hudson Bay.

Linnaeus's collections were purchased in October 1784 by a wealthy young English physician, James Edward Smith, for a thousand guineas and the twenty-six chests were brought to London where their presence helped to stimulate the founding of the Linnean Society of London in 1788.[42]

Over fifty years after Linnaeus's death, a committee of the British Association for the Advancement of Science, chaired by Hugh Strickland with Charles Darwin and Sir John Richardson as members, produced a report that, as Paul Farber tells us, "established the law of priority, utilized Linnaeus's binomial nomenclature, and designated the twelfth edition of *Systema Naturae* as the starting point of reference."[43] The report, generally referred to as the Strickland committee report, "was in the best Linnean tradition: clear, practical and simple ... The reform of nomenclature gave zoology, and ornithology in particular, a common language, which not only facilitated communication and removed much unnecessary confusion, but also was a major step in helping ornithologists towards the common goal they shared: a complete catalogue of the birds of the world."[44]

JOHANN REINHOLD FORSTER (1728–1798)

Johann Reinhold Forster, a descendant of George Forster who had emigrated from Scotland to Prussia in 1630, was born at Dirschau near Danzig. He obtained an extraordinary knowledge of both classical and modern languages at the Joachimsthal Gymnasium in Berlin and then became the pastor of a church in the little village of Nassenhuben near Danzig. However, when he was sent by Count Orlov on a nineteen-month survey of land intended for German colonization along the lower Volga River, assisted by his enthusiastic eleven-year-old son, Georg, he lost his parish.[45] In desperation the family moved to England, where Forster eked out a living as a teacher and translator while establishing himself as "one of the best-read, most discerning and leading naturalists in Britain in the 1760's"[46] (Figure 1.2).

Figure 1.2
J.R. Forster, portrait by Anton Graff. From Hoare 1976

Unexpectedly, an opportunity arose for Forster to accompany Captain James Cook on his second round-the-world voyage on the *Resolution*. Having charted the New Zealand coastline on his first expedition, Cook's emphasis this time was "more on zoogeography,"[47] although one historian has suggested that "his most important duty was to establish the British empire on the bottom side of the globe."[48] Naturalists Joseph Banks and Daniel Solander, Cook's naturalists and companions on his first voyage from 1768 to 1771, had declined to accompany him, complaining that the ship's cabins were too small. Forster leapt at the opportunity and took his son Georg, eighteen, as his assistant.

The *Resolution* had already left Sheerness on 22 June 1772. Forster spent £1500 of his advance of £1795 to acquire a large library of well-bound scientific volumes and a number of new instruments; then, on 26 June the Forsters took a post-chaise, reaching Plymouth dock on 29 June. They need not have hurried so; the *Resolution*, behind schedule, did not sail from Plymouth until 13 July.[49] Forster barely had time to submit his assessment of the Hudson Bay specimens to *Philosophical Transactions* before he sailed.

At Capetown, South Africa, the second Cook expedition picked up Anders Sparrman, a student of Linnaeus's. They traversed the Indian Ocean, visited New Zealand and Tahiti, and discovered the Tonga Islands, the New Hebrides, New Holland, and Norfolk Island. Drawings were made by Cook's draughtsman, Sydney Parkinson, and by Georg Forster.

Forster returned from the Cook voyage in 1775 "with an incomparable haul of scientific specimens,"[50] including "thousands of plants" of at least 220 new species.[51] Father and son published a botanical catalogue,[52] but were ordered by the British Admiralty to publish nothing more. J.R. Forster obeyed the letter of this order but allowed Georg to scoop Cook's official narrative by a few weeks with *A Voyage round the World in his Britannic Majesty's sloop Resolution, commanded by Captain James Cook, during the years 1772–75.* "Never before was a scientific expedition described more thoroughly, comprehensively or thoughtfully," wrote Stresemann, the doyen of world ornithological history.[53] Publication brought father and son the ill-will of the Admiralty and of Cook's friends, engendering criticism "with more ill-nature than good judgment" from William Wales, the astronomer of the expedition.[54]

These insoluble disagreements with both Cook and the Admiralty had unfortunate and serious consequences: the Forsters were not paid the £1,000 owed them; their collections were scattered, and Georg's watercolours went to their creditors. Hoare, Forster's biographer, tells us that "Forster's foolish, obstinate behaviour, and a certain degree of scientific 'jealousy,' clearly lay at the bottom of the deteriorating relationships ... Forster's besetting ignorance was of men."[55]

J.R. Forster was deeply in debt and even spent some time in debtor's prison before he was offered the professorship of natural history at Halle, Germany, near Leipzig.[56] He then became librarian in Mainz, where Georg, who had become professor of natural history in the University of Wilna in Lithuania, unwisely became a member of the provisional government after Mainz was captured by the French. Georg's wife and four children deserted him. Georg went to Paris as one of three deputies, "with a price on his head, exiled by the Emperor and widely branded as a traitor in Germany ... he died a lonely, tragic pauper's death in a Paris garret on 10 January 1794."[57] J.R. Forster died in Halle on 9 December 1798.[58]

Forster's *Descriptiones Animalium,* the text of which was completed while on the voyage with Cook, was not published until 1844, almost half a century after Forster's death, with a bungled commentary by Martin Heinrich Karl Lichtenstein.[59]

It is ironic that Forster gained permanent priority of citation for five specimens from the much smaller collections of Graham and Marten from Hudson Bay and yet was unable to achieve publication of his own, much larger collection from the Pacific Ocean. His difficult personality and lack of tact had conspired against him. It was left to Dr John Latham, in 1781–85, to describe about two hundred of Forster's new bird species.

As Hoare has said of Forster, "his work was always more attractive than his personality for, despite high standards of personal probity and morality,

Forster was fiery, often obdurate, always in debt yet unswervingly generous."[60] To be fair, Hoare had said earlier: "Forster was a competent scholar, not only in natural history but also in philology, languages, ancient geography and classical studies, and he also wrote about agriculture, geography and ethnology ... Pennant's opinion of J.R. Forster as a zoologist and ornithologist was high indeed."[61] When on the *Resolution* with Cook, Forster had developed the concept of "biological provinces," long before the development of biogeography as a discipline.[62]

Specimens of sixty birds and twenty mammals, sent from Hudson Bay, had arrived in London in November 1771 and been presented by the "Governor and Committee of the Hudson's Bay Company" to the Royal Society, who, as Forster wrote, "did me the honour to refer them to me for examination."[63] Forty-one of the bird specimens and at least eight of the mammals and three fish had been collected by "Mr. Andrew Graham, the collector of the Natural History specimens at Severn River in Hudson's Bay."[64] Of the birds, another six had been collected by Humphrey Marten at Albany, eight by Moses Norton at Churchill, and two by Ferdinand Jacobs at York Factory. The Ruby-crowned Kinglet, first described by Linnaeus in 1766 from a Philadelphia specimen, is listed by Forster but is not mentioned by Graham or Hutchins. From the specimen label, Forster quoted an exact date for the spring arrival of the Snow Bunting at Severn, 11 April 1771, whereas Graham had merely given the month. The collection contained five species of fish; although three were new to science, Forster gave a full description of only one of these, the type specimen of the Longnose Sucker, to which he gave the name of *Cyprinus catostomus*, now *Catostomus catostomus*.[65]

THOMAS PENNANT (1726–1798)

Thomas Pennant was born on 14 June 1726 to a distinguished and relatively wealthy Welsh family at Downing in Flintshire, northeast Wales. He went to school at Wrexham and matriculated at Oxford in 1744. Horace Walpole found Pennant "full of corporal spirits, too lively and impetuous," though "a very honest, good-natured man."[66] Pennant's love for natural history began at the age of twelve, when a relative gave him a copy of Willughby's *Ornithology* (1678). He studied law at Queen's College, Oxford, but did not obtain a degree. Elsa G. Allen characterizes him as a traveller and antiquary, a businessman, a man of letters, and a naturalist.[67] His journals of his travels on horseback around Scotland, Wales, and various parts of England (the first of his eleven travel books) went into many editions and earned him Samuel Johnson's praise as "the best traveller I ever read; he observes more things than any one else does."[68] Pennant is "perhaps the best known of the

Figure 1.3
Thomas Pennant, portrait by Thomas Gainsborough,
engraved by T. Shermin. From Hoare 1976

British zoologists of the eighteenth century ... an elegant scholar and refined gentleman"[69] (Figure 1.3).

Pennant began corresponding with Carl Linnaeus in 1755. Linnaeus early recognized Pennant's competence and arranged for his election to the Royal Society of Uppsala in 1757.[70] Pennant published *British Zoology* between 1761 and 1766, and *Arctic Zoology* in 1784–85, with a second edition in 1792. He also published *Indian Zoology* in 1769 and *The Genera of Birds* in 1773. Because he refused to go along with the new Linnacan system of binomial Latin names, later authors such as Gmelin are given the priority for giving Latin names to new species first described by Pennant; a small caveat is added in each instance: "based on the ... of Pennant." Two such examples are the type specimens for currently recognized North American subspecies of the Horned Grebe, *Podiceps auritus cornutus* (Figure 1.4), and the Rock Ptarmigan, *Lagopus mutus rupestris*.[71]

Sir William Jardine said that Pennant's works on natural history "contained the greater part of the knowledge of their times." Pennant was also "commended for making dry and technical matter interesting."[72]

Figure 1.4
Horned Grebe. Edwards 1750, 3:145

Pennant was elected a Fellow of the Royal Society in 1767. The University of Oxford conferred the honourary degree of DCL in 1771. The famous portraitist Thomas Gainsborough painted Pennant's portrait in 1776.

Gavin de Beer, quoted by Urness, considers Pennant "the leading British zoologist after Ray and before Darwin ... his services are to be recognized not only in the published works under his name, but also in his encouragement of Gilbert White [1720–93], of whose *Natural History of Selbourne* the first part is in the form of letters addressed to Thomas Pennant."[73] The Fisher, *Martes pennanti*, was named for Pennant by Erxeleben in 1777. Pennant died on 16 December 1798.

From the first Pennant had access to the observations of Andrew Graham and Samuel Hearne. Two paragraphs of acknowledgments, titled "Advertisement" and dated "Downing, February 1, 1785," were in the first edition of *Arctic Zoology*:

To Mr. SAMUEL HEARN [sic], the great explorer by land of the *Icy Sea*, I cannot but send my most particular thanks, for his liberal communication of many zoological remarks, made by him on the bold and fatiguing adventure he undertook from *Hudson's Bay* to the *ne plus ultra* of the north on that side.

Mr. ANDREW GRAHAM, long a resident in *Hudson's Bay*, obliged me with numbers of observations on the country, and the use of multitudes of specimens of animals transmitted by him to the late museum of the Royal Society, at the instance of that liberal patron of science, my respected friend the Honorable DAINES BARRINGTON.

Very early in the first edition of *Arctic Zoology*, after only five species had been described, Pennant inserted a footnote:

At the time this sheet was printing, I had the good fortune to meet with *Mr. Hutchins*, surgeon, a gentleman many years resident in *Hudson's Bay*; who, with the utmost liberality, communicated to me his MS. observations, in a large folio volume; in every page of which his extensive knowledge appears. The benefits which this work will, from the present page, receive, is here once for all gratefully acknowledged.[74]

From this footnote forward, some of the specimens treated in both editions of Pennant, though collected by Graham at Severn, were inappropriately credited by Pennant to Hutchins. For example, under Long-eared Owl, Pennant says: "Observed by Mr. Hutchins about *Severn* settlement in *Hudson's Bay*."[75] The female of a new species, the Yellow-headed Blackbird, was described by Pennant but not listed by either Hutchins or Graham (it was not given a Latin name until Bonaparte did so in 1825).[76] Pennant also received a partial albino blackbird. Pennant's accounts of species such as the Gray Jay and the female Snowy Owl contain the same information as in E.2/12, HBCA, PAM,[77] but rewritten. For some species he has additional information from Hudson Bay, as when he says of the Sharp-tailed Grouse, "The young, like others of this genus, run as soon as hatched, and make a puling noise like a chicken ... The flesh of these birds is of a light brown colour, plump, and very juicy."[78]

Pennant published a supplement to *Arctic Zoology* in 1787. In it he describes Hudson Bay specimens of the Hudsonian and Marbled Godwits obtained from Dr John Latham. There is no mention of the collector, perhaps Andrew Graham. The Red-breasted Merganser and Hooded Merganser came from Hutchins, and the Blue Goose from Albany (and hence Hutchins), where the Snow Goose was very scarce. These accounts reappeared, sometimes with changed wording, in the second edition of *Arctic Zoology* in 1792.

The Advertisement in Pennant's second edition was three pages longer than it had been in 1785. Acknowledgments of help received from Hearne and Graham were repeated unchanged, except that Hearne's surname was now spelled correctly. The previous notices were now preceded by a new entry:

To the late Mr. THOMAS HUTCHINS, a gentleman greatly distinguished for his philosophical enquiries, I was unspeakably obliged for his judicious remarks made during sixteen years residence in Hudson's Bay, of which he most liberally indulged me with the perusal.[79]

In addition to the written accounts, Pennant had access to Hudson Bay specimens of most species. He gave the specific locality of "Hudson's Bay" for ninety-four species, and one colour phase, the Blue Goose.[80] However, he occasionally accepted erroneous hearsay, as when he listed the Bean Goose, Greylag Goose, Barnacle Goose, and Brown Pelican as from Hudson Bay. Similarly, the Fulvous Whistling-Duck was credited to Hudson Bay, where the fur-trader term of "Whistling Duck" clearly applied to the noise produced by the wings of the Common Goldeneye.

JOHN LATHAM (1740–1837)

John Latham was born at Eltham, Kent, on 27 June 1740, the son of Dr John Latham, a practising surgeon. His mother was a Sotheby from Yorkshire. He attended the Merchant Taylors' School and then studied anatomy under William Hunter (1718–83), the first great teacher of anatomy in England and the elder brother of the famous surgeon John Hunter (1728–93).[81]

Latham began his remunerative medical practice in the little town of Dartford, Kent, in 1763. He was an enthusiastic collector and a man of "dogged industry" who "channelled his curiosity into the study of Linnaean systematics."[82] He corresponded with Linnaeus and Pennant. Between 1781 and 1785, in *A General Synopsis of Birds*, published in three volumes, Latham was the first to describe about two hundred new bird species that the Forsters had brought back from Cook's second voyage and some from Cook's third voyage. He next published *Index Ornithologicus* in 1790 and *A General History of Birds* in 1821–28. He designed, etched, and coloured all the illustrations himself. He was unfortunately sloppy with inadequate and often erroneous descriptions; one-third of the time he even got the country of origin wrong.[83] Professor Alfred Newton, in *A Dictionary of Birds*, wrote that "Latham did not possess the inborn faculty of picking out the characters wherein one species differs from another ... the number of cases in which he erred as to the deter-

Figure 1.5
John Latham, portrait. Reproduced from *Ibis*, series 13, 1:467, 1931

mination of his species must be very great."[84] William Swainson added, in *A Bibliography of Zoology*, "The works of Latham will be long quoted, because, although exhibiting more of unwearied zeal, and extensive research, than of critical acumen or comprehensive judgement, they ... are cited by almost every writer ... the vastness of his plan, which aimed at no less than the description of all known birds, was too great for his talents. His memory was not good; hence he has frequently described the same species by different names."[85] However, Latham was the first ornithologist "who achieved anything like completeness in treating of the birds of the world."[86]

Like Pennant, for twenty-four years Latham thought Latin names were superfluous. He capitulated only in his 1790 edition of *Index Ornithologicus*, a year too late to obtain priority for the new species he had described. The one exception was the North American race, now a subspecies of the Whimbrel, *Numenius phaeopus hudsonicus*.[87] Otherwise, Gmelin's thirteenth edition of Linnaeus's *Systema Naturae* (1788) had usurped the priority for Latin names otherwise due to Latham. In this manner, as David E. Allen phrases it, his pioneering labours were "effectively buried."[88]

Latham retired to Romsey, Hampshire, in 1796. The University of Erlangen in Germany had conferred the degree of MD on him the year before he retired[89] (Figure 1.5). Latham published two volumes of a supplement to his *General Synopsis* in 1805 but Newton remarked "his defects as a compiler, which had been manifest before, rather increased with age, and the consequences were not happy."[90] In his nineties Latham completely updated his *Synopsis* in three large handwritten volumes; these were deposited in the British Museum but not published.[91] Latham died on 4 February 1837 at ninety-six years of age, deeply in debt, nearly blind, but "active, patient, cheerful to the end."[92]

Latham's *General Synopsis of Birds* listed at least forty-eight species of birds from Hudson Bay. He had read and may possibly have made the pencilled annotations on one of the copies of the Hutchins-Graham manuscript E.2/10 in Hudson's Bay House, correcting and supplementing the natural-history notes. Latham may even have had thoughts of preparing that manuscript for publication about 1790.[93]

REV. DR JOHN WALKER (1731–1803)

Walker, a man of many parts, was the principal founder of the Royal Society of Edinburgh in 1783.[94] His resulting connection with Andrew Graham and collections from Hudson Bay has received little attention. Walker was the second man to hold the joint post of professor of natural history at the University of Edinburgh and keeper of the university's Natural History Museum, following Robert Ramsay, a physician by training, who held both titles from 1767 to 1778.[95] Walker was simultaneously a Church of Scotland minister. He obtained his Master of Divinity degree in 1753[96] and served parishes in Kirkcudbrightshire, 1754–58; Glencorse near Edinburgh, 1758–62; the distant border parish of Moffat, 1762–83; and Colinton outside Edinburgh, 1783–1803. Eleven years into his ministry, in 1765, he obtained his Doctor of Divinity degree from Edinburgh University.[97] He became moderator of the General Assembly of the Church of Scotland in 1790.[98]

In 1764 Walker surveyed the Hebrides, walking three thousand miles in seven months. His studies were published posthumously in 1812 in two volumes titled *An Economical History of the Hebrides*.[99] Although Walker began his university and museum appointments with enthusiasm on 3 November 1779, only with great difficulty did he balance his two full-time jobs – the church at Moffat on weekends and the university and museum during the week. Not until 1783 did he obtain a transfer to Colinton, where he continued as parish minister throughout his term as a professor and until his death in 1803.

At the University Walker's lectures focused on the practical economic usefulness of natural knowledge, including agriculture. He taught a *utilitarian* natural history: "Taken in a speculative view its object is to discover new and useful productions in nature, to promote the cultivation of the useful arts; to contribute to the entertainment and improvement of individuals; to advance the public good and to turn the truths of nature and science to the public good."[100] Walker's definition of natural history, appropriate for his time, was broad indeed and included "meteorology, hydrography, geology, mineralogy, botany and zoology."[101] He was one of the first academics in Great Britain to consistently use Latin bird names from the Linnean classification, as can be seen in his acquisition catalogue of 1772.[102]

Withers has tabulated the names and origins of 709 students taught by Walker between 1782 and 1800; of these, 248 were registered as students of medicine, 188 of physick, 19 of philosophy, and only 19 of divinity. His students came from all over Europe, from the United States, and even from India and Brazil.[103]

Walker's teaching faltered in the winter of 1801–02, when he became blind. He was succeeded in 1804 by Robert Jameson (1774–1854), who had been his star pupil in 1792 and 1793.[104]

In 1787 Andrew Graham donated his collection of ethnographic and natural history items, including Hudson Bay specimens of "beavers, divers and plants" to the Edinburgh Royal Society.[105] The Royal Society of Edinburgh minutes of 22 January 1787 record these as "natural productions and artificial rarities ... presented ... in the course of the last year."[106] (The block of pages, 157 to 198, dealing with acquisitions from Hudson Bay is reproduced in Document 5.)[107]

One can only speculate whether Graham's specimens came to Edinburgh directly or via the HBC office in London, why common birds known in Europe were chosen, and why six specimens of one species, the Three-toed Woodpecker, were entered into the collection. It is tempting to think that surgeon Thomas Hutchins, during the last three years of his career in Hudson Bay (1766–82) or during his years as secretary in the HBC office in London (1783–90), might have influenced Andrew Graham to send these specimens directly to Professor Walker in Edinburgh.

SAMUEL WEGG (1723–1802)

Samuel Wegg's (Figure 1.6) invaluable contributions are little known in the history of science. Wegg was born in Colchester, Essex, on 17 November 1723. He studied at St John's College, Cambridge, and was called to the Bar in 1746. On his father's death in 1748 Samuel inherited half his father's stock in the Hudson's Bay Company; in 1760 he bought the other half from his

Figure 1.6.
Samuel Wegg Esq., governor, Hudson's Bay Company, 1782–99.
Artist unknown. Silhouette on glass. HBCA PAM F–92 (N4067)

brother and became a member of the HBC committee. Elected to fellow-
ship in the Royal Society in 1753, when only thirty, he served thirty-seven years
as its treasurer. In 1767 Wegg was the go-between for the Royal Society and
the Company, responsible for sending William Wales to Churchill to observe
the transit of Venus.[108] For the rest of his life he fostered two-way co-operation between the Company and the Society.

In November 1768 Wegg was one of the auditors of the HBC accounts.
He encouraged Andrew Graham to submit his specimens and observations
to the head office in London. It has been suggested that Wegg had introduced
Graham to Thomas Pennant in 1769 when Graham was on leave in
London.[109] Similarly, Wegg introduced Samuel Hearne to Pennant when
Hearne was in London during the winter of 1782–83.[110] Graham acknowl-
edged Wegg in his title-page dedication: "A meteorological journal kept at
York Fort in Hudson Bay in the year 1775 and 6 for Sam[l] Wegg esq[r]."
Hearne's narrative, published post-humously in 1795, was also dedicated pri-
marily to Wegg.

Wegg became deputy-governor of the HBC in 1774, the year that Samuel
Hearne founded the first major inland post, Cumberland House.[111] Four
years later, with Wegg's encouragement, the company hired Philip Turnor,
a trained map-maker. Wegg gave Alexander Dalrymple[112] and Aaron Arrowsmith[113] full access to HBC information, used to produce fifteen successive

revisions of the Arrowsmith family maps of the interior of North America. Wegg's

executive acumen must surely have exceeded that of his immediate associates in breadth of outlook and of imagination. None of his fellow Committeemen, during his years of office, appear to have been exposed as he was to the same range of educated thought, to new concepts in the natural and physical sciences, to burgeoning geographical data about the world, of which Rupert's Land was a connected part, and to such leading men of ideas and of action. Couple this with the opportunity which he took of integrating into some coherent economic geographic structure the mass of information penned at trading posts located over thousands of miles of the North, from explorers far out on the trail, from ships' captains plying difficult seas, and from experienced servants home on leave. If one correlates all these elements with his knowledge of the intricacies of the financial and trading world, one can appreciate that in Samuel Wegg the Hudson's Bay Company benefited greatly from the services and leadership of an unusual man during a signal period of its history.[114]

Wegg became governor of the HBC in 1782 and served in that capacity until 1799.[115] As governor, "unlike his predecessors, Wegg welcomed geographers,[116] naturalists and explorers into the Company archives."[117] He died at his home in the suburban village of Acton, northwest of London, on 19 December 1802.[118]

Wegg exemplifies the encouragement from the HBC head office and board that led to the remarkable contributions to science made by Hudson Bay fur-traders. Hudson's Bay Company workers brought a strength of common purpose to further the trade, improve the lot of native hunters, expand knowledge and, eventually, further the Company's well-being.

This was an era before government or private industry sponsorship of science. Little of the work of the Company employees would have reached England, let alone scientists there, if Wegg in particular had not afforded the incentive, encouraged the opportunity, and provided the connections.

ALEXANDER LIGHT

(dates of birth and death unknown)

━━◦ ⋯⋯⁙⋯⋯ ◦━━

Alexander Light was the first collector to provide type specimens from Hudson Bay. During his second tour of duty at the Bay, from 1738 to some time in the late 1740s, he collected five taxa of birds (all but one new to science), two mammals, and a turtle, each illustrated by George Edwards. Light was also a successful fur trader and one of the Company's earliest explorers. We offer those scattered fragments of information that are available.

Initially hired as a shipwright, Light was sent by the HBC to Churchill in 1733 for four years at thirty-three pounds per annum.[1] No doubt he travelled on the *Mary*, which arrived at Churchill on 4 August.[2] He had skills beyond those of a shipwright, explorer, and fur trader. John Richardson, surgeon-naturalist on the first two Arctic exploring expeditions led by John Franklin in the 1820s, mentions that about eighty years earlier Light had been "sent out ... by the Hudson's Bay Company, on account of his knowledge of Natural History."[3]

EXPLORATION AND FUR TRADE SERVICE

Light came to notice as an explorer in 1737. During the fourth year of his first tour of duty at the Bay, the company sent two ships north to explore Roe's Welcome Sound, between Southampton Island and the mainland. The initial aim was to search for a North West Passage, but the HBC later reversed the order of priorities and gave instructions to "develop trade with the Eskimos and test for minerals."[4] The *Churchill* was under the command of James Napper, with Alexander Light as mate; and the *Musquash* was under Robert Crow.[5] A letter from Prince of Wales's Fort, Churchill River, on 17 August 1736, reported that "whereas Mr. Light is appointed to be mate of the *Churchill* sloop who is to go to the northward upon discovery, we shall be greatly in want of a carpenter to keep our craft of the river in repair in Mr. Light's absence and to do other carpenter's work as is continually wanting to be done."[6]

The northern exploration was not successful. The two ships got no farther than Whale Cove at 62° 10' North, thereby failing to explore Chesterfield
Inlet, Wager Bay, or Repulse Bay. Worse, James Napper died at Whale Cove
on 7 August. Light took charge immediately, sailed for Churchill on the 15th
and arrived there on 18 August; Crow's accompanying sloop, the *Musquash*,
arrived four days later on 22 August.[7] Norton felt it would not be worth
sending sloops on the same quest another year, "the coast being perilous, no
rivers navigable that they could meet with nor no woods, and the trade trifling
and inconsiderable."[8] One day after his return from the exploration, Light,
whose first term had expired, boarded the *Mary* with Captain Coats and
reached London on 23 September 1737.[9]

On his return to the bay in late August 1738, the *Beaver* sloop "was to be
commanded and repaired by Alexander Light, 'a very good Shipwright,'"[10]
and stationed at Moose. In 1740 Light was master of the *Beaver* until it
reached Albany on 20 August. Two days later Light was appointed to officer
status: "3d in Council and Master of ye *Moose* sloop and Trader at ye Eᵗ
Main."[11] He was listed as "master and trader" at Eastmain post in 1741, its
second year of operation.[12]

ANTHROPOLOGY AND NATURAL HISTORY

On his 1837 furlough, Light carried with him skinned bird and mammal specimens for George Edwards, who portrayed them in his book. He also visited Sir Hans Sloane's private aviary-zoo "at His House in Russel Street near
Bloomsbury, London."[13] However, we know in greater detail the anthropology collection he made when Inuit came on board the *Hudson's Bay* as it
passed through Hudson Strait during the return trip in 1738.[14] Light obtained
thirty-five items from them, including pieces of ivory and an Inuit basket
made of twigs, for which he gave knives and brass buttons in return. Three
larger items were the butt end of a harpoon staff, a harpoon, and a lance.
Smaller ivory tools included a drill, a swivel for a fishing line that could be
fixed to the kayak side for lines to run out on; a fosset to blow up sealskins;
a pipe used in skinning seals; a piece of ivory that was attached to a harpoon
staff and used for dressing skins; and a comb. Other items were ornaments
for the nose, and to hang from women's breasts, and a child's doll.[15] In his
letter that accompanied the specimens, Light told Sloane that he had "not
been much on Shore as yet but this Looks Like a Pleasant Country and in
it thayr seems to be a Great Deall of Room for Industry. I see at Albany sum
Pettryfied Stones and severall fine flowers and I doubt not but here is the same
at Moos River, all of which I will Indeavour to make as Good a Collection
as I Posably would."[16]

Figure 2.1
Spruce Grouse, collected by Alexander Light. Edwards 1750, 3:71

Light's natural-history collections were probably a response to an initial request from the company to its officers to collect specimens, particularly plants, since the company's letter to Thomas White, Factor, dated 2 May 1735, was at least a second request: "We must repeat our formal order that you at a proper season plant in boxes some roots of the several sorts of herbs, plants, grass and shrubs that are in your parts and save at a proper season some of the seeds, berries, cones or kernels of all growing in your country and send them to us. Also lett [sic] your surgeon give us a particular description thereof and their names and qualities and what use the natives put them to and send us an account in writing of the particulars of what you put on board of that kind. This order we require may not be neglected for the future." This request was reiterated in 1736, 1737, and 1738.[17]

The company surgeons ought to have responded to these requests, but their response was not overwhelming. In 1738 the surgeon at Moose Factory, Edward Thompson, sent a 152-page "book of Carthredge paper ... with different sorts of plants, flowers and leaves," part manuscript and part collection. Sadly, this seems not to have reached London.[18] James Isham's four

Figure 2.2
Willow Ptarmigan in summer plumage. Edwards 1747, 2:72

boxes of "trees, herbs &c.," sent from York Factory, similarly went astray.[19] More excuses than results were produced. An August 1738 letter from Moose Factory states that the next surgeon there, Robert Pilgrim, collected only a few herbs, plants, and shrubs. Robert Macduff, surgeon at York Factory, also made a small collection, noting that "We have taken care to send your honours some plants, shrubs etc., this with the names and qualities the surgeon will give some account of."[20] James Dudgeon, the surgeon at Albany, sent nothing: "All herbs, plants, shrubs, cones or kernels that we can at convenient times gather with their names and qualities given by the surgeon, shall be placed and sent home ... but have not any at present, this summer proved so cold which frustrated all our endeavours."[21] Although individual company surgeons were known to be lazy or chronically inebriated, our best guess is that many HBC surgeons simply lacked an interest in botany. In the absence of participating surgeons, the gap was filled in part by the special competence of Alexander Light.

Linnaeus recognized Light's Spruce Grouse as a new species, now *Canachites canadensis* (Figure 2.1). Light also collected a Snowy Owl, a species

Figure 2.3
Northern Hawk-Owl. Edwards 1747, 2:62

already known to Linnaeus from northern Europe. In the case of three of Light's specimens, Linnaeus correctly considered them to belong to the European species, but later "splitters" recognized small differences that warranted a new Latin name, today recognized as the North American subspecies of each. The Willow Ptarmigan was named *Tetrao albus* by Johann Friedrich Gmelin, who edited the thirteenth edition of Linnaeus' *Systema Naturae*; it is now a subspecies, *Lagopus lagopus albus* (Figure 2.2). The Northern Hawk-Owl was named *Strix caparoch* by P.L.S. Müller in 1776; it is now a subspecies, *Surnia ulula caparoch* (Figure 2.3).

Light's specimen of a subspecies of the Gyrfalcon, *Falco obsoletus rusticolus*, was illustrated as the "Ash-coloured Buzzard" by George Edwards, with credit to Light for the specimen.[22] In another instance, Light's specimen, which "came on board a Ship sailing on the coast of Maryland, a good Distance from Shore, in an Off-land Wind," is now known as the Red-necked Phalarope (Figure 3.12).[23]

Linnaeus gave the name *Falco canadensis* to an eagle portrayed correctly by Edwards as having feathered tarsi but with a whitish base of the tail.[24]

Figure 2.4
Golden Eagle. Edwards 1743, 1:1

This eagle was said to have been brought alive to England by an unnamed "Gentleman employ'd in the Hudson's-Bay Company's Service,"[25] in all probability Alexander Light. Not until the fourth *American Ornithologists' Union Check-list* was this specimen designated the type for the North American subspecies of the Golden Eagle, now *Aquila chrysaetos canadensis* (Figure 2.4).[26]

Light also collected one new species of mammal named by Linnaeus, the American Porcupine, *Erethizon dorsatum*, and a new subspecies of the Wolverine, *Gulo gulo luscus*, from Hudson Bay. He is likely the person who brought from Hudson Bay the live Wolverine given to Sir Hans Sloane in London.[27] Light later presented George Edwards with a live Box Turtle from South Carolina.[28] While Light may also have been the "Gentleman in the HBC Service" who sent specimens of the Great Horned Owl and Wild Swan, the timing was wrong for him to have been the unnamed collector of the live Peregrine Falcon that Edwards described as having been "pitched on ship" in Hudson Strait in August 1739.[29]

Light told George Edwards that "there is a Goose which comes in Summer to *Hudson's-Bay*, having its Forehead as it were scorched with Heat, and the Natives firmly believe, that these Geese to avoid the Winter's Cold, fly toward the Sun, and approach so near that it singes its Forehead against his Orb. It is hard to convince these Savages that there are Climates on this Earth warmer than their own, to which Birds may fly for Food and Shelter during their rigid Winters." Edwards correctly presumed this to be the blue colour phase of the Snow Goose,[30] anticipating by more than two centuries the decision of the American Ornithologists' Union, which finally combined the Blue Goose and Snow Goose into one species in 1973.[31]

The last known mention of Light was by George Edwards, who noted that Light was still in the HBC service at Albany on 10 August 1747;[32] Edwards again called him "a friend of mine residing at Hudson's Bay." Edwards had written to Light to inquire about the porcupine and received the following reply from him:

"The Porcupine in this country is a beast which makes its nest or den under the roots of great trees, and sleeps much; it feeds on the bark of juniper and other trees, but chiefly on juniper; in winter it eats snow instead of drinking, and laps water in summer like a cat or dog, but carefully avoids going into it. His hair and quills remain all summer without alteration of colour; but, as the weather grows warmer in the spring, the fur grows thinner, as in all creatures in this country. But you may depend on better information next year, for they are very plentiful on the east main, several of my trading Indians depending on them for food at some seasons of the year."[33]

We salute a man who began as a shipwright, met two of the leading scientists in Britain, rose to officer status, and contributed to exploration, anthropology, and natural history.

JAMES ISHAM

(1716–1761)

James Isham was a capable but plodding man who neither sought glory nor received much recognition. Although he has a substantial biography in the specialized *Dictionary of Canadian Biography*, he is not listed in the *Encyclopedia Canadiana* (1957) nor the *Canadian Encyclopedia* (1985, 1988). Isham's writings did not come to light in time for mention by Elsa Guerdrum Allen in her synopsis of early North American ornithology in 1951; she was unaware that *Isham's Observations and Notes, 1743–1749,* had been edited by E.E. Rich for the Champlain Society and published in 1949. Rich (1949) summarized Isham's qualities: "at once a skilled and understanding trader, a perceptive planner and strategist, and a conscientious and observant natural historian."[1] Only in 1997 did a brief profile of Isham appear in a compendium of naturalists' biographies.[2]

The son of Whitby Isham and Ann Skrimshire, James was born in the parish of St Andrew's, Holborn, London, in 1716. He had a good general education for his time but no special training in natural history. On 11 May 1732, at the age of sixteen, he was hired as a "writer" (and accountant) by the HBC. After a long voyage on the *Mary*, the third HBC ship of that name, he arrived at York Factory during the first three days of August 1732.

Described by his new chief as "very sober, honest & diligent," Isham received unusually rapid promotion.[3] On 4 May 1737, when only twenty-one years old, he became the chief at York Factory. He next became chief at the then-headquarters post of Fort Prince of Wales at Churchill on 16 August 1741.

Isham's first winter at Churchill was marred by the presence of the troublesome overwintering crew of the naval exploring expedition led by Captain Christopher Middleton, the former HBC ship's master, to search for the North West Passage. The HBC had warned the Admiralty secretary in advance (on 30 May 1741) of inadequate provisions and the consequent "Danger and ill Consequences that may attend the Company if Capt. Middleton should Winter at any of their Settlements."[4] Middleton lost thirteen of his men that winter, eleven to scurvy alone, before his summer explorations of the west coast of Hudson Bay north to Wager Inlet and Repulse Bay excluded the presence of a practical North West Passage.[5]

The icy blasts from the bay at Churchill did not agree with Isham; he thought they aggravated his gout. Partly for this reason he was transferred back to York Factory, where he arrived on 3 August 1746 on the *Prince Rupert II* following his furlough in England. Probably he first met George Edwards during this furlough. At York in 1746–47 he hosted the officers and men of the even more contentious discovery expedition led by William Moor in the *Dobbs* and Francis Smith in the *California*, prior to their disappointing northward expedition of 1747; like Napper and Light in 1737, they found no evidence of a North West Passage.

In 1748 Isham was recalled to London to help the Hudson's Bay Company Committee defend its monopoly against attacks by Arthur Dobbs and others.[6] Within a few days of his arrival in London on the *Prince Rupert II* on 29 October 1748, the thirty-two-year-old Isham married twenty-one-year-old Catherine Mindham of the parish of St Martin's-in-the-Fields. In all probability she knew nothing of Isham's native woman at the Bay.[7] On this prolonged second furlough Isham visited the naturalist George Edwards, who paid tribute to Isham's "commendable curiosity."[8]

Isham returned on 18 August 1750 on the *Prince Rupert II*. Catherine remained in England, where she gave birth to their daughter.[9] Isham was in charge of York Factory once again: his replacement during his absence, John Newton, had drowned while swimming in the icy water on 28 June 1750.[10] In 1754 Isham organized the unprecedented inland trip of Anthony Henday, who wintered that year with the Blackfoot Indians near the Rocky Mountains.

Isham's third and last furlough was during the winter of 1758–59; he made the journey to London and back in the *Prince Rupert II*, now an old and leaky ship under Captain Jonathan Fowler, Sr.

His last two years at York were miserable: his gout became worse and for two months he complained of "weakness & stoppage in his throat."[11] He died on Monday, 13 April 1761, and was buried with a twenty-one-gun salute. Catherine had recently predeceased him so all his property passed to his mixed-blood son, Charles Price Isham (also known as Charles Thomas Isham), who by 1790 had risen to become master of several smaller fur-trading posts, the first of the native-born to reach this rank.[12]

ANTHROPOLOGY

James Isham's valuable observations on the customs and language of the native Indians, as well as on mammals and birds, were transcribed from the

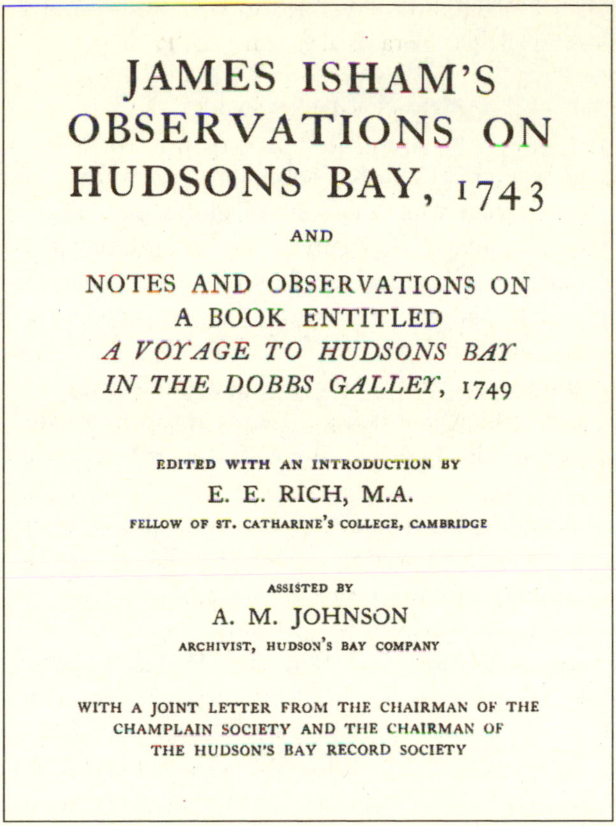

JAMES ISHAM'S OBSERVATIONS ON HUDSONS BAY, 1743

AND

NOTES AND OBSERVATIONS ON A BOOK ENTITLED *A VOYAGE TO HUDSONS BAY IN THE DOBBS GALLEY*, 1749

EDITED WITH AN INTRODUCTION BY

E. E. RICH, M.A.

FELLOW OF ST. CATHARINE'S COLLEGE, CAMBRIDGE

ASSISTED BY

A. M. JOHNSON

ARCHIVIST, HUDSON'S BAY COMPANY

WITH A JOINT LETTER FROM THE CHAIRMAN OF THE CHAMPLAIN SOCIETY AND THE CHAIRMAN OF THE HUDSON'S BAY RECORD SOCIETY

Figure 3.1.
Title page of Isham's *Observations*, edited by E.E. Rich, 1949

original notebooks in the HBC Archives by E.E. Rich, a Fellow of St Catharine's College at Cambridge University. In 1949 they appeared as a 457-page book, *James Isham's Observations on Hudson's Bay, 1743–1749* (Figure 3.1).

Isham's *Observations* included a respectable first attempt at a Cree-English dictionary, together with some words in the Siouan Assiniboine language. This dictionary included what may be the first (1743, though not published until 1949) use of what have become English "loan words," *pimmegan*, now spelled *pemmican*, and *ti pee* or *ti pi* (for tent).[13] The *Dictionary of Canadianisms* credits Isham with being the first known person to bring four more Cree words into English: *ne may cu sheeck* as the first rendition of *namaycush*, the Cree name for lake trout; *shaganappi* as a Cree word for rawhide thong; *wa pis ka john,* which became shortened to whiskey jack for the Gray Jay; and *weywey* or wavey for Snow Goose.[14]

NATURAL HISTORY

Isham was the second Hudson Bay collector of important natural-history specimens. Unfortunately for Isham, although his specimens were among the first to receive binomial Latin names bestowed by Linnaeus himself, they were collected before it was fashionable to name new species after the collector. There are no species named *ishami,* and few modern ornithologists have even heard his name.

Isham responded to the Company's first requests for samples of plants in 1737 and 1738 by sending four boxes of plants from York Factory each year. There is a strong possibility that his surgeon, Robert Macduff, collected the plants on his behalf.[15]

At Churchill, during a long bout of illness from 23 December 1742 through 1 February 1743, Isham found time to write his *Observations,* listing twenty-four species of birds. Of these, twelve species and one subspecies, the small Canada Goose, were not delivered to Edwards or were not considered to be new and thus were not illustrated by Edwards.[16] Further, Isham failed to identify the species of eagle, owl, "kite"(hawk), and swallow that were present at York Factory.

Isham described the American White Pelican as "a Large bird, with a great Bill Long neck't and short Legd. Carrying their neck Like a Swan ... under the throat hangs a bag, which when fill'd wou'd hold 2 Gallons, the Substance of itt is a thin membrane, of a sky Colour, they fly Very heavy and Low, and fish is their Chiefest food, the Bouch, as well as stomach has fish found in itt. The Bouch or bag is purely to Keep their food in; they are Eat by some."[17]

Concerning the Passenger Pigeon, Isham wrote: "Its Very Rare to see any Pidgeons or doves, in these parts, or Downe by the sea side, tho in Land some hundred miles are Very Numerous, once in 12 Year I Did see some millions of them, which Came from the Southwd. flying in Ranges as the Goose does, &c.: they are of a Blew Grey and abou't as big as a dove pidgeon and Very Good Eating."[18]

When he left for England on 27 July 1745 on his first furlough, Isham took with him the specimens he had collected; large, interesting, or edible birds were overrepresented. Landing at London on 28 September, he was welcomed by the HBC Committee on 30 September. George Edwards, to whom he entrusted his specimens, depicted a number of them in his splendid four-volume work, *A Natural History of Uncommon Birds*, between 1743 and 1751.[19] Edwards referred to Isham, who had

obliged me extremely by furnishing me with more than thirty different Species of Birds, of which we have hitherto had little or no Knowledge, the far greatest Part of them being non-descripts.[20] As I shall in the Course of this Work have Occasion frequently to mention the above curious Gentleman's Name,[21] it will be here necessary to let the Reader know, that Mr. Isham has been employ'd for many Years in the Service of the Hudson's-Bay Company, and has for some years past, been Governor under them at different times, of several of their Forts and Settlements in the most Northern habitable Parts of America; where at his leisure Times, his commendable Curiosity led him to make a Collection of all the Beasts, Birds, and Fishes of those countries ... The Furs of the Beasts, and the Skins of the Birds were stuffed and preserved very clean and perfect ... and brought to London in the Year 1745.[22]

NEW BIRD SPECIES AND SUBSPECIES COLLECTED BY ISHAM

Edwards' volumes in turn were one of the main sources of information for the definitive species list compiled by Linnaeus in Uppsala, Sweden, in 1758. Birds collected by Isham and painted by Edwards became the official type specimens[23] for the following twelve species. (Those also mentioned in his *Observations* are marked with an asterisk):

Ardea herodias	Great Blue Heron (Figure 3.2)
Anas caerulescens	Snow Goose (blue morph) (Figure 3.3)*
Anas perspicillata	Surf Scoter (Figure 3.4)
Tetrao phasianellus	Sharp-tailed Grouse (Figure 3.5)*
Ardea americana	Whooping Crane (Figure 3.6)*
Ardea canadensis	Sandhill Crane (Figure 3.7)*
Rallus carolinus	Sora (Figure 3.8)*
Scolopax fedoa	Marbled Godwit (Figure 3.9)
Scolopax haemastica	Hudsonian Godwit (Figure 3.10)
Tringa fulicaria	Red Phalarope (Figure 3.11)
Tringa lobata	Red-necked Phalarope (Figure 3.12)
Hirundo subis	Purple Martin (Figure 3.13)

Another three birds collected by Isham, mentioned in his manuscript and illustrated by Edwards, had not yet been differentiated from similar species occurring in Europe. One, the bittern, was and still is an occasional vagrant, crossing the Atlantic to Iceland and the British Isles; another, the Canada

Figure 3.2
Great Blue Heron. Edwards 1750, 3:135

Figure 3.3
Blue Goose (blue morph of Snow Goose). Edwards 1750, 3:152

Figure 3.4
Surf Scoter. Edwards 1750, 3:155

Figure 3.5
Sharp-tailed Grouse. Edwards 1750, 3:117

Figure 3.6
Whooping Crane. Edwards 1750, 3:132

Figure 3.7
Sandhill Crane. Edwards 1750, 3:133

Figure 3.8
Sora. Edwards 1750, 3:144

Figure 3.9
Marbled Godwit. Edwards 1750, 3:137

Figure 3.10
Hudsonian Godwit. Edwards 1750, 3:138

Figure 3.11
Red Phalarope. Edwards 1750, 3:142

Figure 3.12
Red-necked Phalarope. Edwards 1750, 3:143

Figure 3.13
Purple Martin. Edwards 1750, 3:120

Goose, had already been introduced to estates in England (see Appendix E).
The third column lists the year they were recognized as separate species:

Botaurus lentiginosus	American Bittern*	1813
Cygnus columbianus	Tundra Swan*	1815
Anser albifrons	Greater White-fronted Goose*	1769

The following species, sent by Isham from Hudson Bay (though none was
described in his manuscript), illustrated by George Edwards, and then listed
by Linnaeus in 1758, had also been collected elsewhere, all but one of them
in Europe. The country acknowledged as the official type locality is given
after the species name:

Gavia arctica	Arctic Loon	Sweden
Podiceps auritus	Horned Grebe	Finland
Histrionicus histrionicus	Harlequin Duck[24]	Newfoundland
Somateria spectabilis	King Eider	Sweden
Clangula hyemalis	Long-tailed Duck	Sweden
Arenaria interpres	Ruddy Turnstone	Sweden
Stercorarius parasiticus	Parasitic Jaeger	Sweden
Picoides tridactylus	Three-toed Woodpecker	Sweden
Plectrophenax nivalis	Snow Bunting	Lapland
Pinicola enucleator	Pine Grosbeak (male & female)	Sweden

Two additional species had already been painted by Mark Catesby, the
Canada Goose from "Canada" – that is, Quebec – and the Belted Kingfisher
from South Carolina. Both also appeared in the Isham collection, were illustrated in Edwards' 1750 book, and then were listed by Linnaeus in 1758. A
third species, the American Golden-Plover, was illustrated by Edwards in
1750, but Linnaeus failed to appreciate its plumage differences from the rather
similar European Golden-Plover; Müller in 1776 named the American
species from a specimen collected in Hispaniola.

Branta canadensis	Canada Goose*	Quebec (and Hudson Bay)
Ceryle alcyon	Belted Kingfisher	South Carolina (and Hudson Bay)
Pluvialis dominica	American Golden-Plover	Hispaniola

One other race, named by Linnaeus from an Isham specimen illustrated by
Edwards, was the only Hudson Bay taxon whose description by Linnaeus
was delayed until his twelfth edition in 1776: *Falco hudsonius*, now a subspecies
of Northern Harrier, *Circus cyaneus hudsonius* (Figure 3.13).

Figure 3.14
Northern Harrier. Edwards 1750, 3:107

Isham also showed George Edwards a tobacco box set in silver, which had the lower shell of a tortoise for its bottom and the upper shell for its cover. What Isham called a land-tortoise, "in Hudson's-Bay," was probably a Painted Turtle, *Chrysemys picta*, or, less likely, a Snapping Turtle, *Chelydra serpentina*.[25] In either case, the turtle shell came from somewhere inland, probably at or near Lake Winnipeg.

Isham performed a valuable service. Not only did he collect specimens of new taxa but he prepared them well and delivered them to George Edwards at an optimal time. Isham lacked the direction and assistance that Andrew Graham and Thomas Hutchins, his successors, were to derive fifteen years later from Pennant's book *British Zoology* (1761–66). Access to these volumes helped Isham's successors to maintain the pre-eminence of Hudson Bay as the main centre of ornithological study in the giant area that would one day form a large part of Canada.

On the last page of volume 3 of his *Natural History*, published in 1750, Edwards paid tribute to Isham, "to whose Curiosity and good Nature I am beholden for the greatest Part ... of my *History of Birds*; and I believe the curious Part of the world will not think themselves less obliged to Mr. Isham than I acknowledge myself to be."

Isham was revered as the "Grand Old Man" of the fur trade, the "beloved friend" and "worthy master" of the new generation of factors, and above all as "The Idol of the Indians."[26]

HUMPHREY MARTEN

(1729?–1790?)

Humphrey Marten was born about 1729.[1] An unusually clear-headed man, he was engaged by the HBC in the capacity of "writer" on 1 March 1750.[2] In the opinion of the distinguished historian Richard Glover, Marten was "devotedly loyal" to the Company throughout his life, "had besides the none too common gift of being able to depute authority," and had "a very clear insight into Indian character."[3] Marten sailed in the *Prince Rupert II* in May and arrived at York Factory on 18 August 1750. Following employment as clerk and steward, he became acting chief at York Factory during James Isham's furlough in 1758–59. He next rebuilt Severn in 1759 and was chief there for two years.[4] He then took command at York Factory for a year, spent a year on furlough in England, and returned to serve at Albany, including two terms as chief, 1764–68 and 1769–74.

Furloughs because of ill health resulted in Marten's spending winters in England in 1768–69 and again in 1774–75. He was next placed in charge of the headquarters post, York Factory. Here in 1774–75 he both directed and supported Samuel Hearne's founding of the Company's first major inland fur-trading post at Cumberland House, in present-day Saskatchewan.

Glover has said that Marten's writings, describing the competition between the Hudson's Bay Company and the fur traders from Montreal, "contain perhaps the best, clearest and most informative brief pictures of the early days of what is called the strife between the companies."[5] Each year Marten took special pains to go through the journals of the inland posts and assemble their most important points in well-organized, numbered paragraphs, "unsparingly blunt" and "mercilessly bare."[6]

Edward Umfreville, a sworn enemy of the Company which he had previously served for eleven years, claimed that Marten treated Indians badly, sometimes beating them cruelly.[7] Such a statement hardly squares with evidence that Marten had a persuasive way with the Indians, who carried goods inland to supply Cumberland House and, after 1777, a more distant second inland HBC post at Hudson House, west of present-day Prince Albert.

The Hudson's Bay Company could undersell the French traders from Montreal, but it couldn't move sufficient trade goods inland. Since the

Orkneymen, who made up the bulk of the workers at the post, would not go inland unless Marten met their exorbitant wage demands, he increased their pay in defiance of orders from London; fearing the consequences of such disobedience, he said "sleep, health and peace of mind are to me no more."[8] The lives of the inland servants were frequently threatened "by the Canadians[9] who's numbers are as 15 to 1; frequent hungry bellys; wet and cold lodgings are amongst the many other hardships they undergo."[10]

Marten did not go inland because of his age and ill health, especially his gout. When he wrote to surgeon Thomas Hutchins at York Factory, describing his symptoms of depression, Hutchins replied,"Use exercise my dear sir – nothing better."[11] In an attempt to improve his health Marten took long rides on horseback. In 1777, presbyopia obliged him to give up reading, one of the foremost pleasures in his life.

Marten had a difficult life in winter; journals could be written only after the ink thawed, and strong beer froze solid in bottles two feet from a stout fire. Yet in summer he undertook some of the first farming northwest of the St Lawrence River valley, maintaining a fine garden and a flourishing population of cattle and pigs. His first native wife, Pawpitch, daughter to the captain of the fort's goose hunters, died "at 10 minutes before 3 O Clock" on the morning of 24 January 1771,[12] leaving him a son, John America Marten, whom he later educated at great expense in England. The bill for the boy's "maintenance and education" in 1780 was £50, the equivalent of at least $5000 in 2003 currency. Marten's second native woman bore him three children, two of whom survived. Before he left York Factory in the fall of 1781, Marten arranged for her father to come from Albany to take her and the two children under his care.

After his leave to Britain in 1781–82, Marten returned to York Factory on 15 August, just two days before three French warships led by the celebrated French navigator Jean-François de Galaup, Comte de la Pérouse, arrived offshore. One week earlier they had sacked Hearne's Prince of Wales's fort at Churchill. These two surprise attacks by the French were the only acts of aggression in the bay during during the American War of Independence.[13] The French aim was not to conquer but "to destroy the prosperous Hudson's Bay Company fur trade." Marten had no choice but to surrender to the last French squadron[14] ever to attack a British trading post on Hudson Bay. La Pérouse burned the fort. Unlike Hearne, whom La Pérouse allowed to sail from Hudson Strait to the Orkneys, Marten was taken to France and held a prisoner there.

After Marten's release to England, the Company persuaded him to take charge of York Factory once more. He arrived on 15 September 1783, twelve days after the signing of the Treaty of Paris, to learn that William Tomison

Figure 4.1
Albany Fort, 1791–92. Artist unknown. Courtesy HBC Archives, PAM.

from Cumberland House had been at York Factory from 6 August until 8 September 1783, waiting in vain for supplies for the next trading year, but had had to return inland empty-handed.[15] In 1785 Marten was cheered by the arrival of David Thompson as his assistant. A year later, on 30 August 1786, Marten left York Factory for good on the *King George III* and reached London on 4 October.[16]

Marten is last mentioned in HBC records of 1787, may possibly have been alive in 1790, and was termed "the late Humphrey Marten" by Hearne in 1792.[17] Because he had had constant pain in his left kidney area while ill in 1779, he asked that an autopsy be done after his death, hoping that the knowledge so gained might be of benefit to others.[18]

NATURAL HISTORY

Between 1769 and 1774, during his second term as chief factor at Albany (Figure 4.1), Marten was called upon to provide the Royal Society of London with natural-history specimens and information.[19] He admitted his "ignorance in Zoology" and hoped "to find the surgeon versed in these matters,"[20] but by 1770–71 he had developed increasing enthusiasm for the project. In some instances he relied on the local natives for "the best Indian intelligence

I could get" instead of making personal observations. Moreover, he wished that "when I received orders from my masters to make a collection of birds, etc., that the *Naturalists Journal*, as also *British Zoology*, had been sent to me, for which I should have paid with thanks; fine seed shot, birdlime, glass bottles with ingredients for preparing liquor, would have enabled me to have given more satisfaction to the gentlemen concerned as well as myself than it is possible for me now to do."[21]

Marten's initial shipment, sent with other specimens from fellow trader Andrew Graham in 1771, contained seventeen skins of seven species. Among them was the world's first scientific specimen of the Eskimo Curlew, given the name of *Scolopax borealis* by Johann Reinhold Forster.[22] In 1771 Marten also sent home "a fine brace of Partridges a Cock & Hen," both alive, and a pair of snowshoe hares; only the male hare survived the voyage. Forster lists the Ruffed Grouse, Sharp-tailed Grouse, Black-bellied Plover, Yellowlegs, Eskimo Curlew, Yellow-shafted (Northern) Flicker, Black-billed Magpie, Horned Lark, Black-capped Chickadee, and White-crowned Sparrow as belonging to the 1771 collection from Albany. The Downy Woodpecker specimen from Albany[23] probably came from Marten. He thus became (with Andrew Graham) one of the first two natural-history collectors in what is now Ontario. In 1771 he was, to the best of our knowledge, the first person to put up bird boxes in what is now Canada: "this spring I caused breeding Boxes to be placed in many places within and without the Fort; to one of which boxes, a brace of those Birds took kindly, and hatched their Young, and became so tame as to permit me to come within two Yards of them." These were Tree Swallows.[24] Marten also informed Hutchins that Blue Geese were commoner than Snow Geese at Albany, the first indication of the preponderance of the blue morph in the eastern part of the flyway, an important observation made known by Thomas Pennant in 1787 and 1792.[25]

Marten's second shipment of specimens, sent to Britain in 1772, comprised twenty-six specimens of twenty-one species. To accompany them, he provided descriptions of the colours of soft parts that might fade before reaching England, described the colour of the pupil of the eye (!), gave the Cree Indian name, and for all but the Snow Goose, which nested farther north, reported the number of eggs. In 1949 and 1950, when Elsa G. Allen was writing her landmark history of early North American ornithology, her researches took her to the Royal Society offices in London. The librarian found for her a Marten manuscript entitled "A Short Description of the Birds in a Box" (reproduced in Document 3).[26] This manuscript had initially accompanied Marten's box of twenty-six specimens and had given their native names; Mrs Allen published Marten's account of the swallow.[27] Since Marten's notes were

Figure 4.2
Daines Barrington, 1770 portrait by Slater,
engraved by C. Knight, 1795. From Hoare 1976

intended to accompany specimens, there was no need for him to provide a full description, and in four instances one cannot even guess which species is represented.

W. Earl Godfrey, author of *Birds of Canada*, agrees with our identification of the Tree Swallow, Bank Swallow, Snow Goose, and Common Nighthawk, and with "best-guess" tentative identifications of Gray Jay (or Northern Shrike?), Gyrfalcon, Herring Gull, Whimbrel, Arctic Tern, Red-breasted Merganser, Common Goldeneye, Northern Goshawk, Eskimo Curlew, and Pine Grosbeak. A small yellow bird was probably a Yellow Warbler, since Albany is too far north for it to have been an American Goldfinch. A bird with red on its head, size not indicated, could have been a redpoll. As Godfrey comments, "Marten ... was merely trying to comply with orders from headquarters ... Specimen identification and consequent application of names came from Indians of various experience and ability, as did much of the life history data ... It's like trying to do a jigsaw puzzle, most of the pieces missing or mutilated."[28]

Marten kept spring arrival dates for birds such as swallows, and reported late fall departure dates for snow buntings. He attempted unsuccessfully to have a domestic hen incubate eggs of the Sharp-tailed Grouse.

Marten's handwriting was much better than average but, as was common in his era, his spelling, punctuation, and capitalization were all idiosyncratic. Although he exaggerated the incubation period of the Tree Swallow and believed they carried their young with their claws, his other natural-history accounts were unusually sound for the time. At least he was not misled by the widespread belief that birds do not migrate, an erroneous view held in Britain by no less a personage than Daines Barrington (Figure 4.2), compiler of *The Naturalists' Journal* and a major influence on Gilbert White of Selborne.[29]

Samuel Hearne was the first to decry the lack of recognition given to Marten. Hearne gives us a better idea of the size of the various collections sent home by Marten – "several hundred specimens" – and felt that when Hutchins succeeded Marten at Albany in 1774, "every thing that has been sent over from that part" was thereby credited to Hutchins. This is our first evidence of Hutchins taking credit for the work of others. Hearne writes that Thomas Pennant, "who with a candour that does him honour, has so generously acknowledged his obligations to all to whom he thought he was indebted for information ... has not mentioned his [Marten's] name."[30] Hearne is correct; Marten's achievements were poorly recognized during his lifetime and for over 200 years since.

ANDREW GRAHAM

(1733–1815)

Andrew Graham was born about 1733, probably near Edinburgh. Nothing specific is known about his childhood, but his writings suggest that he obtained a good Scottish education. In 1749, as a youth of about sixteen, Graham joined the service of the HBC as servant to the master of the sloop *Churchill*, sailing up and down Hudson Bay for three years. In September 1753 he travelled overland from Churchill to York Factory to become assistant writer under James Isham. On a return overland trek to Churchill in January 1754, to retrieve his possessions, he froze his feet so severely that they narrowly escaped amputation.[1] Graham was so proficient as a clerk and accountant that he became acting chief at age twenty-five while Isham took a furlough to Britain in 1758–59; thereafter, until 1761, he was second-in-command at York Factory. He was then promoted to master at Severn House, where he served until 1774.[2] Following the unexpected deaths of Moses Norton, chief, and Isaac Leask, second, at Churchill, Graham left Severn on 5 February 1774 and travelled overland in midwinter to complete his Company service by taking command at Churchill on 3 March 1774. He turned over this, his last brief command, to Samuel Hearne in the summer of 1775.

FUR TRADE

Graham's most important contribution in terms of Company service was to plan the inland expansion of the Hudson's Bay Company. This began with two big steps in 1772. First he sent Matthew Cocking on an exploratory trip inland in 1772–73. However the Indians assembled by Cocking to make the trip to York Factory instead sold most of their furs to rival Montreal traders on the Saskatchewan River at Nipawi, thus solidifying the need for a permanent inland trading post.[3] Second, Graham's landmark memorandum of 26 August 1772 laid out plans for the famous explorer Samuel Hearne to found the first HBC inland trading post, Cumberland House on the Saskatchewan River, in 1774.[4] Founding of this post thus "led to ... a new era in the rivalry with the Montreal traders."[5] During the second year of its operation,

Mathew Cocking, second-in-command at York, was sent to take charge of Cumberland House.[6]

The marital affairs of men living in the wilds of Hudson Bay were often complicated. On 6 May 1770, while home on his first furlough, Graham had married Patricia Sherer in Edinburgh; he spent only four weeks with her before returning to Hudson Bay. Nothing more is known of her. Graham also had a native wife at Hudson Bay; when he retired he took his six-year-old daughter, born about 1769, back to England on the *Prince Rupert IV*, which sailed on 26 August 1775. Graham left his two-year-old son, Joseph, with his native mother.[7]

From Edinburgh, Graham acted as agent for the HBC from late 1786 through early 1791, and sent regular payments to the company's servants in the Orkney Islands. The date of Graham's second Edinburgh marriage, to Barbara Bowie, is not known, but may have followed his retirement to Edinburgh in 1775. Barbara died in 1812 or 1813. Graham may have had a liaison with another Scottish woman, for his will left the rather large sum of £700 in trust for "Andrew Graham ... the son of Menzie Waterstone."[8] From 1802 until his death at Prestonpans, Scotland, on 8 September 1815, Graham received a generous annual thirty-guinea gratuity from the Company.

One cannot accept Graham's overly modest disclaimer, typical of the formal etiquette of his time, that he wrote descriptions of bird and mammal specimens only for his own amusement. The version titled E.2/7 was directed to Robert Merry of Red Lion Square, Middlesex.[9] Graham's motive may have been to show how competent and knowledgeable he was, in the hope of obtaining a permanent promotion to be chief at York Factory. Indeed, in E.2/5 he tells how anxious he was to be appointed permanent head at York Factory, a big promotion from the smaller post at Severn.[10] He had already served twice as interim chief factor at York in 1765–66 and in 1771–72, when Ferdinand Jacobs was on leave. Graham writes in E.2/5, "I have made it appear that I know the affairs of York Fort as well as any person whatever."[11] But Graham's efforts were in vain; he failed to receive the promotion.

ANTHROPOLOGY AND CARTOGRAPHY

Another lasting achievement was Graham's careful documentation of "Life and Trade in the Bay," "Indians," and "Eskimos."[12] Since their publication by the Hudson's Bay Record Society in 1969, these sections of Graham's *Observations* have proven to be among the best primary resource material available anywhere for the eighteenth century. Unlike the bird section, they were written by Graham alone, as were most of the notes concerning forty-one mammals and seventeen fish. Graham also played a small but important role

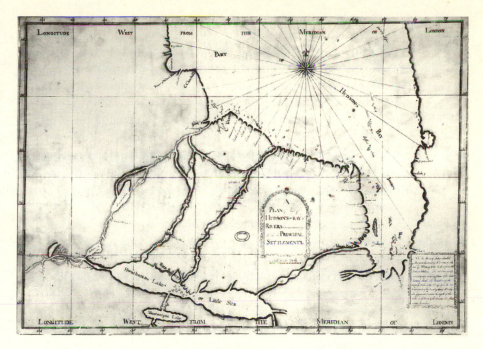

Figure 5.1
Graham's map G.2/15. HBC Archives, PAM

as "the first of the map makers of the bay to depict the complicated network of interior waterways." Graham's first rough sketch-map, sent to London in 1774,[13] is shown in Figure 5.1.

NATURAL HISTORY

In 1770, on his return from his first English furlough after his arrival at the bay in 1749, and stimulated by Thomas Pennant, who had published his *British Zoology* in 1768,[14] Graham began to enthusiastically collect natural-history specimens at Severn. He encouraged Humphrey Marten at Albany to do the same. The Indians learned of his interest in ornithology and brought him skins, "stuffed and dried," from inland.[15]

Pennant wanted skins of birds and mammals in order to publish additional books. He had already enlisted John White, the brother of England's first celebrated naturalist, Gilbert White, to send him specimens from Gibraltar. Gilbert White's friend, the Honourable Daines Barrington, had also applied to the HBC for natural-history specimens on behalf of the Royal Society, and the Company asked its officers to "send home 'Sundry Species.'"[16] Barrington put Graham's specimen of either a snowshoe or arctic hare to good use and published an "Investigation of the specific characters which distinguish the Rabbit from the Hare" in early 1772.[17]

At Severn, Graham made a permanent mark in the annals of natural history as one of the earliest to collect specimens (including new bird species) in North America and to provide observations on bird and mammal behaviour. He became "the most industrious and systematic" collector among the Company factors, and "for the most part a discriminating observer," as Glyndwr Williams said in a 1968 information brochure.[18] Among the sixty-four skins of thirty-nine bird species Graham sent from Severn in 1771 were the type specimens for the Great Gray Owl *Strix nebulosa*, Boreal Chickadee *Parus hudsonicus*, Blackpoll Warbler *Muscicapa striata* (now *Dendroica striata*), and White-crowned Sparrow *Emberiza leucophrys* (now *Zonotrichia leucophrys*). The Snow Goose, *Anas nivalis*, was recognized by the first three AOU check-lists as a subspecies. A Gyrfalcon, named *Falco sacer*, was accepted until 1882 as a full species.[19] These and one fish, the Longnose Sucker *Cyprinus catostomus* (now *Catostomus catostomus*), were given their definitive Latin names and complete Latin descriptions in 1772 by Johann Reinhold Forster, who quoted from Graham's accompanying notes and gave Graham sole credit for them, as he richly deserved.

Sadly, Forster made two errors of commission and two of omission with Graham specimens. He described the Slate-colored Junco as a new species, whereas it had already been described by Linnaeus from a Catesby Carolina specimen. He gave a new name, *Falco spadiceus*, to what later proved to be merely the dark phase of the Rough-legged Hawk.[20] But he passed up two opportunities to describe new species from Graham specimens. He recognized the Rusty Blackbird as new and different,[21] yet gave it no name. He mistakenly assumed that the American White Pelican[22] was the same as the somewhat similar (white) Oriental Pelican described by Linnaeus. Graham's accompanying notes described the nesting habits of the Cliff Swallow, a species not formally described and named until 1823, but the swallow specimen sent Forster was a Tree Swallow.

Graham provided valuable information, still true today, about the distribution of the Ruffed Grouse. He said it was "pretty common" inland at Henley House and at Moose Fort on James Bay, but seldom seen farther north than Albany. Given this statement, Graham's Ruffed Grouse specimen, sent from Severn, most probably came from some distance inland. Forster published Cree names supplied by Graham for twenty-three bird species, but only two Cree names for fish and none for mammals.

In E.2/5 Graham wrote of the Snow Bunting: "we kill some of them with a net made for that purpose, which is put in a frame and set on the ground, one side being kept up by two sticks, and under it is scattered a little oatmeal or seeds of grass, and when they come to feed, the two sticks having a string fast to them is hawled out at pleasure, when the net falls down and all that are under made prisoners."[23] Concerning the "Whiskajohn" or Gray Jay, he said, "A person no where in [the] woods can stop ten minutes but he is surrounded by them, whistling and making an agreeable noise. They are very troublesome to the English when tenting abroad, picking the baits out of the martin traps, and pilfering the provisions off the stages that are without the tents. ... Piece of pork or bacon is their delight ... I have known them in six hours eat and carry away twelve pound wt of bacon, two salt geese, and two pieces of pork ... they are so impudent as to go into the tents when the Men are out on duty, and examine all about; nay, they will sometimes settle on you when standing in a steady posture."[24] One can see why Forster assessed Graham as "a careful observer, and an indefatigable collector."[25] Graham, however, admitted that he was "quite ignorant of plants."[26]

Few authors wait 154 years after their death for their writings to be published and recognized. This was Andrew Graham's fate. He deserves to be remembered. For the first time Graham's own unassisted natural-history observations (E.2/5) may be viewed in Document 1.[27]

THOMAS HUTCHINS

(1742?–1790)

Thomas Hutchins, surgeon, fur trader, and meteorologist, whose name is perpetuated in Hutchins' Goose, *Branta canadensis hutchinsii*, first appears in Hudson's Bay Company records as surgeon on the *King George II*. The annual supply ship from London under Captain Jonathan Fowler, Jr, unloaded supplies and loaded the season's furs at York Factory between 6 and 16 September 1765; it returned to London by 20 October. Hutchins was paid £11/3/2 for his service during the voyage.[1] On 12 February 1766 he accepted an appointment as surgeon at York Factory at £36 per annum, arriving on the *King George* on 11 August. It is of some interest that, had Samuel Hearne been unable to found the first inland post at Cumberland House, Andrew Graham's second choice would have been Hutchins, who was equally proficient as a fur trader.[2] Hutchins was undoubtedly the most distinguished of the long list of York Factory surgeons of his century[3] (Table 6.1).

In 1774, when Hutchins returned to the bay from his first furlough, he became chief at Albany. Hutchins brought with him George Sutherland from Wick, Scotland, as his servant.[4]

When Philip Turnor, the first inland surveyor and map-maker of the HBC,[5] visited Albany from 23 December 1779 through 19 February 1780, he contrasted Hutchins' well-run operation at Albany ("every thing seems in good Repair a Sufficient stock of Firewood and Timber on the Plantation and business seems to go on smooth and even") with the sorry state of Moose Fort ("A person could hardly suppose this place and Moose Fort has the same owners") (Figure 6.1).[6]

Hutchins and Germain Maugenest, a French trader in the employ of the HBC at Albany, were also involved in the first known correspondence concerning "pointed" blankets.[7] On 23 December 1779 the committee at Hudson's Bay House in London placed an order with Thomas Empson of Witney, Oxfordshire, who had previously supplied the HBC with blankets and duffels. The first order requested 100 pairs each of 1-, 1½-, 2-, 2½-, and 3-point blankets. The company then proposed that two "made beaver" be the purchase price for the 1½-point blanket and four beaver for a 3-point blanket, but Thomas Hutchins wrote from Albany that the Indians expected

Table 6.1

Eighteenth-century surgeons, Hudson's Bay Company, York Factory, 1714–1801

From	To	Surgeon	Comments
1714	1717	John Carruthers	
1718	1723	William Moncrieff	
1724	1726	William Roberts	
1726	1731	James Graham	
1731	1735	William Roberts	
1735	1738	Robert Macduff	
1738	1741	John Potts	Chief at Moose Factory, 1747
1741	1744	Giles Wills	
1744	1747	Charles Brady	
1747	1751	William Reynolds	
1751	1753	Benjamin Picart	
1753	1754	William Reynolds	Alcoholic, died May 1754
1754	1755	Thomas Hopkins	Sent for from Churchill 19 May 1754 after Reynolds died
1755	1756	John Lloyd	Mentally ill, sent home
1756	1757	John Price	
1757	1760	Thomas Hopkins	
1760	1762	James Bloxham	Alcoholic
1762	1763	Thomas Hopkins	
1763	1766	Paul Cauldwell	
1766	1773	Thomas Hutchins	Chief at Albany, 1774–82
1773	1777	Robert Body	
1777	1781	William Stephenson	
1781	1782	Alfred Robinson	
1782	1783	John Turner	
1783	1788	Alfred Robinson	
1788	1789	Norman Dauntsey Southall	
1789	1796	Thomas Thomas	to 3 July 1795
1796	1797	John Wright	Colen said Wright was unfit, ideas exhausted, dangerous, and obstinate
1797	1798	No surgeon	Fur trader Tate did bloodletting in absence of surgeon
1798	1799	Thomas Thomas ?	
1799	1801	Mark Stephen Fielding	

Figure 6.1
East view of Moose Factory. Watercolour by William Richards, 1804–1811.
HBC Archives, PAM

to trade even, one beaver for each point of blanket. One "made beaver" was "a unit of exchange equivalent to the value of one prime beaver pelt."[8] Hudson's Bay point blankets[9] and blanket coats remain a standard item two and a quarter centuries years later, having been worn on expeditions to Mount Everest and the Antarctic. In December 2001 a beaver pelt fetched fifteen to twenty dollars, while a 4-point blanket, big enough for a double bed, cost $299.[10]

MEDICAL PRACTICE

The late Dr William B. Ewart abstracted medical information from each year's York Factory journal, covering more than two centuries from 1714 through 1939.[11] During Hutchins' six-year tenure, 1776–73, twelve Indians and nine Europeans died at York Factory. Six of the Europeans drowned, two died from tuberculosis, and one from old age. Surgical problems included a dislocated shoulder, a fractured arm, amputations, and drainage of abscesses. Medical problems included tertiary syphilis, pleurisy, pneumonia, tuberculosis, rheumatism, gout, frostbite, and epidemics of influenza and diarrhea. Graham added bronchitis and snowblindness to this list of conditions seen in other years.[12] In February 1771 Andrew Graham, who was acting chief factor, reported, "Doctor fully employed. Never less than 3 or 4 patients at one time," and on 15 March 1771 he added that the surgeon works "night as well as day."[13] Graham also described the conduct of Hutchins and other surgeons whenever native "objects of pity present themselves ... The hungry are fed, the naked clothed, and the sick furnished with medicines, and attended by the factory surgeon; all this gratis."[14]

On Christmas Eve 1777 Hutchins treated John Daniel for an abscess on his right hand. "I opened the hand which was swelled and greatly inflamed ... put a poultice made of green ointment with a little oil and vinegar over the hole and dressed it again ... at night ... found it more swelled and thick at two or three places and let out matter, dressed it again." Daniel survived.[15]

The journals from Albany 1774–82 have not to our knowledge been studied in detail, but Albany appears to have escaped the smallpox epidemic that swept the plains in 1781–82, Hutchins' last winter on the Bay. In the spring of 1782 there were six smallpox deaths at York Factory, involving six Indians who arrived with furs from inland.[16] Imposition of isolation and quarantine by Hutchins' successor, surgeon Alfred Robinson, prevented what otherwise would have been the inevitable spread of smallpox through the aboriginal population of York Factory.[17]

In a letter to Maugenest on 23 May 1782, Hutchins listed the plants used in the treatment of scurvy: "vegetable is the truest remedy when they can be had, sorrel [*Oxyria digyna?*],[18] dandelion [*Taraxacum lacerum*], fat hen [pigweed, *Chenopodium album*], nettles [*Urtica procera*], scurvy grass [*Cochlearia officinales*], water cresses [*Rorippa islandica*], are all excellent and many grow wild in this country, the liquor of the birch tree [*Betula glandulosa*] obtained by tapping is a very good remedy, there can be no fear of this scurvy affecting your people until the spring of the year as fish and vegetable berries in particular are to be had all summer and autumn."[19]

METEOROLOGY

Hutchins had a scientific bent and found it a great boon when William Wales, mathematician and astronomer, visited Churchill in 1768–69. Wales had been sent by the Royal Society to observe the transit of the planet Venus. He set a good example for Hutchins by keeping a full set of observations "on the state of the air, winds, weather, &c."[20] Samuel Wegg's desire to establish world-wide weather stations led to Wales leaving his instruments behind at Hudson Bay.[21]

Figure 6.2
Compass with thirty-two directions. From Houston, *Arctic Ordeal*, 201

Hutchins made his first careful measurements of temperature and atmospheric pressure during 1771–72, when he was with Andrew Graham at York Factory. His recordings of wind direction, in terms of the thirty-two main directions of the compass (Figure 6.2), were observed "by the vane on a flagstaff about fifty feet high."[22]

CONGELATION OF MERCURY AND THE COPLEY MEDAL

At Albany in the winter of 1774–75, Hutchins made his first careful observations on the dipping needle, an instrument used to measure one dimension of geomagnetism. On 19 January 1775, with the assistance of Mr Jarvis, the surgeon, he experimented with the congealing of mercury in severe cold. A second experiment took place on 11 February.[23] As a result of these initial experiments, Dr Joseph Black of Edinburgh undertook to write to Andrew Graham (but *not* to Hutchins!) on 5 October 1779 (Figure 6.3), detailing how they might improve on Hutchins' initial experiments.[24] Seven winters after his initial experiments, and once more at Albany, Hutchins conducted ten

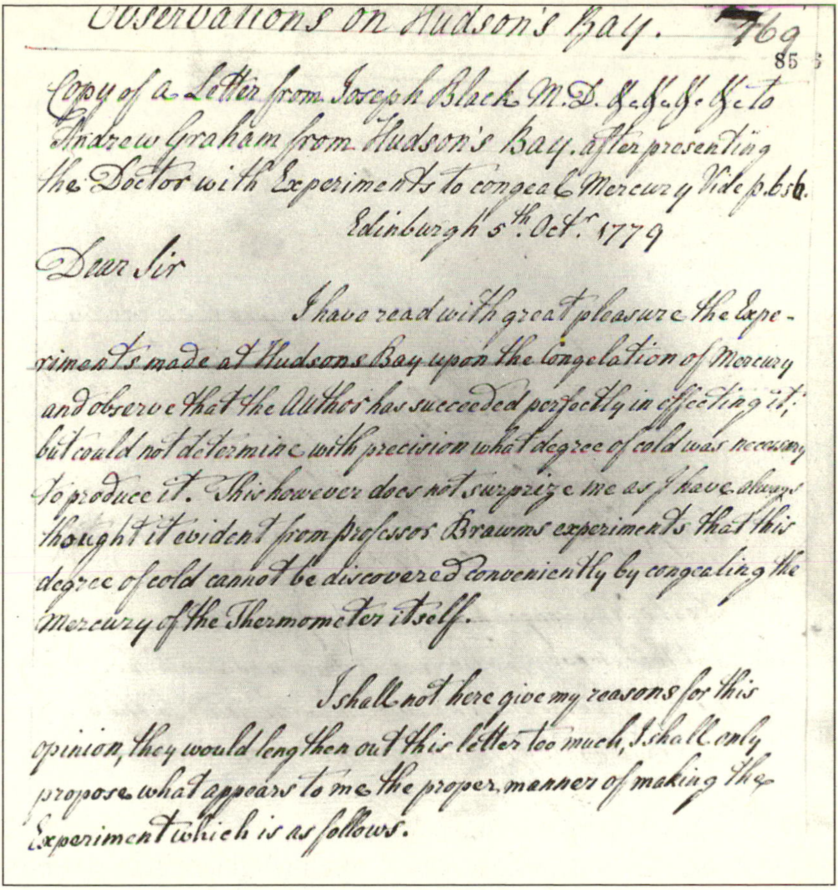

Observations on Hudson's Bay. 769

Copy of a Letter from Joseph Black M.D. &c.&c.&c.&c. to Andrew Graham from Hudson's Bay. after presenting the Doctor with Experiments to congeal Mercury Vide p.656.

Edinburgh 5th Oct.r 1779

Dear Sir

I have read with great pleasure the Experiments made at Hudsons Bay upon the congelation of Mercury and observe that the Author has succeeded perfectly in effecting it; but could not determine with precision what degree of cold was necessary to produce it. This however does not surprize me as I have always thought it evident from professor Braun's experiments that this degree of cold cannot be discovered conveniently by congealing the Mercury of the Thermometer itself.

I shall not here give my reasons for this opinion, they would lengthen out this letter too much, I shall only propose what appears to me the proper manner of making the Experiment which is as follows.

Figure 6.3
Letter from Joseph Black to Andrew Graham. HBC Archives, PAM

careful experiments, using eight different thermometers. He began on 15 December 1781: "This experiment was made in the open air, on the top of the fort, with only a few deerskins sewn together placed to windward for a shelter; there was plenty of snow (18 inches deep upon the works) and the thermometers were close at hand."[25] The last measurement was made on 22 February 1782. The experiments occupied sixty-eight pages in the *Philosophical Transactions*, less two pages of commentary by Dr Black.[26] Hutchins reported that quicksilver could be cooled a few degrees below the congelation or freezing point of mercury, and that it contracted in bulk. The "freezing point" of mercury was −39° Fahrenheit.[27]

Hutchins' careful research received immediate praise from leading scientists. His long report was followed by another ninety-five pages of laudatory comments in the *Philosophical Transactions* from Henry Cavendish and Charles Blagden. Cavendish, ordinarily a man of few words, filled twenty-five pages with praise for Hutchins' experiments.[28] Dr Blagden, physician to the army, next gave a prolonged, sixty-nine-page historical assessment of preceding research on the long-debated topic of the freezing point of mercury: "The late experiments at Hudson's Bay have determined a point, upon which philosophers not only were much divided in their opinion, but also entertained, in general, very erroneous sentiments." Blagden summarized the mistaken ideas about the freezing point of mercury held by various named authorities and explained how their experiments had gone wrong. Hutchins, in Blagden's words, "resumed this subject with such brilliant success." Blagden expressed "confidence in the experiments made at Hudson's Bay, in which no hypothesis was adopted, and therefore no prejudice can be apprehended."[29]

Blagden continued, "The principal advantage, however, is to furnish an important lesson to authors, which can never be too strongly inculcated, that their accuracy must be brought to the test of future discoveries. As knowledge advances, their errors, their misrepresentations, their suppression of the truth, or fictitious additions to it, shall all be infallibly detected, and heap upon their head proportionable ignominy; while the simple and candid narrative, the exact and unbiased relation of facts, will acquire redoubled lustre from the fiery trial."[30]

With such commendation resulting from his two publications in the *Philosophical Transactions* (1776, 1783), it is not surprising that Hutchins was presented with the Copley gold medal by the Royal Society in December 1783.[31] He was the second Hudson's Bay man to be awarded this coveted prize, following Christopher Middleton, who received the Copley Medal in 1742 for "The extraordinary degrees and effects of cold in Hudson's Bay."[32] As Stearns said in 1945:

Thomas Hutchins' award was a handsome termination to a century and a quarter of reciprocal association between the Royal Society and the Hudson's Bay Company, a period marked by more meaningful interrelation than any like numbers of years since ... The Hudson's Bay Company materially assisted Fellows of the Royal Society and their scientific colleagues throughout the world to improve their knowledge of geography and to correct maps of the Hudson's Bay area and the Arctic region, to enlarge their knowledge of oceanography, astronomy, and weather forecasting, to fill in gaps in natural history, and to add to their information regarding the native peoples of the New World ... And while the Hudson's Bay Company contributed to the advancement of knowledge, it also reaped profits in the form of improved maps, safer navigation, wider and more economical use of the raw materials of the Hudson's Bay region, and infinite good-will.[33]

On 10 September 1782, perhaps unaware that La Pérouse had captured Churchill and York Factory the previous month, Hutchins left Albany for good, on the *Beaver* and *Albany* sloop, and arrived in Moose Factory on 15 September. There he boarded the *Seahorse* on 20 September, arriving in London on 26 November.[34] Hutchins took with him "two squirrels and a bat, received from Germain Maugenest."

On 23 July 1783 Hutchins was appointed corresponding secretary of the Company in London at £150 per annum. Here "in his dual role as amateur naturalist and secretary of the HBC [he] supplied ... information on Canadian wildlife ... 'Natural history is my delight,' he told Pennant in 1784."[35] One of Hutchins' duties may have been to provide inquirers with information about the natural history of Hudson Bay.

Hutchins remained corresponding secretary of the HBC until 1790, though by then his health was deteriorating. When he died at work at Hudson's Bay House in London on 7 July 1790,[36] he was described as "late of the Parish of Allhallows Staining in London."[37]

NATURAL HISTORY

Hutchins was the first person at Hudson Bay to bring a scientist's approach to diverse aspects of nature observation. In 1969, almost two hundred years after they were written, Hutchins' reports of sixteen species of birds, eleven of which had not been listed by Andrew Graham, fourteen species of fish, and seven species of mammals were published.[38]

A seventeenth bird species, called the *Chepethewuck* by the Cree Indians but now known as the Greater Prairie-Chicken, weighing about twenty-five ounces, is described in E.2/9:

Pinnated Grous: is found about Henley Settlement in Hudson's Bay, legs covered with soft brown feathers, toes naked & pectinated. The tufts which distinguish this species from all others are rooted high on the neck, not far from the hind part of the head.[39]

This specimen from the trading area of Henley House, just below the junction with the Kenogami River, about one hundred miles upstream from Albany, was correctly attributed to Hutchins by Pennant.[40]

As one might expect from a well-trained and observant surgeon, careful notes of the colours of soft parts that might subsequently fade accompanied Hutchins' bird and mammal collections from York Factory in 1772. This information has been reproduced, with permission of the owner, the Royal Society of London, England, as Document 2.[41] New material not given in HBRS 27 is in boldface for emphasis. In the Royal Society document, Hutchins provides measurements and weights of birds, perhaps the first person to record this information in North America; 160 years later, in 1936, Dr T.S. Roberts, in writing *Birds of Minnesota*, could still find only one reliable source, a taxidermist named Lano, for figures concerning weights of different bird species.[42] Hutchins provides Cree names for many additional species, something that Graham had initiated for twenty bird species in 1771. He provides complete descriptions of both male and female Lapland Longspurs, having made a greater effort than Graham to collect small songbirds, including warblers.

As proof that Hutchins shared with Graham and Pennant a firm understanding of bird migration, in his Ornithology section in Document 2 Hutchins divides birds under two headings, Migratory Birds and Stationary Birds. This was at a time when Daines Barrington of the Royal Society was still claiming migration to be a preposterous concept. Graham and Hutchins, aware of Barrington's claim that swallows lie dormant during winter,[43] made specific inquiries of Indians, both young and old, to confirm that none of them had observed such a phenomenon. Hutchins correctly recognized that the Rock Ptarmigan migrated down from the north and stayed only during winter.

Additional evidence of Hutchins' scientific approach is the notation by Pennant concerning the Burbot, *Gadus lota*: "Mr. Hutchins counted, in a single fish, 671,248 ovaria."[44] How many hours must Hutchins have spent in such a count? However many days this project required, it is evidence of an inquiring mind and an unusual degree of perseverance.

At York Fort, Hutchins included occasional natural-history notes in his meteorological journal of 7 September 1771 through 9 June 1772. These represent the earliest phenology dates from Hudson Bay, precious because of their rarity anywhere in North America in the eighteenth century. They were abstracted by the late Dr Bill Ewart:

1771
Sept. 8 – Poplars and Willows are turning yellow
Sept. 12 – Snow birds appear
Sept. 21 – Snow birds & white geese plentiful.

Sept. 23 – White geese very plentiful
Sept. 27 – Snow birds increased today – geese almost gone
Oct. 4   – Ducks, geese & plover left us
Oct. 26   – Martin are now in season for trapping
Nov. 2   – Snow birds taking their departure
Nov. 14   – Saw a flock of winter small birds like Tom Tits [chickadees]

1772
Mar. 29 – A snow bird was heard this day. This is the earliest of the migratory tribe,
            assumed the harbinger of Spring.
Apr. 7   – This day an Indian man saw a *Sa qua to ma* [Rough-legged Hawk]. It is
            of the migratory species of the hawk tribe.
Apr. 8   – Another called by the native *A nouch che chas ieu* [Northern Harrier?]
Apr. 19 – An Indian find a Grey [Canada] Goose
Apr. 20 – 2 ducks were seen
May 10   – Birds of flight are now in small flocks upon our banks
May 15   – This day a plover was seen. First this season
May 16   – White geese was seen for the first time
May 19   – Many flocks of geese
May 21   – Many flocks of white geese – Snipes & small water fowl are gathering
            in the marsh
May 29   – Creaking [= croaking] of frogs was heard
June 9   – White whale [Beluga] in the river.[45]

An unusual potential for profit from upper-class feminine fashions resulted
from Hutchins' 1772 collection, and thirty years later swan skins had become
a profitable item of trade for the company.[46] The Committee of the Royal
Society reported to the HBC on 5 May 1773:

As you have presented ... a specimen of the wild Swan, we have put the Skin into
the hands of an importer, and we shall perhaps surprize when we inform you that
if it had been in a state to be properly dressed, it would have been worth at least a
Guinea and an half, so scarce is this commodity at present and so great is the demand for Powder puffs, the best sort of which can only be made from Swan down.[47]

Two new species mentioned in the Hutchins Royal Society manuscript
(Document 2) did not appear in Williams 1969: the Ruddy Turnstone, called
the *Misshiggitee Kisquathenapishish*, and an unidentifiable gull.

    Under the Gray Jay, Hutchins said, "Mr. Graham last year [1771] sent
home a specimen of this Bird and an account of it's food manners &c. We

have again procured several, ... [N° 8] of the present collection."[48] Hutchins made similar specific references to the previous year's collection by Graham in his accounts of the Boreal Chickadee, Red Crossbill, Snow Bunting, American Robin, Willow Ptarmigan, and Northern Hawk Owl.

In his account of the Pectoral Sandpiper, Hutchins tells of examining several bird-lice under his microscope, an instrument that even a surgeon in England would have been fortunate to own in 1772. The lice appeared like "very beautiful Tortoise-Shells."[49]

Not every observation belongs to Hutchins, Graham, or Indians. The date of 10 October as the departure date of the Snow Geese from Albany was no doubt submitted by Humphrey Marten, who was there from 1763 to 1774. Fur trader William Falconer contributed a Whooping Crane specimen from Severn, surgeon Edward Jarvis a Bohemian Waxwing from Severn, and trader William Tomison a Belted Kingfisher from Cumberland House.

Both Hutchins and Graham were understandably dependent on Indians as their source of knowledge: "We have endeavoured to gain the account of each Bird with all the exactness possible, but different Natives relate different particulars."[50] Under Red Crossbill, Hutchins said, "The account I have now to give of this Bird varies greatly from that Sent by Mr Graham last year; but when it is remembered that there are a great resort of Natives to York Fort in comparison of what go to Severn, it will be imagined with justice that we are nigher the truth having more opportunities of gaining intelligence, or information."[51]

During the fur-trade year of 1772–73, after Graham, his collaborator, was no longer the acting chief at York and had returned to his usual post at Severn, Hutchins continued to collect specimens at York Factory.

BRANTA CANADENSIS HUTCHINSII

Hutchins is the only Hudson Bay naturalist to have a bird named for him. In 1832 in *Fauna Boreali-Americana*, volume 2, *The Birds*, John Richardson wrote:

On Captain Parry's second voyage, several flocks of Geese were seen on Melville Peninsula, which were thought by the officers of the Expedition to be the *Anser leucopsis* or Barnacle ... A number of specimens were secured ... I have since obtained information, which leads me to believe that they actually belong to a distinct species, hitherto confounded with the *A. Canadensis* [Canada Goose]. They are well known in Hudson's Bay by the Cree name of *Apistiskeesh*, and are generally thought by the residents to be merely a small kind of the Canada Goose, as they have the white kidney-shaped patch on the throat, which is deemed peculiar to that species ... We have designated the *Apistiskeesh* by the name of *Hutchinsii*, in honour of a gentleman from whom Pennant and Latham derived most of their information respecting the Hudson's Bay birds.[52]

Richardson appended the following footnote: "Some mistake occurs in Forster's account of the Canada Goose (*Phil. Trans.*, lxii); the habits of *A. Hutchinsii* (Small Grey Goose of Graham) being ascribed to the *A. Canadensis*; while the Large Grey Goose, mentioned in the same passage, is undoubtedly the Canada Goose, which we know to be the only species that breeds abundantly about Severn River."

When P.A. Taverner, ornithologist at the National Museum of Canada, undertook a revision of the various races of the Canada Goose in 1931, he confirmed the "very small size and light breast and underbody ... Weight ... rarely as much as 5 pounds" of the geese from the Arctic islands, and felt Richardson's measurements were consistent except that Richardson gave the culmen [bare unfeathered part of the bill] measurement as 1 inch, 8½ lines, or 43.5 mm, far too long. Taverner said, "To anyone who has measured many Canada goose bills the solution is apparent. The feathering on the fore crown was worn away and did not give the true exposed culmen line ... there can be no doubt that it was this little goose that Richardson designated *hutchinsii* and not its much larger relative to which the name has hitherto been attached. In order to avoid confusion with older references and to connect this bird with the man who first detected its distinctness I propose that it be known vernacularly as Richardson's goose."[53]

Now that subspecies of birds are no longer given vernacular names but retain only their Latin name, "Richardson's goose" has the single name of *hutchinsii*, and thereby honours the surgeon and naturalist who spent about twenty-six years at Hudson Bay. The following light-hearted anonymous verse in support of Hutchins' Goose meriting full species status appeared in 1926:

Now the question of *Branta* – pale or cinereous –
Is no subject for banter but one that is serious.
F's claim is ridiculous that subspecies are made
(A claim most pernicious) from feathers that fade!

To a man of broad mind *Branta c. hutchinsi*
Is a race clear defined as a star in the sky.
But oh! what's the use? And as to this man, sir, –
Well, speaking of goose, he, himself, is the anser. [54]

It is possible that a future edition of the *American Ornithologists' Union Check-List* will accord this small goose full specific status, as proposed in 1946 by a noted taxonomist, John W. Aldrich, based on differences in size, colour, voice (a cackle instead of a honk), nesting habits, habitat, and time of migration.[55]

As secretary of the HBC in London, Hutchins gave further information to Pennant. Most important was one of the first, if not the very first, North American observations of a jay caching food. Concerning the Gray Jay, paraphrasing Graham's account in E.2/5, Hutchins said, "They feed on black moss, worms, and even flesh. When near habitations or tents, they are apt to pilfer every thing they can come at, even salt meat. They are bold, and come into the tents to eat victuals out of the dishes, notwithstanding they have their hoard of berries lodged in the hollows of trees.[56] They watch persons baiting the traps for Martins, and devour the bait as soon as they turn their backs. These birds lay up stores for the winter; and are seldom seen in January, unless near habitations ... When caught, they pine away, and die, tho' their appetite never fails them. Detested by the natives of Hudson's Bay."[57]

The bird accounts in E.2/12 are clearly a collaborative effort between Hutchins and Graham. Earlier authors gave Hutchins too much credit, but Glover (1969) gave Hutchins too little. This we explain in Appendix C.

MOSES NORTON

(1735?–1773)

———— ❦ ————

From 1795 through at least as late as 1979, authorities claimed that Moses Norton was the mixed-blood son of the former factor Richard Norton, who served at Churchill under Richard Staunton and Nathaniel Bishop, and later in 1731 took charge of Churchill.[1] Historical research by Sylvia van Kirk, however, has unearthed evidence in Moses Norton's will that he was the son of a white woman, Susannah Dupeer, possibly born of an illicit union when Richard Norton was on furlough in England in the 1730s.[2]

Young Moses Norton spent nine years in England, and as Samuel Hearne tells us, "considering the small sum which was expended in his education, had made some progress in literature."[3] Moses followed in his father's footsteps by becoming the governor at Churchill in 1763.

The Nortons, father and son, rarely receive their due as early explorers, although they were among the first to realize the futility of searching for a navigable North West Passage. Between 1717 and 1723 Richard Norton went inland once and north three times, once with Henry Kelsey and once with John Scroggs. Richard Norton's main achievement was to find in 1722 the human skeletons from the 1719 expedition of James Knight at Marble Island; the men had succumbed to starvation after two years of vain and anxious waiting.[4]

Exemplary and definitive explorations of Chesterfield Inlet, based on Churchill, occurred in 1761 and 1762. Captain William Christopher first sailed into this inlet in 1761. The next summer, he and Moses Norton sailed from Churchill on 13 July, with the ceremony of "7 guns and three cheers" indicative of the importance of their endeavour. A cutter named *Strivewell* was fitted with washboards so it could be towed behind their sloop, named *Churchill*. After sailing the length of Chesterfield Inlet, Norton discovered Baker Lake and sailed around this large lake in the *Strivewell*, 3 to 5 August 1762.[5] The head of Baker Lake was 275 kilometres inland from Hudson Bay; it offered the earliest but subsequently unwisely ignored evidence that Chesterfield Inlet was not and could not be the hoped-for navigable North West Passage. Indeed, Norton's unequivocal opinion to this effect was sent to the HBC Committee: "I am Certain and Shure that there is no Passage into the Western Oc[e]an in this Hudsons Bay."[6] He received a gratuity of £40 for this exploration.

On his return to Churchill, Norton sent two Chipewyan Indians, Idotliazee and Matonabbee, to explore northern rivers; they returned with samples of free copper in 1767 after a five-year journey.[7]

While on furlough in London in 1768–69, without any prior consultation with Samuel Hearne, Norton proposed that Hearne be sent on an overland exploratory trip to the Coppermine River to ascertain the exact location of the copper deposits. On his third attempt, Hearne finally reached the Coppermine mouth. Hearne, not fond of Norton, later said of him, "At his return to Hudson's Bay [after nine years' education in England], he entered into all the abominable vices of his countrymen. He kept for his own use five or six of the finest Indian girls which he could select ... With all these bad qualities, no man took more pains to inculcate virtue, morality, and continence on others ... [yet he] was known to live in open defiance of every law, human and divine."[8]

Moses Norton maintained an English wife, Sarah, but had a daughter named Mary (Polly) born to a Cree woman in the 1760s. He died at Prince of Wales's Fort of "inflammation of the bowels" on 29 December 1773.[9] While Rich praises Norton, especially for his "uncommon energy and perception,"[10] Glover denounces him as "a very sinister man,"[11] and Hearne calls him a "notorious smuggler."[12]

NATURAL HISTORY

Norton sent a pair of moose calves back to England in 1767. The female survived and reached London on 22 October. *The Royal Magazine* of 4 February 1768 reports that the moose was shipped up the Thames to Richmond Castle on 2 February 1768, after the HBC had spent the considerable sum of £9 10s. 11d. feeding it to that time.[13]

When the Company called for natural-history specimens, Norton complied. He sent seventeen specimens to London in 1771, including interesting species such as the Surf Scoter, Long-tailed Duck (formerly known as Oldsquaw), Hudsonian Godwit, Parasitic Jaeger, Arctic Tern, and three owl species, the Northern Hawk, Short-eared, and Snowy owls. Norton was also guilty of at least one omission; Hearne tells us that a Ross's Goose specimen came to hand at Churchill when the collection was being made, but that Norton failed to forward it to London.[14]

SAMUEL HEARNE

(1745–1792)

Samuel Hearne's exploits as an explorer, fur trader, and author have been appreciated for more than two centuries (Figure 8.1). He was the first European to reach the Arctic coast of North America, travelling on foot with a group of Chipewyan Indians from Churchill to the mouth of the Coppermine River. In 1774 he founded the first inland trading post of the Hudson's Bay Company at Cumberland House, now Saskatchewan's oldest settlement, and thus kept the Hudson's Bay Company in competition with the much larger North West Company. And as James Marsh has written, Hearne's "literary artistry ... secured his fame in letters."[1]

The *Dictionary of National Biography* describes Hearne as "a man of enlightened and benevolent character, as well as of great courage and perseverance, and a close observer."[2] The *Dictionary of Canadian Biography* states that he "represents an interesting combination of physical endurance and intellectual curiosity."[3] Yet modern naturalists rarely refer to Hearne's original and often incredibly apt observations. Apart from Elliott Coues, who says that "the whole story of 'honest old Hearne' is interesting as well as veracious ... [he left] a good, faithful account of his observations,"[4] and Elsa G. Allen, who states that "he had the stamina of an experienced explorer combined with the scientific integrity of a modern investigator,"[5] ironically only the historians appear to appreciate what a good naturalist Hearne was.

Hearne was born in London in 1745, the son of Samuel Hearne of the London Bridge Water Works and his wife, Diana. He was schooled in Beaminster in Dorset "without noticeable success. To the end of his life Hearne's spelling remained quaintly phonetic, his grammar erratic and his mathematics dubiously reliable."[6] He entered the navy at the age of eleven, and was servant to Admiral Hood for six years. In 1766 he joined the Hudson's Bay Company as a seaman and mate of the *Charlotte*, a position he held for three years, sailing out of Churchill.

Figure 8.1
Samuel Hearne. *The European Magazine* 1797.
Artist not known

EXPLORATION

Hearne was chosen by Moses Norton for the company's first major Arctic exploration by land, a search of distant Dené territory in hope of finding their fabled *Neetha-san-san-dazey* or "Far Off Metal River,"[7] now known as the Coppermine River. Hearne's first journey began from Churchill on 6 November 1769, but lasted only one month and five days, failing because his party of Chipewyan Indians lacked women to make moccasins and do other chores and because Hearne was deserted by his Indian guide, Chawchinahaw. His second attempt, with an Indian guide named Conne-e-queese, began on 23 February 1770 and lasted eight months and five days. This time he was forced to return when he broke his quadrant and was unable to make astronomical observations to ascertain his whereabouts. During the return journey overland, with inadequate clothing and little remaining ammunition, Hearne was rescued on 20 September by the chance arrival of Matonabbee, a skilful leader of great prestige among the Chipewyan Indians.[8] Matonabbee provided him with a warm suit of otter skins and fed him well.

Not easily discouraged, Hearne set out again on 7 December 1770, this time accompanied by Matonabbee. His party reached the mouth of the Coppermine on 17 or 18 July 1771, where Hearne "took possession of the coast, on behalf of the Hudson's Bay Company."[9] His estimate of the latitude, two hundred miles north of its actual position, was grossly in error, possibly because he was using an old, cumbersome, heavy Elton's quadrant, the most difficult of instruments for astronomical observations, that had been provided him by Moses Norton. None the less, he showed understanding of a basic principle when he said "before I arrived at Conge-cathawhachaga, the sun did not set during the whole night: a proof that I was then to the northward of the Arctic Circle."[10]

Ian MacLaren's masterful account of Hearne's previously unpublished "field notes" indicates that Hearne colourfully embellished the most gruesome part of his published narrative, the slaughtering of sleeping Inuit by the Chipewyan in his party. It now appears that Hearne's Indian companions were as much as two days march ahead of him when they performed their dastardly deed near Bloody Falls; thus there was no opportunity for the young woman to twist herself around Hearne's legs as she was being killed. As MacLaren says, "publishers endeavoured to straddle the fence of fact and imagination."[11] After the slaughter, Hearne explored the "copper mines" and found a four-pound piece of copper that justified his long journey. He arrived back at Churchill from his gruelling overland trip of eighteen months and twenty-two days on 30 June 1772.[12]

FUR TRADE

Hearne, although rated by E.E. Rich as "nothing of a trader,"[13] was next assigned in 1774–75 to found the first inland trading post of the HBC. After a journey by canoe up the Grass River to Cranberry Portage, and down Goose River to Goose Lake, he reached Cumberland Lake, where he built his fur-trading post on the south shore. Occupied continuously ever since, Cumberland House celebrated its bicentenary in 1974.

SURRENDER TO LA PÉROUSE

Hearne was similarly rated as "nothing of a fighting man,"[14] because on 8 August 1782 he and his group of thirty-eight civilians surrendered Prince of Wales's fort at Churchill to a French force under La Pérouse. The three French ships had 290 soldiers and 74 large guns,[15] so Hearne was out-gunned, out-manned, and facing soldiers who had landed on high ground behind a fort that had been built solely to defend itself from a sea approach. His surrender was prudent, for it saved the lives of all his men.

La Pérouse found and claimed Hearne's journal, already under revision, as a fair prize. He then returned the manuscript, Richard Glover adds, "on the express condition that he publish it." Although "credit for [Hearne's] final publication has commonly been given to La Pérouse, Glover tells us "it is unlikely ... that this view is correct."[16] If La Pérouse, as Elsa Allen claims, had actually "stipulated as part of the conditions of surrender that the Hudson's Bay Company publish the journal,"[17] it would indeed have been a gentlemanly gesture. John Russell Bartlett, author of the *Bibliotheca [Americana]*, obtained the story from Albert Gallatin, who had it directly from the French navigator.[18] However, we side with Glover in the view that such credit is in error[19] and also that Hearne "was already considering publication before ever La Pérouse imposed it as a condition."[20]

Upon being captured by La Pérouse, Hearne then made a brazen request. He asked that La Pérouse allow him to retain one of the fort's trading sloops, the *Severn*, which had been seized as a fair prize of war. La Pérouse generously acceded. He released Hearne and thirty-two others at Resolution Island at the east end of Hudson Strait; from there Hearne sailed the little craft on a risky journey directly east to the Orkney Islands.[21] La Pérouse made no effort to maintain the new territory for France: "The plan had been to destroy, not to conquer."[22]

HEARNE'S NARRATIVE

Hearne returned to Hudson Bay in 1783 to resume British occupation, take charge of Churchill, and restore the fort. Ill health forced him to retire and return to England in 1787. Following at least three,[23] perhaps five years of slow and "seemingly interminable" work, Hearne finally submitted his manuscript for publication in October 1792 through the good offices of William Wales, who negotiated the sale to Messrs Strahan and Cadell for the almost unprecedented sum of £200.[24] A month later, when only forty-seven, Hearne "died of the dropsy."[25] The book, *A Journey from Prince of Wales's Fort in Hudson's Bay to the Northern Ocean*, his greatest achievement, did not appear in print until 1795.

Hearne's book is one of the greatest travel narratives ever written. It was "directed at the general public rather than at specialists, ... written in a plain, unadorned style. It went through two English editions and by 1799 had been translated into German, Dutch, and French."[26] Frank and often understated, Hearne's accounts of hardship and starvation are still worth reading.

ANTHROPOLOGY AND ART

Trevor Levere, a professor of history, philosophy, and science at the University of Toronto, has paid tribute to Hearne as an anthropologist: "His chapter on the Indians is of real anthropological value, ranging through social organization, marital customs, techniques and implements for hunting and fishing, clothing, amusements, beliefs and ceremonies, treatment of the aged, and more besides. He also prepared a vocabulary of their language, covering sixteen folio pages, but this he had lent to the corresponding secretary of the company, who died soon after, and it was lost among his effects."[27]

Hearne gives us a "an accurate, sympathetic, and patently truthful record of life among the Chipewyan Indians at that time,"[28] and includes much information about how the Indians interacted with wildlife. He notes that Chipewyan were fascinated by the Pine Marten, the member of the weasel family most adapted to tree living; the commonest names for Chipewyan girls in Hearne's time were related to the marten – for example, White Marten, Summer Marten, and Marten's Heart.[29]

Hearne was also something of an artist,[30] and his sketches of Fort Churchill (see Figure I.2) and York Factory (Figure I.3) give us a good idea of how these forts looked in his time.

CLIMATOLOGY

Hearne has provided us with the best evidence we have today of the more southwesterly limits of the tree-line and hence of climatic change during the Little Ice Age, prior to 1770. When Hearne was advised by the Indians that the tree-line in generations past had been farther north, he commented that this was evidence the world was cooling down – an accurate comment at the nadir of the Little Ice Age.[31]

NATURAL HISTORY

While in England for the winter of 1782–83, after his capture by La Pérouse, Hearne did not waste time sulking over his defeat. He met Thomas Pennant and gave him a copy of his natural-history sightings, a dozen years in advance of their posthumous publication in *A Journey ... to the Northern Ocean* (1795). As Glover notes, "the meeting of the two men was valuable to both."[32] Pennant incorporated a number of Hearne's observations into *Arctic Zoology*; the first edition appeared in print in 1784 (mammals) and 1785 (birds), a little over a year after their meeting. Hearne in turn cited Pennant nine times and quoted from him without attribution four times.[33]

In his introductions to the 1958 Hearne edition and the 1969 Graham volume, Glover correctly recognized that "Samuel Hearne was, of course, another first class observer and reporter – in fact, a much better naturalist than [Andrew] Graham"[34] and "head and shoulders superior to every other North American naturalist who preceded Audubon."[35] Glover singles out Hearne's accounts of the Whooping Crane and the beaver as especially well done. He also points out that Hearne had "a real affection for animals – witness his extraordinary collection of pets at Churchill: beavers, mink, lemmings and foxes, eagles, snow buntings, lapland buntings and horned larks, as well as canaries which he must have imported."[36]

An observer, not a collector, Hearne was a century ahead of his time in describing the habits of wild animals. He was the first to give recognizable descriptions of the Ross's Goose and Wood Buffalo, and accounts of the habits of the Arctic Ground Squirrel and Arctic Hare.[37] He was also the first to describe the nesting of the White-crowned Sparrow, on the ground at the root of a dwarf willow or a gooseberry.

Hearne described the base of the bill of Ross's Goose as being studded with little knobs about the size of peas. This small goose was scarce at Churchill but more common two hundred or three hundred miles to the northwest. Nearly a century later, Robert Kennicott's three-year sojourn in the north, 1859–62,[38] stimulated several HBC fur traders, especially Bernard Rogan Ross, chief trader at Fort Simpson (in charge of the entire Mackenzie district, 1858–62), to collect specimens for the Smithsonian Institution. Ross wrote articles in the *Canadian Naturalist and Geologist* in 1861 and 1862 dealing with the birds and mammals of the Mackenzie River district;[39] he listed the "horned wavy goose of Hearne" as a species still without a scientific name.[40] The omission was quickly corrected that very year, 1861, when John Cassin gave the name of *Anser Rossii* to the specimen sent him from Great Slave Lake. Cassin remarked that "this species has never again been noticed from the time of Hearne until the time of the receipt of the present specimens ... but has been constantly insisted on as a valid species in his letters to the Smithsonian Institution by Mr. Bernard R. Ross, an enthusiastic naturalist and careful observer in the service of the Hudson's Bay Company."[41]

Hearne claimed to own "an excellent microscope,"[42] a remarkable possession for a layman in that time and place. However, there is an uncanny resemblance between Hutchins' description of his use of the microscope and Hearne's. Both claim to have examined lice on a small mammal (identified by Hearne as a Northern Lemming). Both note that the lens became damp with moisture from the user's breath in his cold winter room, delaying further use of the microscope until the busy summer season. Such consistency between the two reports raises the possibility of copying or sharing to a degree that would be frowned upon today.

Hearne preceded John Richardson by fifty years in telling how a warble-fly, squeezed out of a caribou skin, was a delicacy, always eaten alive, and "said, by those who liked them, to be as fine as gooseberries."[43] Many of these larvae were as large as the first joint of Hearne's little finger. Warble-fly larvae and domestic lice were the only two items Hearne saw his Indian companions eat that he himself could not stomach.

Hearne was a student of practical zoology. He provides excellent accounts of the Wood Buffalo, Plains Buffalo, and Moose and describes how caribou skins that were to be used for clothing were best if taken from caribou killed in early August. It required the prime parts of eight to ten caribou skins to make a complete suit of warm clothing for a Chipewyan. He was fond of buffalo meat and particularly of buffalo tongue, which he termed "very delicate."[44] Unborn calves cut out of the belly of the buffalo and caribou were reckoned an even greater delicacy and were eaten on the spot, whereas the tongues were often brought down to York Factory as a luxury. Hearne was also fond of caribou meat; he lived on it entirely for more than a year and "scarcely ever wished for a change of food."[45]

Hearne's powers of observation are nowhere better revealed than in his description of the moose with its long large head, rather similar to that of a horse but with nostrils twice as large. He noted that a moose's acute hearing rendered it difficult to approach and kill on land and that the gall bladder is absent in both moose and caribou. He also listed animals with an os penis (a length of bone formed between the two blood reservoirs, the *corpora cavernosa*; it aids the animal in maintaining an erection): bear, wolf, wolverine, fox, marten, otter, fisher, mink, skunk, ermine, and long-tailed weasel – much more information than is given in a modern text of comparative vertebrate morphology[46] and more than one can find today in an hour's search through a large veterinary college library. Hearne pointed out correctly that the caribou's glans penis is not shed annually.

Hearne's information on the Arctic Fox is still of interest. He noted that they had litters of three to five sooty black young, which then turned white by winter except for a few black hairs near the tip of the tail. Up to four hundred were trapped each year within thirty miles of Churchill. Foxes came south along the coast about the middle of October but were not molested until their skins were prime the following month. Once at Churchill, they fed upon the carcasses of dead whales lying along the shores. Some continued on as far as York Factory and even as far as Severn.

Hearne understood sexual dimorphism, remarking that the male Willow Ptarmigan was larger than the female. His description of the range in size of ptarmigans demonstrates his understanding of what was later to be

described as Gaussian distribution.[47] He corrected some of the mistaken conclusions of his predecessor James Isham, and of his contemporary Andrew
Graham, both of whom had erred in claiming that beaver houses had several apartments for various uses and that there were "slave-beavers."

Hearne provided valuable information concerning the numbers of some
species. Within half a mile of Churchill as many as forty Arctic foxes could
be killed in one night, while during one winter 120 foxes, after being caught
in traps within half a mile of the fort, were destroyed by other foxes. In January 1775 at Cumberland House the men one day brought thirteen sledge-
loads of elk meat back to the fort, and on another occasion twenty-six
grouse. In 1774 Hearne's men killed eleven black bears in one day of canoe
travel between York Factory and Cumberland House. At Anawd Lake in the
North West Territories twenty or thirty hares could be snared in a single
night. One Indian could kill twenty Spruce Grouse in a day with his bow
and arrow and some would kill upward of a hundred Snow Geese in a day,
whereas the most expert of the English hunters would think it a good day's
work to kill thirty. At Albany Fort in one season sixty hogsheads of geese were
salted away for winter consumption.[48] Arctic Terns, ranked by Hearne
among "the elegant part of the feathered creation," occurred in flocks of several hundreds; bushels of their eggs were taken on a tiny island.[49]

Hearne once saw a flock of over four hundred Willow Ptarmigan near the
Churchill River. The Indians put framed nets on stakes and placed them over
gravel bait to entice ptarmigan to gather under the net. The stake was then
pulled to drop the net on top of the birds. Using this method, three people
could catch up to three hundred birds in one morning; in the winter of 1786
Mr Prince at Churchill caught 204 with two separate pulls. Ptarmigan
feathers made excellent beds; the feathers sold for three pence per pound.
The smaller Rock Ptarmigan would not go under nets but up to 120 could
be shot in a few hours.

Hearne's observations about the Ruffed Grouse were ahead of their time.
His description of the nest, with twelve or fourteen eggs on the ground at
the foot of a tree, was more precise than Audubon's in the 1830s.[50] Hearne
realized, as most others at that time did not, that the noise of "drumming"
was made by "clapping their wings with such a force, that at half a mile distance it resembles thunder."[51] He noted that the pouch at the base of the
pelican's beak had a capacity of three quarts and that, in the 1770s as today,
muskrat houses were favourite nesting sites for Canada Geese.

Hearne evidently was the first to dissect the "windpipe" of an adult
Trumpeter Swan, noting that the convoluted trachea passed into the broad
and hollow breastbone of the swan and, after passing the length of the
sternum, returned into the chest to join the lungs. He also dissected a

Tundra Swan but failed to appreciate that it lacked the extra perpendicular hump in the trachea that is present in the larger Trumpeter Swan;[52] hence he erroneously reported that the two species had identical anatomy, even though their notes were quite different in pitch.

Cranes, curlews and Passenger Pigeons were regularly shot for food; the latter flew in large flocks in the interior near Cumberland House where he saw twelve killed at one shot. Whooping Cranes, only occasionally seen, were most often in pairs. This largest crane was good eating; its wing bones were so long and large that they were sometimes made into flutes. Hearne was the first to recognize two different species of curlew, the Hudsonian and the Eskimo. He also provided invaluable information concerning the northern edge of the Eskimo Curlew breeding range – Egg River, on the west coast of Hudson Bay at 59°, 30' N, about 150 miles north of Churchill. But he did not restrict his attention to edible birds; he also described small birds such as the chickadee.

Although he understood the concept of bird migration, Hearne recognized the Willow Ptarmigan and Arctic Hare as year-round residents. He described the Trumpeter Swan as the first species of waterfowl to return each spring, sometimes as early as late March, frequenting the open waters of falls and rapids.

By no means was Hearne's interest restricted to mammals, birds, and fish. He described mussels, crabs, scallops, frogs, and spiders. He recognized correctly that the Cloudberry or Bake-apple berry was useful in preventing and treating scurvy.

Hearne made surprisingly few errors, mainly in instances where he may have relied on natives' hearsay rather than upon his own observation. Most flawed is his account of the copulation of the porcupine: "Their mode of copulation is singular, for their quills will not permit them to perform that office in the usual mode, like other quadrupeds. To remedy this inconvenience, they sometimes lie on their sides and meet in that manner; but the usual mode is for the male to lie on his back, and the female to walk over him (beginning at his head), till the parts of generation come in contact."[53] Such misconceptions persisted for nearly two centuries after Hearne. The fact is that a few days prior to copulation, the porcupines will meet, belly to belly, as part of their courting procedure.[54]

Surprisingly few of Hearne's natural-history usages are dated, although the term "willick" for the guillemot, one of the smaller seabirds of the auk family, is now obsolete. He used the word "non-descript" correctly, in late eighteenth-century terms, to mean a species not yet described to science.

Joseph R. Jehl, in his forthcoming book about the birdlife of the Churchill, Manitoba, area, has offered a further assessment of Hearne:

Required to live off the land and take a hands-on approach, Hearne necessarily emphasised the large, economically valuable, and edible species, all of which he knew intimately. Facts that today would be fodder for books on ornithological trivia were matters of survival (Which birds overwinter? Is a Snowy Owl edible? Shorebirds are delectable but turnstones taste "like train-oil") or, occasionally, aesthetics (Horned Larks are pretty but won't sing in captivity). He knew about physiology (the composition of fat changes seasonally), molt and the sequence of plumages (Willow Ptarmigan), and that grouse feathers were "double."[55] Hearne recognized that there were two kinds each of swans, curlews, and ptarmigan, and that some local species (Trumpeter Swan, Ross's Goose) had yet to be described. He was aware of the plumage differences between male and female [Hudsonian] godwits.[56] During an era in which many still believed that birds passed the winter in hibernation or torpor, Hearne was making notes on migration routes and dates, the influence of weather and wind direction, and the extreme premigratory fattening of shorebirds. Most importantly – the mark of a good scientist – he admitted what he did not know or could not learn from the native peoples (e.g., where do Horned Waveys or Snow Birds nest), and he took pains to point these out.

From our point of view Hearne's account of the large subspecies of the Canada Goose best reveals his scientific bent. Most naturalists who read Hearne appear to have overlooked its importance. He met these very large geese on the Barren Grounds, but he did not call them the Barren Geese because they summered there, but rather because of the "exceeding smallness of their testicles."[57]

The modern status of this large goose has been somewhat controversial. Hanson's book, *The Giant Canada Goose*, presents the results of recent research.[58] Hanson believes that the Canada Geese nesting in Minnesota and southern Manitoba and Saskatchewan belong to the giant race *Branta canadensis maxima*, previously presumed to be extinct. This race is characterized by a wingspan of six feet or more in adult males, an unusually long neck, and frequently a white spot above the eye. They weigh anywhere from eight pounds for an immature female to eighteen pounds for an adult male, some reaching the sixteen to seventeen pounds cited by Hearne.

Hanson (1965) and Sterling[59] each tell of the capture in July 1963 of five hundred moulting Canada Geese on the tundra in Keewatin Territory. Twenty-nine of these year-old geese carried bands previously placed on them elsewhere, some as young ones in 1962 before they had learned to fly. Ten were from Rochester, Minnesota, three from southern Manitoba, and one from southern Saskatchewan. They had journeyed about 1,600 kilometres north. Because they came north for moulting or as dispersal of young-of-the-year and not for breeding, they arrived later in the year than the other geese, as Hearne had said. Since they did not breed that summer, they had small testicles. It took nearly two centuries to elucidate the precise scientific explanation for the phenomenon noted with such insight by Samuel Hearne, the most talented of the early naturalists on this continent.

PETER FIDLER

(1769–1822)

—◄••••••••►—

Peter Fidler, a generation younger than the men previously discussed, just barely qualifies as an eighteenth-century naturalist and meteorologist. He was born at Sutton Mill, Bolsover, Derbyshire, on 16 August 1769. Fidler was the only one of our naturalists who began as a labourer, working his way up through the ranks by virtue of hard work and an always inquiring mind. During his career he built six new trading forts.

Fidler signed on as a labourer with the HBC in London on 19 April 1788 and arrived at York Factory on the *King George III* on 18 August. He wintered at York and then was sent inland, where his peregrinating career began at Manchester House, on the North Saskatchewan River at the mouth of the Big Gully, and at South Branch House.[1] In early June 1790 he began studies in astronomy and surveying under Philip Turnor at Cumberland House, with the title of assistant surveyor. This opened a new world and a new career for him.[2] He went with Turnor into the Athabasca region in 1790, was with the Chipewyan north of Ile-à-la-Crosse from January to April 1791, wintered on Great Slave Lake in 1791–92, then went to Cumberland House. He made a winter trip from Buckingham House to the Rocky Mountains and wintered with the Peigan in 1792–93, the first European to trade with the Kootenay.[3] He went to Seal River in 1793, then spent two years at York Factory.

From 1795, the year he built Carlton House on the Assiniboine River,[4] Fidler carried the title of surveyor. In 1796 he was in charge of Cumberland House, wintered at Buckingham House, then was back in charge at Cumberland House, 1797–99. In 1799 he built Bolsover House near Meadow Lake, Saskatchewan, and founded Greenwich House on Lac la Biche in present-day Alberta. He established the short-lived Chesterfield House, near the junction of the South Saskatchewan and Red Deer rivers, 1800–02,[5] Nottingham House, opposite Fort Chipewyan, 1802–06, and was postmaster at Cumberland House in 1806–07. In 1807 he mapped and named Wollaston Lake,[6] then wintered at Swan Lake House in present-day Manitoba. He wintered at Clapham House, Reindeer Lake, in 1808–09. Most years he accompanied the annual fur brigade to York Factory from his current fort of residence. He was in charge at Ile-à-la-Crosse 1810–11, then had a year's furlough in England, and returned to the Red River area, serving as district master, based mainly at Brandon House.

In June 1815 Fidler was temporarily in command at Red River following the burning of the houses and destruction of the crops of the "Selkirk settlers" and the resignation of the colony's governor, Miles MacDonell.[7] On 25 June Fidler had little choice but to sign a capitulation to the Métis that ordered "all settlers to retire immediately from this river."[8] He took the colonists to Norway House, where Colin Robertson met them and returned with some settlers to re-establish the colony in late October. In June 1816, Fidler and his three employees survived the sacking of Brandon House by the Métis captain Cuthbert Grant and forty-seven men.[9] As surveyor and district master until 1819, Fidler established Halkett House in September 1818 on the north bank of the Assiniboine where it joins the Red River, the former site of Fort Gibraltar.[10] He moved to Fort Dauphin in 1819 as district master and died there on 17 December 1822.

Fidler left a munificent estate of more than £2,000.[11] His will again shows his independence of mind, as his extraordinary bequest directed that his money be invested until 16 August 1969, the bicentenary of his birth, and that the principal and interest then be placed at the disposal of the next male heir in direct descent from his son Peter Fidler, Jr. Had his instructions been followed, given compound interest, that descendant would have been a multi-millionaire many times over. Fidler's executors, the governor-in-chief of the HBC, the secretary of the HBC, and the governor of the Red River Colony, evidently considered these terms ridiculous and renounced probate. Hence in 1828, contrary to Fidler's bequest, his estate was divided equally among his ten children.[12]

A cairn to Fidler's memory at Meadow Lake, Saskatchewan, where many of his descendants still live on the nearby Waterhen Indian Reserve, carries the following inscription:

PETER FIDLER
Meteorologist, Surveyor

Throughout his career, Fidler was concerned with justice. Debra Lindsay has noted that "a sense of equality between men, white and native, can be discerned in Fidler's journals ... full of Indian words for geographical sites, common objects, and important people and places."[13]

Fidler had "a basic curiosity about the world around him that is a hallmark of his life."[14] A prolific reader, he "accumulated the largest personal collection of equipment, tables, nautical almanacs and technical books of any of the [HBC] servants. From 1792 to 1799, the ledgers show that he had more than £70 debited to his account for such items."[15] In 1799 alone he spent a remarkable £21/0/6 on books.[16] Some of these books are currently in the Hudson's Bay Company Archives in Winnipeg; Fidler's devotion to them is reflected in the beautiful bindings he made.[17] Judith Beattie tells us how, in 1806, he spent most of a month at Cumberland House "binding 41 volumes. With limited supplies and working under difficult conditions, Fidler managed to stitch and crop the books, apply yellow dye to the edges of the pages, recycle book catalogues and newspapers as end papers, and apply attractive, marbled-paper covers and doeskin spines to create volumes sturdy enough to withstand the rigours of travel."[18]

SURVEYS AND CARTOGRAPHY

Fidler's prodigious cartographic output included maps, 2 large-scale shore-line sketches, 8 smaller-scale integrated maps, and 373 segmental sketches. Richard Ruggles, in his book on Hudson's Bay Company maps, gives high praise to Fidler:

As far as originality is concerned, the most important innovator in the history of company cartography was Peter Fidler, who developed a mapping method for use during expeditions. He drew large-scale sketches of successive sections of river and lake networks in his journals as he travelled, noting distances and compass directions, as well as particulars of the shorelines, rapids, falls and portages. Later, he used these sketches and the information to make composite maps drawn to a smaller scale ... Fidler is remarkable not only for the volume of his output, but for its quality.[19]

Fidler surveyed and mapped 7,300 miles (11,680 km) by canoe, horseback, or snowshoe.[20] In 1792–93 he was the first white man to survey the Battle, Bow, and Red Deer rivers and a small Canadian portion of the Rocky Mountains.[21] He was a major supporter of the new Selkirk colonists on Red River, Manitoba, where in May 1813, summer 1817, and September 1818 he was the first to survey residential lots in western Canada. His last service to the colony was to donate his library of five hundred volumes "in trust for the general benefit of the said Colony."[22]

METEOROLOGY

The Company was impressed by Fidler's enthusiasm for science: it provided him with *two* thermometers. His usual routine was to record the temperature three times a day with a Dollard ten-inch Fahrenheit thermometer (until 1794–95) and thereafter with an eight-inch Carey all-spirits thermometer.[23] For twenty-two consecutive years, including his sojourns at Chesterfield House (1800–02), Cumberland House (1806–07), and Brandon House (1814–15), Fidler kept instrumental meteorological records.

A. Burnett Lowe, a meteorologist at the Winnipeg airport, his curiosity aroused by the inscription on Fidler's cairn, began searching old HBC records. He found that Fidler, as he

moved about from one post to another ... set up his meteorological equipment – his thermometer on the north side of the house where the sun could not get at it; his wind vane up on the roof; and his barometer in a sheltered room inside.

His records were kept faithfully, day after day, for some thirty years and recorded in a fine English hand in his ledger. Usually he read the instruments five times each day; the first reading was at daybreak and the last before going to bed at night; the others were equally spaced in between.

This regular reading of the instruments sometimes presented inconveniences but nothing was allowed to interfere. For instance, the entry for June 26, 1794, at York Factory reads: "House plundered by the Indians. Three men, one woman and two children murdered. Temperature 62. A smart breeze."

His records are full, too, of interesting comments about the changing seasons. He records the migration of the birds, the break-up of the ice in the rivers and bays, the changing colour of the leaves.[24]

During the cold winter of 1794–95 at York Factory, it occurred to Fidler that he should test the purity of the alcoholic beverages in his cellar; and so, in his register, intermingled with data about wind and temperature, the following information is imparted: "December 31 – Holland gin freezes at 17 below." The weather turned colder and the entry for January 5 reads: "English brandy freezes solid at 25 below." The cold continued and grew more bitter so that on January 11 the entry is "Rum freezes at 31 below."[25]

Fidler's journal entry for Fort Dauphin for 30 December 1819 tells what happened in the move to the new fort: "The thermometer of mine that came up in summer was broke on the passage so is not able to keep a Meteorological Journal as usual these last 22 years."[26] At any rate, the value of his records was diminished by his many moves; he could not provide long-term comparisons between years at any single locality. Nevertheless, he was probably the first to document the cyclical droughts on the prairies, with records invaluable for Ball's article on the droughts of 1811–20.[27]

Debra Lindsay tells us that Fidler's scientific interests "far surpassed what was expected by the Company ... He had a duty to science ... accompanied by a spirit of obligation ... [which] led him to observe and experiment, but only a sense of duty could prompt him to include this information in his journals."[28]

Written in this spirit, above and beyond the call of duty, Fidler's General Report of the Red River District for 1819 tells us: "The spring months have sometimes storms of wind and thunder even so early as March. Within these last years the climate seems to be greatly changed, the summers so backward with very little rain and even snow in winter much less than usual."[29] He is reporting the severe drought conditions, worse than the 1930s, that lasted from 1816 to 1819. His information is invaluable in understanding the pattern and mechanisms of drought on the Northern Great Plains. These droughts, which occur on average every twenty-two years in conjunction with the Schwabe twenty-two-year cycle of sunspots, affect all regions of the middle latitudes, especially those areas producing cereal grains, and cause extreme hardship.

NATURAL HISTORY

Here ... is how spring arrived at Cumberland House in the year 1798:

March 13	–	A flock of snowbirds seen – the harbingers of spring.
March 18	–	Large blue meat flies seen in numbers, being early in the season.
April 11	–	A swan seen.
April 14	–	Saw the first goose.
April 23	–	Frogs began to croak.
May 12	–	Mosquitoes pretty plentiful, being rather early in the season.
May 17	–	Trees in bud.
May 18	–	Leaves came out.[30]

Natural history items in Fidler's routine journal entries at Cumberland House in 1797 include an important, detailed, unmistakable description of the Channel Catfish, in a different river system from its later-known range north only to Lake Winnipegosis. In fact, his description antedated by two decades its first description to science by Rafinesque in 1818.[31] Fidler was the first to write of tar sands (15–21 June 1791, near present-day McMurray),[32] coal (12 February 1793, near present-day Drumheller),[33] and the Prickly Pear Cactus (February 1793, near the present site of Trochu, Alberta).[34] Other reports mention the vast flights of the Passenger Pigeon and the already declining numbers of swans. He told of the early nesting of the "whiskeyjack," the Gray Jay, who bring forth young before the snow is gone. At Chesterfield House, 1801–02, Fidler made some of the best estimates of bison numbers on the plains: "vast herds ... thousand on thousand buffalo in sight

from the house ... millions of buffalo all around the house not ¼ mile off –
and from a high eminence the ground is black quite round to a great distance."[35]

Fidler's final contributions to natural history were contained in two official
reports to the HBC: "A general report of the Red River district" (May 1819)[36]
and "Report of district" from Fort Dauphin in the spring of 1820 (Document
6).[37] The latter document contains important wildlife sightings, including the
first evidence of synchronous eight- to ten-year cycles in the snowshoe hare
and lynx ("cats"):

There are in some seasons plenty of rabbits, this year in particular – some years very
few – and what is rather remarkable the rabbits are the most numerous when the
cats appear. This winter the cats have come in considerable numbers, whereas these
several years past there was scarce one to be had – its flesh is good eating, sweet and
tender and they live principally on rabbits. The cats are only plentiful at certain
periods of about every 8 or 10 years and seldom remain in these southern parts in
any number for more than two or three years.[38]

These were extremely perceptive remarks, a century ahead of their time.
Subsequent authorities give Fidler credit for being the first to describe the
ten-year cycle, which involves a number of other bird and mammal species
in addition to hares[39] and lynx.[40] Subsequently, major long-term studies have
been designed to understand the mechanisms that drive Fidler's ten-year
cycle.[41] Based on the solid foundation of the long-term fur-catch data from
HBC records, analysed with increasing sophistication over more than a century and augmented by innovative new research, the story of ten-year cycles
is one of the most fascinating and problematical in biology, and is discussed
in Appendix D.

NATURAL HISTORY

Only one of the Hudson Bay fur traders – Thomas Hutchins – is likely to have had even rudimentary training in science, yet these untutored men developed an interest in natural history and joined the ranks of the earliest successful collectors on this continent. For birds alone, fur traders of Hudson Bay, facing almost insuperable difficulties, collected specimens of nineteen species and nine subspecies that received Latin names from Linnaeus and his immediate followers. Four – Isham, Graham, Hutchins, and Hearne – were more than mere collectors: their natural-history accounts in carefully preserved HBC journals and in published books place them in the ranks of the earliest naturalists in North America. Humphrey Marten's innovative experiments with bird boxes are also noteworthy.

The fur traders were drawn into the burgeoning rise of natural-history studies in part through curiosity, but curiosity coupled with the commitment to their company that was the soaring strength of the HBC's success. In Table 10.1 we list the birds that they collected.

THE COLLECTORS

Alexander Light (1737) Birds: 1 new species, the Spruce Grouse; 1 subspecies; Mammals: 1 species, 1 subspecies.

James Isham (1745) Birds: 12 new species, including the Whooping Crane; 1 subspecies; skins of 30 bird species.

Humphrey Marten (1771) Birds: 1 new species, the Eskimo Curlew; 16 skins of 6 other bird species. (1772): 26 skins of 21 bird species; first use of bird boxes.

Andrew Graham (1771) Birds: 5 new species, from Severn, including the Great Gray Owl; 59 skins of 34 other species; Fish: 1 new species.

Thomas Hutchins (1772) Skins of 16 bird species, 14 fish, 7 mammals; earned Copley Medal for determining freezing point of mercury; small goose subspecies named for him.

Table 10.1

Birds of Hudson Bay, as mentioned in ten eighteenth-century HBC manuscripts

NOTES

HM: species in Humphrey Marten's Birds in a Box, xx – 5 certain; x – 9 probable, ? – 2 questionable.

Other abbreviations: A – Albany; AR – Albany River; AZ – Arctic Zoology; C – Churchill; CH – Cumberland House; H – Henley; M – Moose Fort; nsp – no specimen; s – Severn; Y – York Factory

Pennant (3:267–268) erred in citing the Bean Goose (based on Hearne) and Greylag Goose from Hudson Bay

	Edwards plate #	E.2/5	E.2/7	E.2/9	E.2/10	Hutchins RoyalSoc	E.2/12	E.2/13	HM	Hearne	Forster	Pennant (AZ)	Latham
Red-throated Loon				53	30	63	50	55		276		3:234	345
Arctic Loon	146	76	92	61	30		54	65		276		3:233	345
Common Loon		77		53		63	50	55		276	420c	3:232	339
[Pied-billed Grebe]							error						
Horned Grebe	145			57,61	29,34		53	59,64			420s	3:206	
Am. White Pelican		75	92				95,111			278	419Y	3:306	
Am. Bittern	136	75	92	56	29	88	79	68		272	410s	3:152	
Great Blue Heron	135	74	91	54	28		51	56				3:143	
Black-crowned Night Heron										272			
Gr. White-fronted Goose	153	70		24	48	53	42	26		285	415ns	3:270	464
Snow Goose, blue morph	152	70	90	25	49	55	44	27	xx	284	±15ns	3:269A	445
white morph		68	90	25	48	54	43	26		282	413s	3:271S	

	Edwards plate #	E.2/5	E.2/7	E.2/9	E.2/10	Hutchins RoyalSoc	E.2/12	E.2/13	HM	Hearne	Forster	Pennant (AZ)	Latham
Ross's Goose										284			
Canada Goose	151	67	90	24	47	52	41	25		281	414s	3:265	
B.c. hutchinsii				24	47	53	42	26,30		282	414s		
B.c. maxima										285			
Brant	71	71	90	25	48	54	43	26		286		3:274	
Barnacle Goose							377H					3:275	
Trumpeter Swan		73								280			
Tundra Swan		73	91	28	47	56	48	31		279			
Am. Wigeon				53	28	60	50	54		287			
Mallard		73		28	50	56	47	30		287	419s	3:287	521
N. Shoveler, confused composite					52	58	44						
N. Pintail				26				28		287	419s	3:295s	
Green-winged Teal		73		28	50	57	47			287	419s	3:295s	
Scaup, Greater & Lesser				59	49		53	61			413s	3:290	
King Eider	154									287			
Common Eider		77	92	41,56	49,52	58	48,52	44					
Harlequin Duck					201H		371H			286	419		
Surf Scoter	155			52	51	61	49	29			417c	3:279	479
White-winged Scoter							46	69					482
Black Scoter		76	92	252	54	57,61				287			

Scoter, unidentified female	156												
Oldsquaw (Long-tailed Duck)		73		27	50,210H	61	378H	29		287	418c	3:291	
Bufflehead				26	51	65	45	28			416s	3:282s	
Common Goldeneye		73		59	49	60	82	61	x		417s		536
Hooded Merganser				44	53	64	70	46				3:259	427
Common Merganser												3:257	
Red-breasted Merganser				27	29	64	47	30	x	279		3:258	
Bald Eagle, adult				60	20	45	39	64		256		2:228	
immature				23	20		38	24					
N. Harrier	107			39		43	55	41				2:243	
N. Goshawk									x				
Red-tailed Hawk, immature												2:241	
Rough-legged Hawk subsp. sancti-johannis				42	20	42	57	45			383	2:234	
Golden Eagle		65	90	60,61	20	44	38,40	63,64		256			
Merlin				55	21	57	57	57			382s	2:247s	101
Gyrfalcon	53	81	94	67	57	91	98,376H	88	x	257	383s	2:233A	23,58
Peregrine Falcon immature				40	22,23	40,41	69 / 68	43				2:236	73,78
Ruffed Grouse		80	93	80	63	64	110	98		261	393As	2:352AHM	737
Spruce Grouse	71,118	85	93	74	65	100	105	95		138,263	389s	2:359	735
Willow Ptarmigan	72	80	93	78	62	98	108	96		264	390s	2:360	743
Rock Ptarmigan		80,84	93	79	63	99	110	97		267		2:364	

	Edwards plate #	E.2/5	E.2/7	E.2/9	E.2/10	Hutchins RoyalSoc	E.2/12	E.2/13	HM	Hearne	Forster	Pennant (AZ)	Latham
Sharp-tailed Grouse	117	86	95	73	63	101	104	93		262	394As,425	2:357	732
Greater Prairie-Chicken				80								2:356H	
Yellow Rail				31	53	70	61	67				*	
Sora	144			255	27,203H		91,374H						
Sandhill Crane	133			54	28	77	52	56		272	409s	3:142S	
Whooping Crane	132	74	91	54	28	89	51	55		271	409y	3:141	
Black-bellied Plover						50					412A	3:184	
Am. Golden Plover	140			30	25	77	59	33		275		3:189	
Semipalmated Plover		75		33	23	75	63	36					
Killdeer						76							
Yellowlegs, Greater & Lesser		75	92	291	31	51	58	31		274	410A	3:170	
Solitary Sandpiper				251	31		87	68				3:173	
Spotted Sandpiper				256	36		92	72				3:178	
Eskimo Curlew				62	37		84	66	x		411A,431		
Whimbrel (Hudsonian Curlew)		75	92	50	26	66	76	53	x	273			
Hudsonian Godwit	138			62,251	54	66	54,88	66,69		273	411c	3:169	
Marbled Godwit	137											3:169	
Ruddy Turnstone	141			58	37		81	60		274	412s	3:177	188
Red Knot				257	37		93	74					
Sanderling				62	37		85	72				3:193	

Semipalmated Sandpiper				50	36	77	76	52					
Least Sandpiper				63	37		85	72					
Pectoral Sandpiper				29	45	49	59	32					
Dunlin				47	46	84	73	50					
Dowitcher, short- & long-billed				63	35		86	73					
Common Snipe	143	75		30	26		60	33					
Red-necked Phalarope	142		92	252	35,200H		89,369H	70				3:203	
Red Phalarope													
Jaeger, Long-tailed	148												
Parasitic &c		76	93	52,59 256	32	72	81,83	60,71			421c		389
Bonaparte's Gull				254	32		89	66				3:244	
Herring Gull		77		55	56	71	55,78	56	x	277		3:242	
immature				78	33		55	31					
Glaucous Gull?						73	92						
Arctic Tern		77	93	52	33	73	78	54	x	278	421c		
Black Tern		76			34		78	57				3:239	
Black Guillemot ("willick")													
Mourning Dove, 'far inland'											3:7		
Passenger Pigeon		79	95	59	33		83	62		268	398s	3:1M	661
Great Horned Owl	60	86,87	95	77	58		107	92				2:263	119

	Edwards plate #	E.2/5	E.2/7	E.2/9	E.2/10	Hutchins RoyalSoc	E.2/12	E.2/13	HM	Hearne	Forster	Pennant (AZ)	Latham
Snowy Owl	61	86	95	76	59	94	107	92		257	385c	2:269	132
female				*76*	*58*		*106*	*99*				*2:268*	
N. Hawk Owl	62	86		59	59	91	101	91		258	385cs	2:271	142
Barred Owl												2:271	
Great Gray Owl		86	95	71	58	92	102	91			386s,424	2:268	134
Long-eared Owl				80	25		111	100				2:264s	121
Short-eared Owl				45	59	74	72	48			384s	2:265	
Boreal Owl ?				77			108	93			385s	2:274	151
Common Nighthawk					212H		378H		xx			3:135H	
Ruby-throated Hummingbird							112CH						
Belted Kingfisher	115				204H		96,374H					2:327	637
Red-headed Woodpecker					199H		368H						561
Yellow-bellied Sapsucker												2:322A	
Downy Woodpecker					205H		375H					2:321A	572
Hairy Woodpecker			95				101				388s	2:320	572
Three-toed Woodpecker	114			69	57	95	100	91			388s	2:323	600
Northern Flicker		89					101			260	387A	2:316	597
Pileated Woodpecker					199H		369H			260		2:316AR	554
Northern Shrike				79	61		110	98			386s	2:278	160

Species				203H		373H						
Vireo, Philadelphia &c												
Gray Jay	80	96	65	60		96	87	xx	260	386s	2:289	389
Black-billed Magpie		95	62	29		84	65			387A	2:289	
Am. Crow (inland)			258	60		95	100				2:287	
Common Raven	89	95	78	60	104	108	99		259		2:286	
Horned Lark	75	92	44	44	82,85	71	47		270	398A	3:84	197
female			36	47		66	40					
Purple Martin*	120										3:129	
Tree Swallow	75	92	257	39		93		xx		408s	3:128	
Bank Swallow	75				89		74	xx	271			
Cliff Swallow									271	408nosp		
Black-capped Chickadee				63		100			271	407A	3:121A	542
Boreal Chickadee			68	61	96	99	89			408s	3:122s	557
Red-breasted Nuthatch			258	42		94	75				3:109	462
Ruby-crowned Kinglet										407s	3:17s	
Am. Robin	66	90	57	40	90	80	59		268	399s	3:22	26
Gray Catbird (?inland-csh)												
Bohemian Waxwing						95						
Yellow Warbler			255	55		91	71	?			3:96	515
Magnolia Warbler				203H		373H						281
Blackpoll Warbler										406s	3:81s	
Am. Redstart				202H		370H					3:92	651
female				200H		371H						
Wilson's Warbler						377H						

	Edwards plate #	E.2/5	E.2/7	E.2/9	E.2/10	Hutchins RoyalSoc	E.2/12	E.2/13	HM	Hearne	Forster	Pennant (AZ)	Latham
Am. Tree Sparrow		75		255	?41		91	67			405S	3:62S	
Savannah Sparrow				36,46	38,45	80,81	67,73	40,49					
White-throated Sparrow				33	43,202H	46	372H	37					
White-crowned Sparrow				32,254	39,43	68	62,90	35,67			403s,426A	3:41As	200,253
Dark-eyed Junco				34	45	47	64	38			406s,428	3:45S	
Lapland Longspur				48	24	79	74	51		270	404s		
Snow Bunting	126	65	90	23	38		40	24		269	403S	3:41S	
Yellow-headed Blackbird												2:306	
Rusty Blackbird		67		23	40	45	41	25			400S	2:305	
Albino Blackbird, species?							377H						422
Pine Grosbeak	123	75,91	92	35	40	48	65	38	x	269	402S	3:33	
Red Crossbill				43	42	89	69	46			402S	3:32S	408
Redpoll, Common & Hoary		75							?	270	405S	3:68	
Hoary Redpoll			92	66	62	97	97	81			404S		263
Total species	33	50	37	92	100	64	112	92	16		60	93	46
Total column, incl italics		51	38	99	108	66	121	99			63	94	
Total entries		54	38	107	114	70	133	106		55	68	94	

Moses Norton (1771) Birds: 1 potential new species, Ross's Goose, not forwarded; 17 skins of 8 species.

Ferdinand Jacobs (1771) Birds: 2 skins, the Whooping Crane and the American White Pelican, their size compensating for their number.

Samuel Hearne (1770s and 1780s) Best descriptions of habits of birds and mammals; first to describe Ross's Goose.

Peter Fidler (1790–1821) Bibliophile and naturalist; first to recognize the ten-year cycle of the hare and lynx; most productive map-maker.

CHRONOLOGY OF 1770S COLLECTIONS

1768 Graham wrote E.2/4 and E.2/5; latter told of 54 species of birds.

1769 Graham wrote E.2/6, which told of company policy.

1771 Graham wrote E.2/7 and E.2/8, which told of 40 species of birds, to accompany first major shipment of specimens to London, one chest sent on the *Seahorse* from York Factory and presumably Severn, and another on the *King George II* from Churchill.[1] A box each came from Albany and Moose Factory on the *Prince Rupert IV*.[2] Forster described specimens from Graham at Severn and Marten at Albany.[3]

1772 Graham was fully occupied as acting chief at York Factory, the main fur trade depot for the HBC, during the busiest two weeks of the year. He was busy supervising packing of a year's collection of furs, the financial mainstay of the company. Hutchins, by default, was "responsible for packing and labelling the specimens sent home"[4] on the *King George II*, as well as writing the Royal Society manuscript that accompanied them.[5] Graham was fortunate in having Hutchins available to help him; 1772–73 was the only winter they were together. Hutchins' training in comparative zoology and Latin qualified him for the task of describing the specimens. He was not merely a diligent scribe but had helped with the collecting. It was Hutchins who shot the Gyrfalcon in the fall of 1771 and Hutchins, not Graham, who shot two Horned Larks on 12 May 1772.

1773 When Hutchins returned from York Factory to England on furlough in 1773, he took with him "a few samples of subjects of seeds, plants, cones, birds, sea fish and quadrupeds and will continue to collect fish and insects and plants as may prove acceptable."[6] Their receipt was acknowledged by the committee of the Royal Society on 22 December 1773, yet it is not known whether new species were involved; no publication resulted.[7]

1774 A final "package of natural curiosities" was brought home from Moose Factory by the *Prince Rupert* in 1774 (Leveson Gower 1934, 66).

DISSEMINATION OF HUDSON BAY SPECIMENS

Hudson Bay specimens became known beyond England. Georges Louis Leclerc Buffon, in his *Histoire naturelle des oiseaux* (in nine volumes, 1770–83), gave French names to each species; for the Purple Martin he chose "L'Hirondelle de la Baye de Hudson"[8] and gave the type locality correctly (see discussion following) as "the territory of Hudson's Bay."[9] Buffon also opposed the rigid classification of Linnaeus and spoke of "two equally dangerous obstacles ... The first is having no method, and the second is desiring to subsume everything under a specific system."[10] He anticipated the biological species concept, propounded so eloquently in the twentieth century by Ernst Mayr when he wrote, "One should regard as belonging to the same species those animals who by way of copulation can perpetuate themselves and conserve the character of the species."[11] Buffon felt that "related species were probably separated from one another by only the influences of the climate, of nutrition, and by the passage of time."[12]

THE DESIGNATION "HUDSONIAN"

Hudson Bay is well represented in scientific terminology by the adjective "hudsonian" as part of the name, either common or scientific, for some species and as a "type locality" for others. There is a certain geographic ambiguity inherent in the citation of a vast inland sea, up to 1,600 km in length and 1,000 km in width. Yet the term "hudsonian" encompassed a much larger area of 3.6 million km² extending west to the Rocky Mountains, the entire area that drained into Hudson Bay (see Figure I.1). Named Rupert's Land in honour of Prince Rupert and the 1670 charter, it was occupied and governed by the Hudson's Bay Company until 1870.

When in 1823 Joseph Sabine described what in July 2000 became recognized as a full species, the North American form of the Black-billed Magpie, *Pica hudsonia*,[13] from a specimen collected by John Richardson and painted by Robert Hood at Cumberland House, over 1,000 km by canoe from Hudson Bay, he named it "*Corvus Hudsonius*, Hudson's Bay Magpie."[14] The subspecies of Striped Skunk from "the Plains of the Saskatchewan" near Carlton, about 1,500 km from the bay, was similarly named *Mephitis mephitis* var. *hudsonia*, the "Hudson's Bay Skunk."[15]

Other species and subspecies with a tag indicating their Hudson Bay origin include the Boreal Chickadee, *Poecile hudsonicus*; Whimbrel, *Numenius phaeopus hudsonicus*; and Northern Harrier, *Circus cyaneus hudsonius*. The Hudsonian Godwit remains an official American Ornithologists' Union (AOU) common or vernacular name, and for the first four AOU check-lists, until the North

American taxon was merged with the European as the Whimbrel, the Hudsonian Curlew was another official name. And the official French-language name for the American Tree Sparrow is "Bruant hudsonien."

The next confusion is over when and where not to use an apostrophe after the name Hudson. The body of water is plain Hudson Bay, without an apostrophe. Only the fur-trading company is properly called Hudson's, and its territory the Hudson's Bay Territory.[16] The ambiguous, general type locality "Hudson Bay," used by all seven AOU check-lists, is insufficiently precise or even misleading. The most accurate designation of the type locality would be "Hudson's Bay territory." Indeed, this was the locality designation used by Buffon for the Purple Martin, more correct than that given by Linnaeus, Edwards, and the various AOU check-lists.

DIFFICULTIES IN PRESERVING BIRD AND MAMMAL SKINS

The problems faced in preparing scientific specimens for transport to England and preserving them for future reference were formidable. Bird specimens in the Sloane Collection, which had formed the basis of the British Museum in 1753, soon deteriorated and were discarded. As Logan says,

The first attempts at taxidermy appear to have begun during the middle of the seventeenth to the middle of the eighteenth century, when natural history collecting became a fashionable pastime and a scientific requirement as the advance in sea-travel led to the discovery and exploration of new continents. The initial process was extremely crude. An animal would be opened with a single incision, the inner organs removed and the cavity filled with a mixture of dried moss, straw and spices. Preservation was achieved by air-drying. Often a specially constructed oven was employed.[17]

Timely advice on taxidermy was printed in the *Philosophical Transactions* in 1770. Thomas Davies suggested use of a powder of equal quantities of "burnt allum, camphire, and cinnamon ... sprinkled lightly over the whole carcase."[18] Davies would then have had the collector pour into the body cavity, after evisceration, "a small quantity of camphire dissolved in rectified spirits of wine,"[19] and then fill up the cavity with fine cotton. Finally "a composition of sublimate mercury, tempered with some water [is] rubbed gently over the feathers" to prevent "insects, and other vermin, from destroying the plumage."[20] That same year, T.S. Kuckahn[21] recommended a liquid varnish, composed of camphor and turpentine, and a dry compound of corrosive sublimate, saltpetre, alum, flowers of sulphur, musk, black pepper, and coarse ground tobacco. He stuffed the cavities with tansy, wormwood, hops, and tobacco. The next year J.R. Forster gave the recipe for his liquor (an ounce of Sal Ammoniac dissolved in a quart of water, to which is added two ounces of corrosive sublimate mercury, or four ounces of ar-senic in two quarts of water). His powder consisted of four parts of tobacco-sand, four parts of pounded black pepper, one part of burnt alum, and one part of cor-rosive sublimate or arsenic.[22]

Jean-Baptiste Bécoeur (1718–77), an apothecary in Metz, France, and owner of a magnificent bird collection, used a paste containing arsenic, soap, salt of tartar, camphor, and powdered lime to preserve bird skins but kept the ingredients of his profitable recipe a commercial secret. Not until thirty years after Bécoeur's death did Louis Dufresne make the ingredients known; the National Museum in Paris thereby became the standard by which other museums were judged.[23]

ADVENT OF THE LINNAEAN CLASSIFICATION SYSTEM

Alexander Light and James Isham would have been surprised if they could have seen their specimens shown in hand-painted, page-sized illustrations in a book by George Edwards, a devoutly religious man who wished to par-ticipate in what was beginning to be a world-wide passion, the cataloguing and classification of the wonders of God's creation. In turn, Edwards must have been delighted when Linnaeus gave Latin names to a number of the species illustrated in his book. This improbable sequence of events put our fur traders at the very forefront of scientific ornithology and taxonomy. (Par-enthetically one might observe that, over two centuries later, the contribu-tions of competent amateurs still play a role in ornithology.)

When the fur traders made their natural-history collections, they were unaware of Linnaeus's newly created system in which each species had a unique binomial Latin name. Before *Systema Naturae* in 1758 there was no stan-dardized system. A bird species might have one name in one town and a dis-similar one in the next county. At Hudson Bay, one trading post or one tribe might use an appellation unknown elsewhere. One name could be used for two or more species and a single species might have more than one name. Plumages varied by sex and age, so that the drake and hen could have sep-arate names, and various age plumages – in eagles, for example – had sep-arate names. Although specimen-collecting was the first essential step in the process, there were no authoritative books and no reference collections to settle such questions.

As we move into the third millennium, the standard authority for North American bird species taxonomy, the *AOU Check-list*, continues to change species' names and the sequence of their presentation with each edition. As knowledge accumulates, some forms are lumped (the Blue Goose and Snow Goose are now one species), and others are split (the Solitary Vireo was recently split into three species). Because their plumages are not too different, the collectors at the fur-trade posts lumped each of the following pairs into one species: the Common and Red-breasted Merganser, the Black-bellied Plover and American Golden-Plover, the Bonaparte's and Laughing Gull, the Common and Hoary Redpoll, and the Lesser and Greater Yellowlegs. Yet the Cree Indians and Hutchins clearly separated out from the "Large Grey Goose," the much smaller version of the Canada Goose, now known as Hutchins' Goose, using the Cree adjective for small, "apis." Less understandable is the making of two dissimilar ducks a compound species under one name, as the Graham-Hutchins collaboration did with the Northern Pintail and Northern Shoveler. Although the four different species of swallow at Hudson Bay have very different plumages, all of the swallow accounts in the HBC archives remained confused between habitats and descriptions.

CORRECTION OF PREVIOUS ERRORS AND OMISSIONS

Five earlier overviews of the Hudson Bay collections are incomplete or inaccurate, largely because they pre-dated publication of Isham's journal in 1949 and of the Graham-Hutchins collaboration in 1969.[24]

Stevens (1936) mistakenly credited the Golden-Plover to Edwards and the Greater Yellowlegs and Tree Sparrow to Forster;[25] Baillie (1946) mentions eight species described by Isham when in fact there were thirteen;[26] McAtee (1950) covered Edwards well, but the Hudson Bay provenance poorly;[27] Snyder (1963) suggested an overly restrictive type locality of "northeastern Manitoba" for thirteen species.[28]

All five authors overlooked the perceptive historical research of Edward Preble of the United States Biological Survey.[29] From 17 June to 16 September 1900, Preble travelled by canoe from Norway House to York Factory and then by sailboat to Churchill and north to Seal River, returning by the same route. Preble mentions the specimens previously collected at Hudson Bay by Alexander Light, Andrew Graham, and Thomas Hutchins, and the observations of Samuel Hearne. Preble had learned of the "Hutchins manuscript" from Ernest E. Thompson [Seton], and had visited the Hudson's Bay Company Archives in London, England.

In 1951 Elsa Guerdrum Allen[30] published *The History of American Ornithology before Audubon*, a detailed and valuable look into long-neglected and previously untapped sources. However, Humphrey Marten's *Observations* were published after completion of most of her study; she was also unaware of Preble's and Seton's researches and so omitted James Isham and Alexander Light.[31]

MOTIVATION OF THE COLLECTORS

The Hudson Bay collectors dealt with in this book were involved in the first of two short-lived periods of natural-history endeavour in the HBC territory. The second occurred from 1859 to 1867, when HBC employees collected specimens at the instigation of Robert Kennicott of the Smithsonian Institution. Debra Lindsay has studied this period extensively and suggests that the first Hudson Bay collectors shared the field-work of collecting specimens, and that both groups delegated some of this work to unnamed and unrecognized natives. Although the eighteenth-century Hudson Bay traders, like Kennicott's devotees, showed "aptitude ... for fieldwork," they largely lacked the "social status, prestige, recognition among scientists, and Baird's appreciation,"[32] which together rewarded four later enthusiastic HBC fur traders, Bernard Rogan Ross, Roderick Ross MacFarlane, James Lockhart, and George Barnston. Lindsay argues that the more sophisticated 1860s fur traders were nevertheless "susceptible to the inducements of consumer goods, especially alcohol and books ... Their contributions were empirical and functional rather than theoretical or inventive ... Fieldwork on the scale envisioned by Baird was more than a genteel hobby. It was indeed work."[33] In the instance of the eighteenth-century collectors, the only "status and prestige" they achieved was limited to mention of their names in the books by Edwards, Pennant, and Latham – and many died without knowing that they had gained even this.

Through their collections the early fur traders contributed their talents in a constructive, if unexpected, fashion. They lived in an exciting period. Elsewhere, more sophisticated and better educated explorers and collectors (Joseph Banks was one example and Alexander von Humboldt another) were conversant with most of the information available in both science and literature, arguably the last time in human history when this was possible.[34]

CLIMATOLOGY

❖

Weather is known to have been cyclical for over 700,000 years.[1] Concerns about changes caused by these cycles included "the Malthusian threat of global overpopulation, rapid resources depletion, and the spectre of environmental deterioration,"[2] and, more recently, Global Cooling as prophesied by Lowell Ponte in 1976 and exemplified by the Pinatubo eruption in June 1991,[3] or Global Warming resulting from factors that could include El Niño[4] and postulated ozone depletion.[5] A major dilemma faced by science today is to separate natural climate variations from those induced by humans.

Long-term data are extremely limited. A 1999 study by the National Research Council in Washington, DC, drew attention to the problem: "Deficiencies in the accuracy, quality and continuity of the records ... place serious limitations on the confidence that can be placed in the research results."[6] A few long-term records, such as tree rings and ice cores, can be analysed, but few parts of the world have available historical records. Modern weather records rarely exceed fifty years; Environment Canada considers that meaningful records began in 1948. As one proceeds backwards from that date, for most areas on earth instrumental and secular records decrease rapidly in number and length.

Gordon Manley in 1974 produced a temperature record for central England, from 1695 to 1973, but it was created by overlapping many very short sets.[7] Ship's logs provide standardized daily weather observations, but only for the length of the voyage.

THE DEVELOPMENT OF WORLD METEOROLOGY

The earliest instruments from Greek and Roman times were wind and rain gauges. Ironically, neither was maintained by the Hudson's Bay Company, unless you count a flag at the top of a mast pole as a wind gauge.

Sir Christopher Wren (1632–1723), the famous English architect, saw that great promise lay in the development of meteorological data. He and Robert Hooke together developed such instruments as a rain-gauge, an automatic

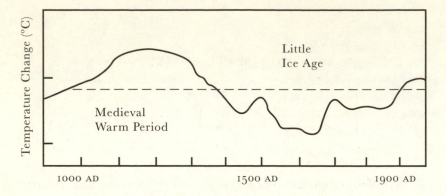

Figure 11.1
Graph: Climate change over five centuries: Little Ice Age, 1560–1830.
Working Group I, Intergovernmental Panel on Climate Change

wind recorder, a thermometer, a barometer, and a hygroscope.[8] Galileo
produced the first fluid thermometer in 1611, followed by Torricelli's barometer in 1643. Regular instrumental observations began in Florence in 1654
and continued to 1670. Similar record-keeping began in Paris in 1658 and
crossed the channel to Oxford and London in 1659.[9] Less sophisticated
weather records had been kept earlier by a handful of individuals, though
not published until hundreds of years later. Reverend William Merle kept
one of the earliest weather diaries at Driby, Lincolnshire, 1337–44 (published
by Symons in 1891); W. Haller in Zurich, Switzerland, kept weather records
from 1546 to 1576 (published in 1872 and analysed in 1949); Tycho Brahe kept
weather and wind observations on the island of Hven, between Denmark
and Sweden, from 1582 to 1597 (published in 1876); Landgrave Herman IV
of Hessen kept observations from 1621 to 1650 (analysed in 1960).[10]

A world-wide weather observation network was first proposed in 1724 by
Dr James Jurin, secretary of the Royal Society in London. Jurin, rated "one
of the most learned men of his day,"[11] had imbibed Newtonian philosophy
from Newton himself.

In 1811 the Royal Society again encouraged people to take observations,
and also worked diligently to develop reliable standards of scale and to build
precision instruments.

If we are ever going to grasp even the basics of global climate, we have
to reconstruct past patterns as accurately as possible. The Intergovernmental Panel on Climate Change (1996)[12] (Figure 11.1) identifies the following
climatic periods since AD 700:

Medieval Warm Period	700–1300 AD
"Sporer Minimum"	1300–1500
Brief Climatic Warming	1500—1560
"Little Ice Age" ("Maunder Minimum")	1560–1830
Brief Warmer Period	1830–1870
Brief Cooler Period	1870–1910
Brief Warmer Period	1910–1940
Brief Cooler Period	1940–1980

It is now recognized that significant climatic change occurs, often over quite short time-periods. Hare and Thomas indicate that such knowledge has important applications for many disciplines: "Physical scientists, geographers, biologists, historians, economists, archaeologists and anthropologists are all interested in climatic change as it affects their discipline."[13] As I have written previously, "Geography and history are inseparable; history is the play and geography the stage on which it is enacted."[14]

We readily accept that climate has an influence on flora and fauna and anthropologists speak of climate change as it affects "primitive" societies. Yet climate change affects history more than has been appreciated. The Highland Clearances began when global temperatures fell rapidly prior to 1580; Scotland lost half the area available for food production in approximately one century. This forced Highland clans into conflict with the Lowland clans and triggered the clan wars. The landlords' reaction, much criticized, was to force remaining tenants off the land, an action that to historians became the "cause,"[15] because they failed to appreciate that climate had changed so quickly or so much. History is a major source of information about previous climate changes, which in turn will change the understanding of history.

More important, we need to determine the natural variability and causes of long-term climate change because only then will we know the extent, if any, of the impact of human actions on climate. Virtually no weather-recording stations are present in the 70 per cent of the world that is ocean, nor in vast stretches of the polar regions, mountains, and deserts. Hence, "the world climatic picture, both temporal and spatial, remains barely an outline sketch."[16]

THE CLIMATE OF HUDSON BAY

Hudson Bay, an extremely large inland sea, has a marked influence upon the weather characteristics of all of North America.[17] Temperatures are modified by the presence of open, relatively warm water in early winter, and by the existence of ice well into summer. Alexander Mackenzie had a remarkable understanding of continental weather, and in 1801 phrased this better than most could today:

The climate must necessarily be severe in such a country ... which displays so large a surface of fresh water. Its severity is extreme on the coast of Hudson's Bay, and proceeds from its immediate exposure to the North-West winds that blow off the Frozen Ocean. These winds, in crossing directly from the bay over Canada and the British dominions on the Atlantic, as well as over the Eastern States of North America to that ocean (where they give to those countries a length of winter astonishing to the inhabitants of the same latitudes in Europe), continue to retain a great degree of force and cold in their passage, even over the Atlantic, particularly at the time when the sun is in its Southern declination.[18]

The bay is subject to intense outbreaks of cold arctic air during most of the winter and not infrequently in summer. Cyclonic activity brings inclement weather during all seasons, but high winds are especially evident during summer. Ice lasts for nearly eight months, and persists well into July.[19] In the southern portion of the bay, the water temperature rarely exceeds 7.2 degrees Celsius (45° F), while northern sections remain close to freezing throughout the summer. Open leads in the ice occur throughout the winter, resulting in fog known as "frost smoke" or "sea roke" to the fur traders. For much of the year the landscape is similar over land and water, the same white waste whether ice or snow. As Cynthia Wilson's research indicates, "mean airstreams and confluences between airstreams define climatic regions with a distinctive annual march of airstream and air mass dominance... the boreal forest occupies the region between the mean or modal southern boundaries of Arctic air in winter and in summer."[20]

The influence of the bay and the confluence of climates make Churchill today one of the most attractive birding areas in the world. In a relatively small area you have subarctic, boreal forest, freshwater lakes, and saltwater eco-zones. Even two hundred years ago the scientific community in Europe was eager to hear about the variety of plants, birds, and mammals at Hudson Bay.

HUDSON'S BAY COMPANY WEATHER RECORDS

How little is generally known about the extent, diversity, and detail of the HBC records, especially the weather information, was underlined for me when I made my doctoral thesis proposal to Queen Mary College, University of London. I proposed that weather maps be produced for each day, 1810–20, in northern Manitoba. The proposal was initially rejected because the committee said that there were insufficient recording stations for reasonable interpolation. Committee members were astounded when told that there were three times as many stations then as there are today.

Indeed, no other region of the world has such an extensive and detailed record of climate and environment over such a prolonged period. The records are "probably as consistent as any in history."[21] The data, offering the largest and longest series of such observations anywhere in North America and possibly the world, cover a critical area of climate along the Arctic Front, where change is most immediately and dramatically felt. They also cover a period before the growth of human industrial activities that purportedly are causing climate and environmental change.[22] The extent of this impact cannot be determined unless we understand the extent of variation before such human input occurred.

Fortuitously, both Churchill and York Factory, with their uniform terrain, level ground, and lack of trees, are ideal sites for measuring long-term climate change.[23] Churchill is right at the tree-line, itself a response to the climate boundary between the arctic and boreal forest regions, on permafrost that is approximately 60 metres (195 feet) deep.[24] The average year-round temperature for the period 1930 to 1960 was a chilly −7.3° C. Annual prevailing winds are from the northwest, although they change dramatically with the seasons. The movements of the polar front through the region in spring and fall bring snow, strong winds, and severe windchills. The annual total precipitation is a low 25 centimetres because cold air holds little moisture.

The tree-line is coincident with the mean summer position of the Arctic Front and the 10° C summer (June, July, August) isotherm.[25] Churchill is very near the south edge of the arctic climatic region, and York Factory is at the northern edge of the boreal climatic region. Prior to 1760, for roughly the first three centuries of the Little Ice Age from 1450 to 1850, the mean summer position of the arctic front was farther south and both York and Churchill were in the arctic climatic region. After 1760, as the climate warmed, the line moved north. Conditions remained unchanged in the arctic region at Churchill, while York Factory became part of the boreal forest region, with more days of rainfall.[26] Because of the slow rate of thaw, both stations continue to have discontinuous permafrost. Detailed tree-ring analysis at Churchill shows that 1760 was pivotal for climate trends.[27]

Alexander Mackenzie was also aware of the improving climate:

It has been frequently advanced, that the difference of clearing away the wood has had an astonishing influence in meliorating the climate in [America]; but I am not disposed to assent to that opinion in the extent which it proposes to establish, when I consider the very trifling proportion of the country cleared, compared with the whole. The employment of the axe may have had some inconsiderable effect; but I look to other causes. I myself observed in a country, which was in an absolute state of nature, that the climate is improving; and this circumstance was confirmed to me by the native inhabitants of it. Such a change, therefore, must proceed from some predominating operation in the system of the globe which is beyond my conjecture, and, indeed, above my comprehension.[28]

A shift in frequency of wind direction is further evidence of change. From 1721 to 1731 southerly winds at York Factory were less than 7 per cent of total winds, but from 1841 to 1851 they were over 10 per cent, bringing with them an earlier onset of spring.

The frequency of north winds shows a similar pattern, with an increase reflecting the shift from a zonal flow (west to east) to a meridional flow (north to south). These reflect greater north-south meandering of the jet stream, with greater variability of temperature and climate. These shifts are of great significance in subpolar and mid-latitude climates. When zonal flow amplitude of the planetary waves in the polar front is low, winds are generally from the northwest in winter and southwest in summer, and weather patterns are relatively predictable. Such a situation existed in the Brief Cooler Period from 1940 to 1980. With meridional (north-south) flow, the amplitude of polar front waves is much greater; winds are much more often northerly in the winter and southerly in the summer, and the weather overall is more variable and unpredictable. This was the condition during the Brief Warmer Period from 1910 to 1940.

Meteorological records for York Factory and Churchill date back to 1714 and 1718 respectively.[29] We must be extremely grateful for the demands for diligent, accurate record-keeping imposed on their employees by the HBC governors. They understood the importance of accurate records because they depended on them for their business decisions. Now their records provide us with valuable information about weather during the Little Ice Age and the Brief Warmer Period.

Catchpole and Moodie note that "the records of the Hudson's Bay Company provide a corpus of chronicles unrivalled in North America."[30] Journals for 210 different fur-trading posts are preserved in the HBC archives; 28 were kept for over thirty years prior to 1871, as shown on the map (Figure 11.2) and circular diagram (Figure 11.3).[31] In addition, ships' logs in the HBC archives cover 216 years of records for twenty-seven different ships over 121 years, with only three years, 1839, 1840, and 1841, missing.[32]

Dedicated meteorological journals were available for Churchill, 1837–39 and 1840–45. Instrumental recordings at Churchill began in the fall of 1768,

Figure 11.2
Map of thirty HBC posts with weather records for more than thirty years.
Courtesy Alan Catchpole (Catchpole 1980, *Syllogeus* 26:37)

providing a cross-check on the daily weather entries. (Mercury thermometers, of course, cease to record temperatures below minus −38.8° C or −37.9° F.)[33]

York Factory (57° N, 92° W) had the most complete and longest record among the HBC posts, although Albany weather records began slightly earlier, in 1705–06.[34] As the administrative centre for the HBC, York had better-qualified officers, and they generally maintained the best records. The first weather entries at York Factory were made on 6 September 1714 by James Knight, who had arrived there with Henry Kelsey to receive the surrender of the French garrison under Nicolas Jérémie after the Treaty of Utrecht returned all Hudson Bay territories to Great Britain.[35] Between 1714 and 1914 (when the RCMP took over weather recording) there were 100,698 qualitative observations recorded at York Factory, 63,230 for temperature alone and 21,833 for precipitation events.[36] Specific, dedicated meteorological journals were available for 1771–72, 1794–95, 1829–30, 1831–32, 1847–49, and 1850–52.

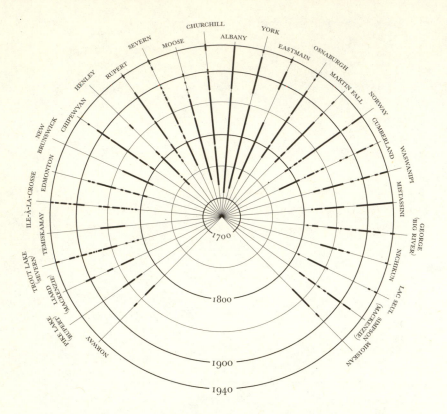

Figure 11.3
Circular diagram showing numbers of years of weather observations at HBC posts.
Courtesy Alan Catchpole. (Catchpole 1980, *Syllogeus* 26:37)

The two centuries of post journals and other fur-company records have been more accessible to Canadians following their transfer to the Provincial Archives of Manitoba (PAM) in 1974,[37] and more recently by having most of them available on microfilm. Although individual journals, for some posts for some years spanning the period 1705 to 1940, "have been lost, or destroyed in fires or in shipping accidents," the HBC archives "provide a unique chronicle of the evolution of half a continent from the stone age to the modern era."[38]

HBC weather observations for Churchill, entered on a computer, total 61,443, of which 22,601 were for temperature alone and 13,505 recorded precipitation events.[39] For Churchill and York Factory together there are a total of 162,147 observations. Barometric readings for the two sites combined total 35,400. Because each weather observation had an average of five recordable

details, there were approximately 810,735 specific pieces of climatic information available for my analysis.

It took me four years to transcribe the data from the daily entries in the
York Factory and Churchill journals alone, and occasional meteorological
journals from these two posts. Computer entry of these data took the better
part of a fifth year. All calendar entries before 1752, the year of Gregorian
calendar reform, had eleven days added. Harington was correct to mention
"the tremendous investment in time that is presently required to distil a useful
drop of paleoclimatic [and modern, he might well have added] data from
archival and other sources."[40]

I was fortunate to have chosen Hudson's Bay Company records for my
thesis project. No other company, anywhere in the world, can boast of such
a complete and extended documentation of its history, commerce, and
influence.

PREVIOUS USE OF WEATHER RECORDS IN THE HBC
ARCHIVES AND ROYAL SOCIETY LIBRARY

The wealth of meteorological data in the Hudson's Bay post journals has
been recognized by a few select scientists, two of whom, both knighted later,
were interested in weather details from western Canada. John Richardson
studied weather records as well as natural-history observations in post journals in the HBC office in London in the 1820s. John Henry Lefroy made magnetical observations at Fort Chipewyan, Lake Athabasca, in the winter of
1843–44 and combined these with Richardson's magnetical and meteorological observations from Great Bear Lake in March and April 1849, made
during his search for the missing men and ships of the third Franklin expedition.[41] More specific use of HBC weather information has been made since
the 1960s.[42]

MacKay and MacKay studied the ice conditions in the Churchill River
from 1719 and the Hayes River from 1714 and found that the variability of
break-up dates was greater than those for freeze-up.[43] The date of freeze-
up reflects local conditions better than does the date of break-up, which is
often due to warm conditions upstream, causing in turn a rise in water levels
downstream, lifting and breaking up the ice regardless of the local temperature. Frequently ice jams form, and the water backs up to flood large areas
– York Factory was moved from its original position because of such occur-
rences.[44] As Catchpole and Moodie say, "thawing and freezing set the tempo
of the water-borne traffic that was the life-blood of the fur trade."[45]

Robert Minns produced a pioneering study of HBC weather records as
his master's thesis at the University of British Columbia in 1970. Despite the

intimidating title, "An Air Mass Climatology of Canada during the Early Nineteenth Century: An Analysis of the Weather Records of Certain Hudson's Bay Company Forts," it was an important advance because it used the scientific method to analyse historical source material. Cynthia Wilson further rewarded the diligence of the record-keepers with precision studies of material kept at forts on the east coast of Hudson Bay, including Eastmain, Fort George, and Great Whale River.[46]

FIRST NATIONS PEOPLE AND FUR TRADE WEATHER

Aboriginal people have lived with the climate of Canada longer than anyone else, suffering and surviving heat, cold, storms, drought, and floods. A recent book, *Voices from the Bay*, documents well the "traditional ecological knowledge of Inuit and Cree in the Hudson Bay region" (the subtitle of the book). The authors appear to have accepted global climate change as fact; they state: "Since the 1940s, weather in northwestern Hudson Bay has become highly variable. There used to be more clear, calm days, winters were colder, and low temperatures persisted longer. By the early 1990s, weather changes were quick, unexpected, and difficult to predict."[47]

We need the valuable information available in First Nations oral history and passed on through their folklore and legends: practical information on how climate influenced decisions and guided daily activities of hunting, fishing, gathering, and migrations, and their strategies for coping with natural disasters. Olive Dickason has shown in *Canada's First Nations* that the fur trade, particularly in its first hundred years, relied heavily on First Nations information and knowledge, particularly for travel.[48]

Europeans have only recently, and belatedly, shown a growing awareness of First Nations knowledge of the environment. Academics sometimes class that knowledge as animistic, defined by the *Oxford English Dictionary* as the "doctrine of *anima mundi* ... the attribution of a living soul to inanimate objects and natural phenomena." No doubt part of the respect typical of animism is reasonable fear or caution, the knowledge that if you don't respect the double-edged sword of bounty and bust, nature can kill.

All human history is influenced by climate, sometimes directly but more often indirectly, such as by limiting food supply. First Nations people appreciate better than most nature's ability to change rapidly in short periods, examples of which occur in any study of long-term records. Sadly, much is being lost as elders die and the oral tradition fades.

Beyond oral history, there is a supplementary source of information: Hudson's Bay Company journals contain a substantial number of First Nations observations about weather, particularly about unusual patterns, passed on by European fur traders. For example, Peter Fidler wrote in his 1819 report, "by the invariable information of the different Tribes I have enquired at agree the country is becoming much drier than formerly."

As with First Nations people, all aspects of fur-trading life were dependent upon the weather for assuring the food supply, called "country provisions"; the weather also affected the wildlife and thus the basis of the trade. Little is recorded about specific weather lore, but frequent comments about unusual weather or rare events indicate that these were topics of conversation between the two races. Comments in the fur-trade journals generally fit two categories, reference to past weather and impact of the weather on current living conditions such as food supply and travel.

Although York Factory was established five years before Churchill Factory,[49] the first entries about First Nations observations of weather at both forts occur in the same year, 1722. An entry for 25 March at Churchill notes, "Indians cannot return to family because of snow they saying they have not seen so much snow upon the ground for many years. Up to their necks in the woods." The entry for 11 October at York Factory reads, "Oldest Indian never new [knew] such moderate weather at this time of year." The entry for 6 July 1803 at Churchill notes, "Eskimau arrived with a very few furs they bring the dreadful intelligence of a great no. [number] of their tribe having perished by famine during the winter which was remarkably cold." The comment of 2 November 1729 at York says, "We have hitherto had such a fine fall as the like has not been known in the memory of the oldest Indian at this place."

Some comments allow one to calculate the period since the previous event. On 31 March 1791 we learn that "an old native now on the plantation tells me he has not seen the snow so deep as it is at this time since the winter after Governor Isham," a span of forty-five years. Or the 23 October 1806 entry at York: "So mild weather at so late a period was never before witnessed by the oldest native about the factory, and there are two now on the plantation who well remember two vessels sent on discovery wintering in Ten Shilling Creek" – a reference to Christopher Middleton and William Moor's ships, *Furnace* and *Discovery*, which wintered over in 1741, sixty-five years earlier. Unusual conditions continued to the following year, because an entry for 31 July 1807 reports that "oldest men say they never saw a summer of greater scarcity at York."

Secondary effects of weather on flora and fauna also add to our knowledge. For example, a Churchill entry for 28 April 1773 tells us, "Indians general complaint that a great part of the country inland has been on fire the last summer it being so vary [very] a dry one to which the natives compute the scarcity of animals." An entry for 25 April 1786 at Churchill reports the arrival of migrating waterfowl: "In the course of this day our people saw three geese and some of the Indians saw two ducks which is the earliest ever knew at this place."

Such selected examples illustrate First Nations knowledge of weather patterns over extended periods and emphasize the care required before conclusions can be drawn about environmental change. If significant changes occur within human memory, have much larger changes not occurred over longer time spans?

WEATHER RECORDING PRIOR TO INSTRUMENTS

Weather observations, commentaries, maps, and measurements, though crude at first, began from the minute Company employees set foot in North America. Prior to 1814, the HBC imposed a considerable degree of uniformity on the contents of each fort's journal entries by specifying those items they considered essential: the provisions given out to the HBC men and Indians, the provisions obtained by hunters and in trade from Indians, the duties performed by each man, and any other data, such as disciplinary action or trading activities, that would be of interest to the governors in London. There were occasional sharp reminders to keep good records. Daily weather information was not one of the requirements, but none the less, wind directions, qualitative wind speed, precipitation, cloud cover, and general weather comments are among the most ubiquitous entries in the journals of the HBC. Typically and fairly regularly, depending on the interests of the writer, the post journals provide information about the first melting, first rain, and first thunder and lightning in spring, the first frost and first snow in fall, and the number of days with rain and with snow.[50]

For example, between 1720 and 1735, the first snowfall moved from the first to the last week in September then back to the last week in August in 1737. Then it moved later until 1765, when it fell back to the second week of September, and by 1815 moved up to the first week in October and became more variable, though shifting sometimes to the second week of September. Days of snowfall per year gradually declined from sixty in 1715 to fifty in 1850, consistent with global warming after the end of the Little Ice Age. The number of days with rain decreased from thirty-five in 1715 to twenty in 1765, then increased rapidly to forty by 1780 (Figure 11.4).[51]

The scientific focus shifted in the twentieth century from concern about cooling in the 1970s to warming in the 1980s and 1990s. In both cases it was assumed that a simple linear trend would continue. That was not the case for cooling, and evidence already suggests it is not so for warming. What is evident, from the historical and the modern record, is how increased vari-

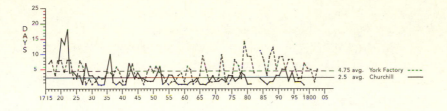

Figure 11.4
Graph: Number of days with heavy or continuous rainfall, Churchill and York Factory
(T.M. Ball)

ability, and therefore unpredictability, creates greater problems and concern for hunter-gatherer and agricultural societies. Our fur traders and naturalists faced similar periods of increasingly unstable weather conditions.

The Company journals are replete with comments on the hardship that weather conditions created in the 1780s and 1790s. Cold and extreme snow conditions that fluctuated between no cover and extreme depths led to a lack of game for food. The natives and Company men suffered from shortages and references to starvation dominate the journals of Joseph Colen.[52] ... A comment for the 5th of February 1792 is indicative of the conditions and reads as follows: "They (Indians) also inform me that the winter set in so early upwards that many Swans and other waterfowl were froze in the lakes and they found many of the former not fledged, they likewise say that the snow is remarkably deep."[53]

The emphasis today is on temperature, but precipitation changes are usually more critical for flora, fauna, and humans. A statistical analysis of rainfall data showed a lack of long-term trends at Churchill but a distinct twenty-two-year dry cycle at York Factory after 1760, similar to the cycle seen on the plains farther south.

The number of days with thunder indicate movement of the mean summer position of the polar front north of York Factory (Figure 11.5). Warmer summer air raises the level of the tropopause (the boundary between the troposphere and the stratosphere), which allows room for vertical development of thunderstorms. Although sparse, there are enough measures to indicate a reversal of this pattern as climate cooled towards the end of the nineteenth century.

The following weather entries are all from York Factory:

5 September 1714: When James Knight[54] arrived at York Factory to establish a permanent post: "Weather proving so bad we had like to have

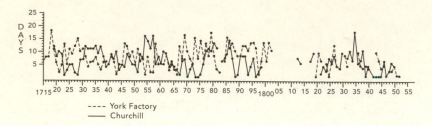

Figure 11.5
Graph: Number of days of thunder at Churchill and York Factory, 1715–1805 (T.M. Ball)

been lost and were in very great danger in being in the same condition there being so violent storm we struck several times by the sea running so high and the weather so thick."

20 September 1752: Joseph Isbister[55] noted at Churchill: "21 years in this country and never see or hear so dismal a night."

10 February 1754: At York Factory there was "very little snow as yet upon the ground in comparison with some years by this time." (James Isham used his thirty years on the bay to make a valuable comment for modern researchers trying to determine precipitation patterns.)

3 April 1732: Thomas Macklish[56] recorded: "here has fallen as much snow since last Thursday night as has fallen the whole winter." (A late winter storm brought important snow, albeit late.)

23 January 1759: "Indian says snow as deep as ever he saw it." (The only thing worse than too much snow is too little. Aboriginal memories of previous weather are especially reliable; oral tradition was the only method of transmission of historical events.)

10 November 1767: "It is very remarkable we have no snow on the ground nor have we had but one day's snow this year, on Saturday, 17 Oct, which thaw'd away very quickly." (Lack of snow at this date was a foreboding of a hard winter. Snow cover was essential for successful survival of plants and animals through the winter.)

6 October 1787: "French Creek is set fast, which is earlier by one month than known for years past." (This comment reflects the change to much colder temperatures that presaged the severe weather conditions at the end of the eighteenth century.)

13 October 1787: "Snow above tops of door." (What was remarkable was the combination of heavy snow and colder temperatures.)

6 June 1791: "Snow is many feet deep in our garden."

18 June 1793: "Ice a half-inch thick."

1 February 1798: "Remarkably mild ... WSW till 3 p.m. when thermometer

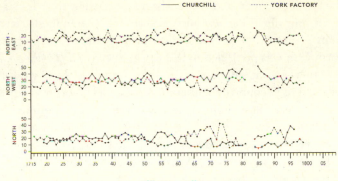

Figure 11.6
Graph: Percent frequency of North wind at Churchill and York Factory (T.M. Ball)

stood at +42, wind changed to NW blowing strong, then rapidly fell to 8 below in evening."

14 July 1798: "53 degrees colder today than it was yesterday."

All these notes indicate that an increase in snow, a decrease in temperatures, and an increase in climate variability at York Factory were associated with the drop in global temperatures during the Little Ice Age.

In keeping with more cold weather, and partially implicated in its cause, was the high percentage of north winds at York Factory in the years 1763–76.[57] Overall, northwest winds predominated in each of the winter months from October through April (Figure 11.6).[58] Cold winters predominated in the Little Ice Age; they occurred fifteen times at both York Factory and Churchill, in 1741, 1748, 1749, 1772, 1786, 1787, 1791, 1792, 1793, 1796, 1799, 1801, 1805, 1806, and 1822. Mild winters occurred at both posts only six times, in 1716, 1744, 1753, 1777, 1807, and 1825. Cold summers occurred at both posts seven times, in 1730, 1734, 1759, 1770, 1777, 1778, and 1801, with one hot summer at both posts in 1781.

The 1770s was an exciting decade, notable for intellectual ferment. Perhaps it was in keeping with the curiosity widely evident that several company employees collected specimens of birds and mammals and others experimented with freezing. For example, some put barrels of water out to see how quickly they froze solid; others would judge colder air temperatures by determining whether mercury could be deformed by pressure of a finger or be cut with a knife.

The surgeon was the most likely person to be involved in scientific observations, but surgeons were present only at the main posts, Churchill, York Factory, Albany, and Moose Factory. Of course, weather diaries and records can be kept by anyone who can read and write.

All the specific meteorological records maintained by the company,[59] but none of the daily fur-trade post journals, were sent on to the Royal Society in London as part of the society's world-wide weather recording. Some of this information was published in the Royal Society's *Philosophical Transactions*, but otherwise the only use of these records has been by modern researchers. This is in contrast to other materials, such as ornithological specimens, which were shared immediately with the scientific community. This failure to share weather data is difficult to explain, especially after the start of the nineteenth century, as scientists became aware of dramatic climate change: by 1840 Professor Louis Agassiz had clearly showed the past existence of ice ages.[60]

On 9 September 1814, when Thomas Thomas[61] took over the Southern Department of the HBC from William Auld,[62] the London governor and committee suggested the following items, which are phenologic or secondary measures of weather, as worthy of recording for possible operational and commercial importance: "Among the circumstances, which are always to be noticed in the journals, is ... the date of the freezing of the lakes & river, the chief falls of snow & their depths, the greatest thickness of the ice, the commencement of thaw, the breaking up and draining away of the ice. These observations are not to be considered as a matter of idle curiosity; but may be of very essential use."[63]

Despite these directions, snow depths, difficult to measure, were rarely recorded, although all the other events were dutifully noted. Modern instrument-makers are still challenged by the task of building an accurate device to measure snowfall amount. The fur traders probably realized that snow depths are generally meaningless because of the amount of drifting, especially in open areas.

Why were weather data recorded? First, because "the fur trade in North America is a good example of an enterprise almost totally dependent upon climate for its survival and success. Climate dictates: the number and quality of furs; ease or harshness of daily life for the trappers and their families; the ease of transport through snow conditions or water levels in rivers and lakes; the ease of shipment across the oceans; the dependency of Europeans of the HBC upon food supply from the land."[64] Weather also determined what crops might be grown and when successful hunting trips might be undertaken, both related to the governors' wish to decrease dependency on expensive provisions sent from England.

Second, weather was part of a ship's log, and some of these men had been trained as mariners; they had developed a "weather eye" as they recorded weather conditions in the ship's log. It had become a habit. Such training produced records with a degree of consistency and homogeneity that is invaluable for modern research. Syntax alters with the years and some terms change, but this does not affect consistency. In fact, the changes offer valuable information about shifting knowledge and understanding of the atmosphere.

Third, weather is the most frequent entry in almost any personal diary, even today. In the company journals it is rare to find a day in which the weather is not the first comment. A fourth reason for recording temperatures was an inherent interest in the natural environment.

Weather information was initially both descriptive (recording wind direction, precipitation, and general weather conditions) and phenologic (including times of freeze-up, break-up, and arrival of the first goose). Wind direction was recorded most frequently and was registered to 32 points of the compass, an indication of the influence of sailing because modern meteorology only records eight points of the compass! Measurements were made from observation of the flags that flew at each post. Wind speed was not measured with instruments, but was observed and recorded using a Beaufort-type scale. Although approximate, this allows a reasonable estimate of wind speed for modern climate reconstructions.

Beaufort introduced his wind-speed scale in 1805,[65] but the journals show that he simply formalized a system already in use. For example, "fresh gale" is defined by Beaufort as wind speeds of 39 to 46 mph, and the visual clue is that "twigs break off trees." An entry in the Fort Churchill journal for 21 February 1725, during a winter storm, reads "NE a fresh gale with a continued snow."

Although there are inconsistencies and deficiencies in the pre-instrumental records, we are left with a substantial understanding of weather conditions around each of the forts on the bay. The fur traders also had some perception of where their climate rated on a world scale. This became apparent after Arthur Dobbs, an Anglo-Irish member of the British Parliament, in 1750 charged the Company with monopoly in North America and requested annulment of the HBC charter. Evidence presented at the lengthy hearings, which resulted in a report to the Privy Council,[66] shows how perceptive people were, even from limited information: although only one or two reports were available from the interior of what is now western Canada, the prairies were correctly compared climatically and agriculturally to the Ukraine and the steppes of Russia.

INSTRUMENTAL WEATHER RECORDING

Part of the intellectual climate of the early period of record – that is, from 1670 onward – was driven by development of instruments. It is beyond my scope to discuss the chicken-and-egg question of whether instruments push ideas or ideas create a demand for instruments. In meteorology it appears that both occur at various times, although instruments created the first great push at the beginning of the seventeenth century.

Today science advances on several frontiers, which can be classed as terrestrial and extraterrestrial. In the past few decades the advent of satellites has dramatically improved our ability to measure activities in the atmosphere, on the surface, and even under the land and water. Perceptions of the earth and our exact location on it are inextricably linked with our perceptions of the place of the earth in the solar system and universe.[67]

In the eighteenth century, extensive and expensive undertakings were designed to measure the solar system. Early in the century, in 1710, the British Admiralty offered a prize of £20,000 for a method of accurate determination of longitude.[68] Sir Neville Maskelyne, the royal astronomer,[69] chaired the committee to determine any winner of this prize.

WALES, DYMOND, AND THE TRANSIT OF VENUS

The HBC was constantly faced with problems of longitude, time, and navigation. An accurate method for determining longitude would have been of both scientific and economic value to the company. For example, Samuel Hearne attempted to map his overland journey to the Coppermine River by using Churchill, his starting point, as 0° longitude. This caused major errors when Hearne or anyone else attempted to transpose his map to modern maps.

How fortuitous and timely, then, was the year-long visit to Churchill by William Wales, an astronomer of the Royal Society,[70] and his assistant, Joseph Dymond.[71] Samuel Wegg, in his dual capacity as committee member with the Hudson's Bay Company and treasurer of the Royal Society had arranged their visit.[72] Wales and Dymond stayed from 10 August 1768 to 7 September 1769 at Churchill in order to spend six hours and twenty-two minutes observing the transit of Venus across the sun on 3 June 1769.[73] They were part of an extensive global effort, with teams deployed widely around the world,[74] driven in part by failure to obtain good measurements of the 1761 transit. Wales was "a good man of plain simple manners, with a large person and a benign countenance ... [and] a perpetual fund of humour, a constant glee about him."[75]

Wales and Dymond made extensive preparations as they crossed the Atlantic. On arrival at Churchill they set up a prefabricated observatory and kept detailed astronomical and weather records. Wales was almost certainly responsible for a unique, multi-faceted sundial found at the fort, now on display in the Parks Canada office in Churchill. That the major face of the sundial was in error for latitude by the same amount as Wales's recorded figures supports such a hypothesis; in addition, it confirms the difficulties of obtaining accurate measurements.

Captain James Cook was in Tahiti on the same errand.[76] By taking simultaneous measurements and knowing the distances between these widely separated sites, it was planned, by triangulation, to determine the diameter of the sun and the distance of the sun from the earth. Wales was later to sail as navigator with Cook on his voyage to Australia, then to teach mathematics, astronomy, and navigation at Christ's Hospital School in London. Wales and Dymond had been instructed by Sir Neville Maskelyne in procedures for determining latitude and approximate longitude only three weeks before Maskelyne gave similar instruction to Charles Mason and Jeremiah Dixon, who were about to begin work on the Mason-Dixon line.[77] The interconnection among these men, the extent of their travels, and their contribution to knowledge is representative of the science of their age.

In part because of Dymond's inaccurate watch-piece, which had gained two minutes thirty-one seconds by the time the measurements were made, and the inadequacy of the other equipment, Wales measured the distance from the earth to the sun at 95 million miles, whereas at that time of year it was closer to 93.5 million miles. Wales was so embarrassed by the poor results that he initially refused to submit them to the Royal Society.[78]

When Wales and Dymond returned to England, their instruments – thermometers, barometers, timepieces, and a portable observatory – were left for use at Churchill and for the use of Dr Thomas Hutchins at York Factory. In using them, Hutchins followed the instructions of Dr James Jurin as propounded in Latin in the *Philosophical Transactions*.[79] The thermometer, for instance, was at all times kept on a north wall in the shade. Hutchins found the instruments made by Francis Hawksbee the younger to be unreliable, so he switched to a barometer and thermometer made by Nairn. A continuous three-year instrumental record was maintained at York Factory from 1770, the first year by Hutchins and the next two years unsigned. The mercury thermometers used by Wales and Dymond had been provided to measure temperature without any realization by the manufacturer that mercury froze just short of −40 degrees.

Likely as a result of Wales's presentation to the Royal Society on his return to London, the Society rewarded the Company and its employees for their support and interest. The council minutes for 23 December 1773 state: "It was moved and ordered by ballot, that two barometers, four thermometers and two ambrometers[80] be purchased at the expense of the Society, and sent as an acknowledgment to the Hudson Bay Company, for their considerable and repeated benefactions; with a view that they be conveyed to some of their officers at their settlements to make observations of the state of the weather and send them from time to time to the Society." Wegg recorded this; for specific meteorological data in the Royal Society library, see Table 11.1.

From 1773, instruments, particularly thermometers, were an integral part of the equipment at many Company posts. The Royal Society continued its generosity by sending instruments out to support its 1811 request for a wider network of observers. As a result, there is no weather record anywhere in the world that is so consistent or extensive. It covers an important region and time period for reconstructing past climates.

Elsewhere in North America, there are large temporal and spatial gaps in weather records, which tend to be either short-term, anecdotal, widely scattered, or all of these. As one interesting anecdotal reporting of extremes, see the two books by David Ludlum entitled *Early American Winters*.[81]

The fur-trading-post managers and surgeons were men of religion, but they were also from an age of reason, of rational thinking, and of action. Curiosity was given full rein. The Company constantly sought new economic opportunities and encouraged exploration and investigation. North America was virgin territory for the naturalists; the climate was dramatically different – colder in winter and warmer in midsummer – from Britain's. What better opportunity for the most dedicated of observers, the amateur naturalist, whose blueprint was developed by Gilbert White in *The Natural History of Selborne* (1789, and in print ever since).

White was curate in the English village of Selborne, where he combined his religious views with a scientific perspective, much as Samuel Hearne did. Interestingly, he corresponded with Thomas Pennant and in 1768 wrote Pennant, saying "All nature is so full that that district produces the greatest variety which is the most examined."[82]

White also spoke in terms that parallel the views of the entrepreneurs of the fur trade: "Nature is a great economist, for she converts the recreation of one animal to the support of another."[83] White's advanced concept of the interconnectedness of nature and of nature's recyling can be compared with the concept implied in the Hudson's Bay Company motto, *Pro pelle cutem*. Debate rages about accurate translation of this motto, but the literal translation is "skin for skin."[84]

The journal-keepers' interest in the weather parallels their curiosity in the surrounding wildlife. It went beyond the mundane concerns of their daily lives, its effect on business, or their interests as amateur scientists. In an age when people were increasingly aware of the natural world, they observed and recorded with curiosity and often with remarkable perception. Of course the degree of interest varied among individuals, and also from one

Table 11.1

HBC meteorological records held in the library of the Royal Society, London

4M87	Contents of reel
MA.69	Isle à la Crosse, 1 Oct. 1809–31 May 1810 by Peter Fidler
"	Clapham House, Deer Lake, 16 Oct. 1808–9 May 1809 by Peter Fidler
"	Isle à la Crosse, 27 May 1810–3 June 1811 by Peter Fidler
MA.139	Athapascow, 20 Oct. 1791–1 May 1792 by Joseph Colen
MA.145	Cumberland House, 14 Oct. 1778–31 Dec. 1789 (not inclusive) by Joseph Colen
MA.160	York Fort, 1 Sept. 1774–25 Aug. 1778 by Ferdinand Jacobs
MA.161	Gloucester House, 19 Nov. 1781–9 July 1782 by Thomas Hutchins
MA.162	Henley House, 8 Nov. 1784–25 June 1785 by John McNab
"	Albany Fort 12 Sept. 1786–31 Aug. 1787 by John McNab
MA.163	Henley House Abstracts, Oct. 1784–June 1785 by John McNab
"	Albany, Sept. 1786–July 1788 by John McNab
MA.168	Cumberland House 1778–1779, 1789–1790 by Philip Turnor
MA.172	York Fort, 1 Oct. 1795–17 Aug. 1796, 1 Sept. 1796–5 July 1797 by Joseph Colen
MA.173	Reed Lake House 21 Oct. 1794–29 May 1795 by Joseph Colen
MA.176	Medium of Moose Fort 1 Aug. 1795–5 April 1797 presented by Joseph Colen
MA.182	York Fort, 1 Sept. 1776–7 Feb. 1777 by Thomas Hutchins
MA.183	Eastmain House, 1 Nov. 1777–27 June 1781 (not inclusive)
MA.184	Albany Fort, 1 Sept. 1776–19 Feb. 1782 by Thomas Hutchins
MA.185	Henley House, 3 June–20 Aug. 1787 by John McNab
MA.214	Churchill Factory, 6 Sept. 1792–17 April 1793 by Thomas Stayner

decade to the next. Opportunity also varied with social standing and economic conditions.

This book discusses notable naturalists who were also keen weather observers. There were others who, although less notable, demonstrated their observation skills and provided a measure of general knowledge through their daily entries. For example, the concept of radiation energy from the sun was not scientifically explained until the late nineteenth century. Despite this, from the earliest entries the HBC recorders consistently distinguished between snow that melts in the direct sunlight and snow that melts in the shade. They did not understand the difference between ambient air temperature and radiative heating; their knowledge was purely empirical.

One cannot understand mammal and bird behaviour and changing distributions without knowing climate and climate change.[85] The goose hunt each spring (some years six thousand geese were killed in the spring and eight hundred in the fall at Churchill)[86] was noteworthy because it provided fresh meat as a dietary change as well as a major food for the winter. The date of arrival was correlated with a southerly flow of wind and the onset of spring. Goose-arrival dates, an important phenologic indicator of weather, were kept at both Churchill and York Factory from 1715 to 1851. They gradually became later between 1715 and 1745, then were remarkably stable from 1745 to 1770. Goose-arrival dates then varied widely, though overall they became slightly earlier from 1770 to 1810, then later from 1810 to 1825.[87]

Snow Bunting ("snowbird") spring-arrival dates at York Factory were recorded with somewhat less consistency, even though they could be caught in sufficient numbers, as Andrew Graham said, to "eat very fine in a pye." No major trend is evident from spring-arrival dates for thirty-one years, varying from 9 March to 28 April, the latter only four days in advance of the geese in 1737.[88] The only late fall date for the Snow Bunting was on 7 Dec 1806: "Snowbirds still around."

Beyond their observations, it is their skills in analysis and understanding that distinguish the men in this book, above all Samuel Hearne. His work is in the best tradition of his age of voyages, exploration, and discovery; it therefore demonstrates remarkable awareness of the environment and the changes that were occurring.[89] It is one thing to go into the wilderness; it is another to be aware of the larger picture. Hearne further demonstrated this geographer's view in the maps he produced.

Hearne made three attempts to get to the Arctic coast by following the tree-line west and then north from Fort Churchill; cold, tired, hungry, and alone among the Chipewyans, he continued to observe and record. He saw clumps of dead trees well north of the live trees that were the tree-line at that time. When told by the Indians that the tree-line was farther north in their ancestors' time, he wrote in his journal that this "is proof that the cold has been increasing in those parts for some ages," a remarkably perceptive comment. Hearne was aware that global climate can change and that vegetation would respond to those changes, two concepts that have only recently been entertained by the scientific community.

IN STRIKING CONTRAST: CHARLES TOWN

In all of North America, why was Hudson Bay first in weather recording and second in the number of Linnaean natural-history specimens it provided? Why was Charles Town second for weather and first for natural history specimens? How did these two disparate areas happen to assume leadership roles?

Clearly these two regions, Hudson Bay and Charles Town, were viewed differently by the British government, largely on the basis of differences in climate: of the two, only Carolina had settlement potential. The eighteenth-century weather recorders were year-round residents at each, as were the natural-history collectors at Hudson Bay and the botanist in Carolina; the continent's best early collections of birds, mammals, and fish were the work of a long-term visitor from England to Carolina.

CHARLES TOWN, SOUTH CAROLINA

The prosperous and aristocratic city of Charles Town, South Carolina, was in stark contrast with the remote and icy lands around Hudson Bay. Charles Town had been founded in April 1670 in the "golden days" of its namesake, "Good King Charles" of England. Following their hedonistic namesake king, it had more theatres than any other city in America; its people attempted to enjoy "worldly pleasures to the utmost."[1]

In 1672 Charles Town consisted of 30 houses and 200 people. In 1690 the population was between 1,000 and 1,200, the fifth largest city north of the Rio Grande. At the time, Boston had 7,000, Philadelphia 4,000, New Amsterdam (later New York) 3,900, and Newport 2,600.[2] Farming and menial work were done by slaves, owned by most families. By 1708 Charles Town had 9,800 inhabitants, of whom 3,960 were white free men, women, and children, 120 were white male and female servants, 1,400 Indian slaves, and 4,100 Afro-American slaves.

By 1770, in contrast to Hudson Bay, South Carolina was well-populated. Charles Town was the fourth largest city in British America, with a population of 10,861, of whom 5,030 were whites and 5,831 blacks.[3] That year the annual export-import trade at Charles Town exceeded that of New York City.[4]

From its beginnings, as Fraser relates, "this fascinating city has been rich in paradoxes: slavery and freedom, kindness and cruelty, health and sickliness, enormous wealth and grinding poverty." Well-to-do white Anglican immigrants from Barbados, especially, "worked and played hard, drank and ate too much, spent recklessly, and often died young." Men made fortunes by importing West African slaves – 10,000 in the 1720s – and exporting Indian slaves. In sharp contrast with Hudson Bay, over eighty ships visited each year, at all seasons.

Charles Town was a centre of intellectual ferment and of gentlemen, often well-educated and wealthy, who enjoyed leisure time. Any resident could borrow a book from the public library, established in 1698. Some kept large private libraries. The Charles Town Library Society was formed in 1748, elected John Lining as president the following year, and by April 1750 had 129 members, fifteen of whom, like Lining, were physicians.[5] Some of these men maintained active correspondence with scholars throughout Europe. By 1778, when it was destroyed by fire, the library contained six thousand volumes. Charles Town also boasted the largest bookstore south of Philadelphia, Robert Wells's "Great Stationery and Book-Store on the Bay."[6]

Charles Town's inhabitants took pleasure in reading, but a select few, some of them medical doctors, trained in botany and zoology, were also contributors to medical science and natural history. "There was no more cultivated and attractive group of medical men in the third quarter of the eighteenth century in America than that in Charleston, S.C. ... Of these Bull was a pupil of Boerhaave, and Chalmers, Moultrie, Lining, and Garden were trained in Edinburgh. These men were abreast of the knowledge of the day."[7]

In the 1780s, J. Hector St John de Crèvecoeur[8] described Charles Town as follows:

Charles-Town is, in the north, what Lima [Peru] is in the south; both are Capitals of the richest provinces of their respective hemispheres ... Carolina produces commodities, more valuable perhaps than gold, because they are gained by greater industry; it exhibits also on our northern stage, a display of riches and luxury, inferior indeed to the former, but far superior to what are to be seen in our northern towns ... their wharfs, their docks, their magazines, are extremely convenient to facilitate this great commercial business. The inhabitants are the gayest in America.[9]

METEOROLOGY

Thriving, wealthy Charles Town was the first locality in the future United States to begin a meteorological recording station, in 1738. Weather there was important for opposite reasons to York Factory: at Charles Town it was too hot in summer rather than too cold in winter, and some wealthy citizens spent their summers at Newport, Rhode Island, to escape the extreme heat and recurring epidemics of yellow fever: "Carolina is in the spring a paradise, in the summer a hell, and in autumn a hospital."[10]

Dr John Lining (1708–1760)

Dr John Lining was born in Walston, Lanarkshire, in April 1708, studied medicine in Scotland and at Leyden in Holland, and moved to Charles Town from Scotland between 1728 and 1730, "Versatile, industrious, astute, and painstaking,"[11] by 1755 he was considered the "most able doctor" in Charles Town.[12] His published account of yellow fever was the first in English and the first from North America.[13] Observing that yellow fever flourished only in the warm months, he undertook in 1737 a study of the relation of climatic conditions to epidemic disease. He used a portable barometer, a Fahrenheit thermometer and a Heath thermometer. His hygroscope was a whip cord, divided into one hundred equal parts, which expanded and contracted five inches with variations in humidity. For eight years he took observations upon arising, at 3 p.m., and at bedtime. Acknowledged as the first American meteorologist, he published the results of his weather recording in the world's leading scientific journal, *Philosophical Transactions*.[14]

Dr Lionel Chalmers (1715–1777)

Dr Chalmers was unusual because he moved to Charles Town in 1737 without having earned a medical degree. He nevertheless learned on the job, built up a lucrative practice, became a medical partner of John Lining's and President of the Charles Town Library Society. He was awarded his MD from St Andrew's University in Scotland in 1756.[15] His noteworthy paper on "Opisthotonus and tetanus" was published in England.[16]

As an associate of Lining's he carried on weather observations in Charles Town from 1750 to 1759 and published them in two volumes.[17]

NATURAL HISTORY

Mark Catesby (1683–1749)

Mark Catesby, an Englishman, made the only eighteenth-century North American bird collection larger than that from Hudson Bay. Catesby was born on 24 March 1683 to John Catesby and Elizabeth Jekyll, probably in the village of Castle Hedingham in Essex. He had a life-long interest in natural history. The marriage of his sister Elizabeth to Dr William Cocke, secretary of state under Governor Andrew Spotwood of Virginia, allowed Catesby to be a visitor of leisure in the American colonies from his arrival in Williamsburg on 23 April 1712 through 1719. He explored westward to the Appalachians and made a trip to Jamaica.

On his return to England, Catesby delivered a collection of plants – said by Robert Hunt "to have been the most perfect which had ever been brought to this country"[18] – to Samuel Dale, a physician practising in Braintree, Essex. To support a return visit to North America by Catesby, Dale wrote to William Sherard (1659–1728), who had founded the chair of botany at Oxford University.[19] As a result, Sir Hans Sloane (1660–1753), president of the College of Physicians, Charles DuBois (d. 1740), treasurer of the East India Company, and his Grace the Duke of Chandos (1673–1744) were among the ten influential people, primarily botanists, whose sponsorship made possible Catesby's second, but three years' shorter, collecting trip to North America.[20]

Catesby sailed in April and arrived at Charles Town on 3 May 1722. After a first summer of collecting along the coast of South Carolina, he was afflicted with "a swelling of the cheek" that laid him low for three months and required surgical incision and drainage of pus on several occasions. Part of his second year was spent near Fort Moore on the banks of the Savannah River, across the river from the present site of Augusta, Georgia. In 1725 he moved to the Bahamas, where he remained as the guest of George Phenney, the governor, and visited the islands of Eleuthera, Andros, and Abaco before returning to England in 1726.

Elsa Allen explains that "botany was the great science of the day and zoology in all its branches had to take second place ... [Catesby] could not go in search of birds but took them mostly as they crossed his path while he was collecting plants for his patrons in England."[21] His biographer characterizes him as an "enigmatic and forgotten figure in American natural history."[22] An overview of early American naturalists has rated Catesby as "an exception to the general rule of incompetence or worse among early eighteenth-century naturalists."[23]

It took Catesby the better part of his second four years in America and another three years after his return to learn the arts of engraving and colouring. In 1731 he produced his sumptuous two-volume work *The Natural History of Carolina, Florida and the Bahama Islands*.[24] It was a large book, measuring 51 by 37 cm, and as Allen says, "unduly ornate ... [with] showy and expensive plates ... Catesby was not an artist either by training or talent."[25] Eleven twenty-plate installments were sold at two guineas each between May 1729 and November 1732 to complete volume 1, which contained 100 plates of birds, including representations of 110 individuals of 102 recognizable species. Fifty-six birds from South Carolina and the Scarlet Ibis from unspecified "Carolina" were the type specimens for new species cited by Linnaeus. There were another five new species from the Bahamas, four from

Virginia, and one each from New Jersey, Georgia, Pennsylvania, Cuba, West Indies, and Quebec.[26] Volume 2, dealing with amphibians, fishes, insects, and only nine quadrupeds, was published between 1734 and 1743. The appendix to volume 2 appeared in 1747, with an additional seven species of birds, including two new species from South Carolina, the Bob-white and the Nighthawk (Table 12.1).

A German translation appeared posthumously in 1756, as did a reprint with a Linnaean index of Latin names in 1771. As Frick and Stearns indicate, Catesby's was "the only colonial attempt to give the whole natural history of any of the North American colonies,"[27] thus earning him Allen's appellation, "the Founder of North American Ornithology."[28] Allen was particularly impressed by Catesby's ahead-of-his-time suggestion that "the main cause inducing birds to migrate was the search for food."[29]

Catesby was admitted a Fellow of the Royal Society in 1733. A genus of shrubs in the *Cinchonaceae* order, *Catesbaea*, and the largest frog in North America, *Rana catesbeiana*, were named for him.[30] He died in London on 23 December 1749.[31]

Dr Alexander Garden (1730–1791)

Garden was born in Birse, Scotland, in January 1730. He apprenticed to the professor of medicine at Marischal College, Aberdeen, and served as a surgeon's mate on navy ships for two years. He then attended Edinburgh University for a year, studying medicine and botany. He emigrated to Charles Town in April 1752. Within four years he had built up the largest medical practice in the port, earning an income of £500 per year,[32] complaining that "from seven in the morning till nine at night, I cannot call half an hour my own."[33] He suffered episodes of hemoptysis (spitting blood) over nearly thirty years.

Garden had a passion for botany. In 1760 he began sending specimens of plants and vast quantities of plant seeds to Linnaeus in Sweden,[34] and to John Ellis in London. His "botanical collecting kept him in contact with the lively circle of European and colonial natural historians."[35] These included "a number of new genera and species" of plants, but few of these were credited to him since he did not publish himself. Linnaeus named the beautiful flowering shrub, *Gardenia*, in his honour. He was knowledgeable and experienced enough to argue against both Linnaeus and Ellis; for example, he was correct in his beliefs that *Zamia* was not a fern, the Carolina Jessamine was not a Bignonia and that the palmetto was not a Yucca.[36]

Garden discovered a new family of eel-like amphibians, named sirens (*Sirenidae*). But his contributions to ichthyology have been documented best of all. Many of the fish species in Pennant's *Arctic Zoology* were specimens sent

Table 12.1.

Catesby's new North American bird species

From Catesby, Natural History of Carolina, etc., 1731

Catesby Plate #	Species name, scientific name	Source
TYPE LOCALITY GIVEN AS "SOUTH CAROLINA" BY AOU CHECK-LIST (58 SPECIES)		
1	Bald Eagle, *Haliaeetus leucocephalus*	Linnaeus 1766
2	Osprey, *Pandion haliaetus carolinensis*	Gmelin 1788
3	Merlin, *Falco columbarius*	Linnaeus 1758
4	Swallow-tailed Kite, *Elanoides forficatus*	Linnaeus 1758
5	American Kestrel, *Falco sparverius*	Linnaeus 1758
7	Eastern Screech-Owl, *Otus asio*	Linnaeus 1758
9	Yellow-billed Cuckoo, *Coccyzus americanus*	Linnaeus 1758
11	Carolina Parakeet, *Conuropsis carolinensis*	Linnaeus 1758
12	Common Grackle, *Quiscalus quiscula*	Linnaeus 1758
13	Red-winged Blackbird, *Agelaius phoeniceus*	Linnaeus 1766
14	Bobolink, *Dolichonyx oryzivorus*	Linnaeus 1758
15	Blue Jay, *Cyanocitta cristatus*	Linnaeus 1758
16	Ivory-billed Woodpecker, *Campephilus principalis*	Linnaeus 1758
17	Pileated Woodpecker, *Dryocopus pileatus*	Linnaeus 1758
18	Northern Flicker, *Colaptes auratus*	Linnaeus 1758
19A	Red-bellied Woodpecker, *Melanerpes carolinus*	Linnaeus 1758
20	Red-headed Woodpecker, *Melanerpes erythrocephalus*	Linnaeus 1758
21A	Downy Woodpecker, *Picoides pubescens*	Linnaeus 1766
21B	Yellow-bellied Sapsucker, *Sphyrapicus varius*	Linnaeus 1766
23	Passenger Pigeon, *Ectopistes migratorius*	Linnaeus 1766
24	Mourning Dove, *Zenaida macroura*	Linnaeus 1758
25	Ground Dove, *Columbina passerina*	Linnaeus 1758
28	Brown Thrasher, *Toxostoma rufum*	Linnaeus 1758
29	American Robin, *Turdus migratorius*	Linnaeus 1766
32	Horned Lark, *Eremophila alpestris*	Linnaeus 1758
33	Eastern Meadowlark, *Sturnella magna*	Linnaeus 1758
34	Eastern Towhee, *Pipilo erythrophthalmus*	Linnaeus 1758
36	Dark-eyed Junco, *Junco hyemalis*	Linnaeus 1758
38	Northern Cardinal, *Cardinalis cardinalis*	Linnaeus 1758
39	Blue Grosbeak, *Guiraca caerulea*	Linnaeus 1758
41	Purple Finch, *Carpodacus purpureus*	Gmelin 1789
43	American Goldfinch, *Carduelis tristis*	Linnaeus 1758
44	Painted Bunting, *Passerina ciris*	Linnaeus 1758
45	Indigo Bunting, *Passerina cyanea*	Linnaeus 1766
47	Eastern Bluebird, *Sialia sialis*	Linnaeus 1758
49	Orchard Oriole, *Icterus spurius*	Linnaeus 1766

50	Yellow-breasted Chat, *Icteria virens*	Linnaeus 1758
52	Great Crested Flycatcher, *Myiarchus crinitus*	Linnaeus 1758
54	Red-eyed Vireo, *Vireo olivaceus*	Linnaeus 1766
55	Eastern Kingbird, *Tyrannus tyrannus*	Linnaeus 1758
56	Summer Tanager, *Piranga rubra*	Linnaeus 1758
57	Tufted Titmouse, *Parus bicolor*	Linnaeus 1766
64	Northern Parula, *Parula americana*	Linnaeus 1758
65	Ruby-throated Hummingbird, *Archilochus colubris*	Linnaeus 1758
69	Belted Kingfisher, *Ceryle alcyon*	Linnaeus 1758
71	Killdeer, *Charadrius vociferus*	Linnaeus 1758
76,77	Little Blue Heron, *Egretta caerulea*	Linnaeus 1758
79	Yellow-crowned Night Heron, *Nycticorax violacea*	Linnaeus 1758
80	Green Heron, *Butorides virescens*	Linnaeus 1758
82,83	White Ibis, *Eudocimus alba*	Linnaeus 1758
90	Black Skimmer, *Rhynchops niger*	Linnaeus 1758
91	Pied-billed Grebe, *Podilymbus podiceps*	Linnaeus 1758
94	Hooded Merganser, *Lophodytes cucullatus*	Linnaeus 1758
97	Wood Duck, *Aix sponsa*	Linnaeus 1758
100	Blue-winged Teal, *Anas discors*	Linnaeus 1766
Appx	Chimney Swift, *Chaetura pelagica*	Linnaeus 1758
Appx	Northern Bobwhite, *Colinus virginianus*	Linnaeus 1758
Appx	Common Nighthawk, *Chordeiles minor*	Forster 1771

TYPE LOCALITY, "BAHAMA ISLANDS" (5)

25	White-crowned Pigeon, *Columba leucocephala*	Linnaeus 1758
37	Black-faced Grassquit, *Tiaris bicolor*	Linnaeus 1766
73	Greater Flamingo, *Phoenicopterus ruber*	Linnaeus 1758
89	Laughing Gull, *Larus atricilla*	Linnaeus 1758
93	White-cheeked Pintail, *Anas bahamensis*	Linnaeus 1758

TYPE LOCALITY, "VIRGINIA" (4)

27	Mockingbird, *Mimus polyglottos*	Linnaeus 1758
48	Northern Oriole, *Icterus galbula*	Linnaeus 1758
66	Gray Catbird, *Dumatella carolinensis*	Linnaeus 1766
67	American Redstart, *Setophaga ruticilla*	Linnaeus 1758

TYPE LOCALITY, "CAROLINA"

84	Scarlet Ibis, *Eudocimus ruber*	Linnaeus 1758

TYPE LOCALITY, "CUBA"

68	Cuban Bullfinch, *Melopyrrha nigra*	Linnaeus 1758

TYPE LOCALITY, "NEW JERSEY"

19B.	Hairy Woodpecker, *Picoides villosus*	Linnaeus 1766

Catesby Plate #	*Species name, scientific name*	*Source*
TYPE LOCALITY, "PENNSYLVANIA"		
Appx	Greater Prairie-Chicken, *Tympanuchus cupido*	Linnaeus 1758
TYPE LOCALITY, "QUEBEC"		
92	Canada Goose, *Branta canadensis*	Linnaeus 1758
TYPE LOCALITY, "WEST INDIES"		
88	Brown Noddy, *Anous stolidus*	Linnaeus 1758

by Garden to Linnaeus, illustrating the important, simultaneous connections Pennant had with both Charles Town and Hudson Bay, and with Linnaeus.[37] In 1760 and 1773 Garden sent other fish to Linnaeus, including at least thirty-five new species; these specimens were still extant in the Linnean Society of London when they were studied in 1898. Eighteen of these species, plus a lizard and a turtle, were credited to Garden in Pennant's 1787 Supplement. Another eight new species of fish were sent by Garden to Laurens Gronovius in Holland.

Loyal to the British Empire, Garden returned to England towards the end of the American Revolution, in mid-December 1782. He died in London on 15 April 1791. Unlike Catesby, Garden and the Hudson Bay collectors were of the same generation as Linnaeus, their specimens contributing to his works-in-progress.

APPENDICES

SAILING SHIPS TO YORK FACTORY, 1716–1892

Compiled from Cooke and Holland, The Exploration of Northern Canada. Supplemented from C.4/1, by Judith Hudson Beattie

In columns 4 and 9: D – the Downs; L – London; N – the Nore; O – Orkney; P – Peterhead; S – Shetlands; Y – Yarmouth
In column 6: EM – East Main; C – stop at Churchill first; C2 – stop at Churchill 2nd, after YF; M – Moose
The Old Style (OS) or Julian calendar was used through 1751 and (inappropriately by HBC ships) through 1752
At Hudson Bay, The New Style or Gregorian calendar was used first late in 1752, and thereafter, moving dates 11 days onward from OS dates

Year	Ship	Captain	Lv	Lv	Arr YF	Lv YF	Ar London	Comments
				Julian calendar, "Old Style" dates				
1716	Hudson's Bay III	Ward	?	?	4 Sept	21 Sept	25 Oct	
1717	Port Nelson	Belcher	?	?	14 Aug	8 Sept	?	
1718	Hudson's Bay III	Ward	?	?	25 Aug	26 Sept	13 Nov	delayed departure, ran aground, repairs; Albany to new Churchill
1719	Hudson's Bay III	Ward	?	5 June C	n/a	n/a		wrecked between Churchill & YF; named Ft Prince of Wales
1720	Hannah	Gofton	D	6 June	3 Sept	18 Sept	26 Oct	

Year	Ship	Captain	Lv	Lv		Arr YF	Lv YF	Ar London	Comments
				Julian calendar, "Old Style" dates					
1721	Hannah	Gofton	?	?		24 Aug	12 Sept	?	not listed in C.4/1
1722	Mary	Belcher	Y	27 May		10 Aug	1 Sept	31 Oct	
	Hannah	Gofton	?	?	C	16 Aug	1 Sept	10 Oct	not listed in C.4/1
1723	Mary	Belcher	D	28 May	C	31 Aug	3 Sept	14 Oct	
	Hudson's Bay IV	Geo. Spurrell	D	28 May		13 Aug	23 Aug	10 Oct	Permanent house built at Eastmain
1724	Hudson's Bay IV	Geo. Spurrell	N	23 May		8 Aug	18 Aug	12 Oct	
1725	Hannah	Middleton	N	23 May	C	20 Aug	26 Aug	6 Oct	not listed in C.4/1
1726	Hannah	Middleton	?	?	C	20 Aug	29 Aug	19 Oct	
1727	Hannah	Middleton	Y	29 May	C	12 Aug	20 Aug	2 Oct	First ship, *Mary*, with Gov Macklish, wrecked on voyage out
1728	Mary III	Geo. Spurrell	?	?		1 Aug	10 Aug	10 Sept	Early return! not listed in C.4/1
1729	Hudson's Bay IV	Middleton	?	?		24 July	1 Aug	?	not listed in C.4/1
1730	Hannah	Coats	Y	23 May		10 Aug	18 Aug	16 Oct	[Moose Factory reestablished]
1731	Mary III	Geo. Spurrell	?	27 May	C	2 Aug	8 Aug	22 Sept	
1732	Mary III	Geo. Spurrell	?	?		3 Aug	19 Aug	28 Sept	not listed in C.4/1; James Isham arrives
1733	Mary III	Geo. Spurrell	Y	20 May	C	11 Aug	17 Aug	30 Sept	Alexander Light arrives with four masons
1734	Mary III	Spurrell/Garn	O	20 May	C	4 Aug	13 Aug	14 Sept	Early return, though would be Sept 25 by later Gregorian calendar
1735	Hudson's Bay IV	Coats	Y	14 May		1 Aug	7 Aug	17 Sept	
1736	Mary III	Geo. Spurrell	N	13 May	C	24 Aug	28 Aug	8 Oct	*Hudson's Bay* lost in Hudson Strait
1737	Hudson's Bay V	Middleton	N	25 May	C	29 July	7 Aug	20 Sept	Alexander Light to England

Year	Ship	Captain		Date					Notes
1738	Mary IV	Coats	?	?	C	24 Aug	1 Sept	29 Oct	not listed in C.4/1
1739	Seahorse	Geo. Spurrell	Y	25 May	C	25 Aug	1 Sept	29 Oct	Peregrine Falcon 'pitched on' the ship
1740	Mary IV	Coats	Y	9 May		20 July	30 July	20 Sept	Record early arrival July 20!
1741	Seahorse	Geo. Spurrell	N	28 Apr	C	2 Aug	13 Aug	3 Oct	
1742	Seahorse	Geo. Spurrell	?	7 May	C	3 Aug	15 Aug	?	not listed in C.4/1
1743	Seahorse	Geo. Spurrell	N	11 May	C	10 Aug	19 Aug	30 Sept	
1744	Prince Rupert II	Geo. Spurrell	Y	22 May	C	13 Aug	28 Aug	18 Nov	
	Mary IV	Coats	?	9 May	C	24 Aug	28 Aug	20 Nov	
	Seahorse	Fowler Sr	N	20 May	C2	24 Aug	5 Sept	wintered	
1745	Seahorse	Fowler Sr	?	?	C	30 June	15 Aug	28 Sept	Returned after wintering
	Prince Rupert II	Geo. Spurrell	N	10 May	C	29 July	15 Aug	28 Sept	Isham to London with specimens
1746	Prince Rupert II	Geo. Spurrell	N	7 May		3 Aug	16 Aug	16 Sept	Isham returns
	Seahorse	Fowler Sr	N	7 May	C	7 Aug	17 Aug	29 Sept	
1747	Prince Rupert II	Geo. Spurrell	N	10 May		8 Aug	22 Aug	Y 13 Oct	
	Hudson's Bay V	Fowler Sr	N	10 May	C	18 Aug	22 Aug	16 Oct	
1748	Prince Rupert II	Geo. Spurrell	N	10 May		18 Aug	30 Aug	Y 4 Oct	Isham to London on furlough
1749	Prince Rupert II	Geo. Spurrell	N	19 May		28 July	14 Aug	15 Sept	
	Hudson's Bay V	?	N	19 May		9 Aug	14 Aug	15 Sept	
1750	Prince Rupert II	Geo. Spurrell	N	25 May		18 Aug	3 Sept	D 21 Oct	Isham returns from furlough
1751	Prince Rupert II	Geo. Spurrell	N	23 May		25 July	10 Aug	14 Sept	Coats' 25th and last trip
1752	Prince Rupert II	Geo. Spurrell	N	16 May		24 July	9 Aug	21 Sept	

Gregorian calendar, "New Style" dates, advanced 11 days

| 1753 | Prince Rupert II | Geo. Spurrell | Y | 5 June | C2 | 27 Aug | 8 Sept | D 10 Oct | |

Year	Ship	Captain	Lv	Lv	Arr YF	Lv YF	Ar London	Comments
				Gregorian calendar, "New Style" dates, advanced 11 days				
1754	Prince Rupert II	Geo. Spurrell	N	29 May	1 Sept	11 Sept	13 Oct	
1755	Prince Rupert II	Geo. Spurrell	N	31 May	23 Aug	4 Sept	29 Oct	
1756	Prince Rupert II	Geo. Spurrell	N	29 May	C2 3 Aug	15 Aug	14 Oct	George Spurrell's 35th & last voyage; Seven Years War begins
1757	Prince Rupert II	Fowler Sr	N	21 May	10 Aug	22 Aug	26 Oct	Fowler Jr's first command, on Hudson's Bay V to Richmond
1758	Prince Rupert II	Fowler Sr	N	26 May	7 Sept	17 Sept	27 Nov	Isham to London on final furlough
1759	Prince Rupert II	Fowler Sr	N	27 May	20 Aug	4 Sept	22 Oct	Isham returns from furlough; Severn reestablished
1760	Prince Rupert III	Jos. Spurrell	N	24 May	26 Aug	11 Sept	24 Oct	[Montreal captured by British, year after Quebec]
1761	King George II	Jos. Spurrell	N	31 May	16 Aug	1 Sept	21 Nov	
1762	King George II	Jos. Spurrell	N	29 May	27 Aug	6 Sept	10 Nov	
1763	King George II	Jos. Spurrell	N	5 June	29 Aug	9 Sept	5 Nov	Chas Price Isham to England
1764	King George II	Fowler Jr	N	1 June	13 Aug	25 Aug	8 Oct	
1765	King George II	Fowler Jr	N	25 May	6 Sept	16 Sept	20 Oct	
1766	King George II	Fowler Jr	N	31 May	11 Aug	28 Aug	17 Oct	Thomas Hutchins arrives
1767	King George II	Fowler Jr	N	30 May	29 Aug	8 Sept	22 Oct	
1768	King George II	Fowler Jr	N	1 June	12 Aug	28 Aug	9 Oct	
1769	King George II	Fowler Jr	N	3 June	14 Aug	27 Aug	29 Sept	Graham from Severn to London, meets Pennant
1770	Prince Rupert IV	Jos. Richards	N	2 June	25 Aug	8 Sept	16 Oct	Graham returns from furlough
1771	Seahorse II	Christopher	N	1 June	25 Aug	7 Sept	17 Oct	Andrew Graham specimens

Year	Ship	Commander		Out		(Aug)	(Sept)	Return	Notes
1772	King George II	Fowler Jr	N	20 May		21 Aug	5 Sept	3 Oct	Thos. Hutchins' specimens
1773	King George II	Fowler Jr	N	29 May		23 Aug	5 Sept	10 Oct	Third batch of specimens; Hutchins goes on furlough
1774	King George II	Fowler Jr	N	28 May		18 Aug	2 Sept	6 Oct	Fourth batch of specimens; Hutchins returns
1775	King George II	Fowler Jr	N	27 May		14 Aug	29 Aug	8 Oct	Graham returns to England, retires in Edinburgh
1776	King George II	Fowler Jr	N	2 June		24 Aug	3 Sept	14 Oct	
1777	Prince Rupert IV	Jos. Richards	N	1 June		18 Aug	1 Sept	18 Oct	
1778	King George II	Fowler Jr	N	3 June		24 Aug	6 Sept	25 Dec	More ice than ever before; latest-ever arrival back in England
1779	Seahorse	Christopher	N	3 June	C	3 Sept	6 Sept	22 Dec	
	King George II	Fowler Jr	N	5 June	C	unable	unable	17 Nov	Couldn't get past Churchill
1780	King George II	Fowler Jr	N	31 May	C	15 Sept	17 Sept	10 Nov	
	Seahorse II	Christopher	N	31 May		30 Aug	17 Sept	10 Nov	
1781	Prince Rupert IV	Fowler Jr	N	3 June		1 Sept	8 Sept	31 Oct	
	Seahorse II	Christopher	N	3 June		20 Aug	8 Sept	31 Oct	
1782	King George III	Fowler Jr	N	4 June		15 Aug	24 Aug	27 Nov	Hutchins retires from Albany; YF surrenders to La Perouse 25 Aug
1783	King George III	Christopher	N	1 June		14 Sept	25 Sept	3 Nov	Outward voyage to Hudson Bay delayed by ice; re-established YF
1784	Seahorse III	John Richards	N	29 May		1 Sept	18 Sept	2 Nov	
1785	Seahorse III	John Richards	N	26 May		25 Aug	16 Sept	19 Oct	
1786	King George III	Christopher	N	1 June	C	18 Aug	30 Aug	4 Oct	
1787	Seahorse III	Tunstall	N	27 May	C	27 Aug	9 Aug	16 Oct	
1788	King George III	Christopher	N	2 June	C	18 Aug	31 Aug	4 Oct	Humphrey Marten retires to England

Year	Ship	Captain	Lv	Lv		Arr YF	Lv YF	Ar London	Comments
							Gregorian calendar, "New Style" dates, advanced 11 days		
1789	King George III	Tunstall	N	30 May	C	25 Aug	10 Sept	10 Oct	
1790	Seahorse III	Hanwell	N	5 June	C2	24 Aug	11 Sept	8 Dec	
1791	Seahorse III	Hanwell	N	8 June	C	8 Sept	4 Oct	15 Nov	
1792	Queen Charlotte	Turner	N	8 June	EM	31 Aug	6 Sept	13 Nov	
1793	Seahorse III	Hanwell	N	26 May		20 Aug	17 Sept	22 Oct	
	Prince of Wales	Hanwell	N	1 June		12 Aug	7 Sept	8 Nov	
	Queen Charlotte	Turner	N	1 June	C	23 Aug	7 Sept	4 Nov	
	Beaver sloop	Taylor	N	1 June		13 Aug	stayed		C.1/611
1794	Prince of Wales	Hanwell	N	31 May	C	5 Sept	26 Sept	12 Nov	
1795	King George III	John Richards	N	7 June		27 Aug	21 Sept	25 Nov	
	Queen Charlotte	Turner	N	7 June	C	11 Sept	21 Sept	24 Nov	
1796	King George III	John Richards	N	4 June		20 Aug	13 Sept	12 Nov	
	Queen Charlotte	Turner	N	4 June	C	2 Sept	13 Sept	12 Nov	
1797	King George III	John Richards	N	22 June		24 Aug	15 Sept	4 Dec	
	Queen Charlotte	Turner	N	22 June	C	6 Sept	15 Sept	4 Dec	
1798	King George III	John Richards	L	6 June		6 Sept	26 Sept	23 Nov	
	Queen Charlotte	Turner	L	6 June	C	17 Sept	26 Sept	22 Nov	
1799	King George III	John Richards	L	29 May		30 Aug	21 Sept	15 Nov	
	Queen Charlotte	Turner	L	29 May	C	13 Sept	21 Sept	14 Nov	
1800	Prince of Wales	Hanwell	L	28 May		8 Sept	23 Sept	5 Dec	
	Queen Charlotte	Turner	L	28 May	C	18 Sept	23 Sept	5 Dec	
1801	King George III	Hanwell	L	20 May		10 Sept	21 Sept	4 Dec	
1802	King George III	Turner	L	26 May	C	26 Aug	18 Sept	23 Oct	

1802	Ceres	Ramsey	L	26 May	C	9 Sept	18 Sept	24 Oct	
1803	King George III	Turner	L	4 June		15 Aug	3 Sept	26 Nov	
	Ceres	Ramsey	L	4 June	C	29 Aug	3 Sept	29 Nov	
1804	King George III	Turner	L	1 June		6 Aug	27 Aug	28 Nov	
	Ceres	Ramsey	L	1 June	C	4 Sept	4 Sept	27 Nov	
1805	King George III	Turner	S	6 June	C	28 Aug	7 Sept	25 Nov	
1806	King George III	Turner	L	4 June	C	18 Aug	30 Aug	22 Nov	
1807	Prince of Wales	Hanwell	N	14 June	C	19 Sept	4 Oct	15 Nov	
	Mainwaring	Davison	N	14 June	M2	10 Sept	18 Sept	stayed	ice closest & heaviest in 41 yrs
1808	King George III	Turner	L	20 May		21 Aug	4 Sept	24 Nov	
	Eddystone	Ramsey	L	20 May	C	26 Aug	4 Sept	24 Nov	
1809	King George III	Turner	L	31 May	C	8 Sept	22 Sept	22 Nov	
1810	King George III	Turner	L	31 May	C	19 Aug	4 Sept	5 Dec	
1811	Eddystone	Ramsey	L	?		26 Sept	6 Oct	Y 28 Nov	Selkirk Settlers (105), longest 61-day voyage out, Churchill bypassed
	Edward and Ann	Gull	L	?		26 Sept	6 Oct	Y 29 Nov	
1812	King George III	Turner	N	31 May	C	31 Aug	14 Sept	2 Dec	Selkirk Settlers (80) led by Owen Keveny; Dr McKeevor on board
	Robert Taylor	Davison	?	?		26 Aug	4 Sept	?	
1813	Prince of Wales	Turner	N	2 June	C	26 Sept	6 Oct	26 Nov	Selkirk Settlers (90); five died on ship, 50 reached RR
1814 ·	Prince of Wales	Hanwell	L	25 May		2 Sept	28 Sept	25 Nov	Selkirk Settlers (14); Lieut E Chappell on HMS Rosamund with them
	HMS Rosamond	Stopford	L	?		2 Sept	28 Sept	?	
1815	Prince of Wales	Hanwell	L	25 May		27 Aug	23 Sept	22 Nov	Selkirk Settlers (80) with Semple; 3 ships wintered re ice

Year	Ship	Captain	Lv	Lv		Arr YF	Lv YF	Ar London	Comments
				Gregorian calendar, "New Style" dates, advanced 11 days					
1815	Hadlow	Davison	L	27 May	M2	26 Aug	7 Sept	wintered	wintered with Eddystone at Strutton Sound
1816	Hadlow	Davison	N	12 May		22 Sept	3 Oct	4 Nov	returned after wintering
	Prince of Wales	Hanwell						wintered	Year Without a Summer; ice; wintered Charlton Island
1817	Prince of Wales	Davison	L	9 May	M	?	1 Oct	7 Nov	returned after wintering
	Britania	Edman						wintered	ice; *Britannia* wintered & burned at Severn
1818	Prince of Wales	Davison	L	10 May		14 Aug	8 Sept	14 Oct	Brought Wm Williams, delayed by ice
	Levant	Rennie	L	?		15 Aug	8 Sept	?	Towed partway thru ice en route to Hudson Bay
1819	Prince of Wales	Davison	L	23 May		30 Aug	27 Sept	30 Oct	Heavy ice; Brought Franklin arctic exploring party
1820	Wear	Thompson	L	23 May		30 Aug	7 Sept	wintered	*Wear* c prisoners (5) to Moose, wintered at Nelson R c Shaw and McTavish
	Eddystone	Bell	L	12 May		15 Aug	9 Sept	26 Oct	Brought Rev. John West
1821	Prince of Wales	Davison	L	22 May		22 Aug	14 Sept	8 Nov	*Lord Wellington* with Selkirk Settlers at YF 18 Aug to 1 Sept
1822	Prince of Wales	Davison	L	27 May		10 Aug	7 Sept	21 Oct	Franklin exploring party survivors return to England
1823	Prince of Wales	Davison	L	16 May		15 Aug	11 Sept	25 Oct	More Selkirk Settlers
1824	Prince of Wales	Davison	L	28 May		20 Aug	12 Sept	1 Nov	Advance party for Franklin II arrives, also Dr. Hamlin for Red River

Year	Ship	Master							Notes
1825	Prince of Wales	Davison	L	30 May		15 Aug	2 Sept	25 Oct	
1826	Prince of Wales	Davison	L	30 May		7 Sept	20 Sept	26 Oct	Back, Kendall, David Douglas return to England
1826	Camden	Bell	L	30 May	M	17 Sept	17 Sept	16 Oct	
1827	Prince of Wales	Davison	L	28 May		23 Aug	15 Sept	15 Oct	
1828	Prince Rupert V	Bell	L	3 June		17 Aug	21 Sept	5 Nov	Hanwell Jr captain of *Prince of Wales*, which went to Moose Factory
1829	Prince Rupert V	Bell	L	3 June		11 Aug	15 Sept	22 Oct	home to England via St. Lawrence River!
	Montcalm	Royal	L	?		9 Aug	25 Aug	?	
1830	Prince Rupert V	Bell	L	2 June		25 Aug	17 Sept	29 Oct	home to England via Ungava Bay & St. Lawrence R
	Montcalm	Royal	L	?		15 Aug	27 Aug	?	
1831	Montcalm	Royal	L	2 June		25 Aug	19 Sept	25 Oct	unusually heavy ice in Hudson Strait
	Camden	? Royal	L	1 June		25 Aug	19 Sept	25 Oct	
1832	Prince Rupert V	Bell	L	5 June		22 Aug	21 Sept	25 Oct	*P of W* with Dr. John Rae arrives; ship forced to winter; Rae remains
1833	Prince Rupert V	Bell	L	6 June	C2	6 Sept	27 Sept	wintered	returned after wintering
1834	Prince Rupert V	Grave	L	4 June	C	22 Aug	31 Aug	20 Oct	*P of W* winters at Charlton Is. 1833–34
	Prince George	Grave/Friend	L			22 Aug	12 Sept	21 Oct	
1835	Prince Rupert V	Grave	L	7 June		23 Aug	24 Sept	29 Oct	Took Dr Richard King to London, after Back expedition"
1836	Prince Rupert V	Grave	L	2 June		24 Sept	5 Oct	12 Nov	Beset in ice 23 Aug–19 Sept, returned to London with most of cargo

Year	Ship	Captain	Lv	Lv	Arr YF	Lv YF	Ar London	Comments
				Gregorian calendar, "New Style" dates, advanced 11 days				
1836	Esquimaux	Butterwick	L	2 June	24 Sept		wintered	Driven ashore, men winter at Ten Shilling Creek near YF
	Eagle	Humphreys	L	2 June	7 Oct		wintered	Wintered in Hayes River
1837	Eagle	Humphreys				28 Aug	13 Oct	Return after wintering
	Prince Rupert V	Grave	L	1 June	28 Aug	16 Sept	29 Oct	
	Prince George	Friend	L	?	4 Sept	21 Sept	?	
1838	Prince Rupert V	Grave	L	29 May	28 Aug	17 Sept	21 Oct	Heavy ice in Hudson Strait en route to Hudson Bay
1839	Prince Rupert V	Herd	L	28 May	14 Aug	11 Sept	16 Oct	
1840	Prince Rupert V	Herd	L	3 June	9 Aug	6 Sept	25 Oct	
1841	Prince Rupert VI	Herd	L	2 June	18 Aug	13 Sept	17 Oct	
	Prince Albert	Boulton	L	2 June	18 Aug	13 Sept	19 Oct	
1842	Prince Rupert VI	Herd	L	1 June	16 Aug	16 Sept	23 Oct	
1843	Prince Rupert VI	Herd	L	1 June	9 Aug	21 Sept	9 Nov	
1844	Prince Rupert VI	Herd	L	29 May	11 Aug	15 Sept	18 Oct	
1845	Prince Rupert VI	Herd	L	5 June	10 Aug	11 Sept	13 Oct	
1846	Prince Rupert VI	Herd	L	3 June	6 Aug	19 Sept	21 Oct	
1847	Prince Rupert VI	Herd	L	2 June	25 Aug	24 Sept	29 Oct	Dr John Rae returns, lands Plymouth 25 Oct with Dr Helmcken
	Westminster	Michie	L	?	30 Aug	28 Sept		Supplies for Richardson–Rae Arctic Searching Expedition; left for Nova Scotia
1848	Prince Rupert VI	Herd	L	31 May	18 Aug	11 Sept	14 Oct	

Year	Ship	Captain	L					Notes
1849	Prince Rupert VI	Herd	L	31 May	14 Aug	11 Sept	25 Oct	Graham sank in ice near Mansel Island, 3 August; half the crew perished
1850	Prince of Wales II	Herd	L	6 June	12 Aug	13 Sept	10 Oct	20 men, 46 women & children to Red River ("pensioners")
	Prince Rupert VI	Mamnock	L	6 June	7 Aug	31 Aug	7 Oct	
	Flora	May	L	?	15 Aug	31 Aug	?	
	George	Midwood	L	?	24 Aug	28 Aug	?	
1851	Prince of Wales II	Herd	L	4 June	13 Aug	9 Sept	3 Oct	Robert MacFarlane on board
1852	Prince of Wales II	Herd	L	2 June	15 Aug	16 Sept	26 Oct	
	Marten	Mamnock	L	8 June	19 Aug		remained	
	Superior	Sherris	L	?	25 Aug	1 Sept		left for Newfoundland
1853	Prince of Wales II	Herd	L	8 June	16 Aug	12 Sept	6 Oct	Archibald McDonald on board; longest-serving factor, Ft. Qu'Appelle
1854	Prince of Wales II	Herd	L	7 June	28 Aug	20 Sept	24 Oct	
1855	Prince of Wales II	Herd	L	8 June	4 Sept	25 Sept	25 Oct	
1856	Prince of Wales II	Herd	L	12 June	20 Aug	22 Sept	31 Oct	
1857	Prince of Wales II	Herd	L	11 June	9 Aug	18 Sept	19 Oct	
	Baroness	Limstrong	L	?	29 Aug	18 Sept	?	
1858	Prince of Wales II	Herd	L	9 June	13 Aug	13 Sept	6 Oct	
	Effort	McLaren	L	?	23 Aug	17 Sept		
1859	Prince of Wales II	Herd	L	8 June	25 Aug	18 Sept	22 Oct	Lost en route to Montreal
	Kitty	Ellis			no date	no date		wrecked at Hudson Strait, 5 Sept; cargo, 11 men and one boat lost
1860	Prince of Wales II	Herd	L	6 June	16 Aug	8 Sept	3 Oct	
1861	Prince of Wales II	Herd	L	4 June	22 Aug	9 Sept	9 Oct	

Year	Ship	Captain	Lv	Lv	Arr YF	Lv YF	Ar London	Comments
				Gregorian calendar, "New Style" dates, advanced 11 days				
1862	Prince of Wales II	Herd	L	4 June	13 Aug	9 Sept	5 Oct	
1863	Prince of Wales II	Herd	L	3 June	29 Aug	17 Sept	9 Oct	*Ocean Nymph* beset in ice, failed to reach Hudson Bay, retreated to Labrador
1864	Ocean Nymph	James	L	8 June	23 Aug	20 Sept	23 Oct	*Prince Arthur* also ran aground, abandoned at Mansel Is. on way in
	Prince of Wales II	Sinnett	L	8 June	29 Aug		wintered	*P of W* ran aground c Dr. Brietzke; *P of W* last voyage, return 1865
1865	Prince of Wales II	Taylor	L	?	?	2 Oct	2 Nov	Returned after wintering
	Prince Rupert VII	Bishop	L	8 June	22 Aug	2 Oct	30 Oct	
1866	Prince Rupert VII	Bishop	L	8 June	2 Sept	4 Oct	31 Oct	
1867	Prince Rupert VII	Bishop	L	6 June	12 Aug	17 Sept	15 Oct	Isaac Cowie on board
1868	Prince Rupert VII	Bishop	L	3 June	24 Aug	20 Sept	20 Oct	
1869	Prince Rupert VII	Bishop	L	5 June	19 Aug	26 Sept	24 Oct	
1870	Prince Rupert VII	Bishop	L	8 June	20 Aug	18 Sept	19 Oct	
	Ocean Nymph	Galbraith	L	?	2 Sept	9 Sept	19 Oct	home to England via Rigolet, Labrador
1871	Prince Rupert VII	Bishop	L	1 June	8 Aug	20 Sept	22 Oct	damaged by gales at YF; wintered at Sorel, Quebec
	Ocean Nymph	Galbraith	L	?	11 Aug	2 Sept		
1872	Prince Rupert VII	Bishop	L	6 June	17 Aug	22 Sept	25 Oct	
	Walrus	Tuggey	L	?	23 Sept	winterx2		wintered 2 years

Year	Ship	Master		Departed					Remarks
1873	Prince Rupert VII	Bishop	L	6 June		10 Aug	21 Sept	17 Oct	Remained in Hudson Bay
1874	Mink	Main	L	13 June		10 Sept	20 Sept	22 Oct	
1875	Ocean Nymph	McPherson	L	10 June		12 Sept	22 Sept	8 Nov	
1876	Ocean Nymph	McPherson	L	8 June		12 Sept	21 Sept	25 Oct	
1877	Ocean Nymph	McPherson	L	9 June	C	3 Sept	22 Sept	28 Sept	
1878	Ocean Nymph	McPherson	L	8 June	C	19 Aug	29 Aug	4 Oct	
1879	Ocean Nymph	McPherson	L	11 June	C	22 Aug	1 Sept	17 Nov	
1880	Ocean Nymph	McPherson	L	10 June	C	4 Sept	13 Sept	12 Oct	
1881	Ocean Nymph	McPherson	L	13 June	C	31 Aug	10 Sept	5 Oct	Churchill visited second
1882	Ocean Nymph	Hawes	L	13 June	C2	15 Aug	24 Aug	wintered	Ar Churchill 8 Oct; heavy ice prevented return; wintered
1883	Ocean Nymph	Hawes	L	11 June	C2	13 Sept	22 Sept	8 Sept	Returned after wintering
1884	Ocean Nymph	Hawes	L	10 June	C	21 Sept	c24July	31 Oct	
1885	Cam Owen	Main	L	10 June	C	21 Sept	3 Oct	26 Nov	Prince of Wales wintered at Charlton Is
1886	Cam Owen	Hawes	L	9 June	C	unable	27 Sept	wrecked	Wrecked off Churchill 30 Aug with loss of cargo; men saved
1887	Prince Rupert VIII	Barfield	L	2 June	C	8 Sept	23 Sept	3 Nov	
1888	Prince Rupert VIII	Barfield	L	4 June	C	2 Sept	14 Sept	2 Nov	
1889	Prince Rupert VIII	Barfield	L	5 June	C	3 Sept	13 Sept	31 Oct	
1890	Prince Rupert VIII	Barfield	L	5 June	C	21 Sept	11 Oct	wintered	Winters at Charlton Is after meeting heavy ice & springing a leak
1891	Prince Rupert VIII	Barfield	L		M	2 Sept	?	7 Oct	Returned after wintering
1891	Perseverance	Milne	P	8 June	C2	25 Aug	27 Aug	20 Oct	Churchill visited 2nd; England departure from Peterhead, not London

Year	Ship	Captain	Lv	Lv	Arr YF	Lv YF	Ar London	Comments
			Gregorian calendar, "New Style" dates, advanced 11 days					
1892	Princess	Hawes	L	?	22 Aug		stayed	
	Erik	Gray	L	12 June	C2	?	7 Nov	*Erik* at YF after Churchill; *Erik* first HBC steam vessel to enter Bay!!

Note: In 1892, *Erik*, the first steam vessel, under Captain Gray, left London on 12 June. She visited Labrador posts, Fort Chimo, Churchill, and York Factory. *Erik* had visited Labrador for the HBC in four previous summers, 1888 through 1891, inclusive

C in column 5 means ship stopped at Churchill before YF

Sailing Ships were the only supply ships until 1892!

This chronology contains much interesting information about the ever-present risks incurred by sailing ships in ice-infested waters and offers insight into changing weather conditions over the greater part of two centuries.

PROVENANCE OF HBC JOURNALS

Deidre Simmons

The Hudson's Bay Company Archives were transferred from London, England, to Winnipeg, Manitoba, in 1974. Twenty years later the archives were officially donated by the Hudson's Bay Company to the Province of Manitoba to be maintained and made accessible in the Provincial Archives. As Moodie has observed, "the company remains the longest-lived of the chartered joint stock companies [world-wide] and its archives provide a unique chronicle of the evolution of half a continent from the stone age to the modern era."

In my MA thesis, "Custodians of a Great Inheritance: An Account of the Making of the Hudson's Bay Company Archives"(University of Manitoba, 1994), I relate how the company's "business records ... have been collected, preserved, and protected for over 320 years." A journal was kept at each fur-trading post, and entries made daily; a book covering almost one full year was then sent annually to London with the returning fur cargos. The early records of the company were kept by the committee members in London until a lease was taken in 1696 on premises in Fenchurch Street, not far from the Royal Exchange. The company remained in that building for ninety-eight years until it moved to another building in the same street, where it stayed until 1865. The company and its records were then moved to a warehouse at No. 1 Lime Street, and in 1924 they were moved to the new Beaver House in Trinity Lane, Garlick Hill. In 1928 the administrative offices of the company were relocated to a new Hudson's Bay House at 68 Bishopsgate, and the archival records were moved to the top floor. During the Second World War they were packed up and stored at the governor's home, Hexton Manor, north of London, then moved back to Hudson's Bay House in 1945. In 1955 all of the company's offices, including the archives, were moved into Beaver House, where they remained until the transfer in 1974 to Canada.

The Company formed the Hudson's Bay Record Society in 1938 to publish some of the more interesting journals in its archives after several previous plans had been bogged down either by sheer volume or by the Company's desire to censor apparently minor details. The first volume, *George*

Simpson's Journal and Correspondence for 1820 and 1821, was issued to members of the Champlain Society and the HBC Record Society in 1938. E.E. Rich edited this and another twenty-one volumes through 1959, including a two-volume history of the company. He was followed in turn by K.G. Davies (1960–65) and Glyndwr Williams (1965–75). Each editor received valuable assistance from the Company archivist, Alice Johnson. After the archives moved to Winnipeg, another three volumes were published, with Hartwell Bowsfield as editor, before the HBC Record Society was dissolved in 1983. Between 1950 and 1966 the records were microfilmed, with a copy of each reel available for viewing in the Public Archives of Canada in Ottawa.

An attempt to have the archives moved to Canada, and specifically to Winnipeg, was made in 1964 by the late Dr William B. Ewart, who proposed the idea to the chairman of the Canadian Committee of the HBC, the secretary of the Manitoba Centennial Corporation, and the president of the University of Manitoba. The next year he carried his crusade to the premier of Manitoba, Duff Roblin, and gained his support. He already had the support of the Manitoba Historical Society, the Library Committee of the University of Manitoba, the vice-president of the university, the chairman of Great West Life Assurance Company, and Manitoba historian W.L. Morton. But nothing happened for five years. In the meantime, the HBC transferred its head office from London to Winnipeg. A Winnipeger, George T. Richardson, was the first Canadian company governor, elected on 28 May 1970.

The Public Archives of Canada and the University of Toronto were both competitively interested in seeing the HBC Archives move to Canada. In 1970, Ernest Sirluck, the new president of the University of Manitoba, and Manitoba Premier Edward Schreyer joined the campaign. Two years later the Manitoba government had renovated and reopened the former Winnipeg Auditorium as the new Provincial Archives building. After considering seriously the proposal from the Public Archives in Ottawa, the company made a decision to move the archives to Winnipeg, in the care of the Provincial Archives of Manitoba. An agreement was signed, and the announcement was made public on 31 July 1973, to the extreme joy of Dr Ewart and his many supporters. Shirlee Anne Smith was appointed keeper of the Hudson's Bay Company Archives in September 1973, and the physical transfer of the archives from London was completed in October 1974. The HBC Archives was reopened in Winnipeg in April 1975. Twenty years later the archives were officially donated by the Hudson's Bay Company to the Province of Manitoba to remain accessible in perpetuity in the Provincial Archives.

THE TEN GRAHAM/HUTCHINS MANUSCRIPTS IN THE HBC ARCHIVES: A DETECTIVE STORY

Stuart and Mary Houston

For a naturalist, the most valuable information in the entire HBC archives must be the ten Graham-Hutchins manuscripts (Table C.1). These primary materials contain some of the most detailed eighteenth-century natural-history observations available anywhere in North America. One volume, E.2/12, was chosen for publication as the twenty-seventh volume in the Hudson's Bay Record Society series in 1969 (hereafter HBRS 27), with Glyndwr Williams as editor.[1] There were nine other manuscript versions of similar material to choose from, all written in the 1770s. Soon after we began our studies of these ten volumes, we encountered the question of the authorship of E.2/12: Graham? Hutchins? Graham and Hutchins in collaboration?

For nearly two centuries, Thomas Hutchins had received all or most and Andrew Graham little or none of the credit for the information in the natural-history manuscripts in the HBC Archives. For example, Dr John Richardson, in *Fauna Boreali-Americana*, volume 2, *The Birds*, credited Hutchins for information in the handwritten manuscript he had borrowed from the Hudson's Bay Company.

When Richard Glover[2] wrote the introduction to HBRS 27, he was certain that Andrew Graham was the author of most of the material in all ten versions in the HBC Archives. Hence the volume was titled *Andrew Graham's Observations on Hudson Bay, 1767–1791*. In spite of the book title, the editor, Glyndwr Williams, was much less certain of the authorship. In 1978 he published in *The Beaver* a splendid, tantalizing account of his research, titled "Andrew Graham and Thomas Hutchins: Collaboration and Plagiarism in 18th-Century Natural History." Williams stresses that the materials in HBRS 27 "form an invaluable record of man's experience in the human, wildlife and trading world of the Canadian North over a period of a quarter-century or more."[3] But what a challenge they posed!

During my years as General Editor of the Hudson's Bay Record Society, the most personally stimulating and demanding of the textual volumes issued was undoubtedly *Andrew Graham's Observations on Hudson's Bay, 1767–1791*. Problems of selection,

Table C.1
The ten manuscripts of Andrew Graham and Thomas Hutchins
[Based on Williams, Appendix B, Observations, 1969]

HBCA Desig	Year	Title Page	Hand-writing	Natural History	Species of Birds	Cree Names	Other Topics
E.2/4	1768	Graham	not AG	No	0	No	Life in HBC
E.2/5	1768	Graham	not AG	Simple	54	No	Indians Henday journal Tomison journal
E.2/6	1769	Graham	Graham	No	0	No	Company policy
E.2/7	1771	Graham	not AG	Brief Simple	40	No	Indians, HBC Reply to Clunie
E.2/8	1771	Graham	Other	Brief Same	40	No	Less re Indians
E.2/9	1772–1775	Graham	Other	Technical	93	Yes	Copy of dip needle
E.2/10	nil	nil	Other	Technical	92	Yes	Appendix birds by Hutchins
E.2/11	nil	nil	Graham	.....	0	No	Henday journal Cocking journal Black's letter re Hutchins' experiments
E.2/12	1791	Graham	Graham	Technical	92	Yes	Published 1969
E.2/13	nil	nil	Other	Technical	92	Yes	Hutchins' name embossed on cover
RoySoc	1772	Hutchins	Hutchins	Technical	68	Yes	Hutchins

compilation and annotation were challenging enough; but the most intriguing fea-
ture of the manuscript "Observations" which formed the basis of the volume was
the central problem of authorship. Were they the work of Andrew Graham or
Thomas Hutchins? ... Who was the originator, and who the copyist? Or is that the
wrong question to ask, and should one be looking for a genuine collaboration? A comparison of the ornithological sections ... shows that in practical terms the two men
were working together ... the Hutchins manuscript in particular reveals a conscious
sense of scientific research, of an advancement of knowledge ... also noticeable in
the Hutchins manuscript is a sense of deference to Graham, on grounds not of rank
but of knowledge. Unlike Graham, who by now was an old hand at the business of
writing up his natural history notes, Hutchins refers to "we" observing, measuring,
writing ... The partnership was fruitful, honest, and (as far as we can tell) happy.[4]

We were even more doubtful than Williams about Glover's decision to give
all credit to Graham. We thought it strange, upon reading HBRS 27, that
Graham, a fur trader, would use an adjective such as "pilose," a noun such
as "canthus," or a phrase such as "the toes semi-palmated and beautifully
scolloped, each finely serrated." Familiar with the writings of surgeon-nat-
uralists such as Dr John Richardson, we were convinced that the descriptions
of bird skins must have been written by someone with a more technical, scientific background, careful to emphasize the fresh colour of soft parts before
the specimen dried and the colours changed. The style was that of a man
with a combined Latin, zoological, and medical education.[5] Who but a scholar versed in Latin, in naming three bird species with no known Cree name,
would use terms such as "innominata," "Hudsonias crane," or, on the birthday of King George III, "Avis Natalis"? We accepted the well-documented
evidence that Graham was author of the perceptive and interesting accounts
of the fur trade and the Indians, and most of the mammal accounts, but it
seemed to us that the surgeon, Thomas Hutchins, was responsible for at least
the technical descriptions of the birds. As substantiating evidence to support
our hypothesis, we noted that Hutchins' bird descriptions from E.2/10, presented as Appendix C in HBRS 27, are written in the same style as those
Glover ascribed to Graham earlier in the book.

The comments of Geraldine Alton Harris, in the introduction to her thesis,
are relevant in this regard:

The principle of provenance, first articulated by European archivists in the nineteenth
century, maintains that in order to protect the integrity of the records as evidence
of the actions of their creators, the creators of the records must be known. It follows that to protect the integrity of the information in the records, the records of a
particular creator must neither be confused with those of another creator, nor have

Figure C.1
Photo of the ten volumes of *Observations*, series E.2, by Andrew Graham and Thomas
Hutchins. HBC Archives, PAM. Reprinted from *The Beaver* 308(4) (Spring 1978):4–5

their identity effaced or obscured by physically intermixing them with the records
of one or more other creators.[6]

In five visits to the Hudson's Bay Company Archives in Winnipeg and one
week transcribing two microfilms on loan, the two of us painstakingly read,
transcribed, and indexed the bird sightings in the Graham/Hutchins manuscripts. Not only did we increase our confidence in our hypothesis, but we
found two entirely different styles of presentation in the ten manuscripts, the
non-technical manuscripts and those with technical terminology.

Manuscripts E.2/4, E.2/5, E.2/6 (which has virtually nothing on natural
history), E.2/7, and E.2/8 clearly state on the title page that they are written
by Graham. E.2/8 is merely a copy of E.2/7, with changes only in punctuation, using more semicolons and fewer periods, more use of "and" and less
of "&," and a tendency to use lower case for the first letter of a month: for
example, may instead of May. E.2/9 is also attributed to Graham. E.2/11 is
a copy in Graham's handwriting of the journals of Anthony Henday and

Matthew Cocking, together with letters and some other material; it contains no natural history.

The remaining three manuscripts, E.2/10, E.2/12, and E.2/13, are replete with detailed descriptions of plumage, technical terminology, colours of soft parts, and a nearly complete set of Indian names for each bird species. These bird accounts are as different as night and day from the three early Graham accounts that deal with natural history. They are similar in style and terminology to the Appendix of E.2/10, written by Thomas Hutchins, and reproduced in full as Appendix C, pages 365–81, in HBRS 27. In E.2/12 the accounts of forty-one species of mammals and seventeen species of fish, unlike the birds, contain less technical terminology and hence are predominantly Graham's. E.2/13 has "T. Hutchins" embossed in gilt lettering at the bottom of the spine bound in leather (Figure C.1).

By this time we were convinced that Hutchins and Graham were indeed collaborators, and Hutchins not a mere copyist, as Glover had inferred. While Graham had been treated badly for two centuries, with Hutchins receiving recognition from Latham and Pennant for his and Graham's joint observations, Glover's introduction, it seemed to us, failed to give sufficient recognition to Hutchins.

With whom does one share one's findings and doubts about a point of authorship, crucial to the early history of Canadian ornithology? Since W. Earl Godfrey, the author of *Birds of Canada*, acted as a consultant to Professor Glover during the preparation of his introduction to HBRS 27, we sent our material to Godfrey. We asked him whether either Glover or Williams was still alive, and if so, whether either was still *compos mentis*.

Meanwhile, Tim Ball and Jennifer Brown of the Ruperts Land Research Centre in Winnipeg were organizing a fur-trade colloquium in the Orkney Islands for June 1990. We had attended the previous fur-trade colloquium at Churchill in 1988 and had then visited York Factory, the hub of the HBC operations for about 150 years. Orkney was an equal attraction for us, as the origin for, at times, up to 85 per cent of HBC employees.[7]

To our delight, Glyndwr Williams was the distinguished keynote speaker at the Orkney colloquium, making our trip even more worthwhile. A professor of history at Queen Mary College, University of London, his research has now shifted away from Hudson Bay. We had expected that a man who had done such important work in the 1950s and 1960s would be appreciably older than ourselves, but this was not the case. His publications had begun at an early age.

We hesitantly presented, in written form, our Hutchins/Graham hypothesis to Glyn. The three of us agreed that the next important step in con-

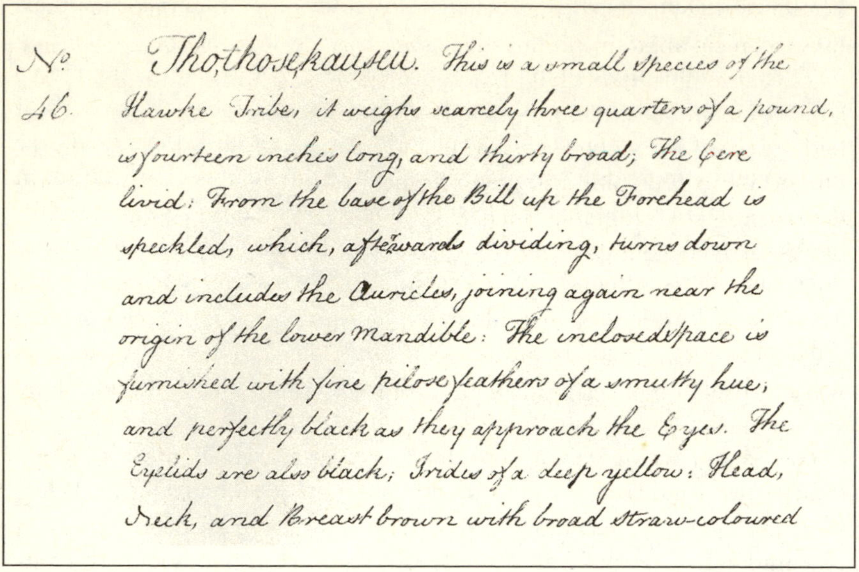

> Nº 46. *Tho,those,kau,seu*. This is a small species of the Hawke Tribe, it weighs scarcely three quarters of a pound, is fourteen inches long, and thirty broad; The Gere livid: From the base of the Bill up the Forehead is speckled, which, afterwards dividing, turns down and includes the Auricles, joining again near the origin of the lower Mandible: The inclosed space is furnished with fine pilose feathers of a smutty hue, and perfectly black as they approach the Eyes. The Eyelids are also black; Irides of a deep yellow: Head, Neck, and Breast brown with broad straw-coloured

Figure C.2
Sample page from Hutchins' Royal Society journal. Account of *Tho,those,kau,seu*,
the Short-eared Owl. Courtesy Sheila Edwards, librarian, Royal Society of London.

firming or refuting our hypothesis was to gain access to the neglected Hutchins manuscript in the Royal Society Archives in London, so that we could transcribe it. Glyn was able to arrange for copies to be made for himself and for us. With some trepidation, after years of intermittent struggling with the handwriting of other fur traders and explorers, often difficult to decipher, we awaited arrival of the electrostatic copy of the Hutchins manuscript.

HUTCHINS' ROYAL SOCIETY MANUSCRIPT

Contrary to the modern stereotype of a surgeon's nearly illegible handwriting, Hutchins' proved to be neat, regular, and eminently legible, delightfully easy to transcribe (Figure C.2).

Throughout the Hutchins Royal Society manuscript are the terms we had seen repeatedly in HBRS 27, copied from E.2/12. In both manuscripts there is substantial evidence of a writer with a scientific, medical background. Who, other than a medical doctor used to describing a measles rash as a macular rash, would use "macula" instead of "spots," as Hutchins did for the markings on the feathers of the Snowy Owl? Hutchins describes the bill of the Three-toed Woodpecker as "angular and cuneiform" – although this is rendered as "angular and formed like a wedge" in E.2/12. Hutchins repeatedly uses technical anatomic nouns such as *apertures*, auricle, *canthus*, cere, *fissure*, *irides*, *laminae*, lorum, nucha, *rugae*, scapulars, *undulations*, vent feathers, vibrissae (those in italics are not defined in Pennant's glossary in *British Zoology*, and hence would not have been available to an owner of that book).[8] In his bird accounts Hutchins also uses adjectives such as assiduous, cineritious, decorticated, fer[r]uginous, incurvated, livid, maculated, palmated, pectinated, serrated, smutty, sulcated, tinctured, and variegated. Phrases such as "cere livid," and "divided into two hemispheres" smack more of the educated doctor than of Graham, the observant fur trader who wrote E.2/5-7-8.

Hutchins' Royal Society manuscript allows us to sort out the previously controversial and perplexing identification of the "wapacuthu" owl,[9] now known to have been assigned to the wrong species in the fifth *AOU Check-list* in 1957, and perpetuated even more recently in an otherwise highly scientific book, *Owls of the World*, published in 1999.[10] It is certain from reading Hutchins' original notes[11] that he described a Snowy Owl, not a pale Great Horned Owl.[12]

It is not surprising that large birds are overrepresented in the early collections from Hudson Bay. Because of their size, the geese, ducks, and upland game birds were annual sources of food. Wading birds were smaller but delectable morsels, and well represented in the Hudson Bay collections. The numerous little snow buntings were a delicacy at table but were caught under nets rather than shot. The guns at that time and for another century were "blunderbusses" that tended to blow the smaller birds into smithereens, making preparation of study skins difficult or impossible. Further, the taxidermy methods of the time were inadequate for long-term preservation of specimens.

EVIDENCE FOR GRAHAM-HUTCHINS COLLABORATION

After studies of each of the versions in the HBC Archives and particularly after complete transcription of the manuscript unequivocally by Hutchins in the library of the Royal Society (Document 2), we wish to summarize evidence for the following six propositions:

1 Hutchins is undoubtedly the author, and not merely the copyist, of the manuscript in the Royal Society Archives, which is in his handwriting. The Hutchins manuscript was written to accompany the second large shipment of numbered bird skins sent back to London from York Factory in 1772, the only year that Graham and Hutchins were together at York Factory. This Royal Society manuscript, containing seventy-seven entries for sixty-

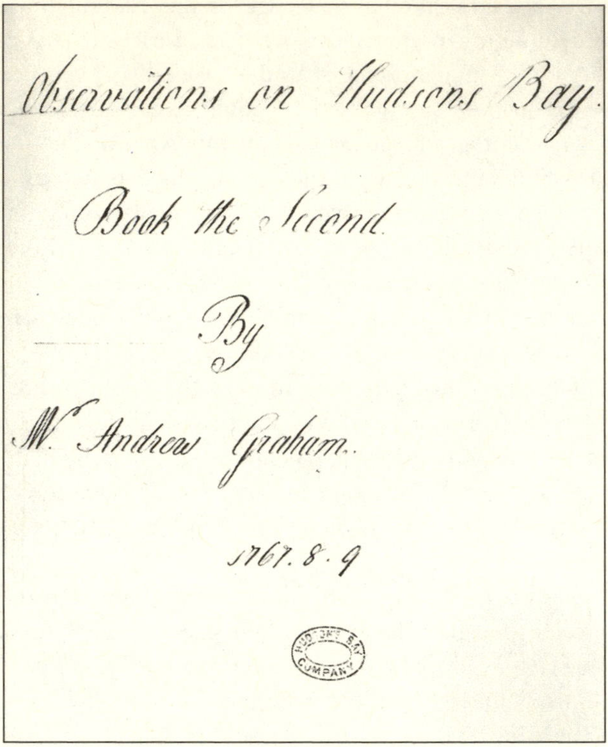
Observations on Hudsons Bay.

Book the Second

By

Mr Andrew Graham.

1767. 8. 9

Figure C.3
Andrew Graham's handwriting: Title page of *Observations on Hudson Bay*.
HBC Archives, PAM

nine bird species (sixty-four with specimens and five without),[13] allows a better understanding of the collaboration between Hutchins and Graham than any of the ten manuscripts in the HBC Archives.

2 Graham had asked Hutchins to write the "scientific descriptions," using the zoological nomenclature in which Hutchins as a surgeon had been trained. Hutchins says in his introduction, "In pursuance of Mr. Graham's advice, I have described the plumage of the birds."[14]

3 Hutchins's approach to both observation and writing was entirely different from that of Graham. His training as a surgeon made him more attuned to the "scientific method." He used technical terminology, more often providing details about measurement, weight, and the colour of soft parts.

4 The ten volumes in the HBC archives fall readily into two categories, simple (by Graham) and technical (by Hutchins).

5 While at Severn, Graham alone wrote E.2/4, E.2/5, E.2/7 and E.2/8. E.2/6 dealt with company policy (Figure C.3).

6 Many of Graham's early observations in E.2/4, E.2/5, and E.2/7 were not repeated in the later versions such as E.2/9, E.2/10, E.2/13, nor E.2/12, the source of the bird accounts of 92 species published in HBRS 27.

GRAHAM'S RELATIONSHIP WITH HUTCHINS

We strongly suspect that Graham was somewhat in awe of Hutchins' superior book-knowledge and technical vocabulary and may well have regarded himself as a junior and less significant partner in the enterprise. Graham sometimes spoke with awe of "The Learned." This modesty could help to explain the lack of rancour on Graham's part when Hutchins passed off some of Graham's observations as his own. As Earl Godfrey has said, perhaps both Graham and Hutchins regarded their collaboration as a joint effort: "It seems very significant to me that E.2/9 (the father of E.2/12) was written mostly in 1771–1772 when the two were together at York."[15]

Some of the examples of plagiarism by Hutchins of material written by Graham seem blatant and indefensible. This concern has been expressed best by Glyn Williams, who wrote to us:

I must accept your proposition that the difference in literary style, technical terms, etc., between E.2/5, E.2/7 and E.2/8 on the one hand, and E.2/9 and the later volumes on the other, stems from Hutchins' input to E.2/12 in 1771–1772. This is an important element in the York collaboration between Graham and Hutchins which I underplayed in my generalised reference to "the help and stimulus which the presence of Hutchins brought to Graham."[16] The balance of interpretation of the collaboration therefore needs to be shifted from the one I advanced in 1978, which basically saw Graham as the "leader," if you like, and Hutchins as the willing novice.

I don't think I can follow your more general conclusions ... I still find quite damning Hutchins' letter to Pennant of February 1784, where unequivocal plagiarism was evident in Hutchins' appropriation of Graham's observations of the White Whale as his own, as reported in *The Beaver* pp. 12 and 13. In 1784 Hutchins was using Graham's material to answer questions from Pennant, not a very heinous crime perhaps in an age when literary conventions concerning acknowledgments were slacker than they are today; but by the following year he was allowing, if not encouraging, both Pennant and Latham to assume that the "Observations" he had permitted them to copy were his own work.

This does not, to my mind, cover Hutchins' behaviour while corresponding secretary of the Company. It was during those years, the mid-1780s, that Graham disappears from view.[17]

We share Williams' amazement that Graham, who outlived Hutchins by twenty-five years, showed no annoyance and apparently held no grudge concerning the sole credit given to Hutchins a number of times by Pennant and Latham for some of Graham's observations from Severn, and for circulating the manuscript of E.2/10 as though it were Hutchins' alone. Did Graham simply acknowledge that Hutchins was more qualified than he to interpret the significance of their combined observations?

Graham also suffered plagiarism by Edward Umfreville, whose *The Present State of Hudson's Bay* in 1790 took "several of the more reliable sections ... straight from Graham's manuscript journals."[18] And Hearne may have copied from Hutchins (see chapter 9).

GRAHAM'S OBSERVATIONS

The earliest manuscript, E.2/5, written by Graham at Severn in 1768, allows us to assess Graham's knowledge and experience when he began; he was at that time familiar with fifty-four species of birds. Three years later, in E.2/7 (not the manuscript that accompanied his 1771 specimens), he mentioned only forty bird species. Graham made two notable errors in his early reports: in E.2/7 he averred that robins do not sing, and claimed that neither the legs nor the feet of the Spruce Grouse are feathered.[19] Even between Graham's two versions there were inconsistencies; the goose dance correctly named in E.2/5[20] became a swan feast in E.2/7. The "bald-coot" in E.2/7 may have been one of the scoters already listed rather than an American Coot, not mentioned in any of the other versions.[21]

Document 2 now makes available to the public for the first time the birds and mammals described by Graham alone in E.2/5 and E.2/7. Graham material not printed in HBRS 27 is shown in bold-face in Document 1 (http://www.mcgill.ca/mqupress/homepa/eighteenth-centurynaturalists. html).

In editing these passages, we appreciate Graham's simple, unaffected writing style, without technical jargon. He wrote in simple, direct terms of the Snow Bunting, "They eat very fine in a pye."[22] Unlike the better-educated Hutchins, Graham had occasional lapses in grammar and a somewhat smaller vocabulary. Although Graham often failed to achieve agreement between his nouns and verbs – "geese comes," "all the sea-birds visits us," "gentlemen was" – he generally wrote well, using correctly words such as stratas, promiscuously, indolence, pernicious, interlopers, impracticable, disingenuous, prolixity, pernicious, and indolence. He was by no means a dullard. In his fresh and spontaneous style, he wrote mainly of birds' habits, though he relied heavily on reports by Indians and others. Sometimes he simply listed categories of birds such as "hawks," or provided accounts of capturing ptarmigan. At the very end of the bird section in E.2/5, he gave long but simple descriptions, without technical terminology, of plumages for only four species of birds: Great Horned Owl (his most detailed), Northern Flicker, Hairy Woodpecker, and Red Crossbill. A perceptive observer, Graham was two centuries ahead of his time in his opinion that the Blue Goose was merely a colour-phase of the Snow Goose.

Graham's mammal accounts include mention of two skins of small, whitish caribou. Glover hypothesized on plausible but somewhat tenuous assumptions that this was the first description of the far northern subspecies of the caribou, *Rangifer tarandus pearyi*, and that the two skins were brought by Matonabbee and the Chipewyan Indians to Churchill, perhaps from Victoria Island, "a place where there was little or no day," about 1774.[23]

PREVIOUS LOANS OF THE TEN MANUSCRIPTS PRIOR TO 1800

Over the years the HBC made various versions of these manuscripts available to naturalists. On occasion a clerk may have been assigned to make an additional hand-written copy. Hutchins, by now in London as corresponding secretary to the HBC, in 1783 or 1784 provided Thomas Pennant with a version of text "of which no exact copy can now be found."[24] In 1785, in the first edition of *Arctic Zoology*, Thomas Pennant acknowledged his indebtedness to both Andrew Graham and Dr Thomas Hutchins for copies of their observations, and to Graham for the specimens he had deposited in the Museum of the Royal Society (see the accounts of Pennant and Walker in chapter 1).

CLARIFICATION CONCERNING BIRD ACCOUNTS

E.2/9 is the only manuscript that tells of an important, unusually far north observation of the Greater Prairie-Chicken: "Pinnated Grous is found about Henley Settlement in Hudson's Bay. Legs covered with soft brown feathers, toes naked and pectinated. The tufts which distinguish this species from all others are rooted high on the neck, not far from the hindpart of the head." Pennant called it the Pinnated Grouse: "Described from the real bird by Mr. Catesby, and by myself from the specimens in Mrs. Blackburn's cabinet, which were sent from the province of Connecticut. Is frequent about a hundred miles up Albany river, in Hudson's Bay."[25] Pennant presumably had access to E.2/9; his use of "frequent" no doubt exaggerated the abundance of this largest member of the North American grouse family, 600 km north of the former accepted northern limit of the Greater Prairie-Chicken range.[26]

The various manuscripts to which Hutchins contributed vary in the number of bird species described. In HBRS 27, there are 119 accounts of birds from the Hutchins/Graham collaboration, but 11 species are described twice and the Bald Eagle 5 times, in different plumages. Thus 102 species are represented, plus 1 recognizable subspecies, the Hutchins' Goose, and 1 colour phase, the Blue Goose. In E.2/10, reproduced as Appendix C of HBRS 27, Hutchins records an additional ten species and has duplicate records for another six. E.2/9, E.2/10 and E.2/13 omit the Bohemian Waxwing, Northern Harrier, and American White Pelican. E.2/9 and E.2/13 both omit the Belted Kingfisher. E.2/13 omits the Sora.

Unfortunately, Richard Glover was selective in asking opinions from Godfrey; without Godfrey's help, Glover also misidentified a Horned Grebe as a Pied-billed Grebe, failed to comprehend that the Pigeon Hawk is an earlier name for the Merlin, and did not appreciate that the main range of the Barrow's Goldeneye is the Rocky Mountains and west.

Table 10.1 presents information concerning the species mentioned in each of the HBC journals.

GRAHAM'S NO-LONGER-EXTANT 1771 BIRD LIST, EXTRACTED BY FORSTER

A special committee, chaired by Samuel Wegg, was appointed by the Royal Society on 26 March 1772 to preserve and arrange the 1771 specimens received from Andrew Graham.[27] Johann Reinhold Forster was "commissioned to examine and describe them. With Pennant's help the papers were prepared and read by the new Fellow before the Royal Society." This matter occupied Forster's time until June 1772.[28] Among the specimens collected in 1771, Forster discovered two additional species in the collection, the Ruby-crowned Kinglet and the Blackpoll Warbler. He chose to describe sixty species and the blue morph of the Snow Goose in *Philosophical Transactions*, quoting fairly extensively from notes written by Graham to accompany the specimens from Severn. One presumes that Graham's accompanying manuscript, a potential twelfth manuscript for our series, differed from any of those available for perusal in the archives, and that the differences are too great to be ascribed simply to liberties taken in paraphrasing by Forster.

Forster, a newly elected Fellow of the Royal Society,[29] was designated "FRS" in all four of his papers published in the Royal Society's *Philosophical Transactions*. The first paper from the Graham material was a letter from

Forster at Somerset Stable-yard, Strand, written to William Watson, MD, and read before the society at their meeting of 27 February 1772. It dealt with dyes obtained by Indians from certain roots.[30] Forster evidently attended three Royal Society meetings to present, on 21 May, "Account of several quadrupeds from Hudson's Bay"[31] and on 18 and 25 June 1772, in two parts, "An account of the birds sent from Hudson's Bay."[32] One presumes Forster's final two presentations were extremely hurried (the editor's note acknowledged they were given "before his departure on an expedition"), because Captain James Cook's *Endeavour* had already sailed from Sheerness on 22 June, causing Forster to hurry to Plymouth to board the ship before final departure. The final Forster natural-history account, on the fishes of Hudson Bay, was on 28 January 1773, read in absentia to members of the Society, more than six months after his departure.[33]

NEAR-MISSES: HOW ONE HUTCHINS-GRAHAM MANUSCRIPT (E.2/10) TWICE CAME NEAR TO PUBLICATION

Twice, roughly a century apart, effort was expended on preparing for publication a manuscript from the Hutchins-Graham collaboration in the year 1771–72. Tantalizing snippets concerning these near-misses proved to be one of the most interesting aspects of our nineteen years of investigation.

Professors Richard Glover and Glyndwr Williams did the initial sleuthing. Glover concludes that Dr John Latham, a country doctor from Dartford in Kent and a cataloguer of natural history, had once been in possession of a copy of E.2/10.[34] In studying that manuscript, Williams found that "practically every page contains pencilled alterations and comments in another hand." These "correct and supplement ... [the] natural history notes, add source references to them, modify the style, and in a few places censor the contents ... Occasional pencilled remarks in yet another hand add to the puzzle. These appear to include the initials 'J.C.' and this may have been Joseph Colen, the bookish factor at York Factory who is known to have had a copy of Graham's 'Observations' in his possession in 1795–97 ... It was also this volume which Latham used, and which he credited to Hutchins ... there is strong circumstantial evidence to indicate that at some time around 1790 the publication of one of Graham's volumes was seriously considered."[35] Glover gives good arguments for his suggestion that Pennant, like Forster, had access to another, different version, no longer extant.[36]

Glover[37] similarly learned that Ernest Thompson Seton[38] in 1891, C.G.A. Gosch in 1897,[39] and Edward A. Preble[40] in 1902 had gained access in the Hudson's Bay Archives in London to (probably) E.2/10.[41] Seton gives the following citation:

1782. Hutchins, T. Observations on Hudson's Bay, 654 pp.; pp. 45–180 treats of birds. An interesting unpublished manuscript volume in the library of the Hudson's Bay Company in London, with marginal annotations by Pennant ... the last date mentioned is July 10, 1782, and it seems safe to conclude that it was issued about this date.[42]

Glover appears to have been unaware that Seton's close friend Miller Christy had also been involved. Indeed, Christy (who had edited the voyages of Luke Foxe for the Hakluyt Society and who also wrote an unpublished book-length manuscript dealing with the history of the Hudson's Bay Company)[43] had made a copy of the original and obtained permission from the HBC to publish "the Hutchins MS." He had the entire manuscript typed and sent a copy to Seton.

But how did Seton and Christy get together in the first place? When Ernest Thompson Seton studied art in London, from 28 August 1879 to 26 October 1881, he visited a cousin by marriage, George Porteous, at Saffron Walden, forty-two miles north-northeast of London. One of Porteous's subordinates in the local bank was Miller Christy – as Seton said, "exactly my own age and ... wholly like myself in natural history tastes."[44]

After Seton returned to Canada, Christy was selected by the James Hack Tuke Emigration Committee[45] to go to the United States to assist the settling of starving families sent there following the Irish potato famine of 1881–82.[46] In 1882, following the completion of his duties, Christy continued north to Manitoba to visit Seton at Carberry. Christy returned to western Canada twice more: in 1884 to complete his 302-page book *Manitoba Described*, written as an incentive to prospective settlers,[47] and again in 1887.[48]

While preparing the introduction to *Ernest Thompson Seton in Manitoba, 1882–1892*,[49] we contacted Eleanor Pratt, director of the Ernest Thompson Seton Museum, Boy Scouts of America, at Cimarron, New Mexico, for further information about the Seton-Christy connection. She sent the title-page of the "Hutchins mss.," tentatively dated 1910 (Figure C.4). Christy had enlisted as co-authors Robert Bell in geology, W. Hague Harrington in entomology, F.W. Dodge in ethnology, John Macoun in botany, Edward A. Preble in ichthyology and mammalogy, and R.F. Stupart in meteorology, but did not list Ernest Thompson Seton at this time.

Later, while doing research on the William Swainson-John Richardson correspondence in the Linnean Society at Burlington House in London, we were led by Gina Douglas to a query placed in the *Journal of Botany* in 1921 by its editor. James Britten had asked, "Who collected [plants] in Hudson's Bay in 1773?"[50]

Miller Christy answered in 1922, in a note titled "An early Hudson Bay Collector," as follows: "They were collected by [Thomas Hutchins] ... bringing

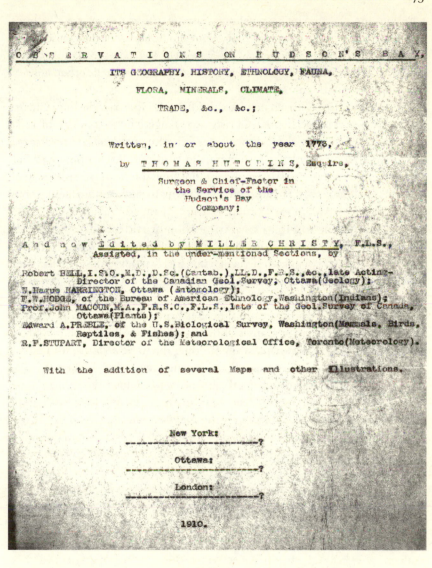

OBSERVATIONS ON HUDSON'S BAY,

ITS GEOGRAPHY, HISTORY, ETHNOLOGY, FAUNA,

FLORA, MINERALS, CLIMATE,

TRADE, &c., &c.;

Written, in or about the year 1773,

by THOMAS HUTCHINS, Esquire,

Surgeon & Chief-Factor in
the Service of the
Hudson's Bay
Company;

And now Edited by MILLER CHRISTY, F.L.S.,
Assisted, in the under-mentioned Sections, by

Robert BELL,I.S.O.,M.D.,D.Sc.(Cantab.),LL.D.,F.R.S.,&c.,late Acting-
    Director of the Canadian Geol.Survey, Ottawa(Geology);
W.Hague HARRINGTON, Ottawa (Entomology);
F.W.HODGE, of the Bureau of American Ethnology,Washington(Indians);
Prof.John MACOUN,M.A.,F.R.S.C.,F.L.S.,late of the Geol.Survey of Canada,
    Ottawa(Plants);
Edward A.PREBLE, of the U.S.Biological Survey, Washington(Mammals, Birds,
    Reptiles, & Fishes); and
R.F.STUPART, Director of the Meteorological Office, Toronto(Meteorology).

With the addition of several Maps and other Illustrations.

New York:
------------------------------?
Ottawa:
------------------------------?
London:
------------------------------?

1910.

Figure C.4
Title page of Miller Christy's proposed edition of Hutchins' observations, 1910.
Courtesy Eleanor Pratt, Ernest Thompson Seton Memorial Library and Museum,
Philmont Scout Ranch and Explorer Base, Cimarron, New Mexico.

with him the manuscript of a volume entitled 'Observations on Hudson's Bay.' Many years ago my friend Mr. Ernest Thompson Seton and myself were permitted to have a copy made of it, with a view to its publication under my general editorship, and the help of a specialist in each department of knowledge treated. Unfortunately however, the work, though nearly ready for publication, has not yet been issued. On the outbreak of war, I sent the MS. to Mr. Seton in New York, where he is arranging for this publication."[51] Evidently publishers in the United States felt sales would not be sufficient.

Christy had an even more ambitious project under way. Based on his extensive research in the HBCA in London, he wrote a detailed history of the HBC. In this regard, Judith Hudson Beattie brought to our attention a letter in the HBC Archives in Winnipeg, from Christy to William Ware of the HBC, dated 20 February 1909. Christy told how he had found it "impossible to make any substantial progress with my intended History of the Hudson's Bay Company, for which I am still collecting information; but sooner or later I shall be able to go ahead with it again." Christy continued, "You remember, I believe, that long since I received the Company's permission to publish the old Hutchins MS (about 1770), relating to the natural history of the North-West, which is in the Company's library and is of considerable scientific interest. I had the manuscript in my keeping for some months, and had a copy made of it but, unfortunately, all arrangements for publishing it fell through in consequence of the death of the late Mr. Henry Seebohm,[52] who had agreed to bear all the expense. Now, however, I think I see my way to make other arrangements for publishing the manuscript."

Christy was a successful author and a Fellow of the Linnean Society. He had published three books, *Manitoba Described* in 1885, *The Birds of Essex* in 1890, a two-volume voyages in the prestigious Hakluyt series in 1894,[53] two monographs, and a number of scientific articles. What a pity that his two major manuscripts dealing with Hudson Bay, one the Hutchins' E.2/10 manuscript and the other a detailed history of the HBC,[54] were never published.

HUDSON'S BAY COMPANY FUR CATCHES DEMONSTRATE TEN-YEAR CYCLES

Canada has been front and centre in the study of one of the most perplexing problems in biology. The process began through use of HBC data dating back as far as 1736,[1] and summarized in table form as far back as 1752.[2] It is a captivating story.

The ten-year cycle of the Snowshoe Hare, which in fact averages about 9.5 years and fluctuates, as Keith and MacLulich have shown, "with remarkable regularity and synchrony,"[3] "has become an almost classic example of an animal that undergoes periodic fluctuations in numbers."[4] Other species, but especially the lynx, are on the same ten-year cycle. Extensive, long-term Canadian studies of this cyclical phenomenon began with studies of the HBC long-term fur-sales records. Because lynx furs were in more constant demand, lynx numbers are the most reliable indicator of the cycle. Elton and Nicholson's 1942 account of the "regularity and great amplitude of the rhythm" of lynx fur-catches is a classic.[5]

Subsequent authorities give HBC factor Peter Fidler credit for being the first to describe the ten-year cycle, now known to involve Snowshoe Hares,[6] Lynx,[7] Muskrat,[8] Pine Marten,[9] Red Fox,[10] Fisher,[11] Ruffed Grouse,[12] Spruce Grouse,[13] Sharp-tailed Grouse,[14] Great Horned Owl,[15] and Northern Goshawk.[16] There is also a four-year cycle, based on lemmings and voles, that appears to drive the cycle of the Snowy Owl.[17] HBC fur catches have provided the best long-term data of the hare and lynx cycles, retrospectively investigated with increasing sophistication in turn by Peter Fidler (1820), Henry Poland (1892), Roderick Ross MacFarlane (1905), Ernest Thompson Seton (1911), J. Walter Jones (1914), Oliver Hewitt (1921), D.A. MacLulich in the 1930s, and finally the Oxford team of Charles Elton, Dennis and Helen Chitty, and Mary Nicholson (1931–48). Peter Fidler's contributions are detailed in chapter 9. The retrospective studies are summarized below, concluding with two prospective long-term studies led by Lloyd Keith (1961–81) and Charles Krebs (1986–96).

HENRY POLAND

Henry Poland, FZS, was a member of a well-known family of fur merchants.[18] P.R. Poland presented the HBC with the library of his late father,
Ernest Poland, dealing with fur-bearing mammals, the London fur trade, and
the history of the city of London.[19]

In his book, *Fur-Bearing Animals*,[20] intended "to aid persons in the [fur]
trade" and to be "a connecting link between science and commerce," Henry
Poland summarized HBC fur returns for each major species from 1752 to
1890. He gave the date of the fur sale, a year or two after the furs were caught.
He took pains to indicate years in which furs did not reach London from,
for example, York Factory, Moose Factory, or Eastmain. Poland's compilation remains to this day the best source available for fur catches in northern
North America from 1752 through the 1820s, as well as for price ranges for
a skin of each species in 1891.

RODERICK ROSS MACFARLANE

MacFarlane joined the HBC in 1852, sailing from Stromness on 25 June and
arriving at Red River on 14 September. After each stint of one to several years
in charge of Forts Rae, Resolution, Liard, Good Hope, and Anderson, he
was promoted to the charge of four districts in turn: MacKenzie, Athabasca,
New Caledonia, and Cumberland. He collected specimens for the United
States National Museum (the Smithsonian), especially at Fort Anderson, a
fort he founded in 1861 and closed permanently in 1866.[21] We owe to Mac-
Farlane all that is known about nesting of the Eskimo Curlew, apart from a
single nest found by Dr John Richardson at Point Lake, NWT, in 1821. Mac-
Farlane collected data on thirty-three Eskimo Curlew egg sets and five downy
young. His observations on birds and their eggs were published in 1892, but
his notes on the mammals were not published until 1905. Both bird and
mammal accounts were then reprinted by Mair in 1908.

MacFarlane discussed the ten-year cycle of the lynx:

This is one of the principal periodic fur-bearing mammals which regularly increase
and decrease in numbers about every decade ... The catch of lynxes ... fell sometimes as low as 4,000 or 5,000 skins ... The fourth year would double those quantities, the fifth often more than doubled the fourth, the sixth doubled the fifth, while
the seventh almost invariably witnessed the maximum trade of skins. The eighth
would still be good, while the ninth and tenth would each exhibit a startling decline
... the regularity of these peculiar results in seasons of scarcity and plenty is remarkably interesting ... from 1853 to 1877, inclusive, the company sold in London a total

of 507,450 skins of the Canada lynx, or an average of 20,198 a year. During that 25-year period, the minimum sale was 4,448 in 1863, and the maximum year was at the very next peak in 1868, with 76,556 skins.[22]

Thus, following in the footsteps of Peter Fidler, another HBC factor, Mac-Farlane, was the first to calculate the time between lynx-cycle peaks.

ERNEST THOMPSON SETON

Ernest Thompson Seton took a keen interest in snowshoe hare numbers during his intermittent residence in Manitoba, 1882–92. In his *Life-histories of Northern Mammals*[23] he noted that hare numbers had peaked in Manitoba in 1856–57, 1875,[24] 1884–86, 1894, and early 1904. When hare numbers crashed suddenly in late 1904, Seton enlisted Winnipeg's two leading med-ical-laboratory experts to do necropsies, but the dead hares showed no signs of disease.[25]

Seton extracted retrospective numbers from one lynx cycle of roughly ten years in the journal of Alexander Henry the Younger (nephew of a better-known fur trader, Alexander Henry "the Elder"), when Elliott Coues edited and published the younger Henry's journal in 1897. Henry told of the num-bers of lynx skins traded in "Lower Red River," from present Grand Forks, North Dakota, north into southern Manitoba. Although the number of forts on and near the Red River varied from two to eight, Henry compiled annual "Returns from the Lower Red River Department" as 20, 67, 194, 167, 38, 0, 4, and 4 lynx pelts, respectively, for the years 1801 through 1808.[26]

Seton and Edward Alexander Preble made a scientific survey of a por-tion of the North West Territories in 1907. They launched their Peterbor-ough canoe at Athabasca Landing, Alberta, on 18 May. Seton mapped Aylmer and Clinton-Colden lakes for the Royal Geographical Society. Seton listed precise numbers of lynx caught for nine years only, 1900–08 inclusive,[27] but graphed "the Company's [fur] returns for the 85 years – 1821–1905 inclu-sive," for fifteen mammal species.[28] In fact, contrary to the text, he then extended his graphs for three additional years through 1908. These graphs confirmed what Seton called a "decacycle" for lynx and snowshoe hares, a cycle just short of ten years. Concerning the lynx, Seton wrote: "It lives on Rabbits, follows the Rabbits, thinks Rabbits, tastes like Rabbits, increases with them, and on their failure dies of starvation in the unrabbited woods."[29] In peak years, Seton added, female hares

bear not one, but two or three broods in a season, and these number not 2 or 3, but 8 or 10 each brood ... every little thicket has a Rabbit in it; they jump out at every 8 or 10 feet; they number not less than 100 to the acre on desirable ground ... Finally, they are so extraordinarily superabundant that they threaten their own food supply ... The Rabbits of the Mackenzie River Valley reached their flood height in the winter of 1903–04 ... in 1907 there seemed not one Rabbit left alive in the country.[30]

Further, HBC fur-catch tabulations showed that lynx skins peaked just after the hares, reaching 58,850 in 1905 and 61,388 in 1906. With snowshoe hares absent in 1907, the lynx were starving and easily trapped.[31]

J. WALTER JONES

J. Walter Jones, BA, BSA, worked for Dr Cecil C. Jones, chairman of the Committee on Fisheries, Game and Fur-bearing Animals, Commission of Conservation, Canada. The chairman of the Commission on Conservation, 1909–18, was Clifford Sifton, "the man most responsible for promoting immigration to the Canadian west, and one of the ablest politicians of his time."[32]

Walter Jones published *Fur-farming in Canada* in 1914.[33] In it he provided precise (unrounded) annual figures for lynx trapping from 1848 through 1909. From 1851 through 1875 the Jones totals are exactly the same as the official HBC totals. For the years 1881 through 1889 the annual totals of Jones and Poland are within 1 per cent of each other. Variations in the time or area covered probably explain most of the differences in these annual totals. Jones acknowledged assistance received from at least seven people in compiling these figures: "Valuable statistics of fur production and sales were furnished by the Hudson's Bay Co., through the office of the Canadian High Commissioner, by Messrs. C.M. Lampson & Co., Messrs. A. and W. Nesbitt, Mr. Emil Brass, Mr. J.D. Whelpley and others. Messrs. Henry and Ernest Poland, of P.R. Poland and Sons, London, England, courteously revised a number of tables of statistics, in addition to providing considerable new material."

GORDON HEWITT

Gordon Hewitt spent four years compiling *The Conservation of the Wild Life of Canada*, published posthumously after his sudden death from pneumonia just after his thirty-fifth birthday. One chapter, "Fluctuations of fur-bearing animals," described and graphed the numbers of snowshoe hares for 110 years and lynx for 115 years, beginning in 1820. The average cycle for the lynx was 9.5 years, the lynx peak following a year or sometimes more after the hare peak. The Pine Marten cycle also averaged 9.5 years and the Red Fox, 9.6

years. These data had been made available to Hewitt by Norman H. Bacon, HBC fur-trade commissioner from 1913 to 1918.[34]

D.A. MACLULICH

Stimulated by Poland, MacFarlane, Seton, Jones, and Hewitt, D.A. MacLulich, of the Department of Biology, University of Toronto, undertook an extensive four-year study, 1932–35, of the Snowshoe Hare. In three study areas in Ontario he recorded its habitat, numbers, life history, bacteriology, and parasites. His highest count was 3,400 hares per square mile, in Frontenac County in July 1932. The abundance of lynx was "definitely correlated" with that of the hares.[35]

CHARLES ELTON, MARY NICHOLSON, DENNIS AND HELEN CHITTY

The most sophisticated statistical analyses of HBC records of mammal cycles were done by, or under the supervision of, Charles Elton, soon after he completed a first-class honours degree in zoology at Oxford University in 1922.

In 1926, when he was only twenty-six, Elton wrote his classic and enduring text, *Animal Ecology*.[36] He devoted chapter 9 to "Variations in the numbers of animals." In this he dealt with the four-year cycle of the lemming, and mentioned the cycle of the snowshoe hare. Elton quoted J. Dewey Soper as having found "hundreds" of hares on a thirty-acre tract southwest of Edmonton in 1912, at the top of the hare cycle.[37]

Elton had already begun his contact with Sir Robert Kindersley, governor of the HBC. In March 1925 Elton persuaded the company to send out questionnaires to HBC post managers. His relations with the company improved in June 1925 when Charles Sale, deputy governor of the HBC, became governor. Anne Morton has read, in the HBC Archives, the correspondence between Sale and Elton; because Sale "shared a willingness to follow new paths and a desire for knowledge," these letters "make delightful reading."[38] The Depression caused serious financial difficulties for the HBC, forcing Sale's resignation, but fur trade commissioner Ralph Parsons and HBC archivist Richard Leveson-Gower were sympathetic to Elton's work, and the HBC cooperation continued. Morton summarizes Elton's role:

So Elton had, as he put it, "to graft ecology onto history," by delving into the journals, reports and letters of the old fur traders and missionaries. Through his painstaking reading, coupled with his sympathetic and imaginative interpretations of the documents, Elton came to the understanding of the living past in Northern Canada. Although the creators of the records were not trained scientific observers, they were vitally interested in wildlife, and Elton's work has made them posthumous contributors to ecological knowledge.[39]

After his graduation from Oxford University, Elton lived tenuously, having to find outside funding for his research. His investigations into HBC fur returns were supported financially by the New York Zoological Society.[40] He was appointed biological consultant to the HBC, 1925–29, and then a demonstrator in zoology at the University of Oxford. In 1930 Elton met Copley Amory, a philanthropist from Washington, DC, who owned land on the north shore of the Gulf of St Lawrence. Their meeting led in turn to the Matamek Conference on Biological Cycles in 1931, funded by Amory, and thence to the founding of the Bureau of Animal Population (BAP) at Oxford. The BAP was directed by Elton until "he retired and it [the BAP] ceased to exist, in 1967."[41] Even though Elton now had a formal organization, assistants, and graduate students,[42] he "encountered formidable difficulties in obtaining money for the work, [which] usually involved high personal risk to the continued livelihood of some or all of the members."[43]

In the Hudson's Bay Archives in London, England, Mary Nicholson (Mrs Max Nicholson) did most of the extensive tabulations of annual fur-trade returns, species by species, year by year.[44] Elton and Nicholson then published the two most important retrospective papers, assessing the "posthumous contributions" of HBC fur traders over two centuries. "The ten-year cycle in numbers of the Lynx in Canada" analysed a data set of annual company fur returns that began in 1735 and extended 206 years through 1940. This was "one of the longest homogeneous records of the sort for any species of wild animal," probably exceeded only by the hundreds of years of changes in the Baltic herring fisheries. Rather than the rounded numbers, usually to the nearest thousand, used by Seton in 1912 and Hewitt in 1921, Elton and Nicholson used exact figures. Elton moved Seton's figures and Poland's 1912 figures back one year, and moved all of Jones's annual totals and all but the first ten years of Hewitt's back by two years to correspond to the year most of the furs were trapped, rather than the year in which they were sold. Elton and Nicholson used their Table 1 to compare, line by line, the six different sets of figures.[45] Between the peak lynx years of 1752 and 1935, "there were 19 complete cycles, giving an average period of 9.63 years." The peak of the lynx cycle took several years, usually three, to develop and spread across the width of northern North America

To carry the ten-year-cycle study forward into the 1930s and 1940s, the Bureau of Animal Population analysed annual questionnaires from each HBC post manager from 1931 through 1948. The annual reports from the "Snow-shoe Rabbit" questionnaires, 1931–32 through 1942–43, were published in the *Canadian Field-Naturalist*. These gave the results of twelve consecutive surveys, by from 240 (in 1931–32) to 673 observers (in 1934–35) each year. The first two reports were by Elton, the next two by Elton and G. Swynnerton, four by Dennis Chitty and Elton, the ninth by Dennis and Helen Chitty, the tenth by Dennis Chitty and Mary Nicholson, and the final two by Helen Chitty alone.[46] The project concluded with two reports, each covering three years, for 1943–46 and for 1946–48, compiled by Helen Chitty, in the *Journal of Animal Ecology*.

Five reports from the "Canadian Arctic Wild Life Enquiry," dealing specifically with numbers of foxes, lemmings, and Snowy Owls (all by Dennis Chitty, with Charles Elton co-author of the first, and Helen Chitty, the fifth), appeared in the *Journal of Animal Ecology*, dealing with the years 1935–46 through 1939–40.[47] In this study there were 163, 111, 105, over 95, and exactly 100 observers, respectively.

In 1939 Elton sent Dennis Chitty north on the HBC supply ship RMS *Nascopie* from July through mid-September, firmly convinced that he would see masses of lemmings. But that cycle had peaked a year early, so Chitty found only masses of lemming droppings from the previous year (Chitty 1996, 13). Shelford had found that voles were absent near Churchill, Manitoba, in 1931, but in following their numbers over the subsequent three years and again in 1936, he plotted lemming peaks in 1929, 1933, and 1936.[48]

In his book *Voles, Mice and Lemmings: Problems in Population Dynamics* (1942), Elton stated that few animal cycles "achieve the remarkable regularity" shown by the lynx, snowshoe hare, and red fox.[49] Earlier, in the introduction to the first annual report of the Canadian Snowshoe Rabbit Enquiry, 1931–32, Elton had separated out figures for the Mackenzie River District alone. The figures from 1822–39 were obtained by Elton himself; those from 1842–63 came from an old chart in the HBC library; and the final years, 1863–1927, were supplied by Mr Charles French, late fur-trade commissioner. Elton corrected figures to refer to the actual biological years of production, not the years in which the returns were made nor the year the skins were sold in London. Elton then graphed the lynx cycles from 1822 through 1933 (Figure D.1).[50] The mean cycle was 9.6 years, but some lynx peaks were much higher than others: the amplitude between lowest and highest years varied from 1:9 to 1:62.

Elton and Nicholson also made detailed studies of the ten-year cycle of the muskrat numbers. In the muskrat paper they made the following general statement: "There is no doubt that the cycles are real ones ... and not simply the result of market or trapping variations; that they are widespread among different terrestrial species of the forest zone ... that they often

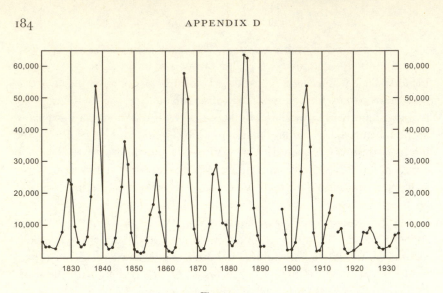

Figure D.1

HBC lynx returns, 1820–1934. Cycle has mean length of 9.6 years
(Elton and Nicholson 1942, 230)

happen over enormous tracts of country; and that there is a tendency for
the years of abundance and scarcity to synchronize regionally ... the muskrat
peak precedes by a year or two the main snowshoe rabbit and lynx peaks."[51]

Dennis Chitty returned to Canada in 1961 to become a professor of
zoology and animal ecology at the University of British Columbia.

WILLIAM ROWAN

Professor William Rowan, the founder of the Zoology Department at the
University of Alberta, did ground-breaking experiments concerning the
effects of daylight on migration (photoperiodism) and also on reproductive
cycles of animals.[52] He showed that artificially increasing daylight hours in
a laboratory would cause gonads to achieve reproductive status earlier, in
keeping with the amount of light to which they had been exposed. Rowan
also studied for thirty years another longer-term problem, cyclic fluctuations
in animals such as the hare and lynx. He and his student Lloyd B. Keith published papers dealing with the reproductive potential and sex ratios[53] and
monthly weights[54] of Snowshoe Hares in Northern Alberta, and, appearing
posthumously in 1959, "Monthly weights of Snowshoe Hares in North-central Alberta."

LLOYD B. KEITH

Lloyd B. Keith went to high school in Edmonton, Alberta. He obtained his BS degree in agriculture and then his MS in Zoology at the University of Alberta under Rowan's tutelage. Keith obtained his PhD under Aldo Leopold at the University of Wisconsin. His book, *Wildlife's Ten-year Cycle*, was published in 1963. From 1961 through 1981 his thorough research on ten-year cycles in the mixed boreal forest near Rochester, Alberta, was assisted by numerous graduate students.[55] The Keith Hypothesis stated that the hare decline began due to winter food shortage, which was followed by a reduction in fecundity.[56]

CHARLES J. KREBS AND ASSOCIATES

Charles J. Krebs grew up in a small Illinois town near St Louis, Missouri, obtained his BSc from the University of Minnesota in 1957 and then moved to Vancouver, British Columbia, for his MA and PhD degrees in animal ecology as Dennis Chitty's first PhD student.[57] During Krebs's four-year studies of mammal cycles at Baker Lake, NWT (now Nunavut), two species of lemmings were at very low numbers in 1959, had a tremendous population growth over the winter of 1959–60, had body weights 20 to 30 per cent above normal at the peak, and then suffered high juvenile mortality during the decline. Food shortage and predation were not causative factors during that single cycle.

On Westham Island, British Columbia, Krebs found that building a fence caused a population explosion among voles within the fenced area. Food and predators are not the answer: later the population crashes, in part because voles kill infant voles in neighbouring nests.[58] This incompletely understood phenomenon is called the Fence Effect or Krebs Effect. In 1978, Krebs wrote a brilliant paper, "A review of the Chitty Hypothesis of population regulation,"[59] and continued research into cycles in Yukon's predator-rich Kluane National Park.

A comprehensive study of the boreal forest ecosystem, 1986–96, was reported in numerous scientific papers. It culminated in a 511-page book, *Ecosystem Dynamics of the Boreal Forest: The Kluane Project*.[60] All the significant parts of the system, including vegetation, were described and quantified in precisely the same place at the same time.

Experimental manipulation of fertilizer, use of herbicide to kill vegetation, food supplementation by addition of rabbit chow, exclusion of hares, and attempted exclusion of carnivorous predators were studied alone, within enclosures, and in combination. Simulations tested twenty-seven individual models.

As expected, addition of fertilizer caused spruce branches to grow more, and hare densities went up 1.3-fold. Removal of mammalian predators doubled the number of hares, and addition of rabbit chow tripled their number. Chow addition and predator exclusion together caused hare numbers to rise 9.7-fold, advanced hare parturition dates by five to twelve days, and increased the number of young weaned per female hare. Food addition postponed the hare population decline.

Special attention was given to the biomass of hares and ground squirrels, and of their main predators, lynx, coyote, and Great Horned Owl. There was a 26- to 44-fold variation in numbers of hares. Coyotes responded with a 6-fold and lynx with a 7.5-fold variation. During the decline and low phases of the hare cycle, many predators did not reproduce.

Most years, over 90 per cent of adult hares that died were killed by predators, and 65 to 75 per cent of these predator killings were by coyotes and lynx. When these mammals were fenced out, Great Horned Owls and Northern Goshawks accounted for 70 to 80 per cent of the predator-killed hares. Great Horned Owls were almost entirely dependent on snowshoe hares during winter, killing at least 5 to 10 per cent of hares present in peak hare years, and up to 38 per cent during one year of hare decline (1992–93). Great Horned Owls were competitively superior to lynx and coyotes.

There were unexpected findings. Great Horned Owl numbers were limited by food even at the peak of the hare cycle; the owl peak lagged two years after the hare peak. The Northern Goshawk was the only predator that switched from hares to grouse during the hare decline. Unexpectedly, Arctic Ground Squirrels numbers were in synchrony with the ten-year cycle of the hares. Spruce Grouse peaked a year ahead of the hares. Hare browsing stimulated productivity of shrubs, rather than diminishing this food supply. Contrary to expectations, sufficient food was available to hares throughout the cycle. It was expected that ground squirrels and red squirrels would function mainly as alternative prey for predators; instead, to everyone's astonishment, both squirrel species ate small hares, killing up to three-quarters of them at the peak of the hare cycle. These squirrel kills thus helped to prevent hares from overgrazing their food supply. The expected four-year vole cycle, evident in Europe, was not seen at Kluane; Red-backed Voles had major peaks eleven years apart, inversely related to peaks in hare populations. Lynx and coyotes accounted for 78 per cent of mortality of radio-collared hares over eleven years. Coyote numbers were highest at the peak of the hare cycle, but lynx lagged a year behind.

Krebs and his colleagues conclude that the boreal-forest community is predominately a top-down system. The major changes are driven by predators; predators could not survive in the boreal forest in the absence of hare peaks. Most hares die from predation and very few from starvation.

MANY ASPECTS OF THE MYSTERY REMAIN UNSOLVED

There are still important unanswered questions, as evident from Dennis Chitty's thought-provoking and somewhat iconoclastic 1996 book, *Do Lemmings Commit Suicide? Beautiful Hypotheses and Ugly Facts.*[61] Early in his career Chitty had postulated that "populations of all species living in favorable environments are capable of preventing unlimited increase in their numbers." But as the years went by he realized that each hypothesis that might direct such a process could be demolished in its turn. He methodically demonstrated that starvation, shock, intra-group aggression, and crowding were all inadequate explanations. Nor did bad weather, predation, disease, dispersal, or hormonal effects of stress suffice. After seventy years of study Chitty remains disappointed by the circular reasoning employed by many of his colleagues, including their tendency to equate effects with causes, their single-cause thinking, their hypotheses that lack the hallmark of scientific corroboration, their overdependence on statistical models, and their failure to use appropriate controls.[62] We know too little about the variables involved in differences between cyclic and noncyclic populations of the same species.

In spite of massive studies, "there is still no answer to this ecological equivalent to the riddle of the sphinx,"[63] why hare cycles recur so regularly at ten-year intervals, and lemming and vole cycles at four-year intervals. As Elton wrote sixty years ago, "the cycle of abundance and scarcity has a rhythm of its own."[64]

Peter Fidler had hoped to settle a fortune on his male heir two centuries after his own birth date. Surely he would be amazed to learn today, after a similar nearly two-century interval, that we still do not understand what drives the repetitive rhythmicity of the synchronous cyclic phenomenon he described.

THE NINETEENTH-CENTURY TRADE IN SWAN SKINS AND QUILLS

C. Stuart Houston, Mary I. Houston, and Henry M. Reeves

Much has been written about the economics of the fur trade in what is now Canada, but little attention has been paid to one important side item of trade, swan skins and swan and goose quills. Few naturalists have realized what prodigious quantities of these two items were shipped from Hudson Bay to Britain. Such overharvesting, superimposed on subsistence use, no doubt contributed to the Trumpeter Swan's decline in numbers and range, and to some decline in the Tundra Swan as well. In an attempt to learn more about the eighteenth-century swan populations in western Canada, we consulted the records in the Hudson's Bay Company Archives (HBCA), Provincial Archives of Manitoba (PAM), in Winnipeg.

Samuel Hearne, who in 1774 founded Cumberland House (in present-day Saskatchewan), the first inland trading post of the Hudson's Bay Company, reported that the Indians killed Trumpeter Swans "in such numbers that the down and quills might have been procured in considerable quantities at a trifling expence; but since the depopulation of the natives by the small-pox ... no advantage can be made of those articles, though of considerable value in England." Hearne also noted that one Trumpeter Swan egg was "a sufficient meal for a moderate man, without bread, or any other addition."[1] One thirty-pound (14 kg) swan, the heaviest bird in North America, provided a great deal of food for hungry people, especially welcome in spring after a winter diet of fish and pemmican.[2] Hearne also reported that the swan skins, "of which the Company have lately made an article of trade," became a trade item only near the end of the eighteenth century. We began our investigation of the trade in swans by consulting the definitive text, *The Fur Trade in Canada: An Introduction to Canadian Economic History*, by Harold A. Innes. Since he fails to mention or index swan skins, our search led elsewhere.

A scattering of early historical nest records confirm that Trumpeter Swans bred on the northern Great Plains from Iowa up through North Dakota into Manitoba and Alberta, north into the parklands and the southern mixed forest.[3] Lumsden suggests that this larger species needed an ice-free period of at least 140 days, and preferably 154 days, to complete its

DIRECTIONS
FOR
CURING AND PRESERVING
Swan Skins.

AS Swans are generally shot, let the Feathers be pulled out while the Bird is hot, with the greatest care not to injure the Fine Down underneath; the Blood that may be upon the Skin may be washed off with Soap and Water, and well dried afterwards; the Bird will be skinned much easier after the Feathers are pulled, and must be done in this manner,—

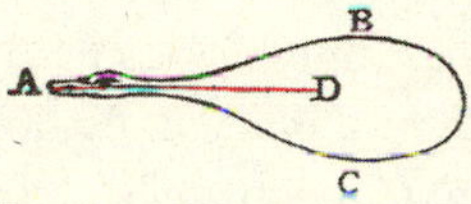

A the Head and Neck,
B ⎫
C ⎬ the Body,
D the Cut from the Neck to the Breast.

The Back must not be cut, and it is not necessary, as the Bird may be skinned by drawing it through the Part cut from the Head to the Breast; when dry, it may be turned the Pelt or Skin outside, which will protect the Down from being injured by Grease, &c. and will come safe in Packages any distance.

N.B. The Swan Feathers should not be mixed with those of the Goose.

Printed by R. Causton & Son, 21, Finch-Lane, Cornhill, London.

Figure E.1
Directions for curing and preserving swan skins, circa 1817. HBCA A.63/22, fo. 3.
Courtesy Judith Hudson Beattie and HBCA, PAM

long breeding cycle, coinciding nicely with what we know about the northern edge of their presumed breeding grounds, south of that of the smaller Tundra Swan.

How common was the Trumpeter east of the Rockies in the 1600s, when they were "to a great extent invulnerable to Indians hunting with bows and arrows"?[4] By extrapolating from the 1968 density of one swan per 20 km^2 in Alaska, and projecting this over an area of 2.6 million km^2 of the potential 4 million km^2, Lumsden made a credible estimate for AD 1600, a "best guess" of 130,000 Trumpeter Swans.[5] He felt that annual removal of 3,000 to 5,000 swans from this population for swan skins, possible only after the advent of firearms, "would not have been an excessive harvest." Such analysis, of course, presumes no drop in population over two or more centuries. There is good evidence that swans were common at Moose Factory in 1674, but following more than a century of gun use by natives and whites alike, the swan flight into James Bay had almost disappeared by 1783–85.[6]

In the interior, before Caucasian settlement, Trumpeter Swans were fairly common. Immediately after Alexander Henry the Younger built Fort White Earth #1, on the North Saskatchewan River at the mouth of White Earth River,[7] he reported that his men brought 70 swan skins from nearby Smokey Lake on 23 July 1810; eight days later he had 208 swan skins in stock.[8] Archaeological excavations of the 1810–13 occupation of this fort have confirmed the presence of three bones of the Trumpeter Swan as a dietary item.[9]

At the 1913 meeting of the American Ornithologists' Union there were predictions that "this magnificent bird was nearing extinction; and would soon disappear forever."[10] Henry Coale could find, in a survey of all museums, only sixteen specimens (five of them from Canada) collected between 1856 and 1909 and preserved with authentic data. E.S. Cameron reported in a letter to Coale on 30 April 1914: "Twenty years ago Trumpeter Swans were common in [north-eastern] Montana, and used regularly to winter here, but are now on the verge of extinction."[11] By 1935 only sixty-nine Trumpeter Swans were known to exist in the wild, although we now know in retrospect that unrecorded flocks also inhabited parts of Alaska and the Grande Prairie region of Alberta.[12]

The Trumpeter was not the only swan to be affected. The Tundra Swan disappeared as a breeding species from the general area of Hudson Bay for over 150 years, from before 1800 through 1969; they have since returned to breed in northern portions of Manitoba, Ontario, and Quebec.[13]

SWAN SKINS

Judith Hudson Beattie has allowed us to reproduce the official Hudson's Bay Company directive that told traders how to prepare swan skins of the highest value (Figure E.1). This printed "broadside" dated from circa 1817, when R. Causton and Son had their office at 21 Finch-lane.[14] Nearly a half-century earlier the governor and committee had given very similar instructions to Ferdinand Jacobs, on 12 May 1773, saying, "We are informed that the skin of the Wild Swan may turn out [to be] of some utility in our trade."[15]

The number of swan skins listed for sale in London increased from a low of 168 in 1804 to a high of 4,305 in 1813. Such soaring numbers must have represented an increase in effort or value or both, rather than a change in the availability of swans of both species. The peak years were 1826, 1827, 1830, 1834, and 1837, with 5,817, 5,052, 5,636, 7,918, and 6,600 swan skins

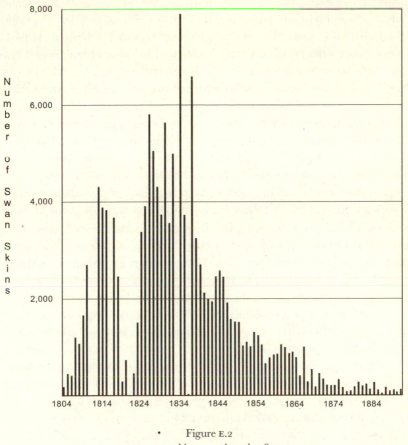

Figure E.2

HBC swan skin annual totals, 1804–91

respectively sold in those years, the five highest on record (Figure E.2). In 1858, 1,038 skins were sold, the last year over 1,000. Average annual numbers for the decades ending in 1820, 1830, 1840, 1850, 1860, 1870, 1880, and 1890 respectively were 2,735, 3,379, 3,876, 1,897, 981, 627, 190, and 120. The final recording was of 108 swan skins in 1891.[16]

These figures correspond only loosely with totals obtained by Roderick Ross MacFarlane from the HBC fur catalogues "for sale in London." From 1853 to 1877 the HBC sold a total of 17,671, or an average of nearly 707 swan skins a year. The HBC catalogues listed seven good years (1853 to 1856, 1861, 1862, and 1867), with sales ranging in those years between 985 and 1,312, the maximum reached in 1854. There were seven poor years (1870 to 1877), with returns varying between 338 and a minimum of 122 in 1877. MacFarlane also provides helpful details concerning the major sources of these skins. From 1854 to 1884, inclusive, Athabasca District turned out 2,705 swan skins, nearly all of them from Fort Chipewyan. Mackenzie River District supplied 2,500 skins from 1863 to 1883. From 1862 to 1877, Fort Resolution, Great Slave Lake, contributed 798. For 1889 Athabasca traded but 33, as against 251 skins in 1853. In 1889 and 1890, Isle-à-la-Crosse, headquarters of the English River District, sent out only 2 skins each year.[17]

Why were these large swans rarely mentioned by explorers and traders passing through? We think it was because the swans retreated to large marshes and small lakes for breeding and moulting, off the path of those travelling by river canoe routes or overland.

Questions remain. Which species was killed for the swan-skin trade, Trumpeter or Tundra (Whistling) or both? Where were they taken? How many were taken only in spring or fall migration? How many in summer, before the immatures could fly, and how many during the adult flightless summer moult? What were these swan skins used for? Partial answers require melding of information from archaeologic sources, fur-trade archives, and published historical records. The following information is the best we have.

Both species were taken, the Tundra Swan only in migration. The most authoritative comment is by Dr John Richardson, who collected birds at Cumberland House and Carlton House in Saskatchewan in the 1820s. He reported: "It is to the Trumpeter that the bulk of the Swan-skins imported by the Hudson's Bay Company belong."[18] As late as 1859 Blakiston concurred that the Trumpeter was still the commoner species at Carlton.[19]

A breakdown of skins traded by individual trading posts on Hudson Bay is available for 1804 through 1819 (Table E.1). Almost 97 per cent (25,218 of 26,052 swan skins) came through York Factory, the direct link with the plains and parkland areas of what are now the prairie provinces, far south of the nesting area of the Tundra (Whistling) Swan.

For the subsequent two decades, 1821 through 1841, numbers of swan skins taken in each trading district have been transcribed from HBCA B.239/h/1 (Table E.2). The first four areas, in descending order of importance, were the Saskatchewan River (Carlton and Edmonton, which traded with Indians on the plains), Churchill River (then called English River), Athabasca, and Swan River. Each of these localities was south of the nesting area of the Tundra Swan. With the exception of 1804, these figures correspond exactly with numbers for sale in London for those years. These inland localities delivered their furs to York Factory.

In Europe, a swan was a principal food item at banquets,[20] as well as a prime item of clothing. In medieval times in England ownership of swans was a mark of social standing. As a food item, the set-piece for banquets, a

Table E.1

Swan skins from Hudson Bay, listed for sale 1804–1819

Year	Churchill	York Factory	Severn	Albany	Moose	Eastmain	Total six posts
1804		168		37			205
1805		435					435
1806		396					396
1807	28	1133		27		4	1192
1808	9	997	1	60			1067
1809	6	1576		70			1652
1810		2706					2706
1811		0					0
1812		0					0
1813	213	4066		4		16	4305
1814		3853			16	15	3884
1815	348	3487					3835
1816		0					0
1817		3666			4		3670
1818		2462			1		2463
1819		273			6		279
Total	610	25,218	1	198	27	35	26,089

Compiled by H.M. Reeves from HBC Fur Trade Importation Book, HBCA, PAM a.53/1

swan was extremely expensive, selling in London in 1274 for 3 shillings (36 pence), compared to 5 pence for a goose and 4 pence for a pheasant. The punishment for stealing swan eggs was imprisonment for a year and a day. For stealing a swan, the thief had to pour wheat over the suspended bird, hung by its beak, until the tip of the beak was covered; the wheat was then paid to the swan owner. Swan skins were also used in the manufacture of powder puffs for women.[21] One wonders, with the large numbers involved, whether the skins might also have been used for coat-linings? Swan skins were also used for making vests, ceremonial robes, and for ornaments such as epaulets on uniforms of high-ranking officials.[22] Swan skins were still valued at five pence (twenty-five cents) a pelt in 1899. The beautiful snow-white down of the Bewick's Swan, when dressed by a furrier, made women's neck-pieces (boas) "of unrivalled beauty."[23] *Early American Dress* illustrates a loose jacket, brought over from Holland by Dutch settlers in New York, "trimmed with fur or swansdown around the neck, down the front, and around the bottom."[24] In Russia the tough skin and warm soft pelt were used for wallets, jackets, and caps. Swan skins were also used for quilts, pillows, and mat-tresses.[25] Jack London, in his short story, "The nighborn," mentions a robe of swan-skins.[26] In *By the Shores of Silver Lake* by Laura Ingalls Wilder, Pa Ingalls shoots a swan and Ma Ingalls makes a small swan cape for the youngest girl.[27]

The demand for swan skins was no respecter of species. Earlier in this cen-tury Frank M. Chapman found "hundreds of thousands" of Black-necked Swan skins in an Argentina warehouse awaiting shipment to be made into women's powder puffs.[28]

SWAN AND GOOSE QUILLS

The flight feathers of all birds have long been known as quill-feathers. Some clues to the increasing interest in quills as a commercial item derive from entries in the 1942 edition of *Encyclopaedia Brittanica*. Under "Feather": "The earliest period at which the use of quill feathers for writing is recorded is the 6th century ... Only the five outer wing feathers of the goose are useful for writing, and of these the second and third are the best, while left-wing quills are more esteemed than those of the right as they curve outward and away from the [right-handed] writer using them ... Swan quills indeed are better than those from the goose."[29] Under "Pen": "In 1809 Joseph Bramah devised and patented a machine for cutting up the quill into separate nibs by dividing the barrel into three or even four parts, and cutting these transversely into "two, three, four and some into five lengths."[30]

Until improved nibs were invented, quills required continual sharpening. The average clerk would use more than one new quill pen per day. "Bed-feathers" were first sold by the HBC in the London market in November 1736,[31] and "goose quills" were first offered in December 1774.[32] Swan quills were in great demand and sold (in bundles of twenty-five or one hundred) at the highest price. Swan and goose quills from Hudson Bay sold in increasing numbers, from 58,000 in 1799 to 566,632 in 1814 and 655,030 in 1817 (think of the tedium involved in counting them!) (Figure E.3). Sales peaked at 1,112,000 in 1834 (the year that a grand total of 18,732,000 quills were sold in London)[33] and 1,259,000 in 1837. At a maximum of ten quills per bird, 1837 saw the sacrifice of over 100,000 swans and geese from Rupert's Land.

There is only a modest correlation between the numbers of swan skins and the number of quills sold in a given year. The four years when no skins and no quills were sold in London were years when the annual ship or ships were unable to return to England; each gap was followed by a higher total the following year.[34]

Table E.2

District fur returns, swan skins, 1821–1842

Fur trade district	1821	1822	1823	1824	1825	1826	1827	1828	1829	1830	1831	1832	1833
Athabasca		260			1404	1407	1413	738	2133	71	1286	1202	485
English (Churchill) R.	52	428	1647	1057	890	1289	800	1128	1271	778	975	1108	
Cumberland House	24	35	112	222	264	390	232	20	44	46	51	176	196
Saskatchewan	256	370	408	533	991	1200	1215	1445	1603	2356	2045	2002	1616
Swan River	34	208	189	624	900	375	447	192	139	0	154	507	556
Lower Red River	17	20	5	60	209	45	0	8	2	19	24	64	66
Upper Red River (Minnesota)	10	48	74					8	3	27	26		3
Winnipeg (Lake)		8	6	34	27	20	12	25	16	6	18		
Lac la Pluie	37						1						
Norway House		2	2	4	15		2	4		1	1	20	20
Island Lake		2		7	24	10	1	4	7	6	14	11	11
Severn		2		3									
Nelson River		63	123	78	120	18	6			12	13	12	6
Churchill		18	18	51	110	90	62	96	362	168	275	327	154
York Factory			73					830		422			
Western Caledonia – nil													
Totals, each of 21 years	432	1462	2660	2670	4954	4844	4191	4498	5580	3922	4882	5429	3040

Table E.2 / continued

Fur trade district	1834	1835	1836	1837	1838	1839	1840	1841	Total
Athabasca	216	340	776	745	736	716	562	560	15050
English (Churchill) R.	534	639	797	783	502	456	384	310	16655
Cumberland House	178	131	71	57	31	42	37	23	2382
Saskatchewan	1447	1087	904	925	628	433	536	481	22491
Swan River	537	488	408	430	385	166	103	118	6960
Lower Red River	246	225	376	199	147	200	171	209	2312
Upper Red River (Minnesota)									199
Winnipeg (Lake)									172
Lac la Pluie									38
Norway House	11	13	8	13	41	28	7	18	210
Island Lake	5	2	4	1	1	7	5	1	123
Severn									5
Nelson River	16	14	18						499
Churchill		159		68	182	42	154	108	2444
York Factory		48	158	258					1789
Western Caledonia – nil									
Totals, each of 21 years	3190	3146	3520	3479	2653	2090	1959	1828	71329

compiled by Mary I. Houston from B239/b/1, HBCA, PAM   Italics = four posts with highest totals

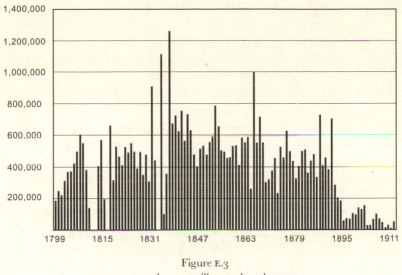

Figure E.3
HBC goose and swan quill annual totals, 1799–1911.
Listed for sale by the HBC, London. Compiled by H.M. Reeves from HBCA A.53/1

In general, sales of the prime "Hudson Bay quills" and of swan skins both peaked in the 1830s. Quill numbers did not fall off as quickly as did swan skins, and remained relatively high through 1891.

At Fort Edmonton, the only source to specifically identify quills as being from swans, 810 swan skins and 460 swan quills were collected in 1810–11, 1,206 skins and 450 quills in 1811–12, and 1,316 skins and 2,740 quills in 1812–13.[35] Other listings of quills may well have been a combined total of both goose and swan quills.

Finlay's informative book *The History of the Quill Pen* shows that at one time crow quills, used for architectural drawing, fetched as much as 9 shillings per 100; turkey quills, for law writing, 7 shillings; domestic goose quills, 15 shillings; and "Hudson's Bay quills" and swan quills each as much as 63 shillings per 100.[36] In England huge flocks of geese were farmed mainly for their quills: in 1812 nine million geese were plucked for the domestic market. The quills of the wild geese from North America were even more highly regarded, since "the best quills came from the coldest countries." Swan quills were even better, "a single swan outlasting as many as fifty made from goose quills." The five largest feathers from each wing were used. The first primary was called a pinion; the second and third were labelled "seconds," and the fourth and fifth, confusingly, "thirds." By tradition, swans'-quill pens were left full feather.[37]

Quills were obviously big business: twenty-seven quill and pen manufacturers and dealers were listed in Pigot's London Directory in 1822, while Newcastle-upon-Tyne had three. Though metal pens became available in the 1820s, most writers and almost all lawyers preferred the quill, as it "enables an expert Scribe to both text and engross in a better style, and to cut the letters more clearly."[38] The last large year for quills from Hudson Bay was 1865, when the total was just one thousand short of the million mark. Numbers dropped to 59,000 in 1895, reflecting increasing competition from the development of metal pen-nibs. In the last two years on record, 1911 and 1912, 12,000 and 52,000 quills respectively were sold (Figure E.3). Manufacture of metal pen-nibs became common in the United States in the 1860s, but it is apparent that some writers in England did not switch for another half-century. As late as 1894, one firm supplied the India Office with more than two million quill pens, and in 1908 swan pens were sold with gold- and silver-plated tips. The last quill company closed its offices in London in 1954, when computer punch-card systems were already in evidence![39]

TRUMPETER SWAN POPULATIONS IN NORTH AMERICA

Bones from early historical sites suggest that the Trumpeter Swan suffered from more drastic declines than other large birds such as the Sandhill and Whooping Cranes. All three species fared poorly after settlement – driven out as land was ploughed and marshes drained. Trumpeters began their decline at least a century earlier than the cranes. Originally breeding from at least Kentucky and from Chesapeake Bay north to the Maritime provinces and wintering south to northern Florida, Trumpeters quickly disappeared from eastern North America as humans advanced inland.[40] Undoubtedly, subsistence taking of its eggs and meat as prime food items antedated recorded history, but later demand for the Trumpeter's skins and quills speeded its demise. As Banko summarized in his classic monograph in 1960, "The effects of such exploitation on the far-flung breeding populations of this species for more than 125 years must have been devastating and largely responsible for its extermination over vast regions, particularly in the heart of its Canadian breeding range."[41]

We strongly suspect that the pre-1900 falling-off in numbers of Canadian swan skins sold each decade in London reflected overharvesting of these large birds, aggravated by collecting of both the swans and eggs in season for food, especially after bison numbers fell drastically in mid-century.

Extinction of the Trumpeter Swan was narrowly averted at the beginning of the twentieth century. With protection, numbers have increased in a gratifying manner, such that the Pacific Coast population in Alaska increased to 9,500 individuals by 1991, while the Rocky Mountain population (including northern Alberta) increased elevenfold to 2,200 individuals. The restored interior population had 629 free-flying birds by 1993, and began re-occupying suitable beaver ponds in the Porcupine Hills of east-central Saskatchewan in 1986.[42] Trumpeter Swan reintroduction programs are gaining speed wherever they have been attempted. In southern Ontario they began in 1982; by 1 September 1995 there were 82 Trumpeters flying free, and one year later, 123. Twenty-nine wild pairs laid eggs in southern Ontario in 2001.[43] The Trumpeter Swan recovery has been sufficiently successful that the species has been de-listed from the federal endangered-species list. However, the dangers of overharvesting, especially in the face of inadequate information, should be obvious from the history of its exploitation.

HOW DID THE CANADA GOOSE GET ITS NAME
BEFORE THERE WAS A CANADA?

C. Stuart Houston

The above question was posed by Dr Bernice Capusten of Red Deer, Alberta. Bernice, a former medical student of mine who chose to specialize in my field of radiology, is the daughter of the late Tony Capusten, an expert in mushrooms and photography.[1] Hers is an inspired question, and the answer becomes a lesson in history.

Because of its supposed resemblance to the bustard in Europe, the early French explorers, beginning with Cartier in 1635, called this large goose the *outarde*.[2] This was not an apt name, the bustard and the goose being completely unrelated, with different habits, and resembling each other only in size. Later English explorers called it the grey goose or, from its call, the honker.

My initial reply to Bernice, published in the *Blue Jay*, was based on the information in six consecutive check-lists of the American Ornithologists' Union, stating that the Linnaean name was "based mainly on" Mark Catesby's Plate 92. The first two check-lists, in 1886 and 1895, had failed to list a type locality; the third, in 1910, gave it as "Canada"; the fourth, in 1931, as "in Canada"; only in the fifth check-list in 1957 did the AOU committee add "based mainly on Mark Catesby's Plate 92" and make a ruling that "Canada = city of Quebec." Thus Quebec City is now the official type locality for the Canada Goose.[3] This restriction of the type locality to one city is in marked contrast to the forward-thinking Linnaeus, who more than two centuries earlier had used *canadensis* to encompass a very much wider area that included Hudson Bay. These check-lists led me to infer that the name had originated with Catesby.

My article prompted Alan Brown of Oakville, Ontario, to make several visits to the Royal Ontario Museum and the Thomas Fisher Library at the University of Toronto. With some difficulty, Brown gained access to a precious volume by Francis Willughby published in Latin in 1676. This great work had been seen through the press by John Ray and published posthumously.[4] Ray's biographer, C.E. Raven, notes that Willughby's book "laid the foundation for serious scientific progress ... a new epoch in its special field."[5] Willughby named, described, and illustrated the Canada Goose.[6] As he was writing in Latin, he gave it the Latin binomial of *Branta canadensis*, fifty-six years before Catesby and fully eighty-two years before Linnaeus proposed binomial Latin names as the standard.

One must now presume that both Catesby and Linnaeus had merely used the name they knew had been bestowed by Willughby. Willughby's phrase *Locum titulus indicat* inferred that the bird illustrated came from "Canada." John Ray, in his 1678 translation of Willughby into English, rendered this as "The title shews the place whence it comes."[7] As Alan Brown said in his covering letter to me: "What could be plainer? Or more obscure?"

Where, when, and how did Willughby become familiar with a goose from North America? I wrote to Clinton Keeling in Guildford, Surrey, to inquire. As early as 1665, he replied, during the reign of Charles II, pinioned Canada Geese were among the king's wildfowl in St James's Park adjacent to the Royal Aviaries and Birdcage Walk. An escaped Canada Goose was shot on the Thames in 1731, and by 1785 domesticated flocks were present "in many gentlemen's seats." By 1845 there were free-flying flocks in seven counties.[8]

In 1750, George Edwards used the name "Canada Goose," and added that "They are found in Canada, and are brought also to us from New England and Hudson's-Bay."[9] Three other Hudson Bay species illustrated by Edwards were named *canadensis* by Linnaeus eight years later: the Golden Eagle,[10] Sandhill Crane,[11] and Spruce Grouse.[12] In this way Linnaeus greatly extended the area considered to be Canada.[13]

As Bernice suggested, the name "Canada" did not come into official use until 1791, when the Constitutional Act of Canada divided Quebec into the provinces of Upper Canada and Lower Canada. In 1841 they were joined to form the Province of Canada, and in 1867 they were joined with Nova Scotia and New Brunswick to form "One Dominion under the name of Canada."[14] Further, the name *Canada* is derived "from the Huron-Iroquois *kanata*, meaning a village or settlement." On 13 August 1535 Jacques Cartier was told, by two Indian youths he was bringing back from France, that the route "to Canada" lay to the south of Anticosti Island. By "Canada" the two young men meant the village of Stadacona, the site of present-day Quebec City. Cartier's use of "Rivière de Canada" was followed by Champlain in 1604. François Du Creux's book *Historia Canadensis* used the term in 1664 to refer to the banks of the St Lawrence River and the gulf of the same name. In 1762, three years after the conquest of Quebec by James Wolfe, General Thomas Gage said that the "limits between Canada and Louisiana" had never been clearly described.[15]

The name Canada Goose was thus well established long before Canada became an official name. The legal use of the name Canada, however, was but official recognition of the name that had since 1535 been widely used to describe an ever-enlarging area that centered on the St Lawrence River basin.[16]

CREE NAMES IN USE AT HUDSON BAY IN THE EIGHTEENTH CENTURY

compiled by C. Stuart Houston and Mary I. Houston,
with regularization of Cree orthography and organization of Cree headings
by Arok Wolvengrey and Jean Okimâsis[1]

The Cree language is a descriptive language and, as George Cardinal says in his introduction to the *Alberta Elders' Cree Dictionary*, "is a beautiful language"; it is also an intricate language. We agree wholeheartedly that this language must be treasured and preserved.

The Cree Indians around Hudson Bay were known in the eighteenth century as "Home Indians," and spoke what is now referred to as the Swampy Cree dialect. Distant from the bay, other dialect groups with self-explanatory names included Plains Cree, Woods Cree, and Moose Cree.[2] Swampy Cree, as yet lacking a dictionary, is the dialect most in use around Hudson Bay. However, some of the words in this appendix appear to be representative of the "th" dialect, or Woods Cree, suggesting a more easterly location for speakers of this dialect than is the case today, or simply the use of inland visitors to the Bay as informants. Not only were the Cree nomadic, but those from inland, bringing a variety of dialects, travelled up to a thousand kilometres to deliver their furs to the bay. Today, some Swampy Cree words are identical to those used in Plains Cree and Woods Cree, some are similar, and others are quite different. Obviously geography explains some of the difference – there are no whales and walruses on the plains and no badgers at the bay.

The Plains Cree use only an "s" sound whereas the Swampy Cree use both the s and š which is pronounced "sh". Hence a duck in Plains Cree is *sîsîp*, pronounced "seeseep" and in Swampy Cree is *šîšîp*, pronounced "sheesheep." Similarly the Plains Cree and Swampy Cree names for Yellowlegs are *sêsêsiw* ("saysaysoo") and *šêšêšiw* ("shayshayshoo"), respectively.

Arok Wolvengrey points out that the common word for "bird" varies as follows: *pithîsîs* in Woods Cree (any word with "th" is a Woods Cree word); *piyêsîs* in Plains Cree (the "y" dialect; Wolvengrey 2001); *pinêsîs* in Swampy

Cree (the "n" dialect); *pilêsiw* in Moose Cree (the "l" dialect; Ellis 2000). With the exception of the Moose Cree form, all dialect forms are diminutives derived from a base: *pithîsiw* in Woods, *pinêsiw* in Swampy and *piyêsiw* in Plains.[3] Evidence from Howse's work in 1844 indicates that the distribution of Cree dialects has changed over nearly two hundred years, for the "th" dialect then was in wide use at the bay, where it has since been supplanted by "n" and "l" dialects.

The present compilers (CSH and MIH) have merely copied what is available. Then, with the help of language professionals from the Saskatchewan Indian Federated College, Arok Wolvengrey and Jean Okimâsis, the names have been alphabetized by Cree entries. To find a Cree name, readers are advised to scan all names beginning with the same letter. "Loon," spelled "makwa" in the past, is here listed under the more correct *mwâkwa*.

It was fortunate that the various English-speaking collectors of specimens near Hudson Bay took the trouble to record the names then in common use by the Cree. The compilers did their best, without the benefit of modern linguistic conventions.

Among English-speaking fur traders, naturalists, and explorers there was a marked variation in phonetic spellings: for example "amisk" or "omisk" for beaver (*amisk*),and "aukuskou", "awkiskow", "oc-kiss-cow", and "yaw-kis-co" for sharp-tailed grouse (*âhkiskow*). Berries were rendered as "min-nick", "menuck" or "meena."[4] The Ruffed Grouse was rendered as "pus-pus-cue" by Samuel Hearne; the modern phonemic or orthographic representation is *paspaskiw*. Standardized orthography has been in sporadic use for three decades, but only in full use in Cree dictionaries published in 1998 and 2001.

Large, edible birds were of great value and were more likely to have a Cree name. Waders (e.g., the now extinct Eskimo Curlew was then both numerous and a supreme delicacy)[5] and the Sora Rail were especially sought for food. A young eagle had a different name from an adult eagle in both Cree and English. Rarely, one species had two, three, or four Cree names. Small birds were of less interest (with the exception of obvious species such as the chickadee, robin, and Gray Jay), because they were difficult to collect: before the days of "dust shot" for museum collectors,[6] a blunderbuss might blow a little bird to smithereens. Further, little birds were rarely eaten, with the notable exception of the Snow Bunting: "they eat very fine in a pye" said Andrew Graham. For most species, terminology has remained constant; the sincere attempts of unskilled English-speaking men to render Cree words into English are of interest, and sometimes offer amusement. James Isham, the first of the compilers listed here, perhaps had the least skill in this regard, and Dr John Richardson, the latest, did the best. Richardson studied birds on the

Saskatchewan River at Carlton (Plains Cree), at Cumberland House (largely Swampy Cree), and at the bay (Swampy Cree), but did not differentiate between dialects.

On occasion, the fur trader would ask a name and fail to recognize that the respondent had reported the sex of the bird pointed at – thus a name beginning with *nâpê-* indicated a male and *nôsê-* a female. Often a name had a prefix, *apiši-* for small, or *miši-* for large. A few names were onomatopoetic, "kawkaw" for a corvid (cf. *kâhkâkiw* "raven"), "ho-ho" for the Great Horned Owl (cf. *ôhow* "owl"), "ha-ha-way" for the Long-tailed Duck, and *pisk* for the Common Nighthawk.

An item without use was less likely to be given a name. T. F. Ball had a tour of Cumberland House with Lily McAuley, a Cree woman who knew the Latin and English names of certain plants yet gave the same Cree name to a succession of different plants that had no specific use in Cree society. In contrast, aboriginal people may have additional terms for fine nuances of difference among items important to their survival. The most striking example known to us is the number of separate terms required by Eskimo people in Alaska to describe ice age and thickness (22), ice conditions and movement (16), and sea-ice topography (47), as reported by Richard K. Nelson from Port Hope, Alaska.[7] A similar rich vocabulary for particular objects, unknown to all but the most discerning of visiting white people, was encountered by Jared Diamond in New Guinea.[8]

Diamond's studies remind us that Caucasian ignorance was probably the greatest handicap in compiling Cree terms. The questioner was unable to learn the name of a bird unless he recognized it himself and asked its Cree name. The relative paucity of bird names in the standard early Cree-French and French-Cree dictionary of Father Lacombe[9] is more an indication of Lacombe's ignorance of ornithology than of the Indians' lack of interest or knowledge. Isham's list of Cree bird names offers unequivocal evidence that the Cree knew of species for which Isham did not know an English name. Of the various early sources for the following lists, only Dr John Richardson had sufficient knowledge of plants and animals to ask for a large number of their names. David Meyer (personal communication) tells me that First Nations people on the Red Earth reserve, east of Carrot River, Saskatchewan, recognize more bird species than the average Caucasian farmer nearby.

Cree and other Indians at times may possibly have tried to please their questioners (including Graham, Hutchins, and Richardson) by inventing a name on the spur of the moment. Richard Glover addressed this: "However primitive a heathen savage the aboriginal Indian might appear to the comfortable and well-to-do, he still had his code of good manners. That code forbade him to disappoint people, and other investigators have told how often they found that Indians thought it more important to give an answer likely to please the questioner than to give the correct answer or to admit they knew no answer."[10] A few names included herein may be mere descriptions.

Not only were there problems in committing an oral language to paper but the "cultural" adaptations so necessary for survival in a harsh climate meant that the original inhabitants of Hudson Bay had a different approach to nature than Caucasian fur traders. Traders were the interlopers whose commercial success depended on the assistance and cooperation of the Indians. Battiste and Henderson, in *First Nations Education in Canada: The Circle Unfolds*, tell us that "processes of categorization are not part of Indigenous thought ... Indigenous scholars choose to view every way of life from two different but complementary perspectives: first as a manifestation of human knowledge, heritage, and consciousness, and second as a mode of ecological order ... we [Europeans] reject the concept of culture ... and instead connect each Indigenous manifestation as part of a particular ecological order. ... those who are possessors of [Indigenous] knowledge, often cannot categorize it in Eurocentric thought." Further, "Indo-European languages and worldviews are based on nouns and most Aboriginal languages are not ... Indication that Aboriginal people were attaining knowledge of a very different nature and purpose from Western peoples is evident in Aboriginal language and culture."[11]

First Nations people had no reason to subdivide as scientists do. Both members of a pair of similar species, the Marbled Godwit and the Hudsonian Godwit, the Black-capped Chickadee and the Boreal Chickadee, the merlin and the kestrel, the gyrfalcon and peregrine, gulls and jaegers, lynx and bobcat, perch and pickerel, shared one Cree name. All grebe species shared the same name. Several Arctic animals had a similar root, *wâpi-*, to indicate their white colour: *wâpask*, polar bear; *wâpihêw*, ptarmigan; *wâpahkêsiw*, arctic fox. Other names included *osâw-* for yellow, or *kaskitê-* for black.

Traditional ecological knowledge, some of it spiritually based, of First Nations people around the bay, has become a topic of recent interest. The summer 1997 issue of *Northern Perspectives* was devoted to this topic, with excerpts from the book *Voices from the Bay*.[12]

Modern spellings and Standard Roman Orthography (SRO) diacritical marks, equivalent to accents used in other languages, are provided for many Cree names in the following list. SRO has been used consistently only in very recent books: *The Student's Dictionary of Literary Plains Cree*, by Wolfart and Ahenakew, and especially the two-volume *nêhiýawêwin: itwêwina / Cree: Words*, compiled by Arok Wolvengrey. For Cree Grammar, see Okimâsis and Ratt, *Cree: Language of the Plains*.[13] For modern spelling and diacritical marks, the reader should consult the introductory chapter on Cree pronunciation and orthography in Wolvengrey 2001, the source for many of the terms in the following lists. When, for geographic reasons, a word is missing from Wolvengrey, or when the usage of Faries is closer to that of the early traders, selected Cree names are offered from the 1938 Anglican English-Cree and Cree-English dictionary of Richard Faries,[14] or from the *Alberta Elders' Cree Dictionary*, written by Nancy Leclaire and George Cardinal, and edited by Earle Waugh.[15] However, forms from these sources have usually been regularized to the Standard Roman Orthography (i.e., when in italics).

Waugh/LeClaire/Cardinal correctly state that "Writing the sounds of Cree has always caused great problems for dictionary writers." In reading these recent entries, remember that: *c* is pronounced as the "tch" in "catch"; the long *â* is pronounced somewhat like the "a" in "father" (though perhaps "fa" in "do, re, mi, fa" is better); the long *ô* is pronounced as in "host"; the long *î* is pronounced as the "ea" in "bead"; the long *ê* as the "a" in "acorn" or the "ei" in "eight".

Even though Cree has no "r" sound except in the Attikamek dialect which does not figure here, insertion of "r" by an Englishman did occur. However, its use merely meant that a vowel sounded similar to vowels in his own speech. For example, the Cree name for Blackfoot, *ayahcithiniw* in Woods Cree, was recorded as "Archithinue."

The reader will recognize that a number of modern geographic names have been based on Cree names for birds, mammals, and plants. Cutler (1994) refers to these "Native American loanwords." Watch for Amisk and Namekos lakes, Makwa, Moosomin, Saskatoon, and many others. In Saskatchewan, an Indian Reserve is named Peepeekisis for a former chief (*pîhpîkisîs* means "little falcon.")

Arok Wolvengrey has been a marvellous resource during the preparation and presentation of this appendix. In particular, he suggested that the list be alphabetized by the Cree terms, rather than by English, allowing for entries for each species to be grouped together despite disparate English spellings. Within each entry, the names that most closely approximate modern use are given first, hence not in strict English alphabetic order.

We hope the following imperfect but valuable list of animal and plant names, in local use between 1750 and 1830, may be of interest to naturalists, anthropologists, linguists, and future compilers of Swampy and/or Woods Cree dictionaries.

SOURCES AND ABBREVIATIONS

AEW = Arok Elessar Wolvengrey, notes

CSH = C.S. Houston, notes. Occasional insertion of spelling transcribed from original mss E.2/10.

E29 – E.2/9, Hudson's Bay Company Archives, Provincial Archives of Manitoba (HBCA/PAM) contains 107 bird entries of 92 species.[16]

E210 – E.2/10, HBCA/PAM, contains 114 bird entries of 100 species, with Cree names of 134 birds, 14 fish, 1 snake, 1 turtle, 1 toad, 14 insects, 32 mammals and 24 plants.[17]

E.2/10 lacks three woodpeckers from the last four lines of E.2/12.

E212 – E.2/12, HBCA/PAM, published by Williams, G., ed., 1969, *Graham's Observations*, Hudson's Bay Record Society, volume 27 (HBRS 27). Contains 119 bird, 14 fish, 4 amphibian, 13 insect, 43 mammal, and 28 plant entries with Cree names. Because this is the published version, it is listed before E.2/9 and E.2/10.

E213 – E.2/13, HBCA/PAM, contains 106 bird entries, 103 with Cree names of 92 species.[18]

Faries – Faries 1938. *A Dictionary of the Cree Language* (Toronto: Synod of the Church of England in Canada).

FBAm – *Fauna Boreali-Americana. Vol. 1, The Mammals, 1828, and Vol. 2, The Birds*, 1831–1832. Dr John Richardson's version of 118 Cree and other Algonquin origin names for birds, 12 for fish, and 44 for mammals.

Forster – *Philosophical Transactions* 62:382–433, 1772. Forster gives 24 Cree names supplied by Graham in 1771 for 20 species of birds and 2 of fish.[19]

Hearne – Hearne 1795. Page numbers are from the Glover edition, 1958. Cree names are provided for 12 birds, 4 mammals and 4 plants.

Hood – Robert Hood, artist and midshipman with the first Franklin expedition (Houston 1974), painted birds at Cumberland House in the winter of 1819–20. He shared Cree names for eight species of birds and one fish; five species had not been given Cree names by Richardson.

Hutchins – Hutchins' Royal Society 1772 list to accompany specimens sent back to England. Contains 70 bird entries for 64 species, with 98 Cree name entries for birds, 4 for fish and 39 for mammals.[20]

HutchinsAppx – pages 368–379 in HBRS 27, Appendix C, 368–379, from the Appendix to E.2/10. Contains 11 new bird species plus 5 species already mentioned in earlier combined account, E.2/12. Seventeen Cree names are given for 16 bird species, 1 frog, 1 mussel and 1 mammal.

Isham – Isham's Observations, 119–131, edited by E.E. Rich, 1949. Contains 61 Cree names for birds.

JRAppx – Richardson's "Botanical Appendix" (VII) to Franklin's *Narrative of a Journey to the Shores of the Polar Sea in the Years 1819, 20, 21, and 22*. Cree names are given for 20 plants, and a few mammals and birds.

JRtxt – Richardson's chapter 3, "Account of the Cree Indians," pp. 59–93 in Franklin (1823), provides Cree names for 16 mammals, 10 fish and 12 plants.

lit: – literally (e.g., *amisk-ôhow* literally means "beaver-owl").

Marten – Marten's "birds in a box" provide 19 Cree names for birds, but for about half of these the species is not known.

Pennant – Thomas Pennant, *Arctic Zoology*, 3 volumes, 1792.

Waugh – Waugh/LeClaire/Cardinal 1998.

Wolfart – Wolfart and Ahenakew 1998.

Wolvengrey – Wolvengrey 2001 or personal communication.

SAULTEAUX/OJIBWAY NAMES

Che-chish-kae-wainae, Hudsonian Godwit, FBAm

Kanwan-seek, Red-breasted Merganser, FBAm [possibly in Cree: kanwâ-nasihk; cf. *asihk* – AEW]

ALGONQUIAN NAME

Quaequaeshew, Gray Jay, FBAm [Algonquin term; *kwêkwêšiw* if Cree]

VOYAGEURS' TERM

Naccaysh [Laquaiche, Scott and Crossman], Goldeye, FBAm

SPECIES WITH NO KNOWN CREE NAME

Avis Natalis, Philadelphia Vireo, Hutchins, HutchinsAppx, E210

Blackpoll Warbler, E212

Bohemian Chatterer = Bohemian Waxwing, E212

Red-headed Woodpecker, Hutchins, HutchinsAppx, E210

Golden Woodpecker or Yellow-shafted Flicker, E212

Hairy Woodpecker, E212

"Hawk's Eye," Black-bellied and Lesser Golden-Plover, Hearne, Pennant

"Hudsonias Crane," Great Blue Heron, E212, E29, E210, E213

Hummingbird = Ruby-throated], E212 [cf. Waugh: "âmopewayisîs", *âmôw-piyêsîs*; Wolvengrey: *âmôwi-piyêsîs*]

Innominata, Tree Sparrow, E212, E29, E210, E213

Innominata, unidentified Sparrow, E212, E210, Hutchins

Scaup Duck of Pennant, Greater Scaup, E212, E29, E210, E213

"Sea-Pigeon," Black Guillemot, Hearne

White Whiskijohn, Northern Shrike, Forster

ALPHABETIC LIST OF HUDSON BAY AREA
CREE NAMES FOR BIRDS, 1770–1830

by Arok Wolvengrey and Jean Okimâsis

In the following list, Cree terms are spelled in italics, following Standard Roman Orthography (SRO). When "(ak)" appears in parentheses at the end of a Cree word, this indicates the plural spelling. Unless otherwise stated, words are from Wolvengrey 2001 with additional material by Arok Wolvengrey and Jean Okimâsis, Cree language professionals from the Department of Indian Languages, Literatures, and Linguistics at the Saskatchewan Indian Federated College (SIFC). Forms from additional sources may occur in square brackets representing a non-SRO spelling, but they have usually been regularized to the SRO. Main headings are given when the derivation seems certain. Questionable forms begin with "??", used as an abbreviation to indicate "possibly" – sometimes with a suggested but uncertain derivation in brackets. The most uncertain suggestions are headed "????"; they are not italicized and should not be taken as SRO representations. An unaccented letter comes ahead of a letter with a diacritical mark. For example, a comes before â. Indeed, each is treated as a separate letter of the alphabet. Similarly s appears before š, a letter whose use is largely restricted to eastern Cree dialects. Hyphenated phrases have been placed ahead of un-hyphenated phrases.

English names are the official names in modern use; they often differ from the vernacular name used at the time.

amisk-ôhow [lit: beaver owl]
   Amisk-Oho, Long-eared Owl, Williams, E29, E210, E213
   Ammisk-oho, Long-eared Owl, FBAm

amiskošip [lit: beaver duck, i.e. lives in beaver ponds]
   Omiskasheep, Hooded Merganser, Williams, E29, E210, Hutchins, E213
   Omiska-sheep, Hooded Merganser, "beaver duck" FBAm
   also: Keeneeconais-sheep, Hooded Merganser, FBAm [Algonquin
      term, although possibly *kînikonêsišip* "sharp mouth duck"]

apisci-mikisiw [lit: little eagle; cf. *mikisiw*]
   Apisk Mickesew, Golden Eagle, Williams, E29, E210, E213
   Appsik-Meekeeshew, immature Bald Eagle, FBAm

apisti-kihîw [lit: small eagle; cf. *kihîw*; falcon = "onicayikowiw" in
  Waugh, possibly *onôcayîkowêw* "frog hunter"]
  Apeestae-kaeoo, Peregrine Falcon, FBAm

apisti-pithês or *apisti-pithêw* [lit: small grouse]
  Apistapethais, Rock Ptarmigan, Hutchins
  Ap pis top pe thau, rock partridge = Rock Ptarmigan, Isham

apistišip [lit: small duck]
  Apeesteh-sheep, Green-winged Teal, FBAm
  Apistesheep, Green-winged Teal, Williams, E29, E210
  Appistis Sheep, Small [Hutchins'] Canada Goose, E213

apistiskiš(iš) [lit: small goose; cf. *apisci-niska* (Wolvengrey) and *apisci-
  niskis* (Mandelbaum, orthography regularized)]
  Apisteeskeesh, Hutchins' Goose, FBAm
  Apisteskiss, Small [Hutchins' small subspecies of] Canada Goose,
    Hutchins, HutchinsAppx, E210.
  Apistiskish, Small [Hutchins'] Canada Goose, Williams, E29, E210,
    E213
  Pisk-a-sish, Hutchins's Goose, Hearne
  Piskeshish, Small Canada Goose, Hutchins

apiši-kâhkâkîs [lit: small raven = magpie]
  Appish a'cawcaw sish, mag pye = Black-billed Magpie, Isham [cf.
    apisci-kâhkâhkîs Wolvengrey]

apiši-kiyâsk [lit: small gull]
  Akeesee Keask, Bonaparte's Gull, E210
  Akeseey Keask, Bonaparte's Gull, Williams, E29, E213
  Akesey-keask, Bonaparte's Gull, FBAm
  Ap pish e'ke ash'k, a sort of swallow, or a tern = ??, Isham

apiši-kîskisiš
  Ap pis h e'kis ke sish, small winter bird = ??Redpoll, Isham

apiši-mwâkwa [lit: little loon]
  Ash e'moquo, Lun'n = Loon, Isham

Asse-Moqua, Red-throated Loon, Williams, E29, E210
Asse-Mouqua, Red-throated Loon, Hutchins
Asse Mouqua, Red-throated Loon, E213

apišišipiš [lit: small duck; cf. *apištišip*]
Apesheshepis, Teal, Hutchins

apišîšišit sihkihp [lit: Grebe which is small; cf. *sihkihp*]
Pishishiset Seekep, Horned Grebe, Williams, E29, E210, E213

??
Aseehum, [unidentified], Marten

?? [possibly: (asicowi)*kocêšiš* "little ?? beak"]
Ashecowecochesish, Red Crossbill, Williams E25
Asitchchouachashish, Red Crossbill, Williams, E210, E29, E213
Asitch,chou,achasish, Red Crossbill, Hutchins

asihk [Merganser; cf. Faries]
Assick, Red-breasted Merganser, Williams, E210, E29, E213
Ouseek, Red-breasted Merganser, Hutchins
Seek, Common Merganser, FBAm

ašikan-pithîsîs [lit: sock-bird]
Sheegun-peetheesees, Snow Bunting, FBAm

athiwâk miši-cîkiskawišiš [lit: even bigger ??]
Athawuck-Misha-Checkiskaweshish, Short-billed Dowitcher, E213
Athawuck-Missha-Checkiskaweshish, Short-billed Dowitcher, Williams, E29, E210

?? [possibly: *athîkîmowišip* "frog-eating duck"]
Atheekemow-weeshep, American Wigeon, FBAm
Atheikimoasheep, American Wigeon, Williams, E29, Hutchins
Atheikimo Asheep, American Wigeon, E213
Atheikimoksheep, American Wigeon, E210

atihkamêk-kiyask [lit: whitefish gull]
Tickomeg-Keask [no Indian name in E.2/13], Herring Gull, Williams, E29, E210

atihko-šêšêšiw [lit: caribou sandpiper; cf. *šêšêšiw, sêsêsiw*]
   Attickew-shaeshaeshew, Solitary Sandpiper, FBAm
   Attickue-Shesheshew, Solitary Sandpiper, Williams, E29, E210
   Attickue-Shesheshue, Solitary Sandpiper, E213
   Atticku-sha-she-shu, Solitary Sandpiper, Pennant 3:173

ayaskîmow-kiyâsk [lit: meat-eating or Eskimo gull]
   Esquimaux-Keask, Parasitic Jaeger, Williams, E29, E210 (twice), E213
   Esquimaux-Keask, Glaucous Gull, Williams, E210
   Esquimaux Shesheep, Common Eider, Williams, E29, E210, E213

âhâsiw [crow]
   Hahasue, American Crow, Williams, E29, E210, E213
   Haw-haw-sew, American Crow, FBAm

?? [possibly: *âhâwêw(ak)* or *âhâwêhwêw(ak)*; Long-tailed Duck, formerly
     Oldsquaw]
   Haw haw haw wa wuck, [old wife sea bird], Isham
   Hahaway, Old-squaw, Williams, E29, E210, E213
   Har-har-vey, Old-squaw, Forster
   Hawhawway, Oldsquaw = Long-tailed Duck, E210
   Haw haw way, Oldsquaw, Hutchins, HutchinsAppx

âhkamiwišîš(ak) (??) [phalarope]
   Accummee-sheeshick, Red-necked Phalarope, FBAm ["willing, make
     an effort" – R. Gallernault]
   Accumushishick, Red-necked Phalarope, Williams, E29, E210, E213
   Ackumeoushish, Red-necked Phalarope, Hutchins, HutchinsAppx,
     E210

âhkiskow [partridge, pheasant; cf. Faries]
   Aukuskou, Sharp-tailed Grouse, Hutchins
   Aukuskow, Sharp-tailed Grouse, Williams, E29, E210, E213; Pennant
   Awkiscow, Sharp-tailed Grouse, FBAm, Hearne
   Oc-kiss-cow, Sharp-tailed Grouse, Forster
   Yaw kis co, pheasant [= Sharp-tailed Grouse], Isham

?? [possibly: âhkwâtiko-*pithêšîš*; *âhkwâtiko* ?? and *pithêšîš* "bird"]
   Aquateko-Pethayshish, Savannah Sparrow, Williams, E29, E210, E213
   Aquateko-Pethaysish, Savannah Sparrow, Hutchins

cahcahkâthow [blackbird; cf. Faries]
  Chachacathew, Rusty Blackbird, Williams , E29, E210, E213
  Chauchuckithou, Rusty Blackbird, 45
  Chaw chaw ko low, bird not known to Isham, Isham [suggests Moose
    Cree: *cahcahkâlow*]
  Chuck-chuck-kaioo, Rusty Blackbird, FBAm [suggests Plains Cree:
    cahcahkâyow]
  Chuck-chuck-kawthoo, Rusty Blackbird, FBAm
  Ohau chuc y thau, Rusty Blackbird, E210

cahcahkiw or *tahtakiw* [Pelican; Faries gives: *sasakiw* or *cahcakiw*]
  Sass-suckue, White Pelican, Williams, Hutchins
  Sha su que, pilacan [sic] = Am. White Pelican, Isham

?? [possibly: cikipašiš(ak)]
  Chikipushishuck, Laughing Goose = White-fronted Goose, Hutchins

?? [possibly: cimâtanasiw]
  Chematunnasue, Arctic Tern, Marten

??
  Che-chish-kae-wainae, Hudsonian Godwit, FBAm [a saulteur = Saul-
    teaux/Ojibwa name]

?? [possibly: *cîkiskawišiš*; cf. *athiwâk miši-cîkiskawišiš* "Short-billed Dow-
itcher"]
  Chaekis-coo-awschesh, Semipalmated Sandpiper, FBAm:
  Checkiskashish, Spotted Sandpiper [k a typo in HBRS 27??] E213
  Chechiskashisk, Spotted Sandpiper, Williams, E29, E210
  Chekiskuashish, Semipalmated Sandpiper, Williams, E29, E210,
    Hutchins, E213

cîpay-ômišîš [lit: little ghost owl; cf. *cîpay-pithîs*]
  Cheepomesees, Boreal Owl, FBAm
  Shipmospish, Boreal Owl, Pennant
  Shipomosish, Boreal Owl, Williams, E29, E210, E213
  Shipomosish, Boreal Owl, Hutchins, FBAm
  Shipomospish, Boreal Owl, Forster, Pennant

cîpay-pithîs [lit: little ghost grouse; cf. *cîpay-ômisîs*]
  Cheepai-peethees, Boreal Owl, FBAm "death-bird"

?? [possibly: cîstihkwanêniwišip]
Cheesteh-qua-nan-weeshep, Blue-winged Teal, FBAm ["shoestring duck" – Richardson]

ithinišip [mallard; lit: ordinary duck; cf. *iyinisip*; cf. *ithinisiw-šîšîp*]
Athinue-Sheep, Mallard,**
Ethee-ne sheep, Mallard, E213
Etheenieship, Mallard, Williams, E29, E210
E'thi thu ship, Indian duck, Isham [suggests: *ithithiwišip*]

ithinito-ômisiw [lit: real or ordinary owl; cf. *ômisiw*, *ithinito-*]
Atheeneetoo Omeesew, Great Gray Owl, FBAm
Atheeneetoo Omeesew, Great Gray Owl, ["real or Indian owl"] FBAm
Omisscu-Athinnito, Great Gray Owl, Hutchins
Omissew-Athinnetoc, Great Gray Owl, Williams, E29, E210, E213

ithiniw-mwâkwa [lit: common loon; cf. *mâkwa*]
Ethinnew-Moqua, Common Loon, FBAm
Ethinue moquo, Indian lun = Loon, Isham

ithiniw-pithêw [lit: common, ordinary or Indian grouse]
Ethi nue pe thau, Indian partridge = Ruffed or Spruce Grouse???, Isham

ithinîsiw [lit: s/he is intelligent]
Eethin-neesew, Osprey, FBAm
[cf. *ê-misikitit piyêsîs (kâ-môwât) kinosêwa* "a big bird (which eats) fish") in Waugh and *apiskway* in Wolvengrey; Waugh's is a description, not a name – AEW]

ithinîsiw-mikisiw [lit: common or intelligent eagle; cf. *mikisiw*]
Ethenesue Mickesue, Golden Eagle, E210
Ethinesue Mickesew, Golden Eagle, Williams, E29, E213

ithinîsiw-šîšîp [lit: ordinary or intelligent duck; cf. *ithinišip*]
Ethin-neesew sheesheep, Mallard, FBAm

?? [possibly just a phrase: *êwako êsa kiyâsk* "that's a gull, I suppose"]
Eko sha ke ash'k, mackerall bird, [a gull, tern or phalarope], Isham

?? [possibly: kanwânasihk; cf. *asihk*]
  Kanwan-seek, Red-breasted Merganser, FBAm [Saulteaux term]

?? [possibly: kasâpâtâ-*pithêšiš*; cf. *pithêšiš*]
  Kausarbacta Pethashish, White-throated Sparrow, Hutchins, Hutchins-
  Appx, E210

?? [possibly: kasâpâtâsiš]
  Cusabatasish, White-crowned Sparrow, E213
  Cusabtasish, White-crowned Sparrow, Williams, E29, E210
  Cussawbawtawseesh, White-crowned Sparrow, FBAm

kaskasikwâtam [cf. nâpê-kaskasikwâtam; note: scoters are the blackest
     ducks – CSH]
  Cuscusicatum, Scoter, Hutchins
  Cuscusiquatum, female Black Scoter, Williams, E29, E210, Hutchins,
     E213
  Cuscusitatum, Black Scoter, FBAm

kaskitêw-wêhwêw [blue goose; lit: black wavey]
  Cathacatew Whewe, Blue Goose, Williams, E29, E210, E213
  Cathcatew-waewaeoo, young Snow Geese, FBAm
  Kurs ka ta wa we wuck, blue weywe = Blue Goose, Isham, Hutchins
  Kuthkiteouwayway, Blue Goose, Hutchins

kaskitêwistikwân [lit: black head]
  Cathchcatew kestequon, Black-capped Chickadee, E210 quoting
     Latham 540

kaskitêwišip [lit: black duck]
  Cuskeetaw-sheep, Ring-necked Duck, FBAm

?? [probably: *kâ-mišâk piponâsiw*; lit: hawk which is big; if so, ungram-
     matical inanimate verb used to describe an animate being – Wolven-
     grey]
  Kommashoc-Paypaynayseu, Gyrfalcon vs Northern Hawk-Owl!!!,
     Hutchins [looks like pêpênêsiw; possibly *piponâsiw*]
  Kommayshoc-Paypaynayseu, Gyrfalcon, Williams, E29, E210, E213

kâ-pitikôš [lit: one who is doubled up; cf. *kâ-pitikow* (Chief) Thunder-
     child]

Cabaducutch, Northern Hawk-Owl, Forster
Cabeticouch, Northern Hawk-Owl, Williams, E210
Cabeticuch, Northern Hawk-Owl, Forster
Cabeticuche, Northern Hawk-Owl, Hutchins ["Paypathekauseu"]
Cabetituch [misspelled], Northern Hawk-Owl, Pennant
Cob-a-dee-cooch *or* Cobadecootch, Northern Hawk-Owl, Hearne,
    Williams, FBAm

kâhkâkiw [raven; cf. Faries]
Caw caw qua, Raven, Isham
Kacakew, Common Raven, Williams, E29, E210, E213
Kaukauk, American Raven, Hutchins
Kaw-kaw-gew, Common Raven, FBAm

kâhkâkiwišip [lit: raven duck; possibly an error of record or
    identification; cf. *âhâsiw*]
Caw caw qua ship, jackdaw = American Crow, Isham

kicikîskošîš [chickadee; see also *picikîskošîš*]
Kiss-kiss-heshis, Black-capped Chickadee, Hearne
Kiss-kiss-ke-shish, Black-capped Chickadee, Forster
Kiss-kiss-she-shish, Black-capped Chickadee, Pennant

?? [possibly: kihci-minakîhamâkašiš; cf. ocîciminâkâmâkâšîš]
Kechemin,nuc,ea,ha,mau,ka,shish, American Redstart female, E210,
    Hutchins, HutchinsAppx

kihci-wâpisiw [lit: great swan]
Keetchee wapeeshew, Trumpeter Swan, FBAm [Wolvengrey]

?? [possibly: kimiwanipêkotêšiš; lit: little rainwater beak ??]
Kimmewanapaykuteshish, Magnolia Warbler, Hutchins, Hutchins-
    Appx, E210

?? [possibly: kinocinêw-kiyâsk; cf. *kiyâsk* "gull"]
Kenoucheneou Keask *or* Kenoucheneow Keask, Arctic Tern, Hutchins,
    Williams, E29, E210, E213

?? [possibly: kiskwâthinapišiš]
Hisquathenapishish [Kisquathenapisish is preferred spelling, E213],
    Semipalmated Plover, Williams, E29, E210

Kisquathenapishish, Semipalmated Plover, Hutchins, E210
Kisquathenapisish, Semipalmated Plover, E213

?? [ends in -*šip* "duck"]
Ketuiaukasheep, Common Goldeneye, Hutchins

kithîw(ak) [eagle]
Hethewuck [Kethewuck is preferred spelling, E210, E213]
Kethewuck Mickesue, Golden Eagle, E210, E213 [cf. *mikisiw*]
Koeoo, Golden Eagle, FBAm [suggests Plains Cree: *kihîw*]

kiyâsk [gull; dim: *kiyâskos* "tern", Faries]
Ke ashk, Sea swallow = Arctic Tern, Isham
Keask, Herring Gull immature, Williams, E29, E210, Hutchins,
    "Herring Gull", Hutchins, E213

?? [possibly: kîkâwâšiw]
Gega washue, Ruddy Turnstone, E210
Gehawaeshew, Ruddy Turnstone, FBAm
Gehawashue, Ruddy Turnstone, Williams, E29, E213

kîsikâwi-pinêsîs [lit: day bird; Swampy Cree; also Woods Cree: *kîsikâwi-*
    pithêsîs]
Keesquaw-the-napaesees, Semipalmated Plover, FBAm
    "keesekow-wipinaysees"

kotak cîkiskawišiš [lit: another sandpiper]
Hetuck-Chekiskaweshish [Ketuck .. is preferred spelling, E213], Least
    Sandpiper, Williams, E29, E210
Katuck Chekiskaweshish, Least Sandpiper, E213
Ketuck Chekiskaweshish, Least Sandpiper, E213

kwêkwêšiw
Quaequaeshew, Gray Jay, FBAm [Algonquin term]

?? [possibly: (kwês)kwêskipâtam]
Que she ba tum, not known to Isham, Isham
Quesqueshepatum, seaweed-eater, unidentified, Marten

mâkwa [loon; see *mwâkwa*]

mâthâpisiw [lit: ugly swan; cf. *wâpisiw*]
Mathapeseu, Swan, Hutchins

?? [possibly: *mâthatimosiš*; lit: ugly puppy]
Mar te ti mu sish, ugly duck = ??, Isham

mâthi-mwâkwa [lit: ugly loon; cf. *mâkwa*]
Mathe-Moqua, Arctic Loon, Williams, E29, E210, E213

mêmêw [lit: pigeon; cf. *mîmîw, omîmîw*]
May-may, Pileated Woodpecker, Hutchins, HutchinsAppx, E210 [cf.
misi-pâhpâscês = Large Woodpecker]

mihtawakay-ômisiw [lit: eared owl; cf. *ohtawakêhow, ôhow*]
Natow okey Omisseu, Great Horned Owl, E210
Netowoky Omissew, Great Horned Owl, Williams, E29, E213
Netowky-omeesew, Great Horned Owl, Hutchins, FBAm

mikisiw [lit: eagle]
Kethewuck Mickesue, Golden Eagle, E210, E213 [cf. *kithîw(ak)*]
Meekeeshew, Bald Eagle, FBAm ["bark of dog": mistakenly translating
the similar form *mikisimo-*]
Me ke sue, Eagle, Isham
Mekissew, Eagle sp., Hutchins
Mickesew, Bald Eagle, Williams, E29, E210, E213
Mickesew, Golden Eagle, Williams, E29

mikisiw-pâhpâstêw [lit: eagle woodpecker]
Meekesew-paupastuow Yellow-bellied Sapsucker, FBAm

mikisîsiš [lit: small eagle]
Meekeeseeseesh, yearling Bald Eagle, FBAm

?? [possibly: *miminihk*; cf. Faries: ominihk "Grey Duck"]
Me me nick, a kind of duck = ? Shoveler, Isham
Mimenick, Northern Shoveler, FBAm
Mimmenic, Whistling Duck, ?Shoveler,
Mimmenick, Whistling Duck, Williams [composite], E29, E210, E213
perhaps also: Ap-Nemenick, Common Goldeneye [Duck], Marten 7

misi-kiyâsk [lit: big gull; cf. *miši-*]
   Misse-Keask, Gull, 73 [New, Not in HBRS 27]

?? [*misi-*?? "big ??"]
   Missequagukawow, ["big ..."], Surf Scoter, Williams E210 51, E29, E213
   Missequaqukawow, Surf Scoter, Hutchins
   Me she qua two wa quish, sea fowl, not known to Isham, Isham

mistahi-cîkiskawišiš [lit: large sandpiper; cf. *cîkiskawišiš*]
   Mistehay-checkiskawaeseesh, Sanderling, FBAm
   Mistehay-Chekiskaweshish, Sanderling, Williams, E29, E210, E213

?? [possibly: *mistahi*-koskowânapišiš "large ??"]
   Mis ta kus qua na pe sish, Stone Plover = Yellowlegs ???, Isham

mistahi-niska [lit: large goose; pl: *mistahi-niskak*; cf. *niska*]
   Mistahay Nesscock [pl], Canada Goose, E213
   Mistehay-Neescah, Canada Goose, FBAm
   Mistuhay Nesscock [pl], Canada Goose (large) E210
   also: Che po me sish, Cobed wuch or Bustard = Large Canada Goose,
      Isham

mistahi-pâhpâkipitêsiw [cf. "corncrake", Faries; cf. *miši-pâhpâkipitêsiw,*
      pâhpâkipitêsiw]
   Mistahaypaupaukepetesue, Sora, Hutchins, HutchinsAppx, E210

mistahi-piskwâpiwiw [cf. *miši-piskwâpiwiw*]
   Mistepesquapewew, Common Goldeneye, Williams, E29, E210, E213

mistiko-pithîw [lit: wood grouse]
   Meescootaeshoo, Spruce Grouse, FBAm [Algonquin term]
   Me stick a'pe thau, wood partridge = Spruce Grouse, Isham
   Mistic-apeetheyoo, Spruce Grouse, FBAm
   Mistic-Apethou, Spruce Grouse, Williams, E29, E210, Hutchins, E213
   Mistick-a-pethow, [** name??....], Hearne

miši-kiyâsk [lit: big gull]
   Meshetheash, unidentified Gull [heash = typo for keask - CSH], Marten

miši-pâhpâkipitêsiw ["corncrake", Faries; cf. *pâhpâkipitêsiw, mistahi-pâhpâkipitêsiw*]
  Misha-Pawpakapatesew, Sora, Williams, E29, E210

miši-piskwâpiwiw [cf. *mistahi-piskwâpiwiw*]
  Meesheh-pesqua-pewew, Common Goldeneye, FBAm

miši-pithîw(ak) [lit: big prairie chicken]
  Chepethewuck, Greater Prairie Chicken, Williams, E29, E210

miši-wâpiskacân [lit: big white whiskeyjack; cf. *wîskacân, wâpiskacân*]
  Meesheh wappisk kaechawn, Northern Shrike, FBAm

?? [possibly: *mišikiti*-kiskwâthinapišiš "big ??"]
  Misshiggitee Kisquathenapishish, Ruddy Turnstone, Hutchins [New, not in HBRS 27]

mišišip [lit: big duck; scoter or eider]
  Mesheshep, unidentified Scoter, Marten
  Me she ship, winter duck = Scoter, Isham
  Mishshesheep, Common Eider, Williams, E29, E210, E213
  Missesheep, Common Eider, Hutchins

mišithîw [lit: big grouse]
  Mish e 'thau, a cock or hen = ? Grouse, Isham

??
  Mettick-Esquimaux, Common Eider, E210

?? [possibly: *(kâ-)mîhâwêsit* "one who is hairy"]
  Mehauvesick, unidentified bird, Marten

mîmîw(ak) [lit: pigeon; cf. *omîmîw; mêmêw*]
  Me me wuck, a pidgeon or dove = Passenger Pigeon, Isham
  Memewuck, Passenger Pigeon, E213
  Memewusk, Passenger Pigeon, Williams, E29, E210
  Mimewuck, Passenger Pigeon, FBAm

mohkahasiw [bittern; cf. Faries]
 Mockcohosew, American Bittern, FBAm
 Mockkohosue, American Bittern, Williams, E29, E210, E213
 Wothquokuseu, American Bittern, Hutchins

?? [possibly: môhcikanakišîš; cf. môhkocikanêšîš]
 Mochicanakasish, Red-breasted Nuthatch, Williams, E210, E213
 Mohchicanakasish [Machicanakasish? – CSH], Red-breasted Nuthatch,
  E29

?? [possibly: môhkocikanêšîš "little planer"; cf. môhcikanakišîš]
 Mohkeechae-cannaeshees, Pileated Woodpecker, FBAm ["hollow-
  cutter"– R. Gallernault]
 Mookutchicanakayshish, Wilson's Warbler, Hutchins, HutchinsAppx
  [note: two names may have been combined or confused here –
  AEW]

mwâkwa [loon; also: *mâkwa*]
 Moqua, Arctic Loon, FBAm

?? [possibly: nâciwêšiw(ak)]
 Nachchewayshewuck, Hutchins [??Lesser Golden-Plover]

?? [possibly: *nâpê*-kaskasikwâtam; lit: male ??; cf. kaskasikwâtam; another
  possibility for the prefix could be *wâpi*- "white"]
 Napew-Cuscusiquatum, White-winged Scoter, E213 [male]
 Nappew-Cuscusiquatum, White-winged Scoter, Williams, E210

niska [goose; plural: *niskak* "geese"]
 Neescah, Canada Goose, FBAm
 Neish cock [pl], grey goose = Canada Goose, Isham
 Neishcoock [pl], grey goose = Canada Goose, Isham
 Nescock [pl], Canada Goose, Williams, E29, E210
 Niscock [pl], Canada Goose, Hutchins

?? [possibly: *nîmiskwê-pithêšîš*]
 Nemiscu A pe thay shish, American Redstart male, HutchinsAppx,
  Hutchins, E210

nîpini-pithêšiš [lit: little summer bird]
 Nepin-Apethashish, White-crowned Sparrow, Hutchins

Nepin-Apetheyshish, White-crowned Sparrow, Williams, E210, E29, E213

ocêhcapisiw or *otêhtapisiw* [lit: "little rider" or "sits on top"]
Chechapishew, Lapland Longspur, Williams, E29, E210, E213
Checheppeseu, Lapland Longspur, Hutchins
Chee-chupeeshew, Lapland Longspur, Hutchins, FBAm
Chee-chup-peesew, "proper appelation of Lapland Longspur according to Hutchins", *not* Horned Lark of Forster, FBAm
Chi-chup-pi-sue, Horned Lark, Forster, Pennant
Ootay-tapaysew, Horned Lark, FBAm
Outaytaypayseu, Horned Lark, Hutchins, E213
Outaytaypaysew, Horned Lark male, Williams, E29, E210
U' che chu a sue, Lark, Isham
Wethaychapisheu, Horned Lark, Hutchins
Wethechepeseu, female Horned Lark, Williams, E29, E210
Wethecheppeseu, female Horned Lark, E213

ocicâhk [crane]
Ochee-chak, Sandhill Crane, FBAm

?? [possibly: ocîciminâkâmâkâšîš; cf. kihci-minakîhamâkašiš]
Oochae-chimmenaw-kawmawkaw-seesh, White-throated Sparrow, FBAm
Ouchechiminaukamaukashish, White-throated Sparrow, Hutchins
Ouchechiminawkamawkashish, White-throated Sparrow, Williams, E29, E210, E213

ohtawakêhow [lit: eared owl; cf. *mihtawakay-ômisiw, ôhow*]
Otowuck-oho, Great Horned Owl, FBAm

okîskimanašiw [kingfisher; also: *kîskimanašiw*]
Kiskemanasue or Kiskeman, Belted Kingfisher, Hutchins, Hutchin-sAppx, E210
Kiskeman-ethtecoo, Belted Kingfisher, Williams, E210
Okces-kae-mannaeshew, Belted Kingfisher, FBAm ["chopped off nose bird" – R. Gallernault]

onôcikinêpikwêšiw [lit: snake-hunter]
Annooch-ke-naepeek-quaeshew, Northern Harrier, "snake-hunter" FBAm

Ounuchshechesquaseu, Northern Harrier, Williams, E29, E210,
Hutchins, E213 [suggests: onôciciskwêsiw; misrecorded?]

osâwâ-ocicâhk [lit: yellow crane]
Sawack Uchechauk, Sandhill Crane, Williams, E29, E210, E213
Usa wa u'te chauk, Gray Crane = Sandhill Crane, Isham

?? [possibly: wêsâwâk piyêsiw "bird which is yellow/brown"; but if so, the
inanimate verb does not properly agree with the animate referant –
AEW]
Wasawuck apaeshew, Marbled Godwit, FBAm ["wasawuck" = color
brown [R. Gallernault] [Faries]

osâwâw-pithêšîš [lit: little yellow bird]
Oosowow-peetheesees, Yellow Warbler, FBAm +
Sowow-Pethayshish *or* Sowow-pethaysish, Yellow Warbler, Williams,
E29, E210, E213
possibly also: Cowessonnrisdocobreashish, little yellow bird, probably
Yellow Warbler, Marten

?? [possibly: *oskanithêw* or *oskanihêw* "bone partridge" ??]
Ooskammahaeoo, Rose-breasted Grosbeak, FBAm
Uscunethau, [bird, English name unknown to Isham], Isham

?? [possibly: *oskanithow*; lit: bone tail; cf. *oskana* = Wascana, "bones" ; cf.
oskuneyases = grosbeak, Faries]
Usecunethong, Pine Grosbeak, Marten
Wuskuneethow, Pine Grosbeak, FBAm
Wuskunithou, Pine Grosbeak, Hutchins
Wuskunithow, Pine Grosbeak, Williams, E29, E210, E213 38

?? [possibly: oskathacîš]
Uscathacheesh, Rock Ptarmigan, FBAm
Uscathachish, Rock Ptarmigan, Williams, E29, E210, E213

?? [possibly: otacikâkiw(ak)]
Utt tu che ka ke wuck, [bird, English name unknown to Isham = ?
Jaeger], Isham

otêh-kiyâsk [lit: heart gull]
Ootaw-kee-askee, Black-billed Magpie, FBAm

Oue-ta-kee aske, "heartbird," Black-billed Magpie, Forster, Pennant
Outa-keask, Parasitic Jaeger, Hutchins
Utay-Keask, Parasitic Jaeger, E213
Utey-Deask, Parasitic Jaeger, Williams, E29, E210, Hutchins
U'cha ke ash'k, Man of War, Isham

?? [possibly: othîkwâ(nâ)naw]
Oothee quan-nornow, Yellow-shafted Flicker, FBAm
Ou' the ca nau, bird not known to Isham, Isham
Ou-thee-quah-nor-now, Yellow-shafted Flicker, Forster

ôhow or *ôhôw* [Owl; cf. *ohtawakêhow* Great Horned Owl]
Ho-ho, Great Horned Owl, Hearne

?? [cf. *mohkahasiw*]
Pas ke ka we na sun nuck, Bittern, Isham

paspaskiw [ruffed grouse; partridge]
Puskee, Ruffed Grouse, Williams, E29, E210 ("Dr. Folster" [sic] written
   in later), Forster, E213
Pus-pus-cue, Ruffed Grouse, Hearne [paspaskiw, Wolvengrey]
Puspuskee, Ruffed Grouse, Forster, Hearne
Puspusquew, Ruffed Grouse, FBAm

pâhpâstêw [lit: woodpecker; cf. Faries]
Paupastaow, Downy Woodpecker, HutchinsAppx, E210
Pau pas taow, Downy Woodpecker, Hutchins
Paupastuou, Woodpecker E210, Three-toed Woodpecker, Hutchins
Paupastuow, Downy Woodpecker, FBAm, E213
Pawpastow [Paupastu] Three-toed Woodpecker, Williams, E29, E210

?? [possibly: *pâkahcowêšiš*, lit: "little ball-playing bird"]
Paukachowisish, Slate-colored Junco, E213
Paukachowishish, Slate-colored Junco, Hutchins
Pawkachowishish, Slate-colored Junco, Williams "genus uncertain",
   E29, E210
Pawkaw-choweeseesh, Slate-colored Junco, FBAm

?? [possibly: *pâpaninêsiw*; cf. *pêpênêsiw*]
Paupunenaysue, Gyrfalcon, E210
Pau pune nay sue, Gyrfalcon, Hutchins, HutchinsAppx

pâhpâkipitêsiw [rail; diminutive: *pâhpâkapitêsîs*; cf. Faries: "corncrake"]
  Paupaukapeteseu, Yellow Rail ("Corn Crake"), Hutchins
  Pawpakapaeteesees, Yellow Rail, FBAm
  Pawpakapatesew, Yellow Rail, E213
  Pawpawkkapetesew, Yellow Rail, Williams, E29, E210
  Pawpapwkaw-paeteesew, Sora [Rail], FBAm [see also: *mistahi-*, *miši-*]

pâhpithîkisiw [cf. Faries: pâpinakisiw "small owl"; cf. *pêpâthîkâsiw*]
  Pawpeereekeesue, Laughter, Marten [There is a Laughing ...]

pâwistikošip [lit: rapids duck]
  Pawawistick-weesheep, Harlequin, "cascade duck" FBAm

?? [possibly: *pêpâthîkâsiw*; cf. *pâhpithîkisiw*]
  Paypathekauseu, Northern Hawk-Owl, Williams, E29, E210,
      Hutchins91 *or* Kommashoc Hutchins91 [see also *kâ-mišâk*]
  Paypathekawsew, Northern Hawk-Owl, E213
  Paypaw thee-cawsew, Northern Hawk-Owl, FBAm

picikîskošîš [lit: chickadee; see also *kicikîskošîš*]
  Peche-ke-ke-shish, Boreal Chickadee, Forster; Pennant
  Pechekiskeshish, Boreal Chickadee, Williams, E29, E210, Hutchins, E213
  Peecheh-keesaeshees, Black-capped Chickadee, FBAm

pihpihcêw or *pihpihciw* [robin; cf. Faries]
  Peepeechew, American Robin, FBAm
  Pee-pee-chue, American Robin, Forster
  Pepechew, American Robin, Williams, E29, E210, E213
  Pepejou, American Robin, Hutchins

piponêsiw [lit: winter (bird); cf. Faries: *piponasiw* "partridge hawk"; cf.
      piponêsiw-kêhkêhk; also: *piponâsiw*]
  Peepooneeshew, Gyrfalcon, "winter bird" FBAm
  Pepoonasue, Gyrfalcon, Marten
  Pe pun sue, winter hawk = Gyrfalcon, Isham

piponêsiw-kêhkêhk [lit: winter-hawk; spellings suggest *pêpênêsiw-*; cf.
      piponêsiw; also: *piponâsiw*]
  Paypaynayseu-Kacake, Peregrine Falcon, E210, E213, E29, Hutchins
  Paypaynaysew Hacake, Peregrine Falcon, Williams, E210 22, E29 40

pithêpâkêsiw [cf. Faries: pânâpâkêsiw "snipe"]
    Pethaypacaseu, Common Snipe, E213
    Pethaypaukaseu, Common Snipe, Hutchins
    Pethaypawcaseu, Common Snipe, Williams, E29, E210
    Pethay-pe-ca-she, Common Snipe, Pennant

pithêšîš [lit: small bird]
    Apetha shish, "small ....", Pectoral Sandpiper, Hutchins
    Pe da sish, little birds, Isham

pithêw [fowl; grouse]
    Pe da 'u, a bird or fowl, Isham

pîhpîkišîš [lit: small falcon, kestrel or merlin; note: a Saskatchewan Indian
    Reserve has this name]
    Pecusish, Merlin, E210
    Peepeekeeshees, American Kestrel, FBAm
    Pepecooseesh, Merlin, FBAm
    Pepecusish, Merlin, Williams, E29, E210, E213
    Peepeequaisees, Sharp-shinned Hawk, FBAM [attributed by
        Richardson to the 'Monsonees' tribe at Moose Factory]

pîmikocêšîš [lit: twisted beak]
    Pemmoo-koo-chae-shees, White-winged Crossbill, "crooked beak"
        FBAm

pîskwa or *pîsk* [Nighthawk; onomatopoeic]
    Paisk, Nighthawk, Marten
    Paysk, Nighthawk, Hutchins, HutchinsAppx, E210
    Peesk, Common Nighthawk, Hutchins, HutchinsAppx
    Peesquaw, Nighthawk, FBAm

pîstêwâciwasow [lit: "he boils till foam appears on top"; possibly used as
    a sound-alike for the Meadowlark's song; cf. *otâpiskâkanêsîs* "little
    scarf-wearer"]
    Peesteh-atchewusson, Western Meadowlark, FBAm

poskacasiw [plover; cf. Faries]
    Pur ske chu nuck, a Plover, Isham
    Pus ku chusch'u, a Plover, Isham

?? [see *poskwacasiw* above]
  Pusquacheseu, Red or Hudsonian Godwit, Hutchins
  Pusquatishishue, Hudsonian Godwit, Williams, E29, E210, E213

?? [possibly: *paskopicêwišip* "weed-pulling (or plucking) duck"]
  Pus quo pu sha we ship, a kind of duck, Isham

sahkwâtamow or *sahkwatêmow*
  Saquatema, Rough-legged Hawk, 7 April 1772, Hutchins B.239/a/67,
  Saquatowmau, Rough-legged Hawk, Hutchins [sâkwahtamow]
  Saquatowmaw, Rough-legged Hawk, Williams, E29, E210, E213

?? [possibly: *sakitakâwišip* "thicket duck"]
  Su ke ta cowe' ship, a kind of duck, Isham

?? [??-*išiš*; identifiable only as referring to a small bird]
  Sasquaa-pisquanishish, Red Knot, Williams, E29, E210, E213

?? [possibly: *sasaskiw*; cf. *cahcakiw* or *sasakiw* "pelican"]
  Sus us cow, Hern = Heron, Isham

?? [possibly: *sâsâskikwê-pithîsiw* "frying bird"]
  Sasassquae-pethesew, White-fronted Goose, FBAm
  Sasasquepethesue, White-fronted Goose, Williams, E29, E210, E213

?? [possibly: (sâ)sâšaninipîšiw]
  Sahysashyninepeshew, Tree Swallow, Williams, E29, E210
  Sashun-peeshew, Purple Martin, FBAm

sêsêsiw or *sêsêšiw* [yellowlegs; cf. Faries]
  Sa-sa-shew, Greater Yellowlegs, Forster 411
  Sasashew, Greater Yellowlegs, FBAm

sêsêsîs or *sêsêšîš* [diminutive; cf. *sêsêšiw, šêšêšiw*]
  Sassasees, Lesser Yellowlegs, FBAm

??
  "Sea-Pigeon," Black Guillemot, Hearne

sihkihp [grebe, hell-diver; cf. Saulteaux: šinkihpîhs]
  Seekeep, Horned Grebe, FBAm

Sekeep, Horned Grebe, Williams, Forster, E29, E210, E213
Shinkepees, Horned Grebe, FBAm [Saulteur = Saulteaux tribe]

sikâk-pithîsiw [lit: skunk bird]
Seecawk-petheesew, Bobolink, FBAm "skunk bird"

sîsipâskwat-pithêšîš [lit: sugarmaple bird]
Seesebasquit-pethaysish, Evening Grosbeak, FBAm "sugar bird"

sîsîkisiw(ak) [cf. Faries: "a sea-pigeon"]
Sesekesewuck, Black Guillemot ("willick,"), Williams, E29, E210, E213
Sesekesewuck, Black Guillemot, FBAm

šêšêšiw [snipe, yellowlegs; cf. *sêsêsiw, sêsêšiw*]
Shesheshew, Greater Yellowlegs, Williams, E29, E210, Hutchins, E213

?? [possibly: *šîkisapâtim*]
She ke su partem, Surf Scoter, Williams, Forster

šîpihko-mîmîw(ak) [lit: blue dove]
Shepecum-Memewuck, Black-billed Magpie, Williams, E29, E210, E213
Shepecum-mewuck, Black-billed Magpie, FBAm [Maskegon tribe]

šîšîp [duck; cf. *sîsîp*]
She ship, duck, Isham

?? [possibly: *šîšîwinipêšiw*]
Shee-shee-winae-paeshoo, Bank Swallow, FBAm
Shishiwinepeshu, Bank Swallow, E213
Shishiwinnepayseu, Bank Swallow, Hutchins

takwâkišip [lit: "fall duck"; cf. Faries]
Tawquawgew-'sheep, Scaup, FBAm

thîkihtaw-wataniy-kiyâsk [lit: forked tailfeather gull]
Athekeetowwatunnee-Keask, unidentified Gull, Marten

?? [possibly: thothosikâsiw]
Tho ro sa ca see, a kind of hawk, Isham
Tho-thos-cau-sew, Short-eared Owl, Hutchins, quoted by FBAm
Thothosecauseu, Short-eared Owl, E213

Thothosecawsew, Short-eared Owl, Williams, E29, E210
Thothosekauseu, Short-eared Owl, Hutchins

?? [possibly: tikamâšiš or ocikâmâšiš]
Tecumashish, Redpoll, E213
Tecumasish, Hoary Redpoll, Williams, E29, E210
Tecumishish, Hoary Redpoll, Hutchins
Tecurmashish, Lapland Longspur [error, should be Redpoll], Pennant
Tecurmaseesh, Redpoll, FBAm
Tercurmashish, Redpoll, Forster 404 [Forster's error was copied by
    Richardson; there is no 'r' sound in CREE – CSH]
Uechacamashish, Redpoll, Marten

?? [possibly: *twêtwêšiw*]
Twae-twae-shew, Blue Jay, FBAm

??
Uvesick, unidentified Duck, Marten

?? [second element could be either *kihîw* "eagle" or *ôhow* "owl"]
Wannah-koeoo, Turkey Vulture, FBAm [Swampy Cree kenew *(kinîw)*
    = vulture, Faries]

wâkikotêsiw [lit: crooked beak; also: *wâkikocêsîs* "curlew", cf. Waugh]
Waukacuttayseu, Whimbrel or Hudsonian Curlew, E213 [Wading bird
    or curlew with crooked beak – CSH]
Waukacuttasew, Hudsonian Curlew, Hutchins
Wawkacuttayseu, Whimbrel or Hudsonian Curlew, Williams, E29,
    E210, E213
Waw-kaw-cuttaysew, Whimbrel or Hudsonian Curlew, FBAm
Wawkeecoottasue, Eskimo Curlew?, Marten
Woc ko ko ta sue, Curlew, Isham

?? [possibly: *wâpasko-pithêšiš* "whitebear bird" or *wipiskâ-pithêšiš* "dirty-
    bodied bird"]
Wapuska-Apatheyshish, Black-bellied and Golden Plover, Williams, E29
Wapusk-Apethaysish, Black-bellied and Golden Plover, E213
Waupuskapethasish, Black-belled Plover, Hutchins
Waw-pusk-abree-shish, Forster

Wipusk-a-pethaysish, Black-bellied and Golden Plover, E210
[also: "Hawk's Eye," Black-bellied and Lesser Golden-Plover, Hearne,
    Pennant]

wâpâ-cahcahkâthow [lit: white sharp-tail or white-blackbird]
    Waupawchauchuchithou, Albino Blackbird, species unknown,
        Hutchins, HutchinsAppx, E210

wâpâ-kiyâsk [lit: white gull]
    Wap pa ke as h'k, white gull, Isham   .

wâpâ-ocicâhk or *wâpocicâhk* [lit: white crane]
    Wapaw-Uchechauk, Whooping Crane, Williams, E29, E210, E213
    Wapow oocheechawk, Whooping Crane, FBAm
    Waupauchechauk, Whooping Crane, Hutchins

wâpâ-wêhwêw(ak) [white snow goose]
    Wapawhewhe, [white] Snow Goose, E213
    Wap pa wa we wuck, white goose = Snow Goose, Isham

wâpâ-wîskacân(is) [lit: (little) white whiskeyjack; cf. *wîskacân, miši-
        wîskacân*]
    Waapau-Whiskijohnish, Northern Shrike, Hutchins
    Wapaw-Whiskijohn, Northern Shrike, Williams, E29, E213
    Wapawa-Wisky john, Northern Shrike, E210
    Wap pa whisker John *or* Wap pis ka John, whisker jack [sic] = Gray Jay,
        Isham
    Wawpow-whiskae janneesh, Northern Shrike, FBAm "white whisky-
        jack"
    White Whiskijohn, Northern Shrike, Forster

?? [possibly: *wâpâkâthow(-ômisiw)* lit: white-tailed (owl)]
    Wapacathew-Omissew, male Snowy Owl, Williams, E29, E210, E213
    Wa pa cullu, white owl = Snowy Owl, Isham [suggests Moose Cree:
        wâpâkâlow]
    Wa pa cu thew, female Snowy Owl, E213
    Wap-a-kee-thou, Snowy Owl, Hearne
    Wapow-keethoo, Snowy Owl, FBAm
    Wawpekatheu, female Snowy Owl, Williams, E29, E210

wâpânowêsip(is) [bufflehead; lit: (little) white-tailed duck] [note: this
name was perhaps misapplied, since the bufflehead has a white-
marked head, rather than tail]
Wappano-'sheep, Bufflehead, FBAm
Wapew neway sepis, Bufflehead, E210
Waupennewaysepis, Bufflehead, Hutchins
Wawpennewaysepis, Bufflehead, E213
Wawpewwewaysepis, Bufflehead, Williams, E29, E210
also: Wakaishee-weesheep, Bufflehead, FBAm
         Waw-haisheep, Bufflehead, FBAm

wâpâwistikwân-mikisiw [lit: white head eagle, cf. *wâpi-kihîw*, Waugh;
cf. *wâpistikwân-mikisiw*]
Wapaw Estiquan Mickesew, Bald Eagle ad, Williams E29, E210, E213

wâpisiw [Swan]
Wa pa seu, Tundra Swan, E210
Wapasew, Tundra Swan, E29, E213
Wapesew, Tundra Swan, Williams
Wap pa sue, Swan, Isham

wâpiskacân [cf. *wâpâ-wîskacân, miši-wâpiskacân*]
Wap pa whisker John *or* Wap pis ka John, whisker jack [sic] = Gray Jay,
Isham

wâpistikwân-mikisiw [lit: white head eagle; cf. *wâpâwistikwân-mikisiw*]
Wapustiquan-Meekeeshew, mature adult Bald Eagle, FBAm

wâpithêw [ptarmigan; lit: white partridge; cf. Faries: "white ptarmigan"]
Wapethew, Willow Ptarmigan, Williams, E29, E210, E213
Wap pa tha'u, white partridge = Ptarmigan, Isham
Waupethou, Willow Ptarmigan, Hutchins
Wawpeethaeo, Willow Ptarmigan, FBAm

?? [possibly: wâpithîkosiš]
Wa pa tha ko sish,?? snowbird = Snow Bunting, Isham
Wapathecusish, Snow Bunting, Williams, E29, E210, E213
Waupethekeshish, Snow Bunting, Hutchins

wâpôhow [lit: white owl]
  Wa pa ho, white owl = Snowy Owl, Isham
  Wapohoo, Snowy Owl, FBAm = white owl

?? [possibly: *wâsâwakâpišiw*]
  Wasawuckapesew, Hudsonian Godwit, Williams, E29, E210
  Wasawuckapeshew, Hudsonian Godwit, E213

wêhwêšiš [lit: little snow goose; cf. *wêhwêw*]
  Waywayashish, Snow Goose, Marten

wêhwêw [snow goose or "wavey"]
  Waewae-oo, Snow Goose, FBAm
  Wayway, Snow Goose, Hutchins
  Way-way, Snow Goose, Forster
  Whewe, Snow Goose, Williams, E29, E210

wîhkiminêsiw [curlew, cf. Faries; lit: "likes eating berries"]
  Wee-kee-me-nase-su, Eskimo Curlew, Forster
  Weekee-meneesew, Eskimo Curlew, FBAm
  Weekemenew, Eskimo Curlew, Williams, E29, E210
  Weekemenesew, Eskimo Curlew, E213

wînipêko-pithêšiš [sandpiper, cf. Faries; lit: stinking- or stagnant-water
    bird]
  Winepeg, Pectoral Sandpiper, E213
  Winnipeg Apethashish, Pectoral Sandpiper, Hutchins
  Winnepeg-Apethayshish, Pectoral Sandpiper, Williams, E29, E210

?? [possibly: *wîsâkopêsiw*]
  Wesawcopaysue, unidentified Curlew, Marten

wîskacân(iš) or *wîskicân(is)*
  Whiskae-shawneesh, Gray Jay, FBAm
  Whisk-e-jonish, Gray Jay, Hearne
  Whiskijohn, Gray Jay, Forster
  Whisky-John, Gray Jay, Williams, E29, E213, Hutchins
  Wiskey John, Gray Jay, E210
  Wiskeejohn, Gray Jay, Marten

wîskicâk [also: *wîskipôs*, Wolfart; *wîskacân(is)*, cf. Faries]
Whiskijack, Gray Jay, Forster

wîskicânêwišip ["wiskeyjack duck = imitation duck" – R. Gallernault]
Whiskeychawn-weesheep, American Coot, FBAm

?? [possibly: wîšî-pithêšiš "belly-fat bird"]
Wishee-pethaysish, Savannah Sparrow, Hutchins
Wishe-pethaysish, Savannah Sparrow, Williams, E29, E210, E213

?? [possibly: *wîthipwâmacêšiš*]
Wir the pee ma tu sish, hawks eye = Golden Plover, Isham
Weethaypomuchaishish, Dunlin, Williams, E29, E210, E213
Wethaypomuchaishish, Dunlin, Hutchins

wîthi-wêhwêw [lit: dirty wavey]
Weetha-waewae, Brant, FBAm

?? [possibly: *wîthi-piskostikwân*, lit: dirty-pated]
Wir the pis quo esti quan, Sea swallow = ? Arctic Tern, Isham

?? [possibly: wîthiwâpawiw(ak), "dirty ??"]
Wir the wap pa wa wuck, Brant, Isham
Withawapawew, Brant, Williams, E29, E210, E213
Wuthewappywuck, Brant, Hutchins

CREE NAMES OF FISH

apisci-kinosêsis [minnow; lit: little fish; cf. Waugh]

atihkamêk [whitefish]
Attihhawmeg, Whitefish, FBAm
Tickomeg, Whitefish, E212, HutchinsAppx, Forster

iyinito-kinosêw [common or ordinary fish, jackfish, northern pike; cf.
   kinosêw "fish"]

kawacimêkošiš [lit: cold fish]
Cowachemaycushshish *or* cowachemaycushish, Capelin, E212, E210

kinošêw [fish]
  Keneshew *or* Keneshu, Jackfish, Northern Pike, E212, HutchinsAppx,
  E210

?? [possibly: *kînikihcikanišiš*; "sharp ??"]
  Kanekee cheegun ishish, Stickleback, Hutchins
  Kaweekee cheegun ishish, Stickleback, HutchinsAppx

mathay [mariah; also: *mithay*]
  Marthy, Burbot, Forster 152
  Mathy, Burbot, E212, HutchinsAppx, E210
  Methy, Merthy, Burbot, FBAm 248, E212

mâsamêkos [speckled trout]
  Masamacush, Arctic Char, Hutchins, FBAm, E210
  Mavamaycus, Grayling, HutchinsAppx [see also *mâthamêk*]

mâthamêk [lit: ugly fish]
  Mathemeg, [*not* the Black Bullhead], FBAm "ugly fish" Burbot, by elim-
    ination – CSH], Burbot, E212, HutchinsAppx, E210
  La Loche, Burbot, FBAm (Voyageurs)

mithkomêpith or *mithko-namêpith* [lit: red sucker]
  Meethqua-maypeth, Longnose Sucker, FBAm
  [perhaps also: Mithjawcass, Red Sucker, HutchinsAppx
              Mitho mapeth, Red Sucker, HutchinsAppx

namêkos [lake trout]
  Namaycush, Lake Trout, E212, HutchinsAppx
  Nammecoos, Lake Trout, FBAm
  Nemacush, Lake Trout, E210

namêpin, namêpiy, namîpith [sucker or "carp"]
  Namapeth, White Sucker, HutchinsAppx
  Namaypeeth, White Sucker, Pennant
  Namepieth, Sucker or "carp," E212
  Nemaypeth, Sucker, E210

namêw [sturgeon]
  Nemew, Lake Sturgeon, E212, HutchinsAppx, E210
  Nemow, Lake Sturgeon, HutchinsAppx

?? [suggests *nâkêš*; perhaps a Cree form of a French term: *la ??*; cf. Faries:
  wîpicisîs, napakamêkos]
  Naccaysh, Goldeye, FBAm (Voyageurs term)

okâw [pickerel, perch]
  Oukuons, Pickerel or Walleye, HutchinsAppx
  Oukow *or* Oukaw, Pickerel, E212, E210
  Ou kow, Yellow Perch, Hutchins
  Okow, Pickerel, FBAm

omiskomêkos [lit: little red fish]
  Omisco Maycus, Perch, E212; Trout-Perch, Hutchins, HutchinsAppx
  Omisco maycus, Sturgeon, HutchinsAppx [probably misidentified; cf.
    namêw]

??
  Uscathicasish, Stickleback, E210
  Usueathickashish, Stickleback, E212
  Uswae-atheek-asheesh, Nine-spined Stickleback, FBAm
    [cf. Kanekee cheegun ishish, Stickleback, Hutchins; Kaweekee
    cheegun ishish, Stickleback, HutchinsAppx]

otônapiy or *otônapîs* [tullibee (diminutive)]
  Ottoneebees, Tullibee, FBAm
  Otonabi – alternate name for tullibee [Dictionary of Canadianisms,
    813]

owîpicîsis [goldeye; cf. Faries: *wîpicîsis*]
  Oweepeetcheesees, Goldeye, FBAm
  [cf. Naccaysh, Goldeye, FBAm (Voyageurs term)]

sâkahikan-atihkamêk [lit: lake whitefish]
  Sockhigan Tickomeg, Guinaid of Pennant, E210

sôsâw(ak), sôsâwis(ak) [cf. *sôsâsiw*, "salmon"]
  Susawesuck, Arctic Char, E212
  Susawuck, Arctic Char, E210

?? [possibly: *thôtinamêk* "wind-fish"]
  Thutinameg, Sculpin, E212, HutchinsAppx, E210

wînipêk-atihkamêk [lit: dirty-water whitefish; cf. *atihkamêk, wînipêk*]
    Winepeg Tickomeg, Sea Guinaid, E210

CREE NAMES OF AMPHIBIANS, REPTILES, MUSSELS

athik or *athîk* [frog; cf. *athîkis, ayîkis*]
    Athick, Frog, E212

êsa(k) [clam, mussel, shell]
    Essack, Mussel, HutchinsAppx

kinêpik [snake]
    Kinepuck, Snake, E212, E210

miskinâhk [turtle; also: *mihkinâhk*]
    Miskinna, Turtle, E212, E210

pipikwathik [toad; cf. *athik, athîk*; cf. Wolvengrey: *pipikwatêhtêw*]
    Pepequathick, Toad, E212
    Pipequathick, Toad, E210

CREE NAMES OF INSECTS

amiskošiš [beetle, cf. Waugh; cf. *amiskosîs* "water insect"]
    Omiskoshish, Beetle, E212

âmow or *âmôs* [bee, wasp]
    Amo, Bee, E210

?? [possibly: *cîstikâwisiw*]
    Chiste caweseu, Wasp, E210 [cf. *âmow*]

cowêhkanâpisiš [dragonfly; also: *cowêhikanâpisis, cwêhohikanâpisîs*]
    Sheukeganapasish, Dragonfly, E212
    Shewacana pesish, Dragonfly, E210

êthik(wak) [ant(s); also: *îthik(wak)*]
    Ethequock, *or* Ethickwuck, Ant, E212, E210

ihkwa(k) [Louse (Lice)]
  Equock, Human Louse, E212
  Etwuck, Lice, E210

?? [possibly: *kokokaminakisiš*; cf. *kamâmak* "butterfly"]
  Cocokamanasakasish *or* Cucucummenakesish, Butterfly, E212, E210

kwâskohcîsis [grasshopper]
  Quasquote sish *or* Quachquasheshish, Grasshopper, E212, E210

manicôs [insect]
  Man juice, small worm, E212, E210

misisâhk [horsefly]
  Misse saac, Bulldog Fly, E212, E210

mohtêw(ak) [worm(s)]
  Mutewook *or* Mutuwuck, Wood-lice, E212, E210 [cf. *ihkwa*; also:
    mitihkomak; see also Sawow tekemuck]

ôcêw [housefly]

pihkošiš(ak), pihkošišiw [cf. *pihkos* "gnat"]
  Pecussishuck *or* Pecus shishue, Sandfly, E212, E210

sakimêw(ak) or *sakimês* [mosquito]
  Succamees *or* Sucke maywuck, Mosquito, E212, E210
  [see also *wînipêk-sakimêw*]

?? [possibly: *osâwâwitihkom(ak)* "yellow louse"]
  Sawow tekemuck *or* Sawow tekemuch, Worm, E212, E210 [cf. *mohtêw*]

?? [possibly: *wâwâskâcišiw*; cf. Faries: *wâskocâwêsîs, wâwâstêsîs* "firefly"]
  Wawaskacheshew, Glow-worm, E212

wînipêk-sakimêw(ak) [lit: "dirty water mosquito; cf. *sakimêw, sakimês*]
  Winipeg Suckemaywuck, another mosquito, E210

CREE NAMES OF MAMMALS

amisk [beaver]
Amisk, Beaver, E210
Ammisk, Beaver, FBAm
Aumisk, Beaver, Isham
Omisk, Beaver, Hutchins

amisk-âpakosîš [lit: beaver mouse]
Omisk Abbecuchish, White-footed Mouse "Beaver Mouse", Hutchins
[cf. *amisk*]

anikwacâs, athikwacâs [squirrel]
Anikatash, Ground Squirrel, E212
Annekcootchass, Red Squirrel, FBAm
Arthickatash, Red Squirrel, Isham
Mestan, Ground Squirrel, E212 [probably shortened from
mistanikwacâs "big squirrel"]
Neku chas, Red Squirrel, Hutchins, E210
Nicutash, Red Squirrel, E212

apistacihkos [antelope, pronghorn; lit: small caribou]
Apeestat-choekoos, Pronghorn, FBAm
Apiste-attick, [lit: "small caribou"], E212

apišimôsiš [deer; lit: small moose]
Apeesee-mongsoos, White-tailed Deer, FBAm
Peshemousish, Deer (White-tailed, Mule), E212; Pronghorn Antelope,
Hutchins
Peshemousish, Pronghorn Antelope, Hutchins [cf. *apistacihkos*]

atihk [caribou]
Ateek, White-tailed and Mule Deer, Hutchins
Atic, Deer, E210
Attick *or* Atic, Caribou, Isham, E212, E210
Attehk, Caribou, FBAm

atim [dog]
Atim, Dog, E212
Attim, Dog, Isham, FBAm

ayahcithiniwikêsiw [lit: Blackfoot-fox; cf. *mahkêsiw*]
   Archithinnue Ka ceu, Swift Fox, Hutchins [Archithinue *(ayahcithiniw)*
      was an early name for Blackfoot Indians, see Dickason 195; this was
      the little fox in Blackfoot Indian territory of what is now the extreme
      southern part of the Alberta and Saskatchewan – CSH].

âhkik, âthkik [seal; cf. Faries]
   Atheek, Seal, E212
   Athkeek, Seal, Hutchins, E210

âpakošîš [mouse]
   Abaceushish, Mouse, Hutchins
   Appa kosish, Mouse, Isham

?? [possibly: *kâ-miyêstawê-âpakošîš* "bearded mouse"; cf.
      cîposcowiyâkanisîs "shrew"]
   Ka nous ta way Ab ba ku shish, Arctic Shrew, Hutchins

kaskitêwikêsiw [lit: black fox; cf. *mahkêsiw*]
   Kuth ke keou-ka ceu, "Grizzle or Grey Fox," Hutchins

kâkwa [porcupine]
   Caqua, Porcupine, E212, E210
   Cawqua, Porcupine, Isham
   Cawquaw, Porcupine, FBAm
   Coquaw, Porcupine, Hutchins

kîhkwahâhkêw or *okîhkwahâhkêw* [wolverine]
   Carcajow *or* Carcajou, Wolverene, E212, E210
   Okeecoohagew *or* Okeecoohawgees, Wolverene, FBAm
   Quiquahaku, Wolverene, Isham
   Quiquhack, Wolverene, E212
   Quiquihatch, Wolverene, Hutchins, E210

kwâskohtit âpakosîš [cf. *âpakosiš kâ-kwâskohtit* "mouse which jumps";
      cf. *âpakosîš*]
   Quas ku tit Abbi ku shish, Meadow Jumping-Mouse, Hutchins

?? [possibly: *kwîskwîsiw*; cf. Waugh: *miscanaskos*, "Marmot", lit: small badger]
  Quisquis-su, Hoary Marmot, FBAm

mahihkan [wolf]
  Mahàgan *or* Mahaygan, Timber Wolf, Hutchins, FBAm
  Mahigan, Timber Wolf, E212
  Mehigan, Wolf, Isham, E210

mahkêšiw, mahkêšîš [fox]
  Makesheu *or* Makeshu, Fox, E212, E210
  Makeshish, Swift Fox or "Little Fox," E212
  Makkeeshew, Red Fox, FBAm
  Mekeshue, Fox, Isham

maskwa [bear]
  Musqua, Black Bear, Isham, E212, E210
  Musquaw, Black Bear, FBAm (plural musquawuck); Black and Grizzly
    Bears, Hutchins

maskwâš [muskrat; cf. *wacask*; *maskwâš* is no longer commonly used]
  Musquash, Muskrat, E212
  Musquash, Muskrat, FBAm, E210

mâthatihk(wak), mâyatihk [sheep, bighorn sheep; cf. Waugh; lit: ugly
    caribou]
  Mathetick *or* Mathi-teik, Pronghorn, E212, E210
  My-attehk, Pronghorn, FBAm (plural My-attekwuck)
  My-attehk, Bighorn Sheep, FBAm
  My-attehk, Pronghorn, FBAm (plural My-attekwuck)

?? [possibly: mâthâstos; cf. *kîhkwahâhkêw*]
  Murtastuss, Wolverene, Isham
  Murthastuce, Wolverene, Isham

mâthi-môs, mâthi-mostos [musk ox, cf. Faries: *mâni-môs*]
  Marthe Moos, Musk-Ox, Hutchins [lit: ugly moose]
  Matheh-moostoos, Musk-Ox, FBAm [lit: ugly bison]
  Mathymoose, Musk-Ox, E212, E210

mêstacâkaniš [coyote]
 Meesteh-chaggoneesh, Coyote, FBAm

misi-maskwa [lit: big bear]
 Meesheh musquaw, Grizzly Bear, FBAm [misi = big, hence "Big Bear";
  see *okistatôwân* below]
 Meshe-Musqua *or* Meshe Musquaw, Grizzly Bear, E212, E210

misi-wâpos [lit: big rabbit; cf. *mistâpos*]
 Misiwapos, Jack-rabbit

mistahi-sihkos [lit: big weasel; cf. *sihkos*]
 Mestihay-Secuse, Long-tailed Weasel, E212

mistamêk [whale, a big whale]
 Mistameg, Bowhead Whale, E212, E210

mistanask [badger; cf. *owâtihkêw*]
 Mistonusk, Badger, FBAm

mistatim [horse; also: *misatim*]
 Mistetim, Horse, E212
 Mistutim, Horse, Hutchins, E210

mistâpos [jack rabbit; cf. *misi-wâpos*]
 Mistapuss, Arctic Hare, E212, Hutchins [lit: "large rabbit"]

?? [possibly misrecorded; suggests: mistikošiš "woody" or mistikôsis
  "small wooden boat"]
 Mistic oushish, Pronghorn Antelope, Hutchins [cf. *apiscacihkos*,
  Waugh, Wolvengrey]

mostos [bison; cf. *paskwâwi-mostos*, "Plains Bison"; *sakâwi-mostos*,
  "Woods Bison"]
 Mistoos, Bison, Hutchins
 Moostoosh, Bison, FBAm, same name less commonly used for Elk,
  FBAm
 Mustus *or* Mustuss, Bison, E212, E210
 Murstuce, Bison, Isham

môswa [moose]
Moosöa, Moose, FBAm 239
Moosu, Moose, E212, E210
Moosue, Moose, Isham
Mooswau, Moose, Hutchins

nanaspâciniskêsiw(ak) [lit: backward paws; cf. *mistanask*]
Nanaspachae-neskesewick *or* Nananaspacheneskesewick, Badger, E212,
E210
Nannaspachae-neeskaeshew, Badger, FBAm

nikik [otter]
Neekeek, Otter, E210, E212
Ne keek, Otter, Hutchins
Ne kick, Otter, Isham

nošê-amisk [lit: female beaver]
Kenosha amisk, she Beaver, Isham [suggests: *kinošew-amisk* "fish-
beaver", but this is less likely]

nôšê-mahihkan [she-wolf; cf. *mahihkan*]
Nosha mehigan, she wolf, Isham

ocêk [fisher]
Otchoek, Fisher, FBAm
Oujack, Fisher, Hutchins
Weejack *or* Wejack, Fisher, E212, Hearne, Hutchins, E210

okistatôwân [grizzly bear; cf. *maskwa*]

?? [possibly: *omîthâcîs;* cf. *kîhkwahâhkêw*]
Ommeethatsees, Wolverene, FBAm

osâwâwikêsiw or *osâwâwi-mahkêsiw* [lit: yellow fox; cf. *mahkêsiw*]
Sow ow-ka ceu, Red Fox, including Cross Fox, Hutchins
U= saw-wa mekeshue, Red Fox, Isham

owâtihkêw [badger; lit: hole-digger]
Awawteekaeoo, Badger, "the animal that digs," FBAm

pahkwâcis or *apahkwâcis* [bat]
  Pasquash, the BAT [was in bird list!] E212, E213

?? [possibly: *piskwâtapiyiw*; cf. *wacask*]
  Peesquaw-tupeyew, Muskrat ("the animal that sits on the ice in a round
    form"), FBAm

pišiw [lynx]
  Peeshoo, Lynx, FBAm
  Peshew, Lynx, Hutchins
  Pir shuee, Lynx, Isham
  Pisshu, Lynx, E212, E210

pôtâcikêsis [pocket gopher; cf. Wolvengrey "mole"]
  Ootaw-chee-goeshees, Pocket Gopher, FBAm

šâkwêš, šâkwêšiw [mink; also: *sâkwêsiw*; cf. *sihkos*]
  Atjackashew, Mink, FBAm
  Jackash, Mink, Hearne, Hutchins, E210
  Sac quaw sue, Ermine, Hutchins [cf. *sihkos*]
  Shacooshew, Ermine, FBAm
  Shacushue, Ermine, E212, E210
  Shakwaeshew, Mink, Isham
  Shakweshue, Mink, E212, E210
  Shekeshu, Ermine, Isham

šâšâkawâpiskos [chipmunk]
  Awappuscus, Chipmunk, E212 [suggests: *-awâpiskos*]
  Sha shaggawun, Eastern Chipmunk, Hutchins [suggests: *šâšâkawan*]

šihkos [weasel; also: *sihkos*]
  Seegoos, Ermine, FBAm

šikâk [skunk; also: *sikâk*]
  Seecawk, Striped Skunk, FBAm
  She cow wuck, Skunk, Isham
  Shicauk *or* Shecauk, Striped Skunk, E212, E210

?? [cf. Wolvengrey: *taswêcanikwacâs* "flying squirrel"]
  Sineskatew ew uck, Flying Squirrel, Hutchins

Tso swa win athickotash, Flying Squirrel, Isham [suggests: *caswêwinathikwacâš*]

wacask(wak) [muskrat(s); *maskwâš, piskwâtapiyiw*]
U=e hus quck, Muskrat, Isham
Wachisk, Muskrat, E212
Wachusk, Muskrat, FBAm
Watsuss, Muskrat, FBAm
Wauchusk, Muskrat, Hutchins

wâpahkêšiw [arctic fox; lit: white fox]
Wappakeshue, Arctic Fox, Isham
Wappekeseu, Arctic Fox, E212
Wau pau kaceu, Arctic Fox, Hutchins

wâpamêk [white whale]
Wapameg, White Whale, Beluga, E212
Wapawmeg, White Whale, HutchinsAppx

wâpask(wak) [polar bear(s), lit: white bear]
Wapusk, Polar Bear, E212
Wap pusk, Polar Bear, Isham
Waupusk *or* Wapusk, Polar Bear, Hutchins, E210
Wawpusk, Polar Bear, FBAm (plural Wawpuskwuck)

wâpatihk [lit: white caribou; cf. *atihk*]
Wappew-tick, Peary=s Caribou, "white Arctic Islands caribou," E212

wâpiskišiw-mahkêšiw [lit: it is white, fox; this seems more likely as a description than a name; cf. *wâpahkêšiw*]
Wappeeskeeshew-makkeeshew, Arctic Fox, FBAm

wâpistân [marten]
Wappastan, Pine Marten, Isham
Wappestan, Pine Marten, E212
Wau pis shan, Pine Marten, Hutchins
Wawpeestan, Pine Martin, FBAm

wâpos [rabbit; cf. *misi-wâpos*; *mistâpos*]
Wappuss, Snowshoe Hare, Isham

Wapuss, Snowshoe Hare, E212, E210
Waupuss, Snowshoe Hare, Hutchins
Wawpoos, Snowshoe Hare, FBAm

wâwâskêsiw [elk]
Waskaseu *or* Washkesew, Elk, Hutchins, E210
Waskesse *or* Wewaskish, Elk, Hearne
Wawaskeeshoe, Elk, FBAm
Waskesew, Elk, E212
Wewaskish, Elk, Hearne
Awaskees, Elk, FBAm

wînask [groundhog, woodchuck; also: *wînasakâtihp*]
Weenusk, Woodchuck, FBAm ["Groundhog"]
Wenusk, Woodchuck, E212, Hutchins
Wenusk, Ground Squirrel, Hutchins; Raccoon = Woodchuck, E210

wîpiciw [walrus; lit: he has teeth; cf. Faries]
Weepitjeu, Walrus, Hutchins
Wepechew *or* Weepeechu, Walrus, E212, E210

CREE NAMES OF PLANTS AND TREES

Because there are no consistent English names for many plants, Latin names have been given when indicated.

acikâšipak(wa) [bearberry; also: *maskomin*]
Jackashey-puck, Jackashipuck, leaves of Bearberry, *Arctostaphylos uva-ursi*, Hearne, E212, E210

amiskomin(ak) ["yellow blackberry" = Cloudberry, *Rubus chaemaemorus*]
Amiscuminic, "Beaver Berry", = Cloudberry, E210
Miskemanaw, Huckleberry family, *Vaccinium*, Isham

?? [possibly: askâtâš]
Askatash [probably Water Parsnip, *Sium suave*, *uskotask*, E212 131],
Parsnip, E210

askiy [moss]
Askee, Moss, E212, E210

askîmin(ak) [lit: "moss berry"]
   Askemenuck *or* Askimwnue, Crowberry, *Empetrum nigrum*, E212, E210

?? [possibly: athâtâwiy(ak); cf. *ayîki-nônâcikan* "mushroom"]
   Athatawiuck, Mushroom, E212, E210

athîkimin(ak) [lit: "frog-berry"; animate]
   Athakimminuck, Currant, Isham
   Atheekimenuck *or* Athicaminuc, Wild Red Currant, *Ribes triste*, E212, E210

athôskan, Raspberry, Wolvengrey [cf. *ayôskan*]
   Athouscan, Raspberry, *Rubus idaeus b canadensis*, JRAppx

âpakosîs-ocêpihk [lit: "mouse root"]
   Appecooseesh-ootchoepeh, Wood Lily, *Lilium philadelphicum*, "termed by the Crees ... mouse-root" JRAppx

?? [possibly: ithiniwâhtik "ordinary tree"]
   Athinue-Artick *or* Athinue Arctic, Balsam Fir, *Abies balsamea*, E212, E210

kâhkâkiwimina or *kâhkâkiwiminak* [juniper berries, inanimate or animate]
   Caw-caw-quew-meena, Ground Juniper [not the "Crowberry" or "Raven-berry" as the Cree name might suggest], *Juniperus communis*, JRAppx [cf. *kâhkâkiwâhtik*, "raven-wood, juniper"]
   Kahawemenuc, Kawkawimenuck *or* kahawemenuc, Juniper berry, *Juniper*, E212, E210

kâkikêpakwa [cf. *maskêkwâpoy* or *maskêkopakwa*, which refers to the beverage made from the plant, Labrador Tea]
   Kawkee-kee pucquaw [or Maskoeg], Always Green, Labrador Tea, *Ledum palustre*, var. *latifolium*. JRAppx

manitômin [black currant; lit: spirit berry]
   Man[i]toomenuck, Black Currant, E212

maskêkomin(a) [cranberry; lit: muskeg-berry; also *maskêkominân(a)*]
   Maskaego-meena, [lit. Swamp Berry], Swamp Cranberry, *Oxycoccus palustris*, JRAppx or *Vaccinium oxycoccus*

maskêkopakwa [labrador tea]
> Cacumpucka, Labrador Tea, *Ledum palustre* or *Ledum palustre* var. *groendlandicum*, E212

maskomin(a) [lit: "bear berry"]
> Musqua-meena, Red Osier Dogwood, *Cornus alba*; [translates as "bear-berry" but this is not the true Bearberry – CSH] JRppx

maskošiy [grass or hay]
> Muscoshee *or* Muskoshee, Grass, E212, E210

mâthi-mîtos [black poplar; lit: ugly tree]
> Matheh-metoos, Ugly Poplar, Balsam Poplar, *Populus balsamifera*, JRAppx [Black Poplar or Cottonwood]

minahik [pine, spruce, or white spruce]
> Meenahi, White Spruce, *Picea glauca*, "The most northerly tree ... Its timber is in common use ... and its slender roots, denominated Watapeh [*watapiy*], are indispensable to canoe-makers for sewing the slips of birch-bark together. The resin which it exudes is used for paying over the seams of the canoes," [JRAppx; cf. Wolvengrey: *sihta* or *minahik* "spruce" and *watapiy* "spruce root"; cf. Waugh: *wâpasiht* "white spruce"]
> Miniakeg, Spruce, Picea, E212
> Miniheg, Pine, E210

misâskwatômin(a) [saskatoon berry]
> Meesasscootoom-meena, Saskatoon Berry, "the finest fruit in the country ... make excellent puddings" JRAppx

misâskwatwâhtik [saskatoon willow, *Aronia ovalis*]
> Meesassquat-athick, wood of the Saskatoon Berry, A*melanchier alnifolia*, "prized for making arrows and pipe stems," JRAppx

?? [possibly: misinîpak(wa)]
> Missinepuck *or* Missanepuck, Scurvy-grass, *Cochlearia officinalis*, E212, E20

mînis [berry]
> Minish, berries, E210 [singular form recorded]

mîtos [poplar]

    Metoos, Trembling Aspen, *Populus tremuloides*, "... is esteemed to burn better in a green state than any other tree in the country," JRAppx

    Metuus, Poplar, *Populus*, E212

môsomin(a) [lowbush cranberry; lit: moose berry]

    Mongsoa-meena, Swamp Cranberry, *Oxycoccus palustris* or *Viburnum edule* JRAppx [recorded form suggests an Ojibwa derivation]

napakâsiht [balsam fir; cf. *napakâw* "it is flat"; the needles of this tree are flat]

?? [cf. *mahihkanimina* "willow berries"; cf. Faries: *nîpisiyâhtik* "green willow" (lit: summer tree)]

    Nekopominuc, Willow-berry, E210

    Neneekamencuk, Willow-berry, E212

niskimin(ak) [lit: goose berry]

    Nishca-minnick, Crowberry, Curlewberry, *Empetrum nigrum*, Hearne

nîpisiy [willow]

    Nepasue, Willow, *Salix*, Isham

    Nipisi, Willow, E212, E210

okinîwâhtik [rosebush; cf. *okiniy* "rosehip"]

    Ogganee-ahtick, wood of *Rosa blanda*, JRAppx

oskâhtakwâhtik [wood of jack-pine]

    Ooskartawuc-ahtick, wood of Cyprès or Jack-pine, *Pinus banksiana*, "... its wood, from the lightness and the straightness and toughness of its fibres is much prized for canoe timbers." JRAppx

okiniy(ak) [rosehip]

    Oukinniack, *or* Oukinneac, Rose [Rose-hip], *Rosa*, E212, E210

?? [possibly: ošikâpakwa; cf. *maskêkopakwa*]

    Wishacapucca, Labrador Tea, *Ledum palustre* and *Ledum groenlandicus*, Hearne, JRAppx

    Wishecumpucwan, Labrador Tea, E210

    Wishekapacwaw, Labrador Tea, E212

otêhimin(a) [strawberry; lit: heart berry]
Otei-meena, Common Wild Strawberry (Heartberry), *Fragaria canadensis*, JRAppx
Outamenuck, Dewberry, *Rubus pubescens*, E212, E210 [suggests animate: *otêhiminak*]

pasasâwêwimina [pincherry; lit: prairie fire berry]
Passeeawey-meenan, Pincherry, *Prunus pensylvanica*, JRAppx [plural suggests possible Ojibwa derivation]

piponimina [lit: winter berry]
Pipon-meena, E212
Peepoon-meena, Low Bush Cranberry, *Viburnum edule*, JRAppx

pithêmin(ak) [lit: partridge berry]
Pethaymenuck, *or* Pethaymenuc, "Partridge-berry," Dry-ground Cranberry, *Vaccinium vitis-idaea*, E212, E210

?? [possibly: pithokotomin(ak); cf. *amiskomin*]
Bethago-tominick, Cloudberry or Bake-Apple, *Rubus chaemaemorus*, Hearne
Pethokotominuck, Cloudberry, *Rubus chaememorus*, E212
Pothokotomewuck, Cloudberry, E210

?? [possibly: sâsâkomina / sâsâkominâhtik]
Sassagoomena-ahtick, Bunchberry, *Cornus canadensis*, JRAppx

?? [possibly: (o)sâwayân "orange hide"]
Sawayan *or* Saw wyan, Bedstraw, *Galium*, E212, E210. ["The Cree women dye their porcupine quills red with the juice of this plant" JRAppx]

skîšikomin(ak) [lit: "eye-berry"; apparently animate; cf. *otêhimin(a)*]
Sheshicimenuc, Strawberry, E210
Skesheckamenuck, Strawberry, *Fragaria*, E212

šâpômin(ak) [gooseberry; lit: through berry]
Shapomenuck *or* shapominuc, Gooseberry, *Ribes oxyacanthoides*, E212, Isham, E210

takwahimin(a) [chokecherry; also: *takwahiminân(a)*]
Tawquoymeena = berry of chokecherry; "Its fruit is not very edible in a recent state, but when dried and bruised, forms an esteemed addition to pemmican."

takwahiminâhtik [Chokecherry tree]
Tawquoy-meen-ahtick, wood of Chokecherry, *Prunus virginiana*, JRAppx

waskway [birch]
Wusquey *or* Wusque, Birch, E212, E210

waskwayâhtik [birch tree]
Wursqi artick, Birch, *Betula*, Isham

wâkinâkan [tamarack; lit: bent one]
Wagginawgan, the Tree that Bends, Tamarack, *Larix laricina*, JRAppx
Wakenogan, White Cedar, *Thuja occidentalis*, E212, E210 [cf. Wolvengrey: *mâsikîsk* "cedar"]

wâpi-mîtos [lit: white poplar]

wâpiskomin(ak) [lit: white berry; animate]
Wapeckumenuck, White Currant, E212

wâpos-ocêpihk [lit: rabbit root]
Waw-poos-ootchepeh, Rabbit Root, Wild Sarsaparilla, *Aralia nudicaulis*, "The Crees use the root of this plant as a remedy against the venereal disease," JRAppx

wîsakimin(a) [low bush cranberry; lit: "bitter berry"; also animate: *wîsakiminak*]
Weesawgum-meena, "Sour-Berry", Dry-ground Cranberry, *Vaccinium vitis-idaea*, JRAppx
Wesakemanuck, Cranberry, Isham
Wusiskumenuck, Cranberry, E212
Wusiskinue, Cranberry

NOTES

INTRODUCTION

1 Ball 1982.
2 A type specimen or *holotype* is that designated as "the type" by the original author at the time of publication, when first describing a new species (Mayr et al. 1953, 239). Before specimens could be adequately preserved, a painting (e.g., by George Edwards or John James Audubon) often served as a substitute for a specimen, hence an *iconotype* (Mills 1998).
3 Cooke and Holland 1978, 32; Clapham 1942, xv–xix.
4 Moodie 1977, 268.
5 Innis 1956, 391–2; Malaher 1998, 1–24.
6 Ruggles 1997, 2:203.
7 Lindsay 1993, 42.
8 Allen 1997, 3:2.
9 Ruggles 1991, 9.
10 Ball 1988, 46.
11 David Geddes was appointed to this position in 1791 (Troup 1990, 2).
12 Clouston 1794, 16:442.
13 Ball 1976.
14 Ball 1988.
15 Ball 1983b, 203.
16 York Factory was first built for the HBC on the north bank of the Hayes River by Pierre Esprit Radisson in 1684, the first year that Cree and Assiniboine Indians made the long trip from inland to the bay (Payne 1989). Held by the French from 1697, it was restored to the English by the Treaty of Utrecht in 1713. York Factory was the most important HBC post, serving as headquarters of the HBC until 1873. Its importance then declined rapidly. It was closed in 1957 and transferred to National Historic Sites in 1968 (Pannekoek 1988, 3:2352).
17 E.2/12, Williams 1969, 249.
18 E.2/12, Williams 1969, 251

19 Avis 1967, 456.

20 E.2/12, Williams 1969, 250.

21 E.2/12, Williams 1969, 251.

22 Payne 1989, 15; Ray 1974, 52.

23 Churchill was founded, with a wooden fort, in 1717, renamed Prince of Wales's Fort in 1719, then rebuilt as a stone fort at Eskimo Point, 1731–71. It was captured and partly demolished by La Pérouse in 1782 (Holland 1994, 147). In 1783 Hearne returned, bringing with him a pre-fabricated building, since the stone fort was unliveable and beyond repair (HBCA B.239/a/81).

24 E.2/4, quoted in Williams 1969, 243.

25 E.2/12, Williams 1969, 248.

26 E.2/12, Williams 1969, 248–9.

27 E.2/12, Williams 1969, 243.

28 Severn had been built by the HBC in 1685, after HBC traders had visited the area for five summers, then was occupied by the French until the Treaty of Utrecht in 1713. The HBC rebuilt it in 1759 (Holland 1994, 123; Voorhis 1930, 162).

29 Fort Albany was founded in 1679, held by the French, 1686–1696, then until the Treaty of Utrecht in 1713 it was the only post held by the HBC. It has been occupied continuously since (Holland 1994, 71).

30 Charles Bayly, the first HBC overseas governor, established Moose Fort in 1673 as a site for occasional occupation (Holland 1994, 69). It was captured by the French in 1686 and held by them for ten years, except for a brief period each in 1693 and 1696. It was unoccupied for thirty-four years until the HBC rebuilt it in 1730 (Voorhis 1930, 119–20).

31 E.2/12, Williams 1969, 242–56.

32 Dickason 1992, 139.

33 Glover 1962, 90. First Nations peoples and fur-traders were each dependent on the other; intermarriage was common. Fur-traders were residents, not merely visitors, like Caucasian observers were in many parts of the world. Greenblatt's (1991, 7) wariness "of taking anything Europeans wrote or drew as an accurate and reliable account ... of the New World lands and its peoples" and his opinion that "European representations of the New World tell us something about the European practice of representation" – and nothing more – is an appropriate caution in general, but is perhaps less applicable around Hudson Bay.

34 Ball 1994, 1152.

35 Rich 1960, 42.

36 Dickason 1992, 143.

37 Rich 1945, 1946.

38 Ruggles 1977, 10.

39 See Chapter 12, pages 130–1.

40 When John Newton was hired at age fifty to command Churchill after thirty years sailing the Mediterranean, several comments implied that this 'outsider' had 'jumped the queue.' Fortunately this was a most unusual circumstance.

41 Nicks 1987, DCB 6:775–7.

42 Ruggles 1977, 10.

43 The Little Ice Age extended from 1560 to 1830, see chapter 11.

44 Dickson 1997, 11–16.

45 Enlightenment was "a system of values – liberal, secular, rational – of continuing moral and political import" (Clark, Golinski, and Schaffer 1999, 9). It "implied an intense preoccupation with some domain ... so that resources of time, money, and labor were willingly spent in pursuit of an aim outsiders deemed trivial or even mad. These commitments had little to do with professionalization. ... nature was the ultimate source of the good, the true, and the beautiful" (Daston 1999, 497, 500, 503). Scotland at this time has been described as a "hotbed of genius," the subtitle of the book by Daiches et al. (1986b). "Everywhere was the aim of improvement ... the seed-bed of much of the later thought of the western world is to be found in this little northern country ... Edinburgh was in a position to vie with Salerno, Padua and Leyden as one of the great medical centres in the western world." (Daiches 1986a, 4–5, 43). In America, "The men of the Enlightenment believed in education" (Cassara 1975, 145, and see his Chronology, 11–14).

46 Macleod 2001, 1.

47 Allen 1993, 335–6.

48 Allen 1993, 336. Sir Christopher Wren's magnificent Bodleian Library at Oxford University has three doors: one to natural sciences, a second to the humanities, and a third in the middle that was the main entrance to the library. In our context these doors illustrated the combining of science, nature and the humanities; in turn they underpin the term naturalist as well as a world view.

49 Alexander Mackenzie's published narrative was known to Thomas Jefferson, who received a copy within two months of publication in London, as part of his standing order for books dealing with North America. Jefferson realized that Mackenzie's trip over the Rocky Mountains to the west coast threatened the American hope for control over the entire continent and led to his recruitment of Lewis and Clark (Gough 1997, 6, 184).

50 "By and large physicians were the only ones who had formal degrees from universities ... only medicine gave students what we might call a graduate training in natural science ... many developed a deep and abiding commitment to natural history" (Cook 1996, 91, 100). The first non-medical specialist societies were the Linnean Society of London in 1788 and the Geological Society of London in 1807, followed by the Zoological Society in 1826 and the Royal Astronom-

ical Society in 1831 (Pyenson and Sheets-Pyenson 1999, 97). Charles Darwin and Alexander von Humboldt were to make their mark in the following century. The American Ornithologists' Union, encompassing Canadians and Americans, was not created until 1883, prompted by the need for nomenclatural reform, to standardize both common and scientific names of birds (Barrow 2000, 7).

51 The concept of such pursuits as a hobby were more than half a century in the future. Between 1830 and 1850, ornithology emerged as a "scientific discipline" but not until 1900 did it begin to be a profession in which numbers could earn a livelihood (Farber 1982, 100).

52 Curious: The *Oxford English Dictionary* (OED) gives the following definitions: "bestowing care or pains, careful, studious, attentive"; "careful as to the standard of excellence"; "careful or nice in observation or investigation, accurate"; "ingenious, skilful, clever, expert"; "desirous of seeing or knowing, eager to learn, inquisitive" but "often with condemnatory connotation ... desirous of knowing ... what does not concern one. prying." Edwards obviously was using some combination of the first four definitions in a laudatory sense, not the fifth definition which is most often inferred in modern usage.

53 The word "scientist" was not coined until 1834 (S. Ross, "Scientist: the story of a word," *Annals of Science* 18:65–85).

54 Dickenson 1998, 191.

55 Allen 1993, 333-5. In this connection, publication of Gilbert White's *The Natural History and Antiquities of Selborne* in 1789 was pivotal.

56 Desaguliers was the only three-time winner of the Royal Sociey's Copley Medal – in 1734, 1736, and 1741 (Royal Society 1940, 345).

57 Stewart 1992, 117, 123, 139, 140, 393.

58 However, Ray's biographer (Raven 1986, 454–5) adds that Ray viewed "reason, strictly disciplined and honestly followed, [as] the supreme instrument in science and religion." The growing popularity of natural theology in British society, and in some far-flung regions of the British empire, had for several decades contributed to the beginnings of the amateur naturalist tradition, decades before William Paley published *Natural Theology* in 1802. Much of Paley's work was based on Ray, to the extent that he has been described as an "unacknowledged plagiarist" of Ray (Keynes 1951, 95).

59 Berger 1983, 33, 41.

60 Geology was also part of natural history, but flowered in present Canada chiefly after 1800 (Zeller 2000, 85–93). The eighteenth century HBC contributions to ornithology and mammalogy were much more important than those to geology.

61 Little is known about the first two botanists whose plants from Hudson Bay are preserved in the Sloane Herbarium in the British Museum of Natural History in London.

Plants collected in 1699 at "Hudgson Bay" by Mr Lide are catalogued as *Hortus Siccae* 318, ff. 78–81, in the James (Jacobi) Petiver collection in the Sloane Herbarium. That year the supply ship, *Dering III*, went only to Albany, the only post still held by the HBC after the 1697 Treaty of Ryswick.

A list of ninety-nine Hudson Bay plants, probably collected in 1708, was compiled by John Smart, ship's surgeon (Reveal et al. 1987, 1–3). The Petiver collection, *Hortus Siccae* (H.S.) 159 contains some of these plants, "specimens much damaged." H.S. 243 also contains some of Smart's Maryland specimens and H.S. 283 contains one. Smart's only dated letter, 2 September 1708, accompanied fourteen plant specimens used for medicinal purposes by the Indians, from the "Sarsafras" River across Chesapeake Bay from Baltimore, Maryland (Dandy 1958, 209; Reveal et al. 1987, 59). A John Smart was among "the servants discharged and come home" in August 1714 from Hudson Bay on the namesake ship, *Hudson's Bay* (Davies 1965, 31). A John Smart, MD (1678–1740) of Chelsea College, London, was listed as a contributing subscriber to a 1729 book, *A Survey of the Globe*, by Templeman (Wallis and Wallis 1988, 549). It is possible, but by no means certain, that these three mentions of John Smart might have referred to the same itinerant ship's surgeon.

Judith Hudson Beattie has been unable to trace Lide and Smart in the HBCA because no ship's logs exist before 1751 (HBCA C.1), the miscellaneous papers for the *Dering* in 1699 contain lists of provisioners only (HBCA C.7/39), and the crucial four years of journals for Albany following 1706–07 are missing.

CHAPTER ONE

1 MacGregor 1995, 79.

2 Brooks 1954, 55, 67. Sloane's *Natural History of Jamaica* was not published until 1707 (volume 1) and 1725 (volume 2).

3 The official journal of the Royal Society of London, *Philosophical Transactions* began publication in 1665. The same year, although three months earlier, the French *Journal des sçavans* came into existence. These two were the first scientific journals in the world (Pyenson and Sheets-Pyenson 1999:219).

4 Dandy 1958; MacGregor 1995, 88.

5 Brooks 1954, 40–3.

6 Clarke 1992, vii.

7 Later, J. Robson, the bookseller and publisher in London, caused no end of confusion when he bound pages from earlier Edwards volumes in a single volume together with a 1776 Linnaeus catalogue and a 1776 memoir of Edwards (who died in 1773), without changing publication dates (Linnaeus 1776; Alden 1969).

8 Mason 1992, 39.

9 Allen 1951, 491.

10 Georges-Louis-Leclerc, Compte de Buffon, 1707–1788, author of the 36-volume *Histoire Naturelle, génerale et particulière*, and Keeper of the Jardin du Roi (Roger 1997). Buffon was one of the "four great lights of the Enlightenment" (Farber 1972, 259). Like Linnaeus, Buffon had a worldwide network of correspondents who sent him specimens, but otherwise he was almost the complete antithesis of Linnaeus; he showed a "mistrustful hostility" to "Linnaeus-style systematizers" (Gerbi 1973, 32), and considered the Linnaean classification artificial. Unlike Linnaeus, Buffon did not view species as fixed but "stressed the adaptability of life to environmental conditions" (Roger 1997, 325–35). Buffon was also a prodigious writer: "The second most frequently owned item in private libraries in France was ...[his] monumental 36-volume encyclopedia of animals." Buffon also built up the Jardin du roi to be the "foremost institution in its day for the study of the living world" (Farber 2000, 2, 14). The "most beautiful in Europe," this Royal Botanical Gar-den was visited by Linnaeus. (Roger 1997, 47–51).

11 Davis and Holmes 1993, 176.

12 Buchanan and Fisher 1951, 93.

13 Dickenson 1998, 4, 144. Dickenson also points out that "the incredible increase in the flow of specimens ... across the Atlantic ... demanded the development of new instruments of understanding, of which the works of Edwards are prime examples" (200).

14 Mason 1991, 2, 7.

15 Mullens and Swann 1917, 194–5.

16 A non-descript species then meant a species not yet described to science. Today it means something very different: "lacking distinctive characteristics, uninteresting, dull."

17 Linnaeus (1758) compiled Latin names for the species portrayed in George Edwards' seven volumes (McAtee 1950, 194–205).

18 Anonymous 1949, 536. All seven volumes were reprinted in English, French, Dutch and German editions (Buchanan and Fisher 1990, 93).

19 In Edwards' last three volumes, *Gleanings*, he included twenty-seven species of birds from William Bartram in Pennsylvania, who first wrote to him in June 1756.

20 Duncan 1840, 250–1. Dickenson (1998, 171) suggests that Linnaeus may have collaborated with Celsius: "Linnaeus had some claim to have invented" the Celsius thermometer.

21 Duncan 1840, 251; Hagberg 1953, 22.

22 Koerner 1999, 67.

23 Gronovius was the author of *Museum Ichthyologicum* (Swainson 1840, 205–6).

24 Koerner 1999, 29.

25 Stresemann 1975, 50.

26 Koerner 1999, 39, 40.

27 Stearn 1959, 20.

28 Stresemann 1975, 50.

29 With the shortened title "Methodus demonstrandi animalia, vegetabilia, aut lapides," an account of the Linnaean method appeared at the back of all subsequent editions of the *Systema* up to and including the ninth (Schmidt 1951, 369). In the tenth, adopted as the foundation for zoological nomenclature, the "Methodus" was dropped, and hence is not familiar to most modern students of taxonomy. Schmidt was the first to translate the "Methodus" into English, from (as he said) the "by no means classical and in certain points obscure" Latin used by Linnaeus. A more recent translation explains how the "Methodus" was "a recommendation to fully-fledged naturalists on the preparation of descriptions of new forms" (Cain 1992, 244).

30 Schmidt 1951, 371.

31 Koerner 1999, 74.

32 Hagberg 1953, 206.

33 The only contemporary European of sufficient stature to challenge Linnaeus was George-Louis Leclerc, comte de Buffon (1707–1788).

34 Seven of Linnaeus' students died during their botanical travels: Carl Fredrik Adler (Dutch East Indies), Anders Berlin (West Africa), Jacob Jonas Björnståhl (Greece), Pehr Forsskål (Arabia), Fredrik Hasselquist (Smyrna), Pehr Löfling (Venezuela), and Christopher Tärnström (China). Fourteen travelling students survived: Adam Afzelius (West Africa), Jonas Carlsson Dryander (England, where he became librarian for Joseph Banks and secretary to the Linnean Society), Johan Petter Falck (Caucasus and Siberia), Johan Gustaf Hallman (China, to spy on the silk industry), Johan Gerard König (Thailand and Sri Lanka), Anton Rolandsson Martin (Arctic Sea), Lars Montin (Lapland), Pehr Osbeck (China), Daniel Rolander (Surinam, where he went insane), Göran Rothman (Morocco), Daniel Solander (Cook's first circumnavigation), Anders Sparrman (Cook's second circumnavigation), Carl Peter Thunberg (Japan), and Olof Torén (China). See Koerner's impressive map of their travels (Koerner 1999, 116), and her citation of a further eight students who did not travel. In total, Linnaeus supervised 186 dissertations – and wrote most of them himself! (Koerner 1999, 124, 202–12).

35 Broberg 1997, 421.

36 Broberg 1997, 422.

37 McAtee 1957b, 291.

38 de Beer 1956, iii–v.

39 Linnaeus 1776.

40 Koerner 1999, 62.

41 Koerner 1999, 129.

42 Gage and Stearn 1988, 5–8.

43 Report of a committee appointed to consider ... the rules by which the nomenclature of zoology may be established on a uniform and permanent basis
1842. *Twelfth Meeting of the British Association for the Advancement of Science*, 106–7.

44 Farber 1982, 115.

45 Along the Volga, Forster and his eleven-year-old assistant, son Georg, collected
207 plants, 23 mammals, 64 birds, 14 reptiles and 16 fish. At Lake Elton, Georg
collected a new species, the Black Lark, *Alauda yeltoniensis* Forster, now *Melanoco-
rypha yeltoniensis* Forster. (Forster 1767, 312–57; Stresemann 1975, 71; Hoare
1976a, 31).

46 Hoare 1982, 1:30.

47 Livingstone 1992, 129.

48 Goetzmann 1986, 44.

49 Hoare 1976a, 75, 82.

50 Stresemann 1975, 73.

51 Hoare 1976a, 135.

52 Entitled *Characteres Generum Plantarum ... Australis.*

53 Forster 1778; Stresemann 1975, 74.

54 Laughton 1949c, 456.

55 Hoare 1976a, 110, 111.

56 Laughton 1949c, 456.

57 Hoare 1976a, 301.

58 Hoare 1976a, 328.

59 Stresemann 1975, 75.

60 Hoare 1976b, 376.

61 Hoare 1972, 10–13.

62 Levere 1993, 177.

63 Forster 1773, 149.

64 Forster 1773, 153.

65 Forster 1773, 158–9.

66 Wroth 1949, 767.

67 Allen 1951, 494.

68 Wroth 1949, 767

69 Mullens and Swann 1917, 464.

70 Wroth 1949, 766.

71 Described respectively on pages 591 and 751 of the first edition of Pennant's
Arctic Zoology and subsequently given Latin names by Gmelin.

72 Wroth 1949, 767.

73 White 1993; Urness 1968, 175.

74 *Arctic Zoology*, 1785, 2:222; this footnote, in the account of the Gyrfalcon, was
repeated in the 1792 edition, 2:233. Hutchins and Pennant also corresponded.

A long Hutchins letter titled "Fish in Hudson's Bay," dated February 1784 and addressed to "Thomas Pennant Esq' Downing Flintshire," was purchased for the Hudson's Bay Company Archives in 1968, HBCA Z .4/1. The letter is reproduced in Williams 1969, 381–5.

75 Pennant 1792, 264. Pennant is in error; this was an Andrew Graham observation. At no time had Hutchins resided at Severn.

76 The Yellow-headed Blackbird was not given a Latin name until Bonaparte in 1825 described a specimen from Pawnee Villages, Loup River, in present Nebraska (American Ornithologists' Union 1998, 643).

77 Hudson's Bay Company Archives, Provincial Archives of Manitoba, mss. E.2/12. In subsequent citations of these manuscripts of the HBCA, PAM will be omitted.

78 Pennant 1792, 2:357–8.

79 Pennant 1792, 1:5–6.

80 McAtee 1963, 103–10.

81 Mathews 1931, 466. Dr John Hunter won the Royal Society's Copley Medal in 1787 (Royal Society 1940).

82 Stresemann 1975, 78.

83 Stresemann 1975, 79.

84 Newton 1896, 12.

85 Swainson 1840, 232–3.

86 Allen 1951, 496.

87 Latham 1790; American Ornithologists' Union 1957, 183; the Hudson Bay specimen probably had been collected by Andrew Graham.

88 Allen 1993, 337.

89 Watkins 1949, DNB 11:605; Wallis and Wallis 1988, 355.

90 Newton 1896, 12.

91 Mathews 1931.

92 Watkins 1949, 606.

93 Williams 1969, 356–7.

94 Withers 1993, 72.

95 Kerr, an Edinburgh University historian, claimed that Ramsay "did not deliver his courses of lectures with uniform regularity, and that, for some years before his death, he did not lecture at all" (Kerr 1811, 288). Thomas Pennant's book *Genera of Birds* in 1780, however, contradicts Kerr; the book contains a two-page dedication to Doctor Robert Ramsay, who had died on 15 December 1778, and the Advertisement on the preceding page states that the book was prepared in 1772 "for the use of the class over which he presided" (Pennant 1781, 2–3).

96 In litt., Charles W. Withers, 19 Dec 1992.

97 Walker 1812; Boulger 1949b, DNB 20:531.

98 Withers 1991, 206.

99 Boulger 1949b, DNB 20:531.

100 Withers 1992, 293.

101 Withers 1988, 106.

102 Edinburgh University Library Special Collections MSS Dc.2.33. I thank Walker's biographer, Charles W.J. Withers and J.V. Howard, Special Collections librarian at the Edinburgh University Library. Walker did not list the collector of the 1772 specimens. Thirty-one pages list specimens from "Hudsons Bay," with the apostrophe omitted.

103 Withers 1991, 3 maps, 214–16.

104 In 1804, Robert Jameson began his fifty-year tenure, 1804–54, and made Edinburgh "one of the few places in Britain where natural history sciences were taught as part of the university curriculum ... Students who had enrolled in medicine were required to take Jameson's courses." As late as 1854–55, the Edinburgh chair was still considered in the "pre-disciplinary status of natural history" (Sheets-Pyenson 1992, 462, 477). In 1808 Jameson founded the Wernerian Natural History Society and in 1819, with Sir David Brewster, he originated the *Edinburgh Philosophical Journal*, and was its sole editor from its tenth volume until his death (Boulger 1949a, 671–2).

105 Withers 1991, 209, and his Table 1, p. 211, which lists 16 items gifted from "Hudson's Bay" [with an apostrophe], 1787, citing Glasgow University Library MS Gen 1061. Withers 1993, 73; Williams 1969, 386–7.

106 Withers 1993, 73. Among the seven volumes which list Walker's acquisitions, including but not restricted to 1766 and 1769–74, acquisitions from overseas are from the West Indies (beginning on p. 70), East Indies (p. 84), New Zealand (p. 86), China (pp. 124–56), and "Hudsons Bay" (with no apostrophe, pp. 157–98).

107 http://www.mcgill.ca/mqupress/eighteenth-centurynaturalists/forster.

108 Ruggles 1976, 11–12.

109 Glover 1969, xxii.

110 Ruggles 1976, 18.

111 Ruggles 1976, 15.

112 Laughton 1949a, DNB 4:402–3.

113 Coote, 1949, DNB 1:595–6.

114 Ruggles 1976, 20.

115 Ruggles 1976, 11.

116 Especially Aaron Arrowsmith, who with Wegg's encouragement, "compiled successive editions of his epochal map of northern North America" (Ruggles 1976, 17). Wegg's openness was in striking contrast to Sir Bibye Lake, governor of the HBC from 1712 to 1743. Lake's defence was "secrecy, an obsessive guarding of the knowledge and expertise accumulated" (Williams 1970, 151).

117. Newman 1985, 1:247; Ruggles 1976, 11.

118. Ruggles 1976, 12.

CHAPTER TWO

1   HBCA A.6/5, fo. 77d, cited in Davies 1965, 187.

2   Cooke and Holland 1978, 58.

3   Richardson and Swainson 1832, 2:ix–x.

4   Williams 1962, 43.

5   Napper's detailed "Orders and Instructions" from the Company were published 12 years later in the *Report from the Committee appointed to enquire into the State and Condition of the Countries adjoining to Hudson's Bay, and of the trade carried on there* (Hudson's Bay Company 1749).

6   Davies 1965, 214. The letter was signed by Richard Norton.

7   Neatby 1969, DCB 2:493.

8   Davies 1965, 242.

9   Cooke and Holland 1978, 60.

10 Davies 1965, 266, fn 3.

11 Davies 1965, 323, 324.

12 Rich 1954, 334; Davies 1965, 324, 326.

13 British Museum Department of Ethnology, Sloane ms 4056, f370. Courtesy Jonathan King, via Glyndwr Williams.

14 Under command of Captain Christopher Middleton, FRS. The Inuit came aboard at 63° North, 72° West.

15 British Museum Department of Ethnology, Sloane ms 4056 f 370, "Fosset" is not a word found in modern dictionaries.

16 Light's accompanying letter to Sloane was dated 25 August 1738, evidently soon after arrival at Moose Factory. The anthropology collection probably reached Sloane in 1739.

17 Rich 1949, xxxvi; HBCA A.6/5, p.5, cited in Lindsay 1993, 41.

18 Rich 1949, xxxvi.

19 Rich 1949, xxxvi.

20 Davies 1965, 263, 268.

21 Davies 1965, 277.

22 Edwards 1743, volume 1, plate 53. Pennant in *Arctic Zoology* 2:208, next described this race of the Gyrfalcon as "the Plain Falcon," from Hudson Bay. When Gmelin in *Systema Naturae* 1(1), 268, gave it a Latin name, *Falco rusticolus*, in 1788–89, he used '*in freto Hudsonias*' in the alternative wider Latin sense of 'the sea in general' as the locality, indicating Hudson Bay.

23 This phalarope specimen was painted as plate 46 in volume 1 of Edwards' first book in 1743. A full-plumaged female specimen brought later from Hudson Bay by Isham was figured in plate 143 in volume 3 in 1750. Sadly, and without regard for chronologic priority, Linnaeus listed the earlier Light specimen second. *The Seventh AOU Check-list*, 1998, 179, citing the plate listed first by Linnaeus, gives

the type locality as "*in America septentrionali*, Lapponia = Hudson Bay," based on the second specimen.

24 Golden Eagles have a large, prominent patch of white near the base of the tail, even more striking than the white in the same area on an immature Bald Eagle. The feathered tarsus is additional confirmation of the correct identification of a Golden Eagle.

25 Edwards 1743, 1:4.

26 American Ornithologists' Union 1931, 70.

27 Edwards 1747, 2:103.

28 Edwards 1751, 4:205; this was an Eastern Box Turtle, *Terrapene carolina*.

29 Edwards 1743, 1:4.

30 Edwards 1750, 3:152.

31 American Ornithologists' Union 1973, 411–19.

32 "1774" was a misprint.

33 Edwards 1743, 1:52.

CHAPTER THREE

1 Rich 1974, DCB 3:301.

2 Houston 1997b, 397–9.

3 Rich 1949, xiii.

4 Barr and Williams 1994, 96.

5 Barr and Williams 1994, 102. Subsequent expeditions, searching for the North West Passage, chose to ignore Middleton's findings; they merely confirmed that he had been correct in his assessment.

6 Dobbs 1744; Rich 1949, lxxii–xcix.

7 For a sympathetic account of relationships between fur traders and native women, see Brown 1980 and Van Kirk 1980.

8 Edwards 1750, 3:107.

9 Rich (1949, xii) referred to Catherine as Isham's "giddy wife in England." Their daughter seems to have been alive in 1757 but no further reference has been traced in the HBC archives (Rich 1949, 323–5).

10 Craig 1974, DCB 3:483–483. John Newton was the father of Rev. John Newton (1725–1807). Bennett 1949, DNB 14:395–8. Rev. Newton has been known through much of the English-speaking world ever since, as the author of "Amazing Grace," as well as other less-well-known compositions still in current hymnals.

11 Rich 1949, 324.

12 Brown 1983, DCB 5:451.

13 Cutler 1994, 58.

14 Avis 1967, 504, 680, 840, 846.

15 There is no evidence that these plants reached London (Rich 1949, xxxvi); see Table 6.1, List of York Factory surgeons.

16 Of the bird species occurring in Europe as well as Hudson Bay, four had already been described from Sweden by Linnaeus – the Brant, Common Eider, Black Guillemot or "willock," and Black-billed Magpie – and he had listed the Yellow-shafted (Northern) Flicker from Catesby's South Carolina painting. But there were missed opportunities. Probably because Edwards failed to recognize them as new species, priority was lost for the following seven Isham species from York Factory: 1) Red-throated Loon (described in 1763 from Denmark by Pontoppidan); 2) Common Loon (1764, from the Faroes Islands by Brunnich) 3) American White Pelican (1788, see chapter 6 in this book); 4) Double-crested Cormorant (not differentiated from other cormorant species until 1831); 5) Trumpeter Swan (separated from the Tundra Swan in 1831, see Appendix D); 6) Passenger Pigeon (although Catesby had painted the Mourning Dove, plate 24, and the Passenger Pigeon, plate 23, Linnaeus did not list the latter separately until his 1766 edition); 7) Gray Jay (a Quebec specimen was not listed by Linnaeus until 1766).

17 Rich 1949, 124.

18 Rich 1949, 125.

19 Edwards 1743, 1747, 1750, 1751. Specimens of the Canada Goose, Greater White-fronted Goose, and Long-tailed Duck or Oldsquaw, were from Hudson Bay but Edwards failed to name the collector of these three.

20 In the 1770s, and indeed for another century, "non-descript" meant "not yet described to science." See Chapter 1, fn. 16.

21 See Introduction, fn. 51.

22 Edwards 1750, 3:107.

23 Because the specimens themselves could not be preserved, the paintings (iconotypes) fulfilled the function of type specimens for all time.

24 The Harlequin was sent from Newfoundland to the royal menagerie, and loaned to Edwards by "Mr Holmes of the Tower of London" (Edwards 1747, 99).

25 Edwards 1751, 4:205; Cook 1984, 102–3. Francis Cook, *in litt.*, 25 November 1995, advises that the upper shell "rising" and the under shell "flattish" and "light horn-colour" would fit the Painted Turtle, perhaps after the scutes had been removed.

26 Rich 1949, cii, 325.

CHAPTER FOUR

1 Tyrrell 1934, 592.

2 Tyrrell 1934, 592.

3 Glover 1952, xxiv–xxv.

4 Severn had been built by the HBC in 1685, then burnt in 1689 to prevent capture by the French, who built a new fort across the river in 1691. The new fort

was captured by the HBC for one year in 1693, then rebuilt by the French at the river mouth in 1701–02 and held by them until the Treaty of Utrecht in 1713 (Voorhis 1930). Meanwhile, except for 1696–97, York Factory had been occupied by the French from 1694 through 1714. Albany, captured by James Knight in 1693, was thus the only post on Hudson Bay under control of the HBC until 1713 (Cooke and Holland 1978, 44–51; Payne 1989, 14–15.

5 Glover 1952, xxix.

6 Glover 1952, xxix.

7 Umfreville, 1790, 34.

8 Glover 1952, xxvii, fn 4.

9 French-Canadian voyageurs in the employ of fur trade companies based in Montreal.

10 Glover 1952, xxxii.

11 Ewart 1995, 40. HBCA B.3/13, 13, 26 June 1776.

12 Tyrrell 1934, 593.

13 Holland 1994, 147.

14 The ships were the *Sceptre, Astrée*, and *Engageante* (Dunmore 1994, liv, lv).

15 Tyrrell 1934, 595.

16 Tyrrell 1934, 596–7; Cooke and Holland 1978, 106.

17 Glover 1952, xxxv.

18 Glover 1952, xxxv.

19 From York Factory, Albany and Moose Fort, the Royal Society received eight boxes of natural-history specimens in 1771, augmented by "further packages" in 1772, and somewhat smaller collections in 1773 and 1774 (Leveson Gower 1934, 31, 66).

20 Glover 1952, xxxiv; Leveson Gower 1934, 31.

21 Williams 1978, 8.

22 Forster 1772c, 411–12; Gollop et al. 1986, 71.

23 Pennant 1792, 2:321.

24 Baillie 1946, 36–9.

25 Pennant 1792, 3:270, added, concerning Albany, "where on the contrary the Snow Geese are very scarce." Clearly this was information from Humphrey Marten, since Thomas Hutchins did not move to Albany until 1774. In his 1787 supplement, Pennant had mentioned Hutchins' goose observations from "Hudson's Bay" on the previous page to the Albany observation, which gave no observer's name.

26 http://mcgill.ca/mqupress/homepa/eighteenth-centurynaturalists/marten.html.

27 Allen 1951, 519. Document 3 corrects Mrs Allen's errors in transcription or printing.

28 W. Earl Godfrey, *in litt.*, 1 January 1990.

29 Daines Barrington was the son of the first Viscount Barrington. "His family's influence, rather than any conspicuous talent, brought him a series of elevated occupations in the course of his life. In the 1750s he obtained high office as a judge" (Holland 1994b, 16). Daines Barrington did better when he wrote of the "extraordinary musical talents" of Wolfgang Mozart, then aged eight years and five months (Barrington 1770).

30 Glover 1952, xxxiv–xxxv.

CHAPTER FIVE

1 Williams 1969, 334.

2 There were three interruptions in Graham's Severn service between 1761 and 1774. Graham was acting chief at York Factory twice when Jacobs went back to England on furlough, 1765–66 and 1771–72. Graham himself went home on furlough, 1769–70.

3 Williams 1983, DCB 5:362–3.

4 Wallace 1934, 39–44. Graham was even more humble in his memorandum than was demanded by the convention of his time, concluding his letter to the Governor and Committee of the Hudson's Bay Company with, "Let me then have cause to bless Your Goodness, Which will ever bind me to be, Honble. Sirs, Your Grateful & obliged Humble Servant."

5 Williams 1968, 4.

6 Tyrrell 1934, 13.

7 Such liaisons with native women were more the rule than the exception. See Chapter 3, fn. 7.

8 Williams 1969, 351.

9 Merry, a member of the Hudson's Bay Company Committee from 1746, had become deputy governor on February 1770 (Williams 1969, 353).

10 E.2/12., Williams 1969, 271

11 E.2/12, Williams 1969, 272.

12 Graham 1969. "Indians," (chiefly the Cree, but including shorter accounts of the Assiniboine, Chipewyan and Ojibwa first nations), pp. 143–212; "Eskimos," pp. 213–41; and "Life and trade in the bay," pp. 242–330. These are every bit as important as his accounts of birds and mammals.

13 Map from HBCA G.2/15; Ruggles 1991, 38 and map 6.

14 Pennant 1768, *British Zoology* (3 vols.).

15 Williams 1978, 7.

16 Williams 1978, 7.

17 Barrington 1772a, 4–14.

18 Williams 1968, 1–4.

19 By *Coues Check List of North American Birds* (1882, 85); "Sacer" means sacred, but this gyrfalcon is not to be confused with the Saker Falcon of central Europe and Asia, *Falco cherrug*.

20 See Cassin 1858, 33.

21 In 1776, from a Carolina specimen, Müller named the Rusty Blackbird *Turdus carolinus*, now *Euphagus carolinus* (American Ornithologists' Union 1998, 645).

22 Forster had access to the pelican specimen sent to Graham and Hutchins from Albany by surgeon Edward Jarvis; another, possibly originating inland, sent by Ferdinand Jacobs; plus a pelican bill sent from Cumberland House by William Tomison. Forster's error was corrected when J.F. Gmelin, in 1789, bestowed the binomial of *Pelecanus erythrorhynchos*, based on the illustration of a Hudson Bay specimen in Thomas Latham's *General Synopsis of Birds*, volume 3, 1785.

23 E.2/12, Williams 1969, 40–1.

24 E.2/5.

25 Forster 1773, 155.

26 E.2/12, Williams 1969, 132.

27 http://www.mcgill.ca/mcqupress/homepa/eighteenth-century naturalists/graham.html

CHAPTER SIX

1 HBCA A.1/42, 152; Wallace 1934, 43.

2 Tyrrell 1934, 28; Wallace 1934, 43.

3 There was also a contemporary American Thomas Hutchins (1730–1789), a military engineer, geographer and cartographer, born in Monmouth County, New Jersey, died in Pittsburgh (Hicks 1932, DAB 9:435–6). Sadly the 1970 reprint of Poggendorff's compilation of world scientists melded the two Thomas Hutchins into one; Harkanyi's 1990 bibliography of scientists (362–3) made the identical error.

4 He paid Sutherland £10 per year for five years. Sutherland later rose through the ranks as labourer, steward, linguist, trader (at £40 per annum) and member of York council (at £80 p.a.), acting chief at York Factory, 1794–95, then chief at Cumberland House 1795-96, and district chief at Edmonton 1796–97 (Brown 1979, DCB 4:726–7).

5 Rich 1979a, DCB 4:740–1.

6 Tyrrell 1934, 264.

7 Thorman 1979, DCB 4:524–5.

8 Avis 1969, 456. The HBC had accepted Germain Maugenest's suggestion that the HBC blankets be traded on the basis of one beaver skin per blanket 'point' (Rich 1959, 109).

9   Introduction of these blankets as a trade item was the "one great success" of the HBC (Rich 1960, 50).

10 Bowes 1993, 59–60; current price of $299 at the Saskatoon Hudson's Bay Company store, 22 December 2001.

11 Ewart 1983, 571–4.

12 Williams 1969, 299.

13 Ewart 1995, 39; HBCA B.239/A/66.

14 Williams 1969, 327.

15 Ewart 1995, 40.

16 Ewart 1983, 573; McIntyre and Houston 1999, 1543–7.

17 Houston and Houston 2000, 112–15.

18 All three species of sorrel have been used to treat scurvy. Mountain sorrel or "scurvy-grass" occurs on the east coast of Hudson Bay and is eaten by the Inuit (Porsild and Cody 1980, 261). Wood Sorrel, *Oxalis acetosella*, and Yellow Wood Sorrel, *Oxalis stricta* or *O. corniculata*, are also edible, refreshing, and antiscorbutic (Erichsen-Brown 1979, 333–5).

19 Ewart 1995, 40; HBCA B.3/b/19, 23 May 1782, 37.

20 The Royal Society, already concerned in 1777 with the quality and the calibration of instruments, sent only the best available with Wales (Williams 1979b, DCB 4:757-8).

21 Ball 1982, thesis, 99.

22 B.239/a/67, Hutchins' meteorological journal, 1771, 2; Ball 1982, 55.

23 Hutchins 1776, 174–81.

24 Black was elected to the chair of medicine and chemistry at the University of Edinburgh in 1766 (Anderson 1986).

25 Hutchins 1783, 303–70.

26 Crowther 1962, 9–13. Crowther considers Black, though he carried on an active medical practice and published only three papers in his lifetime, to be the founder of modern chemistry, the inventor of quantitative analysis, and one of the four chief scientists of the Industrial Revolution.

27 Hutchins 1783, 320.

28 Cavendish 1783. Read at the meeting of 1 May 1783. Cavendish, an eccentric, "tall, thin, morbidly shy bachelor" led the life of a recluse. He discovered hydrogen, thermometry, latent heat, specific heat, thermal expansion, melting points, and the heat changes associated with chemical reactions. His research was "a combination of mathematical precision with ... astonishingly accurate experimental investigations." Cavendish won the Copley Medal in 1766 (Crowther 1962, 274–6, 291, 296; Royal Society 1940, 345).

29 Blagden 1783, 329, 343, 353. Blagden obtained his MD degree from Edinburgh in 1768. A fellow of the Royal Society, later knighted, and a friend of Sir Joseph Banks, the long-term Royal Society president, Blagden became secretary of the

Royal Society in 1784. The most noteworthy of Blagden's physical papers, "Cooling of water below its freezing point," read before the Royal Society on 31 January 1788, gained him the Copley Medal that year (Harrison 1949, DNB 11:617–18 ; Royal Society 1940, 346).

30 Blagden 1783, 397.

31 The Copley Medal, the highest honour bestowed by the Royal Society and in its day the rough equivalent of modern Nobel Prizes, originated in a legacy received from the estate of Sir Godfrey Copley in 1709. Recipients in the eighteenth century included Captain James Cook, Benjamin Franklin, Stephen Hales, Sir William Herschel, Dr John Hunter, Joseph Priestley, and Alessandro Volta. The award has continued into the twentieth century, with Neils Bohr, Sir William Bragg, Albert Einstein, and Ivan Petrovich Pavlov among the recipients (Royal Society of London 1940, 112–13, 345–6; Stimson 1968, 139–40). Sir Godfrey Copley, member of Parliament for Thirsk from 1695 until his death and a friend of Sir Hans Sloane, was elected a fellow of the Royal Society in 1691. Copley brought together a valuable collection of prints and mathematical instruments (Lee 1949, DNB 4:1102). Copley's will bequeathed one hundred pounds in trust to the Royal Society, money which has been used to award a gold medal almost every year since 1731.

32 Middleton 1742. Middleton later resigned from the HBC and at the behest of Arthur Dobbs in 1742 was appointed commander of an Arctic discovery expedition. He sailed in the *Furnace*, with his cousin William Moor in command of the *Discovery*. Middleton explored and mapped Wager Bay and discovered Repulse Bay, but failed to explore Chesterfield Inlet. Dobbs subsequently destroyed Middleton's career "by a malicious campaign of denigration." (Williams 1974, DCB 3:446–50; Barr and Williams 1994).

33 Stearns 1945, 13.

34 Cooke and Holland 1978, 101; HBCA A.11/4, fo. 168; A.6/13, fo. 28d; B.135/a/65; B.135/a/66, all pers. comm. Judith H. Beattie, 8 May 2000.

35 Williams 1979a, DCB 4:377–8.

36 Williams 1979a, DCB 4:377–8.

37 Tyrrell 1934, 263.

38 Williams 1969, Appendix C, 362–85.

39 The Chepethewuck is mentioned but without identifying features or locality in Williams 1969, 111; worse, Glover's footnote mentions the Capercaillie in a confusing manner. However, Glover does not infer that the Chepethewuck is a Capercaillie. Only E.2/9 sets the record straight as to species and locality.

40 In 1828, the farthest north record of the Greater Prairie-Chicken was in Essex County, extreme southwestern Ontario, about 600 miles to the south of Henley House. As settlers cleared land, this species spread eastward to Toronto by 1858 and north to Holland Marsh at the south end of Lake Simcoe by 1875. It then

retreated, until by 1924 it was extirpated from southern Ontario (Lumsden 1966, 33–45). Prairie-chicken spread north in Michigan to Sault Ste.-Marie, then gradually colonized Manitoulin Island (350 miles south of Henley House) from west to east between 1941 and 1962, before being swamped through hybridization with a species newly-arrived from the north, the Sharp-tailed Grouse (Peck and James 1983, 136–7).

41 Located on the World Wide Web at http://www.mcgill.ca/mqupress/eighteenth-centurynaturalists/hutchins.html

42 Hutchins' weights were not yet in print!

43 Barrington 1772b, 265–320. J. Legg knew better, as is evident from his 55-page booklet, *A Discourse on the Emigration of British Birds*, 1780.

44 Pennant 1792, 1:ccxcvii, but not repeated in the species account for Burbot, volume 3:366. This count, 671,248, is also recorded in Williams 1969, Appendix C, 382.

45 B.239/a/67, courtesy of the late Dr William B. Ewart

46 The unfortunate result of the swan skin trade was a drop in the continental population of Trumpeter Swans from 130,000 to perhaps 1,000 by the end of the nineteenth century (Lumsden 1984, 420).

47 Stearns 1945, 13; see Appendix E.

48 Royal Society Hutchins mss., 94.

49 Royal Society Hutchins mss., 50. It should be noted that Graham, who was not known to own a microscope, said that lice "appeared very beautiful when viewed with a microscope" (Williams 1969, 126). Samuel Hearne similarly told of finding lice on lemmings which he endeavoured to examine with his "excellent microscope" at Churchill but "the weather was so exceedingly cold, that the glasses became damp with the moisture of my breath before I could get a single sight" (Tyrrell 1911, 360). Were both Graham and Hearne copying Hutchins or at least reporting on their joint experience with the same microscope?

50 Royal Society Hutchins mss., 101.

51 Williams 1969, 393; Royal Society Hutchins mss., 89–90.

52 Richardson and Swainson 1832, 2: 468–71; "apis" means "small" in Cree (Anderson 1971, 2).

53 Taverner 1931, 28-40.

54 Anonymous. "And the goose honks high." In volume 1, number 1, of a short-lived publication, *The Buzzard*, published by the Cooper Club of Los Angeles in April 1926. (Note the pun; *Anser* was the earlier scientific name for goose, before *Branta*).

55 Aldrich, 1946. Hutchins' Goose breeds mainly on Victoria and Banks Islands in the Canadian Arctic. It is remarkable indeed that both the world's largest and smallest geese are found within what recent authorities recognize as eleven

subspecies of a single North American species, *Branta canadensis* (Dickson 2000, 11, 12, 27).

56   Caching.

57   Pennant 1792, 2:290.

CHAPTER SEVEN

1   Glover 1958, xii–xiii; Thomson 1975, 142–3; Johnson 1974b, DNB 3:489–90.

2   Van Kirk 1979b, DCB 4:583–5.

3   Tyrrell 1911, 107. Did Norton make good progress considering how little was spent? Or is Hearne using classic English sarcasm, telling us that Norton learned little considering the amount spent?

4   Cooke and Holland 1978, 55.

5   Williams 1962, 129.

6   Williams 1962, 132.

7   Glover 1958, xiii.

8   Tyrrell 1911, 107.

9   On Norton's death, Andrew Graham was called to take over Churchill, where he arrived 3 March after a 26-day overland journey (Williams 1969, 347).

10   Rich, 1959, 2:45.

11   Glover 1958, xi.

12   Lamb 1970, 107.

13   HBCA A.1/43, fo. 45.

14   Tyrrell 1911, 405.

CHAPTER EIGHT

1   Marsh 1988, 973. Heather Rollason Driscoll's PhD dissertation adds: "Despite Hearne's lack of formal education and in the absence of a formal scientific method, he managed to develop his own rational and clear method for making observations in the natural world. His intelligence revealed itself, not in his jumbled and often haphazard prose, but in his detailed and careful descriptions of everything around him."

2   Chichester 1949, DNB 9:335.

3   Mackinnon 1979, DCB 4:339–42.

4   Coues 1878, 591.

5   Allen 1951, 322.

6   Glover 1958, vii.

7   Tyrrell 1911, 54.

8   In the late 1750s Matonabbee, a Chipewyan born and raised at Churchill, undertook the dangerous assignment of living as an ambassador among the

Crees; he successfully terminated the hostilities between the two tribes. Later, when living at Churchill, he brought more furs than any other Indian. He committed suicide after la Pérouse captured Churchill in 1782. (Gillespie 1979, DCB 4:523–4).

9 Tyrrell 1911, 186.

10 Tyrrell 1911, 30.

11 MacLaren 1991, 26.

12 The best account of Hearne's route is by Fuller 1999, 257–71.

13 Rich 1967, 148.

14 Rich 1967, 160.

15 Mackinnon 1979, DCB 4:339–42. The need for secrecy had prevented La Pérouse's crew, who sailed from Santo Domingo in the warm Caribbean, from bringing any winter clothing! (Dunmore 1994, liv).

16 Glover 1958, xxxiv.

17 Allen 1951, 524.

18 Bartlett 1865–82, 2:79.

19 Allen's story is interesting but does not ring true. Bartlett and Gallatin were men of unusual influence and authority, yet Gallatin's reminiscences, perhaps relayed late in life to Bartlett, contain obvious errors. At Machias, Maine, Gallatin did indeed meet La Pérouse, in command of the *Amàzone* frigate engaged in convoy duty for the American rebels between early March and early December 1781 (Stevens 1898, 12–16; Dunmore 1994, liii). But this was a year before the Hudson Bay raids in 1782! La Pérouse captured Churchill and York Factory, not Fort Albany.

Bartlett was a historian, linguist, commissioner for the United States-Mexico boundary survey in 1850–53, and author of *Dictionary of Americanisms* (Bartlett 1859). Albert Gallatin, a Swiss, later taught French at Harvard College, was elected to the United States House of Representatives, led his party in the contest that elected Thomas Jefferson, and became Jefferson's secretary of the treasury in 1801 (Stevens 1898, 10–16).

20 Glover 1958, xxxiv.

21 Only Cooke and Holland (1978, 101) tell us that Stromness was Hearne's successful destination on 15 October.

22 La Pérouse sailed on 1 September and arrived at Cadiz, Spain, on 13 October, with four hundred men sick and seventy dead from scurvy. Dunmore 1994, lv, lvi.

23 "The introduction received its final form in the summer of 1790." Glover 1958, xl.

24 Glover 1958, xxxix, xliii.

25 Glover 1958, xliii.

26 Mackinnon 1979, 342.

27 Levere 1993, 102.

28 Tyrrell 1911, 17.

29 Tyrrell 1911, 132.

30 His stylized sketch of "A winter view in the Athapuscow Lake" is reproduced in Houston and MacLaren, *Arctic Artist*, 1994, p. 298 and fig. 24.

31 Ball 1986, 125, 132.

32 Glover 1958, xxxviii.

33 Glover's footnotes in his edition of Hearne mention Pennant another eleven times.

34 Glover 1969, xiii.

35 Glover 1958, xxix.

36 Glover 1958, xxix.

37 Hearne was not the first to describe the Musk-ox. Henry Kelsey had described it north of Churchill on 27 June 1689 (Doughty and Martin 1929, xix). Nicolas Jérémie provided another good description of the musk-ox from the same area about 1694 (Douglas and Wallace 1926, 19–20).

38 James 1942; Zochert 1980, 34-7.

39 This early journal was subtitled *Proceedings of the Natural History Society of Montreal.*

40 Ross 1861, 6:433–4; 1862, 7:137–55.

41 Cassin 1861, 73.

42 Tyrrell 1911, 360.

43 Tyrrell 1911, 215. In October 1821, during the tragic overland trek of the First Franklin expedition, consumption of such warble-fly larvae helped save the lives of John Franklin, John Richardson, George Back, the surviving three interpreters and two of eleven voyageurs (Houston 1984, 196).

44 Tyrrell 1911, 258

45 Tyrrell 1911, 236–7.

46 Webster and Webster 1973, 467.

47 Bühler 1981, 138–40. Karl Friedrich Gauss won the Copley Medal in 1838.

48 Tyrrell 1911, 403.

49 Tyrrell 1911, 397.

50 Audubon 1831–9, reprinted 1967, 5:73–83.

51 Tyrrell 1911, 376.

52 The differences in swan tracheal convolutions were sorted out in 1832 by dissection of specimens from the Hudson bay territory specimen provided by Dr. John Richardson (Yarrell 1832, 1–5, and see Taverner 1940, 75–6).

53 Tyrrell 1911, 355.

54 Even as late as 1935, in a definitive monograph (Taylor 1935) reported that "available accounts of the actual mating process do not agree." Finally, in 1949 Shadle (159–63) observed and photographed porcupine copulation in his lab-

oratory at the University of Buffalo. The male stands on his tail and hindlegs to mount the female while she holds her tail forward over her back. Roze (1989, 145–54) adds that the female is in heat for only twelve hours per year, but pregnant or lactating for eleven months of each year. Prior to the one to five-minute sex act, the male showers his intended with his urine.

55 Is this the second-earliest (after Forster) reference to aftershafts?; they were not mentioned in C.L. Nitzsch's 1833 classic work, *Pterylographiae Avium*, 1840, London. – Joseph R. Jehl, Jr.

56 A distinction known also to John Richardson in 1832 (*Fauna Boreali-Americana*, 2:396–7), and to A.C. Bent in 1927 (Life Histories 142:297), but to almost no intervening authors who, as Bent stated, claimed that "the sexes are alike."

57 Tyrrell 1911, 406.

58 Hanson 1965, 1997.

59 Sterling 1963, 134–5.

CHAPTER NINE

1 Fidler was an employee at Manchester House, 4 October to mid-December 1789, then writer at South Branch House, 21 December 1789 – 2 June 1790 (MacGregor 1966, 18–21).

2 MacGregor 1966, 22.

3 Haig 1992; MacGregor 1966, 63–86.

4 Not to be confused with the long-established Carlton House on the North Saskatchewan River.

5 Johnson 1968.

6 MacGregor 1966, 166. George Hyde Wollaston was a prominent committee member of the HBC in London (Rich 1959, 270). David Thompson had crossed Wollaston Lake in June 1796, but had failed to give it a name (Cooke and Holland 1978, 119, 131).

7 Gray 1963, 110–11.

8 The four Métis were Cuthbert Grant, Bostonais Pangman, William Shaw, and Bonhomme Montour (MacGregor 1966, 199).

9 Houston and Houston 1988, 23–6.

10 MacGregor 1966, 229. Voorhis does not list this Fort Halkett.

11 From 1810 through 1819 his income had been £100 per year (MacGregor 1966, 174, 233).

12 Wallace 1943, 34–5; Fidler 1959, 120–3.

13 Lindsay 1986, 212, 215.

14 Ball 1982, 88.

15 Ruggles 1980, 30–1.

16 Lindsay 1986, 218.

17 Beattie 1993, 4.

18 Beattie 1993, 4.

19 Ruggles 1991, 9, 61.

20 MacGregor 1966, 247.

21 Haig 1992; MacGregor 1966, 63–86.

22 Houston 1997a, 269; Lindsay 1986, 218.

23 HBCA E.3, 2.

24 Lowe 1961, 5.

25 Tests of the freezing of alcohol had a practical outcome, since the men complained of the dilution of the brandy and rum issued them; by testing how quickly each froze, they were testing the amount of dilution by water. So-called English Brandy was actually gin with colouring added – TFB

26 HBCA B.51/a/2.

27 Ball 1992a, 185–95.

28 Lindsay 1986, 215.

29 HBCA B.22/e/1,6.

30 Lowe 1961, 5.

31 Atton 1985, 538–40.

32 MacGregor 1966, 32.

33 Haig 1992, 75.

34 Haig 1992, 80-81.

35 MacGregor 1966, 135.

36 HBCA B.22/e/1,6.

37 http://www.mcgill.ca/mcqupress/homepa/eighteenth-centurynaturalists/fidler.html

38 HBCA B.51/e/1 This paragraph was discovered and cited by Charles Elton and Mary Nicholson (1942) in their renowned, thorough, fifteen-year study of hare, lynx and muskrat cycles as recorded in the archives of the HBC, while these records were still in London, England. Fidler's returns for Lynx from the Manetoba [sic] District were: 2 in 1817, record missing for 1818, 9 in 1819, 483 in 1820, and 863 in 1821.

39 Keith 1990.

40 Brand, Keith and Fischer 1976, 416–28.

41 Keith 1963; Krebs, Boutin and Boonstra 2001.

CHAPTER TEN

1 The *Seahorse II*, under command of Captain William Christopher, left York Factory on 7 September 1771 and arrived in London on 17 October. The *King George II*, Captain Jonathan Fowler, Jr., left Churchill 7 September and reached London 17 October (Cooke and Holland 1978,88). The chests cleared customs about 22 October (Leveson Gower 1934, 31).

2   The *Prince Rupert IV*, Captain Joseph Richards, left Moose Factory 14 September and arrived in London 29 October 1771. Two boxes of specimens from Moose Factory and Albany cleared customs quickly (Leveson Gower 1934, 31).

3   Forster 1772c, 382–433. See Chapter 1.

4   Williams 1969, 394.

5   The *King George II*, under command of Captain Jonathan Fowler, Jr., left York Factory on 5 September 1772 and arrived in London on 3 October (Cooke and Holland 1978, 89).

6   HBCA A.11/115, 23 August 1773.

7   The letter of thanks was signed by Hon. Daines Barrington, Joseph Banks, Daniel Solander and Dr Charles Blagden (Leveson Gower 1934, 66).

8   Buffon 1771–86.

9   Donovan and Ouellet, 1993, 154.

10 Farber 1972, 261.

11 Farber 1972, 262–3.

12 Farber 1972, 279.

13 American Ornithologists' Union 2000, 448.

14 Sabine 1823, 671–2; Houston 1974, 176–7.

15 Richardson 1828, 1:55–6.

16 Avis 1967, 351.

17 Logan 1982, 34.

18 Davies 1770, 185.

19 Davies 1770, 186.

20 Davies 1770, 187.

21 Kuckhan 1770, 312.

22 Forster, 1771, 35.

23 Farber 1977, 54

24 Houston 1983, 95.

25 Stevens 1936.

26 Baillie 1946.

27 McAtee 1950.

28 Snyder 1963.

29 Preble 1902, 23–38.

30 Wife of famous Cornell University ornithologist Arthur A. Allen.

31 Allen 1951.

32 Spencer Fullerton Baird was assistant secretary of the Smithsonian Institution, 1850–78 (Dall 1915). Baird sent his collaborators useful manuals that would aid in identification. He also sent alcohol intended for preserving specimens but on occasion used as a beverage.

33 Lindsay 1993, 121–8.

34 Humboldt, "a superb observer and a far-reaching innovator in the organization of collecting numerical data" (Kellner 1963, 233) is considered by some to

be the last universal man; he died in 1859, the year Darwin published his magnum opus.

CHAPTER ELEVEN

1   Ponte 1976.
2   Catchpole and Moodie 1978, 113.
3   Fiocco, Fuà, and Visconti 1996.
4   Quinn and Neal 1992, 623–48.
5   Jones and Bradley 1992, 649.
6   National Research Council 1999.
7   Manley 1974, 389–405.
8   Cassedy 1969, 193–204.
9   Lamb 1977, 22–3.
10 Lamb 1977, 30.
11 Bettany 1949, 1117.
12 Intergovernmental Panel on Climate Change 1996.
13 Hare and Thomas 1979, 36.
14 Ball 1992b, 197.
15 Prebble 1969.
16 Ball 1982, 22.
17 Meteorology is the study of the physics of the atmosphere. Climatology is the study of weather patterns over time or in a particular area. Weather is the total atmospheric conditions experienced at a given moment.
18 Lamb 1970, 414.
19 Catchpole and Faurer 1985, 121–8; Catchpole and Halpin 1987, 233–44.
20 Wilson 1982, 228.
21 Ball 1994, 1152. The records from the east side of Hudson Bay were subjected to modern Atmospheric Environment Services quality control procedures and passed without difficulty (Bryson 1982, 206).
22 The low aboriginal population density prior to the arrival of fur traders lessened their impact on the environment. Their use of fire, however, was a factor in change. "They deployed fire to improve their access to animals, to improve or eliminate forage for the animals they depended on for food, and to drive and encircle animals ... also ... as a weapon, as a means of communication, and to improve travel" (Krech 1999, 103, 107).
23 Ball 1982, 79.
24 Barr and Williams 1994. Where an area in July has a mean temperature below 13° Celsius, there will be tundra patches; where it is below 10° C., there will be no trees (Hare 1970, 393).

25 That is, north of the isotherm the three summer months of June, July, and August average less than 10° C, whereas south of the line they average above 10° C.

26 Ball 1985, 222.

27 Scott et al. 1988, 199–211.

28 Lamb 1970, 414.

29 Ball 1982.

30 Catchpole and Moodie 1978, 125.

31 Catchpole 1980, 35, 37.

32 For dates of inward and outward passages through Hudson Strait, 1750–1870, and years ships were beset by ice, see Catchpole and Ball 1981, 61, 67. For sea ice conditions in Hudson Bay in 1816, the year of an unusual cold drought, see Catchpole and Faurer 1985, 121–8.

33 Ball 1982.

34 Catchpole 1980, 17–60; Williams 1975, 3, 10.

35 Rousseau 1969, DCB 2:296–300.

36 Ball 1982.

37 Moodie 1977, 268–74; see excerpt from Simmons 1994 thesis (Appendix A).

38 Moodie 1977, 271, 273.

39 During the prolonged construction of Fort Prince of Wales, 1731–62, a journal was kept there and another simultaneously at the fur trade post nearby, Churchill Factory. Since 1884, Churchill has had three different weather stations: from 1884 to 1928 at the old town site on the west side of the harbour; from 1929 to 1951 at the marine port on the east side of the harbour; from 1943 to the present at a modern weather centre at the airport.

40 Harington 1992, 7.

41 Lefroy and Richardson 1855. Both men had the full cooperation of the HBC; as well as making meteorological records available, the HBC furnished "gratituitous canoe conveyance" to Lefroy (Stanley 1955, xix).

42 A.B. Lowe published the first brief piece on weather records when he wrote about Peter Fidler, "Canada's first weather man," in *The Beaver* in 1961. Unfortunately, Lowe's other work has not been published but is available in the Climate Centre in Winnipeg.

43 Mackay and MacKay 1965, 7–16.

44 Ball 1982, 37.

45 Catchpole and Moodie 1978, 134.

46 Wilson 1982.

47 Ball 1992c, 47.

48 Dickason 1992, 143.

49 1684 and 1689.

50 Ball 1992c, 47.

51 Ball 1992c, 57.

52 Chief Factor at York Factory from 1788 to 1802.

53 HBCA PAM B.239/a/97.

54 Dodge 1969, DCB 2:318–20.

55 Van Kirk 1979a, DCB 4:380–1.

56 Often spelled McCleish (Johnson 1974a, DCB 3:414–15).

57 Ball 1982, 211.

58 Ball 1982, 216.

59 These followed the method of Jurin, 1722, and are listed in Ball 1982.

60 Agassiz 1840. His full name was Jean Louis Rodolphe Agassiz.

61 Peel 1987, DCB 6:767–8.

62 Foster 1987, DCB 6:17–18.

63 HBCA A.6/18, 211-13.

64 Ball 1992b, 197.

65 Reproduced by Thomas Topping in the "Memorands for a Meteorological
    Journal" at Churchill, 1811-13, B.42/139a. For Beaufort, see Laughton 1949a.

66 Bryce 1900, 50–7.

67 Copernicus and Galileo both understood that the earth revolved around the
    sun, not vice versa, but after a long trial for publishing this fact, Galileo's dis-
    covery earned him lifetime home confinement under guard.

68 See Sobel 1995. The prize was never awarded but consolation payments of
    £10,000 in late 1765 and of £8,750 in June 1773 were made to John Harrison
    for a watch, H-5, accurate to within one-third of a second per day. This allowed
    an exactitude in longitude determination not previously possible.

69 Maskelyne, the astronomer royal, received the Copley medal in 1775 (Clerke
    1949, DNB 12:1299–301).

70 Carlyle 1949, DNB 20:490–1.

71 Dymond and Wales 1771 Only a few years after this, in 1772–75, Wales became
    the astronomer on the second Pacific voyage of Captain James Cook (Williams
    1979b, DCB 4:757–8). Wales later taught mathematics, astronomy and naviga-
    tion at Christ's Hospital School in London, where his pupils included Samuel
    Taylor Coleridge and Charles Lamb (Williams 1979b, 758; Fernie 1998, 425).
    Wales designed a printed tabular form to gather information from clergy on
    the annual number of baptisms and burials,"political arithmetic [which] com-
    prised the virtues of quantification and the ideals of the Enlightenment" (Rus-
    nock 1999, 60, 66). Dymond disappeared into obscurity.

72 Ruggles 1976, 12–13.

73 The Transit of Venus occurs at intervals of 8, $121\frac{1}{2}$, 8, and $105\frac{1}{2}$ years,
    repeated ad infinitum. The transit occurred again on 9 December 1874 and 6

December 1882, and will recur on 8 June 2004 and 6 June 2012 (Woolf 1959; Phillips 1942).

74 In addition to Wales at Churchill and Captain Cook in Tahiti, there were observers in Newfoundland, Siberia, South Africa, India, and the islands of St Helena in the Atlantic Ocean and Rodrigues in the Indian Ocean. Travel and a £1,400 telescope for each observer made these expensive undertakings (Fernie 1997, 418, 420; 1998, 125, 422).

75. Fernie 1976, 17.

76 Goetzmann (1986, 44) feels, however, that Cook's "most important duty was to establish the British empire on the bottom side of the globe. Science was seen as being of primary assistance in this imperial venture." Captain Cook, incidentally, was awarded the Copley Medal in 1776.

77 The Mason-Dixon line is at 39° 43' 26.3" north latitude, the southern boundary of Pennsylvania.

78 Wales 1771, 100; Proctor 1874; Ball and Dyck 1984, 51–6; the late J. Edward Kennedy, personal communication.

79 Jurin 1722, 422–7.

80 No definition of ambrometer was found in the OED or in a dictionary of scientific instruments.

81 Ludlum 1966 and 1968, *Early American Winters 1604–1820*, and *Early American Winters 1821–1870*.

82 White to Pennant 8 October 1768. www.worldwideschool.org/library/books/geo/geography/TheNaturalHistoryofSelborne/.

83 Quoted in Worster 1994, 7.

84 Rich 1958a; Newman 1985, 72, commented on the HBC motto: "A whimsical derivation of the vengeful biblical 'an eye for an eye' sentiment, it meant, roughly, 'a skin for its equivalent.' The original saying was probably intended to convey the risks incurred by the early adventurers, as in 'we risk our skins to get your pelts.'" Anne Morton informs us that the motto is thought to be based on Job 4:2 (King James version), where Satan says "skin for skin, yea all that a man hath will he give for his life."

85 Climate metaphorically provides the edge pieces for the "jig-saw puzzle"; each specialist has a piece of this puzzle, but has lost the illustration on the puzzle box top that provides the overall picture.

86 Tyrrell 1911, 403.

87 Ball 1983a, 85–93.

88 Spring arrival dates for Snow Buntings at York Factory, the first known from northern North America, were 9 March 1715; 31 March 1728; 25 March 1729; 24 March 1732; 15 March 1733; 19 March 1734; 25 March 1735; 28 April 1737, only four days in advance of geese!; 17 March 1739; 15 March 1746; 25 March

1748; 22 April 1749; 15 March 1751; 24 March 1752; 5 April 1753; 3 April 1754; 6 April 1755; 31 March 1756; 31 March 1757; 24 March 1758; 29 March 1760; 29 March 1761; 9 April 1762; 9 April 1778; 3 April 1784; 6 April 1790; 27 March 1800; 4 April 1801; 9 April 1817; 26 March 1820; 27 March 1851.

89 Ball 1986, 125.

CHAPTER TWELVE

1   Rosen 1992, 21.

2   Rosen 1992, 13.

3   Sellers 1934, 15. Spelling of the city was changed to "Charleston" in 1783, to announce independence from the British Crown, and to reflect more accurately the local pronunciation, CHAHLston (Fraser 1989, 169).

4   Fraser 1989, 128.

5   Mendelsohn, E., 1976, John Lining, 120-134, In: Hindle, B., ed., *Early American Science*. New York: Science History Publications, 1976.

6   Weir 1983, 240.

7   Mendelsohn 1976, 120.

8   His pen name; see Williams 1930, Crèvecoeur, Michel-Guillaume Jean de. *Dictionary of American Biography* 4:542–4

9   Crèvecoeur, Hector St. John de 1782, reprinted 1951, *Letters from an American Farmer*, 158–9.

10 Fraser 1989, 101, 131.

11 Cash 1999, 706–7.

12 Berkeley and Berkeley 1969, 50.

13 Lining 1756, *Essays and Observations, Physical and Literary* 1:386–9; Mendelsohn 1976, 120.

14 Lining, 1743–53, *Philosophical Transactions* 42:491–509; 43:318–30; 45:336–45; 48:284–6; Fraser 1989, 70.

15 Berkeley and Berkeley 1969, 271.

16 *Transactions of the Medical Society of London*; Waring 1964.

17 Chalmers 1776, *Account of the Weather and Disease of South-Carolina*, London; Cassedy 1969, 193-204; Fleming 1990, 6.

18 Hunt 1949, DNB 3:1190.

19 For most of its existence, botany "has been but a branch of medicine – and a subordinate branch at that ... the only justification for distinguishing different kinds of plants ... was assumed to be their potential value therapeutically" (Allen 2000, 335). University teaching of botany began about 1200 A.D., particularly in Montpellier, France, and Basel, Switzerland. Every candidate for a medical degree at Montpellier had to own copies of Galen's various works but there was no requirement that they be showed living plants. About 1550, the botan-

ical garden (*hortus medicus*) and the herbarium (*hortus siccus*) were "invented" so that plants were demonstrated to the medical students (Nelson 1995, 143).

20 In Virginia, botany and entomology were the central interests of John Banister (1650–1692), the first University-trained naturalist to send specimens from America. Banister arrived in Virginia in 1678. The 1680 plant catalogue of this young Episcopal minister, previously the chaplain of Magdalen College at Oxford University, was largely appropriated and published by others, particularly John Ray in his *Historia plantarum* (Ewan and Ewan 1970). Banister died in 1692, accidentally shot while on a collecting expedition.

21 Allen 1951, 473.

22 Feduccia 1985, xiii.

23 Hanley 1977, 3.

24 Catesby 1729–47.

25 Allen 1951, 473.

26 McAtee 1957a, 177–94.

27 Frick and Stearns 1961, 107.

28 Allen 1951, 463.

29 Allen 1937, 475.

30 Hanley 1977, 15.

31 The next centre to contribute natural-history specimens was Philadelphia, whose population grew to 32,200 by 1770. William Bartram's drawings of birds and turtles were made between 1756 and 1761, while he resided in Philadelphia; they were sent to Peter Collinson and thence to George Edwards in England.

32 Fraser 1989, 112.

33 Berkeley and Berkeley 1969, 123.

34 Sanders and Anderson 1999, 13.

35 Mendelsohn 1976, 126.

36 Berkeley and Berkeley 1969, 326.

37 Garden also corresponded directly with Pennant and sent other specimens directly to him (Berkeley and Berkeley 1969, 229, 307).

APPENDIX C

1 Williams at the time was a Professor of History at Queen Mary College, London.

2 Richard Glover was born 21 September 1909. He left the History department at the University of Manitoba in 1964 to become director of the National Museums of Canada and worked there until 1967, when he felt compelled to resign on a matter of principle due to government interference. He then taught history at Carleton University, Ottawa until his retirement in 1979. He died in Victoria, British Columbia, of prostate cancer with skeletal metastases,

on 23 September 1985. In addition to his major contributions to our understanding of the Canadian fur trade and exploration, he was an authority on
the New Testament and European military history (Jones and Bickerton 1985).

3   Williams 1978, 6.

4   Williams 1978, 5–11.

5   In 1819, John Richardson was chosen as surgeon-naturalist for the first Franklin
arctic exploring expedition because he had excelled in zoology and botany while
a medical student in Edinburgh. His thesis for the advanced MD degree was
written entirely in Latin.

6   Harris 1994.

7   In 1799, 416 of the 530 Europeans on the HBC payroll came from the Orkney
Islands (Ball 1988, 43). They considered themselves second to none in their
ability to bear fatigue and toil (Burley 1997, 77).

8   Pennant 1768, 1:110–12.

9   Browning and Banks 1990, 80–3.

10 König et al. 1999, 289.

11 CSH met with Richard C. Banks and Ralph M. Browning of the Smithsonian
Museum of Natural History; together we read Hutchins' original notes; we
reached a unanimous conclusion.

12 Browning and Banks 1990.

13 Four times the same bird species is duplicated in two different accounts; four
times two different Cree names were given to one species.

14 E.2/10, Williams 1969, 389.

15 In litt., W.E. Godfrey to CSH, 7 May 1990

16 Williams 1978, 8.

17 In litt., G. Williams to CSH, 11 December 1990. Graham outlived Hutchins by
twenty-five years, two months.

18 Williams 1983, DCB 5:362–3; Rich 1979b, DCB 4:742–3.

19 These erroneous statements were corrected in E.2/12, the Hutchins-Graham
collaboration.

20 See Meyer, 1991, "The goose dance in swampy Cree religion."

21 Coot, or sea-coot, was also used by northerners for all three species of scoter,
and less commonly, for the Common Eider (Sayre 1996, 110–12).

22 E.2/5, 66.

23 Glover 1960. Banfield 1974, *The Mammals of Canada*, 387, shows *pearyi* only from
the northern tip of Victoria Island, adjacent Banks Island, and "high Arctic"
islands to the north.

24 Glover 1969, xxxv. Since the Greater Prairie-Chicken was known to Pennant,
this suggests the version loaned him was E.2/9.

25 Pennant 1792 2:356–7. The smaller subspecies, the Heath Hen, had been extirpated from New York and Connecticut and then survived only on Martha's

Vineyard, Massachusetts, from 1870 until extinction in 1932 (Schroeder and Robb 1993).

26 In the early 1800s the Greater Prairie-Chicken was still resident in Kent and Essex counties in extreme southwestern Ontario. With forest clearing it spread east as far as Toronto, but disappeared by the early 1900s (Lumsden 1966, 33–45). It invaded the Sault Ste Marie area from Michigan about 1925 and colonized Manitoulin Island, Ontario, until the late 1940s, when it disappeared through interbreeding with the Sharp-tailed Grouse (Lumsden 1970, 57–8). Manitoulin Island is 600 km south of Henley House. The Graham-Pennant record from 1770 has been overlooked or ignored by subsequent authorities.

27 Stearns 1945, 12.

28 Hoare 1982, 1:48.

29 Elected FRS at the meeting of 27 February 1772 (Hoare 1976a, 68).

30 Forster 1772a.

31 Forster 1772b.

32 Forster 1772c.

33 Forster 1773.

34 Glover 1969. Species from Hudson Bay, mentioned in Latham's *General Synopsis of Birds*, are given in the list of birds in Table 11.1.

35 Williams 1969, 356–8.

36 Glover 1969, xiii–lxxii.

37 Glover 1969, xvii.

38 Seton, "first Chief Scout of the Boy Scouts [of America] and charismatic naturalist, artist, author, public speaker, conservationist, and youth movement activist," was one of the "two most important writers for Noble Indians from roughly 1875 through 1940" (Krech 1999, 19).

39 C.G.A. Gosch edited *Danish Arctic Expeditions, 1605 to 1620* (London: Hakluyt Society 1897). Miller Christy wrote the appendix, "Busse Island," in volume 1. Volume two was Jens Munk's expedition to Hudson Bay.

40 Preble 1902. Preble was a biologist with the United States Biological Survey, 1892–1935.

41 Glover 1969, Introduction, xvii.

42 Seton here mistakenly ascribes the annotations to Pennant, but as seen above, they were probably inserted by Latham.

43 A copy of Christy's book mss., *History of the Hudson's Bay Company*, unpublished, is in the HBC Archives. An outline is reproduced in Document 7.

44 Seton 1946, 144.

45 Houston 1988b, 171–7.

46 Ireland had suffered even more severe potato famines in the Great Freeze of 1740–41, and especially in 1845–51 (Dickson 1997).

47 Christy 1885. On his second trip Christy visited Indian Head, Moose Jaw, and Medicine Hat (Houston 1988b, 174).

48 On the third trip Christy travelled north to the York Colony on the Little White-sand River, near the present site of Yorkton (Houston 1988b, 175).

49 Houston 1980.

50 Britten 1922, 239.

51 Christy 1922, 336-7.

52 Henry Seebohm, 1832–1895, was a Yorkshire-born steel manufacturer and traveller, author of *Birds of Siberia* (1901) and *A History of British Birds, with Coloured Illustrations of their Eggs* (1883–95).(Mearns and Mearns 1988, 464).

53 Miller Christy, FLS, edited, in two volumes, *The Voyages of Captain Luke Foxe of Hull, and Captain Thomas James of Bristol, in Search of a North-West Passage*, in 1631–32 (London: Hakluyt Society).

54 http://www.mcgill.ca/mqupress/homepa/eighteenth-century naturalists/ christy.html

APPENDIX D

1 Lynx returns go back to 1736 (Elton and Nicholson 1942b, 231).

2 Annual fur sales from Hudson Bay are given for Beaver, Pine Marten, Otter, Lynx, Fox, Wolverine, Bear, Wolf, Mink, Muskrat, Raccoon and Fisher (Poland 1892, xxii–xxiii).

3 Keith 1990, 119.

4 MacLulich 1937, 5.

5 Elton and Nicholson 1942b, 215.

6 Keith and Windberg 1978, 15–21.

7 Brand, Keith and Fischer 1976, 416–28.

8 Elton and Nicholson 1942a, 99–117.

9 Hewitt 1921, 226–9.

10 Hewitt 1921, 222–5.

11 Hewitt 1921, 229–30. But Fisher numbers show a lower amplitude of fluctuation than the other cyclical mammals.

12 Rusch et al. 2000, 17.

13 Krebs et al. 2001, 246–50.

14 Criddle 1930, 77–80; Rowan 1948, 7–8.

15 Houston 1987, 56–8.

16 Squires and Reynolds 1997, 1,5.

17 Shelford 1945, 592–6.

18 Poland 1930; Anonymous 1933. The Poland firm was operated over many years by family members. In 1866 Edwin L. Poland was master of the Skinners' Company and in 1902 John Poland, FRCS, was master (Wadmore 1902, 195–6). In

1930 Raymond D. Poland was chairman, and F. Rexford Poland was a member, of the British exhibit at the International fur trade exhibition, Leipzig. In 1933 an advertisement for P.R. Poland & Son, Ltd., described the firm as "Pioneers in the Fur Trade in 1781 Import, Export & Commission"; P. Rexford Poland was the managing director. Raymond Denham Poland was later chairman and managing director and also master of the Skinners Company.

19 Anne Morton, personal communication.

20 Poland 1892.

21 Houston 1997c, 487–8.

22 MacFarlane 1905, 692.

23 Seton 1909, 1:640–3.

24 At Portage la Loche, in present west-central Saskatchewan.

25 Drs Gordon Bell and J.H. Cadham. However, Seton (1909 1:646–9) reported that other hares examined in the United States showed a) generalised enlargement of lymph nodes with a systemic *Pyogenes [Staphylococcus] aureus* infection; b) round stomach worms, *Strongylus strigosus*; c) generalised infections with tapeworm cysts, *Caenurus serialis*; d) tuberculosis of the liver.

26 Coues 1897, 184, 198, 221, 245, 259, 281, 422, 440

27 Seton 1909, 1:621–53; 2: 677–99.

28 The species were Beaver, [Pine] Marten, Raccoon, Otter, Badger, [Red] Fox, [Snowshoe] Rabbit, Fisher, Muskrat, Mink, Wolf, Lynx, Wolverine. Seton noted from his personal observations that all had reached a low ebb in 1904–05 (a year or two later for several species, contrary to the generalization in his text). Seton inadvertently omitted Mink and [Striped] Skunk from his "at low ebb" list on page 111. He also graphed fur returns for the [Black] Bear, the returns showing no discernible cycle.

29 Seton, 1912, 96.

30 Seton 1912, 95–6.

31 Seton 1912, 97.

32 Sifton's "greatest achievement" was "securing settlers for the empty [Canadian] west" (Dafoe 1931, 315).

33 Jones, 1914.

34 Morton 1985, 23. Hewitt 1921, 215, gives incorrect initials (W.H.) for Bacon.

35 MacLulich, 1937.

36 Crowcroft 1991, xii.

37 Soper 1921, 101–8.

38 Morton 1985, 25.

39 Morton 1985, 26.

40 Elton 1933, 63–9, 84–6. Disease is "a result rather than a cause" of the snowshoe hare cycle.

41 Crowcroft 1991, ix

42 Including Richard S. Miller, later a professor of Biology at the University of Saskatchewan.

43 Elton 1942,160.

44 Crowcroft 1991, 15.

45 Elton and Nicholson 1942b, 216–7.

46 *Canadian Field-Naturalist* 47:63–9 and 84–6, 1933; 48:73–8, 1934; 49:79–85, 1935; 50:71–81, 1936; 51:63–73, 1937; 52:63–73, 1938; 53:63–70, 1939; 54:117–24, 1940; 56:17–21, 1942; 57:64–8 and 136–41, 1943; 60:67–70, 1946; *Journal of Animal Ecology* 17:39–44, 1948; 19:15–20, 1950.

47 *Journal of Animal Ecology* 6:368–85, 1937; 7:381–94, 1938; 8:247–60, 1939.

48 Shelford 1943, 472–84.

49 Elton 1942, 157.

50 Elton and Nicholson 1942b, figure 7, 230.

51 Elton and Nicholson 1942a:96–7.

52 Rowan 1925, 494–5; Rowan 1926, 147–89; Rowan 1931.

53 Rowan and Keith 1956, 273–81.

54 Rowan and Keith 1959, 221–6. Rowan had died on 27 June 1957.

55 Brilliantly summarized in Keith 1990.

56 Krebs et al. 2001, 143.

57 http://www.science.ca/scientists/scientistprofile.php?piD=11. Krebs is author of *Ecology: The Experimental Analysis of Distribution and Abundance*, now in its fifth edition, a textbook used worldwide to teach ecology.

58 Krebs 1979, 61–77.

59 Krebs 1978. This paper discussed the stress hypothesis, the behaviour hypothesis based on spacing behaviour, and the Chitty hypothesis or polymorphic behaviour hypothesis. The paper was dedicated to Professor Dennis Chitty upon his retirement from teaching at the Department of Zoology, University of British Columbia in June 1978.

60 Keith 1963; Krebs et al. 2001, 143.

61 Chitty 1996, vii, xi, 3, 20, 199, 200.

62 Chitty was born in Bristol, came to Canada in 1930, spent his summers at Frank's Bay on Lake Nipissing (one of three sites where MacLulich studied snowshoe hares), and obtained his BA from the University of Toronto in 1935. Bill Harkness, the director of the Ontario Fisheries Research Laboratory, suggested that Dennis join Charles Elton for a year – a year that stretched to 26. Helen followed Dennis a year later, after completing her MA; they were married 4 July 1936. In 1961 Dennis Chitty joined the Department of Zoology at the University of British Columbia; he earned the Master Teacher award in 1973. He is alive and well, and celebrated his 89th birthday on 18 September 2001 in Vancouver (Lumley, ed., 2001, *Canadian Who's Who*).

63 Chitty 1996, xi.

64 Elton 1942, 3.

APPENDIX E

1   Tyrrell 1911, 399.

2   Mitchell 1994, 1.

3   Banko 1960, 10–25.

4   Lumsden 1984, 416. The earliest extant HBC trade inventory in 1672 included "two hundred fowling-pieces and powder and shot" (Bryce 1900, 21).

5   Lumsden 1984, 420.

6   Lumsden 1984, 418.

7   South of the present town of Smoky Lake, Alberta.

8   Coues 1897, 615–16.

9   Hurlburt 1977, 55–60, 107. (But beware! Hurlburt fails to warn her readers that another Fort White Earth (#2) was also on the North Saskatchewan River, but in the other direction (west 35 miles) from Edmonton, at the mouth of "White Lake Creek" draining Wabamun Lake; it, too, was occupied in 1810 (Voorhis 1930, 132, 177)).

10 Coale 1915, 82.

11 Coale 1915, 87.

12 Mitchell 1994, 2.

13 Lumsden 1984, 419.

14 Harry Duckworth, personal communication.

15 HBCA A.6/11, fo 170d, courtesy Judith Beattie.

16 Fur Trade Importation Book, HBCA A.53/1.

17 MacFarlane 1905, 754.

18 Richardson and Swainson 1832, 464.

19 Blakiston 1863, 137.

20 In medieval times in England ownership of swans was a mark of social standing. As a food item, the set-piece for banquets, a swan was extremely expensive, selling in London in 1274 for 3 shillings (36 pence), compared to 5 pence for a goose and 4 pence for a pheasant. The punishment for stealing swan eggs was imprisonment for a year and a day. For stealing a swan, the thief had to pour wheat over the suspended bird, hung by its beak, until the tip of the beak was covered; the wheat was then paid to the swan owner.

21 Nichols 1990, 12–17.

22 Harold Burgess read this in historical fiction, but no longer remembers the name of the novel.

23 Dawney 1972, 170.

24 Warwick, Pitz, and Wyckoff 1965, 141.

25 Nichols 1990, 12–17; Wilmore 1974, 91.

26 *Jack London Short Stories* 1993 2:1662 (Karen Lunsford, personal communication).

27 New York, Harper and Row, 1971, 125, 176–7, and 193–4 (Brian Burchett, personal communication).

28 Dawney 1972, 169.

29 Pycraft 1942, 9:128–31.

30 Joseph Bramah, 1748–1814, was an English engineer and inventor who invented the hydraulic press, paper-making machinery, a numerical machine for printing bank-notes, and the Bramah lock (*Encyclopaedia Britannica* 1942, 4:25, 17:459–60).

31 Presumably from swans, geese, or ducks.

32 Harry Duckworth, personal communication.

33 M. Finlay 1990, 3.

34 The weather was so bad in 1811 that none of the three ships, including the *Edward and Ann* carrying the first 105 Selkirk settlers bound for Red River, made all its scheduled stops, and one was forced to over-winter in desolate Strutton Sound, en route home (Cooke and Holland 1978, 134). In 1812 the problems of war with the United States may have been reflected as far north as Hudson Bay. In 1816 the *Prince of Wales* was caught in ice and did not return to England; in 1833 *Prince Rupert V* suffered a similar fate. In 1836 two of the three ships had to winter in the bay, while *Prince Rupert V*, after being beset in ice from 23 August to 19 September, returned without fully unloading its inbound cargo.

35 C. Finlay 1994, "Animal populations and habitat changes in the contact period on the North Saskatchewan," presented at Rupert's Land Colloquium, University of Alberta, Edmonton, 27 May 1994.

36 M. Finlay 1990, 91.

37 M. Finlay 1990, 4, 10.

38 M. Finlay 1990, 6.

39 M. Finlay 1990, 7.

40 Rogers and Hammer 1998, 13–29.

41 Banko 1960, 19.

42 Mitchell 1994, 15; Beaulieu 1999, 269–72.

43 Lumsden 2002, 16–18.

APPENDIX F

1 Houston 1988a, 3–4.

2 Avis 1967, 531.

3 American Ornithologists' Union 1957.

4 Willughbei 1676.

5 Raven 1986, 308.

6 Willughby 1676, 276 and Plate 70.

7 Willughby 1678.

8 Clinton H. Keeling, in litt., 30 January 1999; Lever 1977, 259-62.

9 Edwards 1750:151.

10 The North American subspecies of the Golden Eagle, *Aquila chrysaëtos canadensis*, was introduced in the *Fourth American Ornithologists' Union Check-List of North American Birds* (1931).

11 The Little Brown Crane, *Grus canadensis*, was considered a full species in the first three AOU Check-Lists, then was merged with the Sandhill Crane and became *Grus canadensis canadensis* in the 4th AOU Check-List (1931).

12 Always a full species, but known by different English and Latin names: Canada Grouse, *Dendragapus canadensis*, in first two AOU Check-Lists; Hudsonian Spruce Partridge, *Canachites canadensis canadensis*, in 3rd AOU Check-List; Hudsonian Spruce Grouse, *Canachites canadensis canadensis*, in 4th AOU Check-List, and a subspecies of Spruce Grouse, *Dendragapus canadensis canadensis*, in 5th AOU Check-List (1957).

13 Linnaeus often used geographic descriptors; for example, from Catesby he gave Latin names such as *brasiliensis, bahamensis, carolinus,* and *lapponicus*.

14 Lamb 1988, 322.

15 Lamb 1988, 322.

16 The original draft of this account was published in *Blue Jay* 52:141–3, 1995, with a follow-up note after the reply from Alan Brown, in 53:116–17, 1996.

APPENDIX G

1 Arok and Jean are language professionals at the Saskatchewan Indian Federated College and the University of Regina.

2 A dialect used along the Moose River, at Moosonee and Moose Factory.

3 More commonly translated as "thunderbird", especially in Plains Cree.

4 Possibly belying a fluctuation between animate *mînak* and inanimate *mîna* (cf. Plains Cree diminutive *mînisa*).

5 The last Eskimo Curlew specimen was shot in Barbados, 4 September 1963, and the last sight record acceptable to the AOU committee was from Regina, Saskatchewan, 14 May 1982 (American Ornithologists' Union 1998, 160). Gollop (1988), the reigning expert on this species, listed four 1987 sightings as "apparently reliable": in Texas on 17 April and 2 May, in Nebraska on 16 April, and two at Lac Rendez-vous, North West Territories, 68° 54' N, 127° 00' West) on 24 May. Waldon (1996) gave details of a final possible sighting near Killarney, Manitoba, 15 May 1996.

6 Swainson 1840:2.

7 Nelson 1969.

8 Diamond 1989, 26–30.

9 Lacombe 1874.

10 Williams, 1969, xiii.

11 Battiste and Henderson 2000.

12 McDonald, Arragutainaq, and Novalinga 1997.

13 Okimâsis and Ratt 1999.

14 Faries 1938. Edward Ahenakew, then Canon of St. Alban's, Prince Albert, Saskatchewan, was a collaborator.

15 Earle Waugh, Nancy Leclaire and George Cardinal 1998.

16 E.2/9, E.2/10, and E.2/13, represent manuscripts in HBCA. Each shows evidence of collaboration between Graham and Hutchins. E.2/5, E.2/7 and E.2/8 are Andrew Graham's original observations in the HBCA, PAM, Winnipeg

17 But missing Bohemian Waxwing, Glaucous Gull, Northern Harrier, White Pelican, and one plumage form of Golden Eagle. Note that appendix contains eleven new bird species listed under HutchinsAppx above.

18 But missing the Sora and three late add-ons by Williams at very end of migratory bird list: White Pelican, Bohemian Waxwing, and Belted Kingfisher.

19 From one hundred specimens, Forster listed sixty-one species. Probably some species had more than one specimen. Well-known species, such as Mallard, evidently were not deemed worthy of mention.

20 Five of Hutchins's species were without specimens. Four times two forms of the same species are described; on four occasions two Cree names were given to one species.

REFERENCES

Agassiz, L. 1940. "Études sur les Glaciers." Neuchâtel: privately published.

Alden, John. 1969. "A Note on George Edwards's Natural History of Uncommon Birds." *Journal of the Society for the Bibliography of Natural History* 5:135–6.

Aldrich, J.W. 1946. "Speciation in the White-cheeked Geese." *Wilson Bulletin* 58: 94–103.

Allen, D.E. 1993. "Natural History in Britain in the Eighteenth Century." *Archives of Natural History* 20:333–47.

– 2000. "Walking the Swards: Medical Education and the Rise and Spread of the Botanical Field Class." *Archives of Natural History* 27:335–67.

Allen, Elsa Guerdrum. 1937. "New Light on Mark Catesby." *Auk* 54:349–63.

– 1951. "The History of American Ornithology before Audubon." *Transactions of the American Philosophical Society*, ns, 41 (3):386–591.

Allen, J.L., 1997. "Introduction to volume 3." In: *North American Exploration: A Continent Comprehended*. Lincoln: University of Nebraska Press.

American Ornithologists' Union. 1886. *The Code of Nomenclature and Check-list of North American Birds*. New York: American Ornithologists' Union.

– 1895–1998. *Check-list of North American Birds*. New York: American Ornithologists' Union. 2nd ed., 1895. 3rd ed., 1910; 4th ed., 1931; 5th ed., 1957; 6th ed., 1973; 7th ed., 1983; 8th ed., 1998.

– 1973. "Thirty-second Supplement to the American Ornithologists' Union Check-list of North American Birds." *Auk* 90:411–19.

– 2000. "Forty-second Supplement to the American Ornithologists' Union Check-list of North American Birds." *Auk* 117:847–58.

Anderson, Anne. 1975. *Plains Cree Dictionary in the "Y" dialect, revised*. Edmonton: A. Anderson.

Anderson, R.G.W. 1986. "Joseph Black" In David Daiches, Peter Jones, and Jean Jones, *A Hotbed of Genius: The Scottish Enlightenment 1730–1790*. Edinburgh: University Press.

Anonymous. 1926. "And the goose honks high." *The Buzzard* 1(1):6. Los Angeles: Cooper Ornithological Club.

Anonymous. 1933. *British Fur Trade Year Book 1933*. London: Hutchinson and Co.

Anonymous. 1949. "George Edwards." *Dictionary of National Biography* 6:535–6. London: Oxford University Press.

Atton, F.M. 1985. "Early Records of the Channel Catfish, *Ictalurus punctatus*, in Cumberland Lake, Saskatchewan." *Canadian Field-Naturalist* 99:538–40.

Audubon, John J. 1831–39, 1967. *Ornithological Biography: The Birds of America*. Edinburgh, reprinted New York: Dover.

Avis, W.S., editor-in-chief. 1967. *A Dictionary of Canadianisms on Historical Principles*. Toronto: W.J. Gage.

Baillie, James L., Jr. 1946. "Naturalists on Hudson Bay." *The Beaver* 277(3):36–9.

Ball, Timothy F. 1976. "'As cold as ever I knew it.' Joseph Colen, February 22nd, 1802. The changing climate of Manitoba." *Historical and Scientific Society of Manitoba Transactions* ser. 3, 33:61–6.

– 1982. Climatic Change in Central Canada: A Preliminary Analysis of Weather Information from the Hudson's Bay Company Forts at York Factory and Churchill Factory, 1714–1850. Ph. D. thesis, Queen Mary College, University of London.

– 1983a. "The Migration of geese as an indicator of climate change in the southern Hudson Bay Region between 1715 and 1851." *Climatic Change* 5:85–93.

– 1983b. "Preliminary Analysis of Early Instrumental Temperature Records from York Factory and Churchill Factory." *Syllogeus* 49:203–19.

– 1985. "A Dramatic Change in the General Circulation on the West Coast of Hudson Bay in 1760 AD: Synoptic Evidence Based on Historic Records." *Syllogeus* 55:219–28.

– 1986. "Historical Evidence and Climatic Implications of a Shift in the Boreal Forest-tundra Transition in Central Canada." *Climatic Change* 8:121–34.

– 1988. "Company Town: Rugged Stromness in the Orkneys sent Many Men to the Fur Trade." *The Beaver* 68(3):43–52.

– 1992a. "Climate Change, Droughts and their Social Impact: Central Canada, 1811-1820, a Classic Example." In C.R. Harington, ed., *The Year Without a Summer? World Climate in 1816*, 185–95. Ottawa: Canadian Museum of Nature.

– 1992b. "The Year Without a Summer: Its Impact on the Fur Trade and History of Western Canada." In C.R. Harington, ed. *The Year Without a Summer? World Climate in 1816*, 196–202. Ottawa: Canadian Museum of Nature.

– 1992c. "Historical and Instrumental Evidence of Climate: Western Hudson Bay, Canada, 1714–1850." In R.S. Bradley and P.D. Jones, eds., *Climate since A.D. 1500*, 40—73. London: Routledge.

– 1994. "Climate of Two Locations on the Southwestern Corner of Hudson Bay: A.D. 1720–1729." *International Journal of Climatology* 14:1151–68.

– and David Dyck. 1984. "Observations of the Transit of Venus at Prince of Wales's Fort in 1769." *The Beaver* 315(2):51–6.

Banfield, A.W.F. 1974. *The Mammals of Canada*. Ottawa: National Museums of Canada.

Banko, Winston E. 1960. *The Trumpeter Swan*. North American Fauna no. 63. Washington: U.S. Fish and Wildlife Service.

Barr, William, and Glyndwr Williams. 1994. *Voyages in Search of a Northwest Passage, 1741–1747. I. The Voyage of Christopher Middleton, 1741–1742*. London: Hakluyt Society.

Barrington, Daines. 1770. "Account of a Very Remarkable Young Musician." *Philosophical Transactions* 60:54–64.

– 1772a. "Investigation of the Specific Characters which Distinguish the Rabbit from the Hare." *Philosophical Transactions* 62:4–14.

– 1772b. "An Essay on the Periodical Appearing and Disappearing of Certain Birds, at Different Times of the Year." *Philosophical Transactions* 62:265–320.

Barrow, Mark V., Jr. 2000. *A Passion for Birds: American Ornithology after Audubon*. Princeton: Princeton University Press.

Bartlett, J.R. 1859. *Dictionary of Americanisms: a Glossary of Words and Phrases Usually Regarded as Peculiar to the United States*. Boston: Little, Brown.

– 1865–82. *Bibliotheca Americana: A Catalogue of Books Relating to North and South America in the Library of the Late John Carter Brown of Providence, R.I.* Provincetown: privately published.

Battiste, M., and J.Y. Henderson. 2000. *Protecting Indigenous Knowledge and Heritage: A Global Challenge*. Saskatoon: Purich.

Beattie, Judith. 1993. "'My best friend': Evidence of the Fur Trade Libraries Located in the Hudson's Bay Archives." *Épilogue* 8:1–32.

Beaulieu, R. 1999. The New Porcupine Forest Flock of Trumpeter Swans, *Cygnus buccinator*, in Saskatchewan. *Canadian Field-Naturalist* 113:269–72.

Bennett, Henry Leigh. 1949. "John Newton." *Dictionary of National Biography*, 14:395–8. London: Oxford University Press.

Bent, A.C. 1927. *Life Histories of North American Shore Birds, Part 1*. U.S. National Museum Bulletin 142. Washington: Smithsonian Institution.

Berger, Carl. 1983. *Science, God and Nature in Victorian Canada*. Toronto: University of Toronto Press.

Berkeley, E., and D.S. Berkeley. 1969. *Dr Alexander Garden of Charles Town*. Chapel Hill: University of North Carolina Press.

Bettany, G. T. 1949. "James Jurin." *Dictionary of National Biography*, 10:1117–8. London: Oxford University Press.

Blagden, Charles. 1783. "History of the Congelation of Quicksilver." *Philosophical Transactions* 73B: 329–97 [page numbers 329–397 repeated in error].

Blakiston, Thomas. 1863. "On Birds Collected and Observed in the Interior of British North America [part 4]." *Ibis* 5:121–55.

Boulger, George Symonds. 1949a. "Robert Jameson." *Dictionary of National Biography*, 10:671–2. London: Oxford University Press.

– 1949b. "John Walker." *Dictionary of National Biography*, 20:531. London: Oxford University Press.

Bowes, E. "Johnnie." 1993. "Hudson's Bay 'Point' Blankets." *Saskatchewan Archaeology Society Newsletter* 14(3):59–60.

Brand, C. J., L. B. Keith, and C. A. Fischer. 1976. "Lynx Responses to Changing Snowshoe Hare Densities in Central Alberta." *Journal of Wildlife Management* 40:416–28.

Britten, James. 1922. "An early Hudson's Bay collector." *Journal of Botany* 60:239.

Broberg, G. 1997. "Pehr Kalm." In Sterling et al., *Biographical Dictionary of American and Canadian Naturalists and Environmentalists*, 421–3.

Brooks, E. St John. 1954. *Sir Hans Sloane: The Great Collector and His Circle*. London: Batchworth Press.

Brown, Jennifer S.H. 1979. "George Sutherland." *Dictionary of Canadian Biography*, 4:726–7. Toronto: University of Toronto Press.

– 1980. *Strangers in Blood: Fur Trade Company Families in Indian Country*. Vancouver: University of British Columbia Press.

– 1983. "Isham, Charles Thomas (Charles Price Isham)." *Dictionary of Canadian Biography*, 5:450–1. Toronto: University of Toronto Press.

Browning, M. Ralph, and Richard C. Banks. 1990. "The Identity of Pennant's 'Wapacuthu Owl' and the Subspecific Name of the Population of *Bubo virginianus* from west of Hudson Bay." *Journal of Raptor Research* 24:80–3.

Bryce, George. 1900. *The Remarkable History of the Hudson's Bay Company*. Toronto: William Briggs.

Bryson, Reid A. 1966. "Air masses, Streamlines, and the Boreal Forest." *Geographical Bulletin* 8:228–69.

Buchanan, Handasyde, and James Fisher. 1990. "Bibliography." In S. Sitwell, ed., *Fine Bird Books, 1700–1900*, 65–159. New York: Atlantic Monthly Press.

Buffon, George Louis Leclerc, comte de. 1771–86. *Histoire naturelle des oiseaux*. Vols. 4 – 8 inclusive of *Histoire naturelle*. 44 vols. Paris: Imprimerie Royale.

Bühler, W.K. 1981. *Gauss: A Biographical Study*. Berlin: Springer Verlag.

Burley, Edith I. 1997. *Servants of the Honourable Company: Work, Discipline, and Conflict in the Hudson's Bay Company, 1770–1870*. Oxford: Oxford University Press.

Cain, A.J. 1992. "The Methodus of Linnaeus." *Archives of Natural History* 19:231–50.

Cameron, Laura. 1997. *Openings: A Meditation on History, Method, and Sumas Lake*. Montreal: McGill-Queen's University Press.

Carlyle, Edward Irving. 1949. "William Wales." *Dictionary of National Biography* 20:490–1.

Cash, P. 1999. John Lining. *American National Biographies* 13:706–7.

Cassara, Ernest. 1975. *The Enlightenment in America*. Boston: Twayne.

Cassedy, James H. 1969. "Meteorology and Medicine in Colonial America: Beginnings of the Experimental Approach." *Journal of the History of Medicine* 24:193–204.

Cassin, John. 1858. "Raptores." In Spencer F. Baird, *Birds. General Report upon the Zoology of the Various Pacific Railroad Routes*, 3–64. Washington: A.O.P. Nicholson.

– 1861. "Communication in Reference to a New Species of Goose from Arctic America." *Proceedings of the Academy of Natural Sciences*, Philadelphia 13:73.

Catchpole, A.J.W. 1980. "Historical Evidence of Climatic Change in Western and Northern Canada." *Syllogeus* 26:17–60.

– 1992. "River Ice and Sea Ice in the Hudson Bay Region during the Second Decade of the Nineteenth Century." In C.R. Harington, ed., *The Year Without a Summer? World Climate in 1816*, 233–44. Ottawa: Canadian Museum of Nature.

– and T.F. Ball. 1981. "Analysis of Historical Evidence of Climate Change in Western and Northern Canada." *Syllogeus* 33:48–96.

– and M.A. Faurer. 1983. "Summer Sea Ice Severity in Hudson Strait, 1751–1870." *Climatic Change* 5:115–39.

– 1985. "Ships' Log-books, Sea Ice and the Cold Summer of 1816 in Hudson Bay and Its Approaches." *Arctic* 38:121–8.

– and J. Halpin. 1987. "Measuring Summer Sea Ice Severity in Eastern Hudson Bay, 1751–1870." *Canadian Geographer* 31:233–44.

– and I. Hanuta. 1989. "Severe Summer Ice in Hudson Strait and Hudson Bay following Major Volcanic Eruptions, 1751 to 1899 A.D." *Climatic Change* 14:61–79.

– and D.W. Moodie. 1978. "Archives and the Environmental Scientist." *Archivaria* 6:113–36.

Catesby, M. 1729–47. *The Natural History of Carolina, Florida, and the Bahama Islands*. 2 vols. London: published privately.

Cavendish, Henry. 1783. "Observations on Mr. Hutchins's Experiments for Determining the Degree of Cold at which Quicksilver Freezes." *Philosophical Transactions* 73B:303–27 [page numbers repeated].

Chalmers, John. 1776. *An Account of the Weather and Diseases of South Carolina*. London.

Chichester, Henry Manners. 1949. "Samuel Hearne." *Dictionary of National Biography*, 9:335–6. London: Oxford University Press.

Chiel, A.A. 1955. "Manitoba Jewish History – Early Times." *Historical and Scientific Society of Manitoba, Transactions*, series 3, 10:14–29.

Chitty, Dennis. 1996. *Do Lemmings Commit Suicide? Beautiful Hypotheses and Ugly Facts*. New York: Oxford University Press.

Christy, Miller. 1885. *Manitoba Described*. London: Wyman and Sons.

– 1894. *The Voyages of Captain Luke Foxe of Hull, and Captain Thomas James of Bristol, in Search of a North-West Passage, in 1631–32*. London: Hakluyt Society.

– 1922. "An early Hudson Bay collector." *Journal of Botany* 60:336–7.

Clapham, Sir John. 1942. "Introduction" In E.E. Rich, ed., *Minutes of the Hudson's Bay Company, 1671–1674*, xv–xxiv. Toronto: Champlain Society.

Clark, Sir Cyril. 1992. "Foreword" In A. Stuart Mason, *George Edwards: The Bedell and His Birds*, vii–viii. London: Royal College of Physicians.

Clark, William, Jan Golinski, and Simon Schaffer, eds. 1999. *The Sciences in Enlightened Europe*. Chicago: University of Chicago Press.

Clerke, Agnes Mary. 1949. "Nevil Maskelyne." *Dictionary of National Biography*, 12:1299–301. London: Oxford University Press.

Clouston, W. 1794. "United Parishes of Stromness and Sandwick." In J. Sinclair, ed., *Statistical Account of Scotland* 16:409–56.

Coale, H.K. 1915. "The Present Status of the Trumpeter Swan, *Olor buccinator*." *Auk* 32:82–90.

Cook, Francis R. 1984. *Introduction to Canadian Amphibians and Reptiles*. Ottawa: National Museum of Natural Sciences.

Cook, Harold J. 1996. "Physicians and Natural History." In N. Jardine, J.A. Secord, and E.C. Spary, eds., *Cultures of Natural History*, 91–105. Cambridge: Cambridge University Press.

Cooke, Alan, and Clive Holland. 1978. *The Exploration of Northern Canada 500 to 1920. A Chronology*. Toronto: Arctic History Press.

Coote, C.H. 1949. "Aaron Arrowsmith." *Dictionary of National Biography*, 1:595–6. London: Oxford University Press.

Coues, Elliott, 1878. "Bibliographical Appendix." In *Birds of the Colorado Valley*, 567–784. Washington: Government Printing Office.

– 1882. *Coues Check List of North American Birds*. Boston: Estes and Lauriat.

– ed. 1897. *New Light on the Early History of the Greater Northwest: The Manuscript Journals of Alexander Henry and David Thompson, 1799–1814* (3 vols.). New York: Francis P. Harper.

Craig, Joan. 1974. "John Newton." *Dictionary of Canadian Biography*, 3:482–3. Toronto: University of Toronto Press.

Crèvecoeur, Hector St John de [pen name for Crèvecouer, Michel-Guillaume Jean de]. 1782, reprinted 1951. *Letters from an American Farmer*. New York: E.P. Dutton.

Criddle, N. 1930. "Some Natural Factors Governing the Fluctuations of Grouse in Manitoba." *Canadian Field-Naturalist* 44: 77–80.

Crowcroft, Peter. 1991. *Elton's Ecologists: A History of the Bureau of Animal Population*. Chicago: University of Chicago Press.

Crowther, J.G. 1962. *Scientists of the Industrial Revolution: Joseph Black, James Watt, Joseph Priestley, Henry Cavendish.* London: Cresset Press.

Cutler, Charles L. 1994. *O Brave New Words! Native American Loanwords in Current English.* Norman: University of Oklahoma Press.

Dafoe, John W. 1931. *Clifford Sifton in Relation to His Times.* Toronto: MacMillan.

Daiches, David. 1986a. *The Scottish Enlightenment: An Introduction.* Edinburgh: Saltire Society.

Daiches, 1986b. "The Scottish Enlightenment." In David Daiches, Peter Jones, and Jean Jones, eds. *A Hotbed of Genius: The Scottish Enlightenment 1730–90,* 1–41. Edinburgh: Edinburgh University Press.

Dall, W.H. 1915. *Spencer Fullerton Baird: A Biography.* Philadelphia: Lippincott.

Dandy, J.E., rev. and ed. 1958. *The Sloane Herbarium: An Annotated List of the* Horti Sicci *Composing It; with Biographical Accounts of the Principal Contributors.* London: British Museum (Natural History).

Daston, Lorraine. 1999. "Afterword: The Ethos of Enlightenment." In William Clark, Jan Golinski, and Simon Schaffer, eds. *The Sciences in Enlightened Europe,* 495–504. Chicago: University of Chicago Press.

Davies, K.G., ed. 1965. *Letters from Hudson Bay, 1703–40.* London: Hudson's Bay Record Society.

Davies, Thomas. 1770. "A method of Preparing Birds for Preservation." *Philosophical Transactions* 60:184–7.

Davis, Peter, and June Holmes. 1993. "Thomas Bewick (1753–1828), Engraver and Ornithologist." *Archives of Natural History* 20:167–84.

Dawney, Andrew. 1972. "Exploitation" In P. Scott, ed., *The Swans,* 167–80. Boston: Houghton Mifflin.

de Beer, Gavin. 1956. "Introduction." In *Caroli Linnaei: Systema Naturae, a Photographic Facsimile of the First Volume of the Tenth Edition (1758),* 3–5. London: British Museum (Natural History).

Delacour, J. 1954. "Trumpeter Swan." In *Waterfowl of the World,* 1:75–82. London: Country Life.

Desmond, Ray. 1995. *Kew: The History of the Royal Botanic Gardens.* London: Harvill.

Diamond, J. 1989a. "This-Fellow Frog, Name Belong-Him Dakwo." *Natural History* 98(4):16–23.

– 1989b. "The ethnobiologist's dilemma." *Natural History* 98(6):26–30.

Dickason, Olive Patricia. 1992. *Canada's First Nations: A History of Founding Peoples From Earliest Times.* Toronto: McClelland and Stewart.

Dickenson, Victoria. 1998. *Drawn from Life: Science and Art in the Portrayal of the New World.* Toronto: University of Toronto Press.

Dickson, David. 1997. *Arctic Ireland: The Extraordinary Story of the Great Frost and Forgotten Famine of 1740–41.* Belfast: White Row Press, 1997.

Dickson, Kathryn M. 2000. *Towards Conservation of the Diversity of Canada Geese* (*Branta canadensis*). Ottawa: Canadian Wildlife Service, Occasional Paper no. 103.

Dobbs, Arthur. 1744. *An Account of the Countries Adjoining to Hudson's Bay, in the North-west Part of America.* London: J. Robinson.

Dodge, Ernest S. 1969. "James Knight." *Dictionary of Canadian Biography*, 2:318–20. Toronto: University of Toronto Press.

Donovan, L. Gary, and Henri Ouellet. 1993. *Dictionnaire Étymologique des Noms d'Oiseaux du Canada.* Montreal: Guérin.

Doughty, Arthur G., and Chester Martin, eds. 1929. *The Kelsey Papers.* Ottawa: Public Archives of Canada, and Belfast: Public Record Office of Northern Ireland.

Douglas, R., and J.N. Wallace, ed. & transl. 1926. *Twenty Years of York Factory, 1694–1714: Jérémie's Account of Hudson Strait and Bay.* Ottawa: Thorburn and Abbott.

Driscoll, Heather Rollason. 2001. The Journeys, the Journals, and *a Journey*: Samuel Hearne and the Coppermine River Narrative. Ph. D. dissertation, University of Alberta.

Duncan, James. 1840. "Linnaeus." In W. Swainson, *Taxidermy, with the Biography of Zoologists*, 249–53. London: Longman, Orme, Brown, Green and Longman's.

Dunmore, J., transl. and ed. 1994. *The Journal of Jean-François de Galaup de la Pérouse, 1785–1788.* Vol. 1. London: Hakluyt Society.

Dymond, Joseph, and William Wales. 1771. "Observations on the State of the Air, Winds, Weather, &c. Made at Prince of Wales's Fort, on the North-west Coast of Hudson's Bay, in the Years 1768 and 1769." *Philosophical Transactions* 60:137–78.

Edwards, George. 1743, 1747, 1750, 1751. *A Natural History of Birds*, 4 vols. London: published privately.

– 1776. *Some Memoirs of the Life and Works of George Edwards.* London: J. Robson.

Ellis, C. Douglas. 2001. *Spoken Cree, Level 1* [West Coast of Hudson Bay]. Edmonton: University of Alberta Press.

Elton, Charles. 1927. *Animal Ecology.* New York: MacMillan.

– 1933. "The Canadian Snowshoe Rabbit Enquiry." *Canadian Field-Naturalist* 47:63–9 and 84–6.

– 1942. *Voles, Mice and Lemmings: Problems in Population Dynamics.* Oxford: Clarendon Press.

– and M. Nicholson. 1942a. "Fluctuations in Numbers of the Muskrat (*Ondatra zibethica*) in Canada." *Journal of Animal Ecology* 11:96–126.

– 1942b. "The Ten-year Cycle in Numbers of the Lynx in Canada." *Journal of Animal Ecology* 11:215–44.

Encyclopaedia Britannica. 1942. "Bramah, Joseph." 4:25. "Pen." 17:459–60.

Erichsen-Brown, C. 1979. *Use of Plants for the Past 500 Years*. Aurora, Ontario: Breezy Creeks Press.

Ewan, Joseph, and Nesta Ewan. 1970. *John Banister and His Natural History of Virginia, 1678–1692*. Urbana: University of Illinois Press.

Ewart, William B. 1983. "Causes of Mortality in a Subarctic Settlement (York Factory, Man.), 1714–1946." *Canadian Medical Association Journal* 129:571–4.

– 1995. "A Surgeon on the Bay: Thomas Hutchins and the HBC." *The Beaver* 75(4):38–41.

Farber, Paul L. 1972. "Buffon and the Concept of Species." *Journal of the History of Biology* 5:259–84.

– 1977. "The Development of Taxidermy and the History of Ornithology." *Isis* 68:550–66.

– 1982. *The Emergence of Ornithology as a Scientific Discipline, 1760–1850*. Dordrecht: D. Reidel.

– 2000. *Finding Order in Nature: The Naturalist Tradition from Linnaeus to E.O. Wilson*. Baltimore: Johns Hopkins University Press.

Faries, R. 1938. *A Dictionary of the Cree Language*. Toronto: Church of England in Canada.

Feduccia, Alan. 1985. *Catesby's Birds of Colonial America*. Chapel Hill: University of North Carolina Press.

Fernie, J. Donald. 1976. *The Whisper and the Vision: The Voyages of the Astronomers*. Toronto: Clarke Irwin.

– 1997, 1998. "Transits, Travels and Tribulations." *American Scientist* 85:418–21; 86:123–6; 422–5.

Fidler, Vera. 1959. "The Odd Will of Peter Fidler." *Canadian Geographic* 59:120–3.

Finlay, Cam. 1994. "Animal Populations and Habitat Changes in the Contact Period on the North Saskatchewan." Rupert's Land Colloquium, University of Alberta, Edmonton, 27 May 1994.

Finlay, Michael. 1990. *Western Writing Implements in the Age of the Quill Pen*. Carlisle: Plains Books.

Fiocco, G., D. Fuà, and G. Visconti. 1996. *The Mount Pinatubo Eruption: Effects on the Atmosphere and Climate*. Berlin: Springer.

Fleming, R. 1990. *Meteorology in America*. Baltimore: Johns Hopkins University Press.

Forster, J. Georg. 1778. *Observations Made During a Voyage Round the World...* London: G. Robinson.

– and Anders Sparrman. 1776. *Characteres Generum Plantarum ... Australis*. London: B. White, T. Cadell, and P. Elmsly.

Forster, J.R. 1767. "Specimen historiae naturalis volgensis." *Philosophical Transactions* 57:312–57.

– 1771. *A Catalogue of the Animals of North America … to which Are Added, Short Directions … in What Manner Specimens of All Kinds May Be Collected, Preserved, and Transported to Distant Countries*. London: Benjamin White.

– 1772a. "Account of the Roots used by Indians, in the Neighbourhood of Hudson's Bay, to Dye Porcupine Quills." *Philosophical Transactions* 62:54–9.

– 1772b. "Account of Several Quadrupeds from Hudson's Bay." *Philosophical Transactions* 62:370–81.

– 1772c. "An Account of the Birds Sent from Hudson's Bay, with Observations Relative to their Natural History; and Latin Descriptions of some of the Most Uncommon." *Philosophical Transactions* 62:382–433.

– 1773. "An Account of some Curious Fishes, sent from Hudson's Bay." *Philosophical Transactions* 63:149–60.

Foster, J.E. 1987. "William Auld." *Dictionary of Canadian Biography*, 6:17–8. Toronto: University of Toronto Press.

Fraser, Walter J., Jr. 1989. *Charleston! Charleston! The History of a Southern City*. Columbia: University of South Carolina Press.

Frick, G.F. and R.P. Stearns. 1961. *Mark Catesby, the Colonial Audubon*. Urbana: University of Illinois Press.

Frick, G.F., J.L. Reveal, C.R. Broome, and M.L. Brown. 1987. "Botanical Explorations and Discoveries in Colonial Maryland, 1688 to 1753." *Huntia* 7:5–59.

Fuller, W.A. 1999. "Samuel Hearne's Track: Some Obscurities Clarified." *Arctic* 52:257–71.

Gage, A.T., and W.T. Stearn. 1988. *A Bicentenary History of the Linnean Society of London*. London: Academic Press.

Gerbi, Antonello. 1973. *The Dispute of the New World: The History of a Polemic, 1750–1900*. Pittsburgh: University of Pittsburgh Press.

Gillespie, Beryl. 1979. "Matonabbee." *Dictionary of Canadian Biography*, 4:523–4. Toronto: University of Toronto Press.

Glacken, Clarence J. 1967. *Traces on the Rhodian Shore: Nature and Culture in Western Thought from Ancient Times to the End of the Eighteenth Century*. Berkeley: University of California Press.

Glover, Richard. 1949. "York boats." *The Beaver* 279 (3):19–23.

– ed. 1952. "Introduction." In *Cumberland and Hudson House Journals and Inland Journals, Second Series, 1779–82*, xv–xxxv. London: Hudson's Bay Record Society.

– 1958. "Editor's Introduction." In *A Journey from Prince of Wales's Fort in Hudson Bay to the Northern Ocean, by Samuel Hearne*, i–xliii. Toronto: Macmillan.

– 1960. "Andrew Graham, Thomas Hutchins, and the First Record of Peary's Caribou." *Arctic* 13:52–4.

– ed. 1962. *David Thompson's Narrative, 1784–1812*. Toronto: Champlain Society

– 1969. "Introduction." In G. Williams, ed., *Andrew Graham's Observations on Hudson's Bay* (HBRS 27), xiii–lxxiii. London: Hudson's Bay Record Society.

Gmelin, J.F. 1789. *Systema Naturae*. 13th ed. London: J.B. Delamolliere.

Goetzmann, William H. 1986. *New Lands, New Men: America and the Second Great Age of Discovery*. New York: Viking.

Gollop, J.B. 1988. The Eskimo Curlew. In *Audubon Wildlife Report*, 583–5.

Gollop, J.B., Barry, T.W., and E.H. Iversen. 1986. *Eskimo Curlew: A Vanishing Species?* Regina: Saskatchewan Natural History Society, Special Publication 17.

Gosch, C.G.A. 1897. *Danish Arctic Expeditions, 1605 to 1620*. London: Hakluyt Society.

Gough, Barry. 1997. *First Across the Continent: Sir Alexander Mackenzie*. Toronto: McClelland and Stewart.

Graham, Andrew. 1969. "Life and Trade in the Bay." In G. Williams, ed. *Andrew Graham's Observations*, 242–330. London: Hudson's Bay Record Society.

Gray, John Morgan. 1963. *Lord Selkirk of Red River*. London: Macmillan.

Greenblatt, Stephen. 1991. *Marvellous Possesions: The Wonder of the New World*. Chicago: University of Chicago Press.

Guerrini, Anita. 1997. "John Bartram. William Bartram." In K.B. Sterling et al., eds., *Biographical Dictionary of American and Canadian Naturalists and Environmentalists*, 61–5.

Hagberg, Knut. 1953. *Carl Linnaeus*. New York: E.P. Dutton.

Haig, Bruce, ed. 1992. *A Look at Peter Fidler's Journal: Journal of a Journey over Land from Buckingham House to the Rocky Mountains in 1792 & 3*. Lethbridge: Historical Research Centre.

Hanley, Wayne, 1977. *Natural History in America from Mark Catesby to Rachel Carson*. New York: Quadrangle/Demeter.

Hanson, Harold C. 1965. Revised 1997. *The Giant Canada Goose*. Carbondale: Southern Illinois University Press.

Hare, F. Kenneth. 1951. "Some Notes on Post Glacial Climate Change in Eastern Canada." *Royal Meteorological Society, Canadian branch* 2:8–18.

– 1970. "The Tundra Climate." *Transactions of the Royal Society of Canada*, ser. 4, 8:393–9.

– and M.K. Thomas. 1979. *Climate Canada*, 2nd ed. Toronto: Wiley.

Harington, C.R., ed. 1992. "Introduction." In *The Year Without a Summer? World Climate in 1816*, 6–7. Ottawa: Canadian Museum of Nature.

Harkányi, Katalin. 1990. *The Natural Sciences and American Scientists in the Revolutionary Era: A Bibliography*. Westport, CT: Greenwood Press.

Harper, Francis, ed. 1958. *The Travels of William Bartram*. New Haven: Yale University Press.

Harris, Geraldine Alton. 1994. Archival Administrative History of the Northern Stores Department; Hudson's Bay Company, 1959–87. Master's thesis, Department of History, University of Winnipeg.

Harrison, Robert. 1949. "Sir Charles Blagden." *Dictionary of National Biography*, 2:617–8. London: Oxford University Press.

Hearne, Samuel. 1795. *A Journey from Prince of Wales's Fort, in Hudson's Bay, to the Northern Ocean, in 1769, 1770, 1771, and 1772*. London: T. Cadell. [see Tyrrell 1911 and Glover 1958].

Hewitt, C. Gordon. 1921. *The Conservation of the Wild Life of Canada*. New York: Charles Scribner's Sons.

Hicks, Frederick C. 1932. "Thomas Hutchins." *Dictionary of American Biography*, 9:435–6. New York: Charles Scribner's Sons.

Hoare, Michael E. 1972. "'A Strange and Eventful History': The Scientific Correspondents of J.R. Forster (1729–98)." *Records of the Australian Academy of Science* 2(3):7–17.

– 1976a. *The Tactless Philosopher: Johann Reinhold Forster, 1729–1798*. Melbourne: Hawthorn Press.

– 1976b. "'Ulysses' or 'Incubus'?: J.R. Forster's First Period in England, 1766–1772." *Journal of the Society for the Bibliography of Natural History* 7:375–83.

– 1982. *The Resolution Journal of Johann Reinhold Forster, 1772–1775*. 4 vols. London: Hakluyt Society.

Holland, Clive. 1994a. *Arctic Exploration and Development circa 500 B.C. to 1915. An Encyclopedia*. New York: Garland.

Holland, Clive, ed. 1994b. *Farthest North: A History of North Polar Exploration in Eyewitness Accounts*. London: Robinson.

Houston, C.S., ed. 1974. *To the Arctic by Canoe, 1819–1821: The Journal and Paintings of Robert Hood, Midshipman with Franklin*. Montreal: McGill-Queen's University Press.

– 1980. "Introduction." *In Ernest Thompson Seton in Manitoba, 1882–1892*, i–xv. Winnipeg: Manitoba Naturalists Society.

– 1983. "Birds first Described from Hudson Bay." *Canadian Field-Naturalist* 97:95–8.

– ed. 1984. *Arctic Ordeal: The Journal of John Richardson, Surgeon-naturalist with Franklin, 1820–1822*. Montreal: McGill-Queen's University Press.

– 1987. "Nearly Synchronous Cycles of the Great Horned Owl and Snowshoe Hare in Saskatchewan." In R.W. Nero et al., eds., *Biology and Conservation of Northern Forest Owls*, 56–8. Fort Collins, CO: U.S. Dep. Agric. For. Serv. Tech. Rep. RM–142.

– 1988a. "Tony Capusten, 1915–1987." *Blue Jay* 46:3–4.

– 1988b. "Miller Christy, Naturalist and Historian." *Blue Jay* 46:171–7.

– 1997a. "Peter Fidler." In Keir B. Sterling et al., *Biographical Dictionary of American and Canadian Naturalists and Environmentalists*, 268–9.

– 1997b. "James Isham." In Keir B. Sterling et al., *Biographical Dictionary of American and Canadian Naturalists and Environmentalists*, 397–9.

– 1997c. "Roderick Ross MacFarlane." In K. B. Sterling et al., *Biographical Dictionary of American and Canadian Naturalists and Environmentalists*, 487–8.

Houston, C.S., and M.I. Houston. 1988. "The Sacking of Peter Fidler's Brandon House." *Manitoba History* 16:23–6.

Houston, C.S., and I.S. MacLaren. 1994. *Arctic Artist, the Journal and Paintings of George Back, Midshipman with Franklin, 1819–1822*. Montreal: McGill-Queen's University Press.

Houston, C.S., and S. Houston. 2000. "The First Smallpox Epidemic on the Canadian Plains: In the Fur-traders' Words." *Canadian Journal of Infectious Diseases* 11:112–15.

Houston, C.S., M.I. Houston, and H.M. Reeves. 1997. "The 19th Century Trade in Swan Skins and Quills." *Blue Jay* 55:24–34.

Howse, J. 1844. *A Grammar of the Cree Language*. London: J.G.F. and J. Rivington.

http://www.mqup.mcgill.ca/files/houston

http://www.science.ca/scientists/scientistprofile.php?pID =11

http://www.worldwideschool.org/library/books/geo/geography/TheNatural-HistoryofSelborne

Hudson's Bay Company. 1749. "Orders and Instructions to Mr. James Napper, on his Voyage upon Discovery to the Northward in Hudson's Bay, on Board the Churchill Sloop" In *Report from the Committee Appointed to Enquire into the State and Condition of the Countries Adjoining to Hudson's Bay, and of the Trade Carried on There*, 259–60. Reported by Lord Strange, 24 April 1749.

Hunt, Robert. 1949. "Mark Catesby." *Dictionary of National Biography*, 3:1190. London: Oxford University Press.

Hurlburt, I. 1977. *Faunal Remains from Fort White Earth, N.W. Co. 1810–1813*. Edmonton: Provincial Museum of Alberta Occasional Paper no. 1.

Hutchins, Thomas. 1776. "An account of the Success of some Attempts to Freeze Quicksilver at Albany Fort, in Hudson's Bay, in the Year 1775: With Observations on the Dipping-needle." *Philosophical Transactions* 66:174–81.

– 1783. "Experiments for Ascertaining the Point of Mercurial Congelation." *Philosophical Transactions* 73:303–70.

Innis, H.A. 1956. *The Fur Trade in Canada: An Introduction to Canadian Economic History*, revised ed. Toronto: University of Toronto Press.

James, James Alton. 1942. *The First Scientific Exploration of Russian America and the Purchase of Alaska*. Chicago: Northwestern University Press.

Jarrell, Richard. 1994. "Measuring Scientific Activity in Canada and Australia before 1915: Exploring some Possibilities." *Scientia Canadensis* 17:27–52.

Johnson, Alice M., ed. 1968. *Saskatchewan Journals and Correspondence: Edmonton House, 1795–1800, and Chesterfield House, 1800–1802*. London: Hudson's Bay Record Society.

– 1974a. "Thomas McCliesh." *Dictionary of Canadian Biography*, 3:414–15. Toronto: University of Toronto Press.

– 1974b. "Richard Norton." *Dictionary of Canadian Biography*, 3:489–90. Toronto: University of Toronto Press.

Johnson, George. 1995. "William Bissett Ewart" (typescript in possession of CSH).

Jones, J.W. 1914. *Fur-farming in Canada*, 2nd ed., revised and enlarged. Ottawa: Commission of Conservation, Committee on Fisheries, Game and Fur-bearing Animals.

Jones, P.D., and R.S. Bradley. 1992. "Climatic Variations over the Last 500 Years." In R.S. Bradley and P.D. Jones, eds., *Climate since A.D. 1500*, 649–69. London: Routledge.

Jones, R., and C. Bickerton. 1985. "Richard Glover." *Canadian Historical Association Newsletter* 1985:26–8.

Jurin, James. 1722. "Invitatio ad observationes meteorologicas communi consilio instituendas." *Philosophical Transactions* 32:422–7.

Keith, Lloyd B. 1963. *Wildlife's Ten-year Cycle*. Madison: University of Wisconsin Press.

– 1990. "Dynamics of Snowshoe Hare Populations." In H.H. Genoways, ed., *Current Mammalogy*, 119–95. New York: Plenum.

– and L.A. Windberg. 1978. "Demographic analysis of the Snowshoe Hare cycle." *Wildlife Monographs* 58.

Kellner, L. 1963. *Alexander von Humboldt*. London: Oxford University Press.

Kenney, J.F. 1932. *The Founding of Churchill, being the Journal of Captain James Knight, Governor-in-chief in Hudson Bay from the 14th of July to the 13th of September 1717*. Toronto: J.M. Dent.

Kerr, Robert. 1811. *Memoirs of the Life, Writings and Correspondence of William Smellie* (2 vols.). Edinburgh: John Anderson.

Keynes, Geoffrey. 1951. *John Ray: A Bibliography*. London: Faber and Faber.

Koerner, Lisbet. 1999. *Linnaeus, Nature and Nation*. Cambridge: Harvard University Press.

König, C., F. Weick, and J-H. Becking. 1999. *Owls: A Guide to the Owls of the World*. New Haven: Yale University Press.

Krebs, C.J. 1964. "The Lemming Cycle at Baker Lake, Northwest Territories, during 1959–62." *Arctic Institute of North America Technical Paper* no. 15.

– 1966. "Dispersal, Spacing Behaviour, and Genetics in Relation to Population Fluctuations in the Vole *Microtus townsendii*." *Fortschritte Zoologie* 25:61–77.

– 1978. "A Review of the Chitty Hypothesis of Population Regulation." *Canadian Journal of Zoology* 56:2463–80.

– S. Boutin, and R. Boonstra. 2001. *Ecosytem Dynamics of the Boreal Forest: The Kluane Project*. New York: Oxford University Press.

Krech, Shepard III. 1999. *The Ecological Indian: Myth and History*. New York: W.W. Norton.

Kuckhan, T.S. 1770. "Four Letters from Mr. T.S. Kuckhan, on the Preservation of Dead Birds." *Philosophical Transactions* 60:302–20.

Lacombe, Albert, Rev. Père. 1874. *Dictionnaire de la Langue des Cris*. Montreal: Beau-
    chemin and Valois.

Lamb, H.H. 1977. *Climate: Present, Past and Future*. Vol. 2. London: Methuen.

Lamb, W. Kaye. 1970. *The Journals and Letters of Sir Alexander Mackenzie*. Cam-
    bridge: Hakluyt Society.

– 1988. "Canada." *The Canadian Encyclopedia*, 2nd ed.

Latham, John. 1781, 1785. *A General Synopsis of Birds* (3 vols.). London: Benjamin
    White.

– 1790. *Index Ornithologicus*. Volume 2. London: Leigh and Sotheby.

Laughton, John Knox. 1949a. "Sir Francis Beaufort." *Dictionary of National Biog-
    raphy* 2:39–41. London: Oxford University Press.

– 1949b. "Alexander Dalrymple." *Dictionary of National Biography*, 4:402–03.
    London: Oxford University Press.

– 1949c. "Johann Georg Adam Forster." *Dictionary of National Biography*, 7:455–6.
    London: Oxford University Press.

Lee, Sidney. 1949. "Sir Godfrey Copley." *Dictionary of National Biography*, 4:1102.
    London: Oxford University Press.

Lefroy, J.H., and J. Richardson. 1855. *Magnetical and Meteorological Observations at
    Lake Athabasca and Fort Simpson, and at Fort Confidence in Great Bear Lake*. London:
    Longman, Brown, Green, and Longmans.

[Legg, J.]. 1780. *A Discourse on the Emigration of British Birds ... by a Naturalist*. Salis-
    bury, printed privately.

Lever, Christopher. 1977. *The Naturalised Animals of the British Isles*. London:
    Hutchinson.

Levere, Trevor H. 1993. *Science and the Canadian Arctic: A Century of Exploration
    1818–1918*. Cambridge: Cambridge University Press.

Leveson Gower, R.H.G. 1934. "HBC and the Royal Society." *The Beaver*
    265(2):29–31, 66.

Lindsay, Debra. 1986. "Peter Fidler's Library: Philosophy and Science in Rupert's
    Land." In Peter F. McNally, ed., *Readings in Canadian Library History*, 209–29.

– 1993. *Science in the Subarctic: Trappers, Traders and the Smithsonian Institution*. Wash-
    ington: Smithsonian Institution Press.

Lining, John. 1748. "The Weather in South-Carolina, with Abstracts of the Tables
    of his Meteorological Observations in Charles-town." *Philosophical Transactions*
    45:336–44.

– 1753. "The Quantity of Rain Fallen [at Charles-Town, South-Carolina], from
    January 1738 to December 1752." *Philosophical Transactions* 48:284–6.

Linnaeus, C. 1758, 1956. *Systema Naturae*. 10th ed. Stockholm: L. Salvii; reprinted
    London: British Museum (Natural History).

– 1766. *Systema Naturae, Twelfth Edition*. Stockholm: L. Salvii.

– 1776. *A Catalogue of the Birds, Beasts, Fishes, Insects, Plants, &c., Contained in Edwards's Natural History in Seven Volumes.* London: J. Robson.

Livingstone, David N. 1992. *The Geographical Tradition: Episodes in the History of a Contested Enterprise.* Oxford: Blackwell.

Logan, Bari M. 1982. "Charles Waterton's Method of Taxidermy – the Preparation and Arrangement of Animal Skins." *Catalogue of the Waterton Exhibition at Wakefield Museum, Yorkshire.* Wakefield: Yorkshire Communications Group.

London, Jack. 1993. *The Complete Short Stories of Jack London.* Berkeley: Stanford University Press.

Lowe, A. Burnett. 1961. "Canada's First Weathermen." *The Beaver* 292(1):4–7.

Ludlum, David M. 1966. *Early American Winters I: 1604–1820.* Boston: American Meteorological Society.

– 1968. *Early American Winters II: 1821–1870.* Boston: American Meteorological Society.

Lumley, Elizabeth, ed. 2001. *Canadian Who's Who 2001.* Toronto: University of Toronto Press.

Lumsden, H.G. 1966. "The Prairie Chicken in Southwestern Ontario." *Canadian Field-Naturalist* 80:33–45.

– 1970. "A Hybrid Population of Prairie Grouse on Manitoulin Island, Ontario." *Transactions of the Midwest Fish and Wildlife Conference* 32:57–8.

– 1984. "Pre-settlement Breeding Distribution of Trumpeter (*Cygnus buccinator*) and Tundra Swans (*C. columbianus*) in Eastern Canada." *Canadian Field-Naturalist* 98:415–24.

– 2002. "The Trumpeter Swan Restoration Program in Ontario 2001." *North American Swans* 31:16–18.

MacFarlane, Roderick R. 1891. "Notes on and List of Birds and Eggs Collected in Arctic America, 1861–1866." *Proceedings of the U.S. National Museum* 14:413–46.

MacFarlane, Roderick R. 1905. "Notes on Mammals Collected and Observed in the Northern Mackenzie River District, North-west Territories of Canada, with Remarks on Explorers and Explorations of the Far North." *Proceedings U.S. National Museum* 28:673–764.

– 1908. "Notes on the Mammals and Birds of Northern Canada." In Charles Mair, *Through the Mackenzie Basin*, 151–470. Toronto: William Briggs.

MacGregor, Arthur. 1995. "The Natural History Correspondence of Sir Hans Sloane." *Archives of Natural History* 22:79–90.

MacGregor, J.G. 1966. *Peter Fidler: Canada's Forgotten Surveyor, 1769–1822.* Toronto: McClelland and Stewart.

MacKay, D.K., and J. Ross MacKay. 1965. "Historical Records of Freeze-up and Break-up on the Churchill and Hayes Rivers." *Geographical Bulletin* 7:7–16.

Mackinnon, C.S. 1979. "Samuel Hearne." *Dictionary of Canadian Biography*, 4:339–42. Toronto: University of Toronto Press.

MacLaren, I.S. 1991. "Samuel Hearne's Accounts of the Massacre at Bloody Fall, 17 July 1771." *Ariel, A Review of International English Literature* 22:25–51.

MacLaren, I.S. 1994. "Commentary." In C.S. Houston, ed., *Arctic Artist: The Journal and Paintings of George Back, Midshipman with Franklin, 1819–1822*, 275–310. Montreal: McGill-Queen's University Press.

Macleod, Roy. 2001. "Nature and Empire: Science and the Colonial Enterprise." *Osiris* 15:1.

MacLulich, D.A. 1937. *Fluctuations in the Numbers of the Varying Hare (Lepus americanus)*. University of Toronto Studies, Biological Series no. 43.

Malaher, D.G. 1998. "Beavers and Boundaries: The Contribution of the Fur Trade to the USA-Canada Boundary." *Rupertsland Colloquium* 6 June 1998.

Manley, G. 1974. "Central England Temperatures: Monthly Means 1659 to 1973." *Quarterly Journal of the Royal Meteorological Society* 100:389–405.

Marsh, James. 1988. "Samuel Hearne." *The Canadian Encyclopedia, Second Edition*, 2:973. Toronto: Hurtig.

Mason, A. Stuart. 1992. *George Edwards: The Bedell and His Birds*. London: Royal College of Physicians.

Mathews, G.M. 1931. "John Latham (1740–1837), an Early English Ornithologist." *Ibis* ser. 13, 1:466–75.

Mayr, Ernst, E. Gorton Linsley, and Robert L. Usinger. 1953. *Methods and Principles of Systematic Zoology*. New York: McGraw Hill.

McAtee, W.L. 1950. "The North American Birds of George Edwards." *Journal of the Society for the Bibliography of Natural History* 2:194–205.

– 1957a. "The North American Birds of Mark Catesby and Eleazar Albin." *Journal of the Society for the Bibliography of Natural History* 3:177–94.

– 1957b. "The North American Birds of Linnaeus." *Journal of the Society for the Bibliography of Natural History* 3:291–300.

– 1963. "The North American Birds of Thomas Pennant." *Journal of the Society for the Bibliography of Natural History* 4:100–24.

McDonald, Miriam, Lucassie Arragutainaq, and Zack Novalinga. 1997. *Voices from the Bay: Traditional Ecological Knowledge of Inuit and Cree in the Hudson Bay Bioregion*. Sanikiluaq: Canadian Arctic Resources Committee and Environmental Committee of Municipality of Sanikiluaq.

Mearns, Barbara, and Richard Mearns. 1988. *Biographies for Birdwatchers*. London: Academic Press.

Mendelsohn, E. 1976. "John Lining and His Contribution to Early American Science." In B. Hindle, ed., *Early American Science*, 120–34. New York: Science History Publications.

Meyer, David. 1991. "The Goose Dance in Swampy Cree Religion." *Journal of the Canadian Church Historical Society* 33:107–18.

Middleton, Christopher. 1742. "The effects of Cold ... in Hudson's Bay, North America." *Philosophical Transactions* 42:157–71.

Mills, C. 1998. *Images from Nature: Drawings and Paintings from the Library of the Natural History Museum*. London: The Natural History Museum.

Minns, R. 1970. An Air Mass Climatology of Canada during the Early Nineteenth Century: An Analysis of Weather Records of Certain Hudson's Bay Company Forts. Master's thesis, University of British Columbia.

Mitchell, Carl D. 1994. "Trumpeter Swan (*Cygnus buccinator*)." In A. Poole and F. Gill, eds., *The Birds of North America*, No. 105. Philadelphia: Academy of Natural Sciences, and Washington, DC: American Ornithologists' Union.

Moodie, D.W. 1977. "The Hudson's Bay Company's Archives: a Resource for Historical Geography." *Canadian Geographer* 21:268–74.

Morton, Anne. 1985. "Charles Elton and the Hudson's Bay Company." *The Beaver* 315.4:22–9.

Mullens, W.H., and H. Kirke Swann. 1917. *A Bibliography of British Ornithology from the Earliest Times to the End of 1912*. London: Macmillan.

Napper, James. 1749. See Hudson's Bay Company, 1749.

National Research Council. 1999. *Global Environmental Change: Research Pathways for the Next Decade*. Washington: National Academy Press.

Neatby, Leslie H. 1969. "James Napper." *Dictionary of Canadian Biography*, 2:493. Toronto: University of Toronto Press.

Nelson, E.C. 1995. "Review of K.M. Reeds, Botany in Medieval and Renaissance Universities." *Archives of Natural History* 22:142–3.

Nelson, R.K. 1969. *Hunters of the Northern Ice*. Chicago: University of Chicago Press.

Newman, Peter C. 1985. *Company of Adventurers*, vol. 1. Markham, Ontario: Penguin.

Newton, Alfred. 1896. *A Dictionary of Birds*. London: Adam and Charles Black.

Nichols, B. 1990. "Trumpeter." *Michigan Natural Resources* Oct. 1990:12–17.

Nicks, J.S. 1987. "William Tomison." *Dictionary of Canadian Biography*, 6:775–7. Toronto: University of Toronto Press.

Nitzsch, C.L. 1833, 1840. *Pterylographiae Avium*. Halle; translated by W.S. Dawson. London, privately printed.

O'Brian, Patrick. 1993. *Joseph Banks: A Life*. Boston: David R. Godine.

Okimâsis, Jean L., and Solomon Ratt. 1999. *Cree: Language of the Plains: nêhiyawêwin: paskwâwi-pîkiskwêwin*. Regina: Canadian Plains Research Center.

Paley, William. 1802. *Natural Theology*. London: Society for Promoting Christian Knowledge.

Pannekoek, F. 1979. "Humphrey Marten." *Dictionary of Canadian Biography*, 4:517–19. Toronto: University of Toronto Press.

– 1988. "York Factory." *The Canadian Encyclopedia*. Toronto: Hurtig, 3:2352.

Payne, Michael. 1989. *The Most Respectable Place in the Territory: Every Day Life in Hudson's Bay Company Service, York Factory, 1788 to 1870*. Ottawa: National Historic Parks and Sites.

Peck, G.K., and R.D. James. 1983. *Breeding Birds of Ontario: Nidiology and Distribution*. Toronto: Royal Ontario Museum.

Peel, Bruce. 1987. "Thomas Thomas." *Dictionary of Canadian Biography*, 6:767–8. Toronto: University of Toronto Press.

Pennant, Thomas. 1768. *British Zoology*. 3 vols. London: Benjamin White.

– 1781. *Genera of Birds*. 2nd edition. London: Benjamin White.

– 1784–5. *Arctic Zoology*. 3 vols. London: Henry Hughs.

– 1786. *Indexes to the Ornithologie of the Comte de Buffon and the Planches Enluminées*. London: Benjamin White.

– 1787. *Supplement to the Arctic Zoology*. London: Henry Hughs.

– 1792. *Arctic Zoology*. 2nd ed. 3 vols. London: Robert Faulder.

Phillips, T.E.R. 1942. "Venus." *Encylopaedia Britannica*. London: Encyclopaedia Britannica, 23:71–2.

Poggendorff, J.C. [1970]. *Biographisch-Literarisches Handwörterbuch zur Geschichte der exacten Wissenschaften*. Amsterdam: B.M. Israel [reprint].

Poland, Ernest. 1930. "A Short Historical Account of the London Fur Trade." In *Souvenir of the British Exhibition in the Hall of Nations, IPA Leipzig, May-September 1930*, 3–15.

Poland, H. 1892. *Fur-bearing Animals*. London: Gurney and Jackson.

Ponte, Lowell. 1976. *The Cooling*. Englewood Cliffs, NJ: Prentice-Hall.

Porsild, A.E., and W.J. Cody. 1980. *Vascular Plants of Continental Northwest Territories, Canada*. Ottawa: National Museums of Canada.

Preble, E.A. 1902. *A Biological Investigation of the Hudson Bay Region*. North American Fauna no. 22. Washington: U.S. Biological Survey.

Prebble, John. 1963. *The Highland Clearances*. London: Secker and Warburg.

Proctor, Richard A. 1874. *Transit of Venus: A Popular Account*. London: Longmans Green.

Pycraft, W.P. 1942. "Feather." *Encyclopedia Brittanica*. London: Encyclopaedia Britannica, 9:128–31.

Pyenson, Lewis, and Susan Sheets-Pyenson. 1999. *Servants of Nature: A History of Scientific Institutions, Enterprises and Sensibilities*. New York: W.W. Norton.

Quinn, W.H., and V.T. Neal. 1992. "The Historical Record of El Niño Events." In R.S. Bradley and P.D. Jones, eds., *Climate since A.D. 1500*, revised ed., 623–48. London: Routledge.

Raven, C.E. 1986. *John Ray, Naturalist: His Life and Works*. Cambridge: Cambridge University Press.

Ray, Arthur J. 1974. *Indians in the Fur Trade: Their Role as Trappers, Hunters, and Middlemen in the Lands Southwest of Hudson Bay, 1660–1870*. Toronto: University of Toronto Press.

Ray, John. 1691. *The Wisdom of God Manifested in the Works of the Creation*. London: Samuel Smith.

Reveal, J.L., G.F. Frick, C.R. Broome, and M.L. Brown. 1987. "Botanical Explorations and Discoveries in Colonial Maryland: An Introduction." *Huntia* 7:1–3.

Rich, E.E., ed. 1945, 1946. *Minutes of the Hudson's Bay Company 1679–1684*. 2 vols. Toronto: Hudson's Bay Record Society.

– ed. 1949. *James Isham's Observations on Hudson's Bay, 1743* (HBRS 12). Toronto: Champlain Society.

– ed., 1954. *Moose Fort Journals, 1783–85*. London: Hudson's Bay Record Society.

– 1958a. "Pro pelle cutem." *The Beaver* 288:12–15.

– 1958b, 1959. *The History of the Hudson's Bay Company, 1670–1870* (2 vols.). London: Hudson's Bay Record Society.

– 1960. "Trade Habits and Economic Motivations among the Indians of North America." *Canadian Journal of Economics and Political Science* 26:35–53.

– 1967. *The Fur Trade and the Northwest to 1867*. Toronto: McClelland and Stewart.

– 1974. "James Isham." *Dictionary of Canadian Biography*, 3:301–4. Toronto: University of Toronto Press.

– 1979a. "Philip Turnor." *Dictionary of Canadian Biography*, 4:740–2. Toronto: University of Toronto Press.

– 1979b. "Edward Umfreville." *Dictionary of Canadian Biography*, 4:742–3. Toronto: University of Toronto Press.

Richardson, John. 1823. "Botanical Appendix (VII)." In John Franklin, *Narrative of a Journey to the Shores of the Polar Sea in the Years 1819, 20, 21, and 22*, 729–63. London: John Murray.

– 1829. *Fauna Boreali-Americana, or the Zoology of the Northern Parts of British America, Volume 1: The Mammals*. London: John Murray.

– and William Swainson. 1832. *Fauna Boreali-Americana, Volume 2: The Birds*. London: John Murray.

Roberts, T.S. 1936. *The Birds of Minnesota*. 2 vols. Minneapolis: University of Minnesota Press.

Roger, Jacques (transl. S.L. Bonnefoi). 1997. *Buffon: A Life in Natural History*. Ithaca: Cornell University Press.

Rogers, Philip M., and Donald A. Hammer. 1998. "Ancestral Breeding and Wintering Ranges of the Trumpeter Swan (*Cygnus buccinator*) in the Eastern United States." *North American Swans* 27:13–29.

Rosen, Robert N. 1992. *A Short History of Charleston*. 2nd ed. Charleston: Peninsula Press.

Ross, B.R. 1861. "An Account of the Animals Useful in an Economic Point of View to the Various Chipewyan Tribes." *Canadian Naturalist and Geologist* 6:433–44.

– 1862. "List of Mammals, Birds, and Eggs, Observed in the McKenzie's River District, with Notices." *Canadian Naturalist and Geologist* 7:137–55.

Rowan, William, 1925. "Relation of Light to Bird Migration and Developmental Changes." *Nature* 115:494–5.

– 1926. "On Photoperiodism, Reproductive Periodicity, and the Annual Migrations of Birds and Certain Fishes." *Proceedings of the Boston Society of Natural History* 38:147–89.

– 1931. *The Riddle of Migration.* Baltimore: Williams and Wilkins.

– 1948. *The Ten-year Cycle: Outstanding Problem of Canadian Conservation.* Edmonton: Department of Extension, University of Alberta.

– and L.B. Keith. 1956. "Reproductive Potential and Sex Ratios of Snowshoe Hares in Northern Alberta." *Canadian Journal of Zoology* 34:273–81.

– 1959. "Monthly Weights of Snowshoe Hares from North-central Alberta." *Journal of Mammalogy* 40:221–6.

Royal Society of London. 1940. "Appendix 4: Medallists of the Royal Society." In *The Record of the Royal Society of London for the Promotion of Natural Knowledge.* 4th ed., 345–8. Edinburgh: Morrison & Gibb.

Roze, Uldis. 1989. *The North American Porcupine.* Washington: Smithsonian Institution Press.

Ruggles, Richard I. 1976. "Governor Samuel Wegg: The Winds of Change." *The Beaver* 307(2):10–20.

– 1977. "Hospital Boys of the Bay." *The Beaver* 308(2):4–11.

– 1980. "Hudson's Bay Company Mapping." In C.M. Judd and A.J. Ray, eds., *Old Trails and New Directions. Papers of the Third North American Fur Trade Conference,* 24–36. Toronto: University of Toronto Press.

– 1991. *A Country So Interesting: The Hudson's Bay Company and Two Centuries of Mapping, 1670–1870.* Montreal: McGill-Queen's University Press.

– 1997. "British Exploration of Rupert's Land." In J.L. Allen, ed., *North American Exploration: A Continent Defined,* 203–27.

Rusch, D.H., S. Destefano, M.C. Reynolds, and D. Lauten. 2000. "Ruffed Grouse (*Bonasa umbellus*)." In A. Poole and F. Gill, eds., *The Birds of North America,* No. 515. Philadelphia: The Birds of North America, Inc.

Rusnock, Andrew A. 1999. "Biopolitics." In William Clark, Jan Golinski, and Simon Schaffer, eds. *The Sciences in Enlightened Europe,* 49–68. Chicago: University of Chicago Press.

Sabine, Joseph. 1823. "Zoological Appendix V" In J. Franklin, *Narrative of a Journey to the Shores of the Polar Sea in the Years 1819, 20, 21, and 22,* 647–703. London: John Murray.

Sanderson, A.E., and W.D. Anderson, Jr. 1999. *Natural History Investigations in South Carolina*. Columbia SC: University of South Carolina Press.

Sayre, James Kedzie. 1996. *North American Bird Folknames and Names*. Foster City, CA: Bottlebrush Press.

Schmidt, Karl P. 1951. "The 'Methodus' of Linnaeus, 1736." *Journal of the Society for the Bibliography of Natural History* 2:369–74.

Schroeder, M.A., and L.A. Robb. 1993. "Greater Prairie-Chicken." In A. Poole, P. Stettenheim, and F. Gill, eds., *The Birds of North America*, No. 36. Philadelphia: The Academy of Natural Sciences; Washington: The American Ornithologists' Union.

Scott, P.A., D.C.F. Fayle, C.V. Bentley, and R.I.C. Hansell. 1988. "Large Scale Changes in Atmospheric Circulation Interpreted from Patterns of Tree Growth at Churchill, Manitoba, Canada." *Arctic and Alpine Research* 20:199–211.

Sellers, Leila. 1934. *Charleston Business on the Eve of the American Revolution*. Chapel Hill: University of North Carolina Press.

Seton, E.T. 1909. *Life-histories of Northern Animals: An Account of the Mammals of Manitoba*. New York: Charles Scribner's Sons.

– 1912. *The Arctic Prairies*. London: Constable.

– 1946. *Trail of an Artist-Naturalist*. New York: Charles Scribner's Sons.

Shadle, Albert R. 1949. "Copulation in the Porcupine." *Journal of Wildlife Management* 10:159–63.

Sheets-Pyenson, Susan. 1992. "Horse Race: John William Dawson, Charles Lyell, and the Competition over the Edinburgh Natural History Chair in 1854–1855." *Annals of Science* 49:461–77.

Shelford, V.E. 1943. "Abundance of the Collared Lemming in the Churchill Area, 1929-1940." *Ecology* 24:472–84.

– 1945. "The Relation of Snowy Owl Migration to the Abundance of the Collared Lemming." *Auk* 62:592–6.

Simmons, Deidre A. 1994. Custodians of a Great Inheritance: An Account of the Making of the HBC Archives. Joint Master's thesis, University of Manitoba/University of Winnipeg.

Smith, Shirlee Anne. 1979. "Ferdinand Jacobs." *Dictionary of Canadian Biography*, 4:383–4. Toronto: University of Toronto Press.

Snyder, L.L. 1963. "On the Type Locality of Thirteen North American Birds." *Canadian Field-Naturalist* 77:128–9.

Sobel, Dava. 1995. *Longitude: The True Story of a Lone Genius Who Solved the Greatest Scientific Problem of His Time*. New York: Penguin.

Soper, J.D. 1921. "Notes on the Snowshoe Rabbit." *Journal of Mammalogy* 2:101–8.

Squires, J.R., and R.T. Reynolds. 1997. "Northern Goshawk." In A. Poole and F. Gill, eds., *The Birds of North America*, No. 298. Philadelphia: The Birds of North America, Inc.

Stanley, George F.G. 1955. *John Henry Lefroy: In Search of the Magnetic North.* Toronto: Macmillan.

Stearn, W.T. 1959. "The Background of Linnaeus's Contributions to the Nomenclature and Methods of Systematic Botany." *Systematic Zoology* 8:4–22.

Stearns, R.P. 1945. "The Royal Society and the Company." *The Beaver* 276(1):8–13.

Stephens, L.D. 2000. *Science, Race and Religion in the American South.* Chapel Hill: University of North Carolina Press.

Sterling, K.B., R.P. Harmond, G.A. Cevasco, and L.F. Hammond, eds. 1997. *Biographical Dictionary of American and Canadian Naturalists and Environmentalists.* Westport, Connecticut: Greenwood.

Sterling, R.T. 1963. "Wascana Goose Summers on the Arctic Prairie." *Blue Jay* 21:134–5.

Stevens, J.A. 1898. *American Statesmen: Albert Gallatin, 1761–1849.* Boston: Houghton Mifflin.

Stevens, O.A. 1936. "The First Descriptions of North American Birds." *Wilson Bulletin* 48:203–15.

Stewart, Larry. 1992. *The Rise of Public Science: Rhetoric, Technology, and Natural Philosophy in Newtonian Britain, 1660–1750.* Cambridge: Cambridge University Press.

Stimson, Dorothy. 1968. *Scientists and Amateurs: A History of the Royal Society.* New York: Greenwood Press.

Stresemann, E. 1975. *Ornithology: From Aristotle to the Present.* Cambridge: Harvard University Press, 1975.

Swainson, W. 1840. *Taxidermy, with the Biography of Zoologists.* London: Longman, Orme, Brown, Green and Longman's.

Taverner, P.A. 1931. "A Study of *Branta canadensis* (Linnaeus), the Canada Goose." *National Museum of Canada Bulletin* 67: 28–40.

– 1940. *Birds of Canada.* Toronto: Musson.

Taylor, W.P. 1935. "Ecology and Life History of the Porcupine (*Erethizon epixanthum*) as Related to the Forests of Arizona and the Southwestern United States." *University of Arizona Bulletin* 6(5):1–177.

Thacher, J. 1828, 1967. *American Medical Biography.* New York: Milford House.

Thompson [Seton], E.E. 1891. "The Birds of Manitoba." *Proceedings of the U.S. National Museum* 13:457–643.

Thomson, G.M. 1975. *In Search of the North-west Passage.* New York: Macmillan.

Thorman, George E. 1979. "Germain Maugenest." *Dictionary of Canadian Biography* 4:524–5. Toronto: University of Toronto Press.

Troup, J.A. 1990. "The Impact of the "Nor Wast" on Stromness." *Rupertsland Colloquium*, Stromness, Orkney, UK, 5 June.

Tuchman, Arleen M. 1997. "Alexander Garden." In K.B. Sterling, et al., *Biographical Dictionary of American and Canadian Naturalists and Environmentalists*, 301–03.

Tyrrell, J.B., ed., 1911. *Samuel Hearne, A Journey ... to the Northern Ocean.* Toronto: Champlain Society.

– ed., 1934. *Journals of Samuel Hearne and Philip Turnor, 1774–1792.* Toronto: Champlain Society.

Umfreville, Edward. 1790, 1954. *The Present State of Hudson's Bay.* London: Charles Stalker; reprinted Toronto: Ryerson.

Urness, Carol. 1968. *A Naturalist in Russia: Letters from Peter Simon Pallas to Thomas Pennant.* Minneapolis: University of Minnesota Press.

Van Kirk, Sylvia. 1979a. "Joseph Isbister." *Dictionary of Canadian Biography,* 4:380–1. Toronto: University of Toronto Press.

– 1979b. "Moses Norton." *Dictionary of Canadian Biography,* 4:583–5. Toronto: University of Toronto Press.

– 1980. *"Many Tender Ties": Women in Fur-trade Society in Western Canada, 1670–1870.* Winnipeg: Watson and Dwyer.

Voorhis, Ernest. 1930. Historic Forts and Trading Posts of the French Regime and of the English Fur Trading Companies. Ottawa: Department of the Interior (mimeographed).

Wadmore, James Foster. 1902. *Some Account of the Worshipful Company of Skinners of London, Being the Guild or Fraternity of Corpus Christi.* London: Blades, East, and Blades.

Waldon, B. 1996. Possible Sighting of Eskimo Curlews. *Blue Jay* 54:123–4.

Wales, William. 1771. "Journal of a Voyage, Made by Order of the Royal Society, to Churchill River, on the North-west Coast of Hudson's Bay; of Thirteen Months Residence in that Country; and of the Voyage back to England; in the Years 1768 and 1769." *Philosophical Transactions* 60:100–36.

Walker, John. 1812. *An Economical History of the Hebrides and the Highlands of Scotland.* Edinburgh.

Wallace, W.S. 1934. *Documents Relating to the North West Company.* Toronto: Champlain Society.

– 1938. "Sir Henry Lefroy's Journey to the North-west in 1843–4." *Transactions of the Royal Society of Canada* 32:67–96.

– 1943. "Two Curious Fur-trade Wills: I. Peter Fidler Looks Ahead 200 Years." *The Beaver* 274(4):34–5.

Wallis, P.J., and R.V. Wallis. 1988. *Eighteenth Century Medics: Subscriptions, Licences, Apprenticeships.* Newcastle Upon Tyne: Project for Historical Biobibliography.

Waring, J.I. 1964. *A History of Medicine in South Carolina.* Charleston.

Warwick, E., H.C. Pitz, and A. Wyckoff. 1965. *Early American Dress: The Colonial and Revolutionary Periods.* New York: Benjamin Blom.

Watkins, Morgan George. 1949. "John Latham." *Dictionary of National Biography* 11:605–6. London: Oxford University Press.

Waugh, E., N. LeClaire, and G. Cardinal. 1998. *Alberta Elders' Cree Dictionary*. Edmonton: University of Alberta Press.

Webster, Douglas, and Molly Webster. 1973. *Comparative Vertebrate Morphology*. New York: Academic Press.

Weir, R.M. 1983. *Colonial South Carolina*. Millwood, N.Y.: KTO Press.

White, Gilbert. 1993. *The Natural History and Antiquities of Selborne* [1813 edition facsimile with an introduction by P.M.G. Foster]. London: The Ray Society.

Wilder, Laura Ingalls. 1972. *By the Shores of Silver Lake*. New York: Harper and Row.

Williams, Glyndwr. 1962. *The British Search for the Northwest Passage in the Eighteenth Century*. London: Longmans.

– 1968. "Hudson's Bay Record Society." [4-page information pamphlet announcing the forthcoming publication in 1969 of *Andrew Graham's Observations*].

– 1969. *Andrew Graham's Observations on Hudson's Bay, 1767–91*. (HBRS 27). London: Hudson's Bay Record Society.

– 1970. "The Hudson's Bay Company and Its Critics in the Eighteenth Century." *Transactions of the Royal Society* ser. 5, 20:149–71.

– 1974. "Christopher Middleton." *Dictionary of Canadian Biography*, 3:446–50. Toronto: University of Toronto Press.

– 1975. *Hudson's Bay Miscellany, 1670–1870*. Winnipeg: Hudson's Bay Record Society 30.

– 1978. "Andrew Graham and Thomas Hutchins: Collaboration and Plagiarism in 18th-century Natural History." *The Beaver* 308(4): 4–14.

– 1979a. "Thomas Hutchins." *Dictionary of Canadian Biography*, 4:377–8. Toronto: University of Toronto Press.

– 1979b. "William Wales." *Dictionary of Canadian Biography*, 4:757–8. Toronto: University of Toronto Press.

– 1983. "Andrew Graham." *Dictionary of Canadian Biography*, 5:362–3. Toronto: University of Toronto Press.

Williams, Stanley T. 1930. "Crèvecoeur, Michel-Guillaume Jean de." *Dictionary of American Biography*, 4:542–4. New York: Charles Scribner's Sons.

Willughbei, Francisci. 1676. *Ornithologiae*. London: John Martyn.

Willughby, F. 1678. *The Ornithology of Francis Willughby, Translated into English by John Ray* (3 vols.). London: John Martyn.

Wilson, C. 1982. "The Summer Season along the East Coast of Hudson Bay during the Nineteenth Century. Part I. General Introduction; Climatic Controls: Calibration of the Instrumental Temperature Data, 1814-1821." *Canadian Climate Centre Report* 82–4: 1–223. Part II. The Little Ice on Eastern Hudson Bay: Summers at Great Whale, Fort George, Eastmain, 1814-1821." *Canadian Climate Centre Report* 83–9: 1–145.

Withers, C.W.J. 1988. "Improvement and Enlightenment: Agriculture and Natural History in the Work of the Rev. Dr John Walker." In Peter Jones, ed., *Philosophy and Science in the Scottish Enlightenment*, 102–16. Edinburgh: John Donald.

– 1991. "The Rev. Dr John Walker and the Practice of Natural History in Late Eighteenth Century Scotland." *Archives of Natural History* 18:201–20.

– 1992. "Natural Knowledge as Cultural Property: Disputes over the "Ownership" of Natural History in Late Eighteenth-century Edinburgh." *Archives of Natural History* 19:289–303.

– 1993. "Both Useful and Ornamental, John Walker's Keepership of Edinburgh University's Natural History Museum, 1779–1803." *Journal of the History of Collections* 5:65–77.

Wolfart, H.C., and F. Ahenakew. 1998. *The Student's Dictionary of Literary Plains Cree.* Winnipeg: Algonquian and Iroquoian Linguistics Memoir 15.

Wolvengrey, Arok, and Jean Okimâsis. 2001. *Cree Words: nêhiyawêwin itwêwina.* Regina: Canadian Plains Research Center.

Woolf, Harry. 1959. *The Transits of Venus: A Study of Eighteenth Century Science.* Princeton: Princeton University Press.

Working Group I of the Intergovernmental Panel on Climate Change. 1996. *Climate Change 1995. The Science of Climate Change: Summary for Policymakers.* Geneva, Switzerland: Intergovernmental Panel on Climate Change.

Worster, Donald. 1994. *Nature's Economy: A History of Ecological Ideas.* 2nd ed. Cambridge: Cambridge University Press.

Wroth, W.W. 1949. "Thomas Pennant." *Dictionary of National Biography*, 15:765–8. London: Oxford University Press.

Yarrell, W. 1832. "Description of the Organ of Voice in a New Species of Wild Swan (*Cygnus buccinator*, Richardson)." *Transactions of the Linnean Society* 17:1–5.

Zeller, Suzanne. 2000. "The Colonial World as Geological Metaphor: Strata(gems) of Empire in Victorian Canada." *Osiris* 15:85–107.

Zochert, Donald. 1980. "Notes on a Young Naturalist." *Audubon* 82(2):34–47.

INDEX

This index includes some additional information, such as first names or initials not provided in text, and updates of modern species names. Masters of HBC ships are omitted but ship names are included. Most geographic features have not been indexed.

Agassiz, Louis, 128
Ahenakew, Freda, 206
Albany Fort: escapes smallpox, 69; goose consumption at, 88; Hutchins a good manager at, 66; Hutchins departs from, 73, 149; Hutchins' experiments at, 70; Light at, 35, 40; Marten at, 55, 57; Marten's father-in-law from, 56; Ruffed Grouse at, 64, sketch, 57; Snow Goose departure date, 76; specimens from, 24, 27, 57–60, 63, 107; surgeon at, 127; swan skins from, 193; type locality, 8; weather at, 119, 133
Aldrich, John W., 78
Allen, David E.,13, 29
Allen, Elsa Guerdrum, 24, 41, 58, 81, 84, 111, 138–9
American Ornithologists' Union, 110, 190
American War of Independence, 56

Amory, Copley, 182
Ant, 237
Antelope: Pronghorn, 239, 242
Arctic Front, 117
Aristotle, 18
Arrowsmith, Aaron, 32
Artedi, Petrus, 18
Aspen: Trembling, 249
Assiniboine River, 92
Astronomy , 14
Athabasca, 195
Audubon, John James, 86, 88
Auld, William, 128

Back, George, 153
Bacon, Norman H., 181
Badger: American, 242, 243
Bahamas, 138
Baillie, James L., 111
Baird, Spencer Fullerton, 112
Baker Lake, 79, 185
Ball, Tim, 95, 165
Banko, Winston, 198
Banks, Joseph, 22,112
Barnston, George, 112
Baroness, 155

Barrington, Daines, 27, 60, 63–4, 74; portrait, 59
Bartlett, John Russell, 84
Bat, 244
Battiste, M. , 206
Bear: American Black, 88, 241; Grizzly, 242; Polar, 206, 245
Bearberry, 246
Beattie, Judith Hudson, xxxviii, 94, 176, 190
Beaufort, Francis: windspeed scale, 129
Beaver, 88, 204, 239, 243. *See also* made beaver
Beaver, 35
Beaver and Albany, 73
Beaver House, 159
Bécoeur, Jean–Baptiste, 110
Bedstraw, 250
Bee, 237
Beetle, 237
Bell, Robert, 174
Beluga, 75
Berger, Carl, 13
Bewick, Thomas, 17
Birch, 251
Bird-lice, 76

Bishop, Nathaniel, 79
Bison: Plains, 87, 96, 242;
 Wood, 87
Bittern: American, 45, 52,
 99, 222, 225
Black, Joseph, 70, 162
Blackbird: Albino, 106,
 231; Red–winged, 140;
 Rusty, 64, 106, 214;
 Yellow–headed, 27, 106
Blackburne, Anna, 171
Blagden, Charles, 72
Blakiston, Thomas, 192
Blankets, HBC point, 68
Bloxham, James, 67
Bluebird: Eastern, 140
Bobcat, 206
Bobolink, 140, 229
Bobwhite: Northern, 141
Bob-white, 139
Body, Robert, 67
Boerhaave, Herman, 18,
 136
Bolsover House, 92
Bonaparte, Charles
 Lucien, 27
Bowie, Barbara, 62
Bowsfield, Hartwell, 160
Boy Scouts of America,
 174
Brady, Charles, 67
Brahe, Tycho, 114
Bramah, Joseph, 194
Brandon House, 93, 95
Brant, 100, 234
Brass, Emil, 180
Brief Climatic Warming,
 115
Brief Cooler Period, 115,
 118
Brief Warmer Period,
 115, 118
Brietzcke, Henry, 156
Britannia, 152
British Association for the

Advancement of Sci-
 ence, 21
British Museum (Natural
 History), 15, 109
Britten, James, 174
Brown, Alan, 200
Brown, Jennifer, 165
Buchanan, Handasyde, 17
Buckingham House, 92
Buffalo: Wood, 86
Bufflehead, 101, 232
Buffon, Georges Louis
 Leclerc, 17, 108, 109
Bull, William, 136
Bullfinch: Cuban, 141
Bunchberry, 250
Bunting: Indigo, 140;
 Painted, 140; Snow, 24,
 52, 59, 65, 75, 76, 96,
 106, 134, 170, 204, 212,
 232
Burbot, 74, 235
Bureau of Animal Popu-
 lation, 182
Butterfly, 238

Cactus: Prickly Pear, 96
Calendar reform, Grego-
 rian, 121
Cambridge University, 43
Cameron, E.S., 190
Cam Owen, 157
Capelin, 234
Capusten, Bernice, 200
Carberry, 174
Cardinal, George, 203,
 207
Cardinal: Northern, 140
Caribou, 87, 171, 239; as
 food, 8; Peary's, 245
Carlton House [N Sask
 R.] , 108, 192, 205
Carlton House [Assini-
 boine R.], 92
Carruthers, John, 67

Cartier, Jacques, 200–1
Cassin, John, 86
Catbird: Gray, 105, 141
Catchpole, Alan, 118, 121
Catesby, Mark, 16, 52,
 137, 171, 200, 201
Catfish: Channel, 96
Cauldwell, Paul, 67
Causton, R. and Son, 190
Cavendish, Henry, 72
Cedar: White, 251
Celsius, Anders, 18
Chalmers, Lionel, 136–7
Champlain Society, 41,
 160
Chandos, Duke of, 138
Chapman, Frank M., 194
Chappell, Lieut. E., 151
Char: Arctic, 235, 236
Charles Town, 3, 11; first
 for specimens, 135; first
 in meteorology, 136;
 population, 134–5;
 second for weather 14,
 135; too hot in summer,
 137; wealth, 136
Charlotte, 81
Chat: Yellow–breasted,
 141
Chawchinahaw, 82
Chesterfield House, 92,
 95
Chesterfield Inlet, 79
Chickadee, 75, 89, 204,
 206; Black-capped, 58,
 105, 206, 216, 217;
 Boreal, 64, 76, 105, 108,
 206, 226
Chipmunk, 244
Chitty, Dennis, 177, 183,
 187; Chitty hypothesis,
 185
Chitty, Helen, 177, 183
Chokecherry: berry, 251;
 wood of, 251

Christopher, William, 79

Christy, Miller, 174, 175

Churchill, 3; climate of, 116–18, 120–1, 123, 125–7, 130–1, 133–4; fur–trade colloquium at, 165; Graham at, 61; Hearne at, 81–3, 85–9; Isham at, 41–2, 44; La Pérouse at, 56; Light at, 34–5; Moses Norton at, 79–80; pale caribou brought to, 171; population, 8; Preble at, 111; ships stop at first, 145–51, 157–8; specimens from, 107; swan skins from, 193, 195; voles absent one year, 183; Wales at, 69

Churchill River, 192, 195

Clapham House, 92, 133

Clarke, Cyril, 16

Clifford, George, 18

Climate variation: human-induced and natural, 113, 134

Climatic information, Hudson Bay: 810, 735 pieces, 121

Climatology, 14

Cloudberry, 246, 250; to treat scurvy, 89

Coale, Henry, 190

Cocke, William, 137

Cocking, Matthew, explorer, 61; in charge of Cumberland House, 62; journal of, 162, 165

Colen, Joseph, 125, 173

Collinson, Peter, 11

Colonists, Selkirk, 94

Compass, 70

Conge-cathawhachaga, 83

Conne-e-queese, 82

Cook, James, 22, 131, 173

Coot: American, 170, 234

Copley gold medal, 17, 72, 98

Coppermine River, 80, 82

Coues, Elliott, 81, 179

Cove, Whale, 35

Cowie, Isaac, 156

Coyote, 186, 242

Crab, 89

Cranberry: Dry-ground, 251; Low Bush, 250; Swamp, 247, 249

Crane: Sandhill, 45, 102, 198, 201, 223, 224, portrait, 48; Whooping, 45, 76, 86, 89, 98, 102, 107, 198, 231, portrait, 48

Cree: ecological knowledge, 122; Attikamek dialect, 207; Moose ("l" dialect), 203–4; Plains ("y" dialect), 203; Swampy ("n" dialect), 203–4; Woods ("th" dialect), 203. *See also* First Nations

Cree-English dictionary, 43, 203–7

Crèvecoeur, J. Hector St John de, 136

Crossbill: Red, 76, 106, 171, 212; White-winged, 227

Crow: American, 105, 213, 217

Crow, Robert, 34

Crowberry, 247

Cuckoo: Yellow-billed, 140

Cumberland House: elk and grouse at, 88; established by Hearne,

32, 61, 66, 81, 83; Fidler at, 92–5; goods carried inland to, 55, 57; McAuley at, 205; Passenger Pigeons at, 89; specimen from, 76; swans at, 192, 195–6; weather at, 133

Curlew: 89, 204; Eskimo, 58–9, 89, 98, 102, 178, 204, 233; Hudsonian (see Whimbrel)

Currant: Black, 247; White, 251; Wild Red, 247

Cutler, Charles L., 207

Cycle, ten-year, 97

Dale, Samuel, 138

Dalrymple, Alexander, 32

Daniel, John, 69

Darwin, Charles, 21, 26

Davies, K.G., 160

Davies, Thomas, 109

de Beer, Gavin, 19, 26

Deer: White-tailed, 239

des Groseilliers, Médard Chouart, 4

Desaguliers, John Theophilus, 13

Diamond, Jared, 205

Dickason, Olive, 9, 122

Dickenson, Victoria, 12, 17

Dictionary, Cree-English, 43, 203–7

Discovery, 123

Dixon, Jeremiah, 131

Dobbs, Arthur, 129

Dodge, F.W., 174

Dog, 239

Dogwood: Red Osier, 248

Douglas, David, 153

Douglas, Gina, 174

Dove: Ground, 140;

Mourning, 103, 140
Dowitcher: Long-billed and Short-billed, 103, 212
Dragonfly, 237
Drought, 96
DuBois, Charles, 138
Du Creux, François, 201
Duck: Harlequin, 52, 100; "Indian," 215; Long-tailed, 52, 80, 101, 213; "Ordinary," 215; Ring-necked, 216; "Whistling," 220; Wood, 141
Dudgeon, James, 37
Dufresne, Louis, 110
Dunlin, 103, 234
Dupeer, Susannah, 79
Dymond, Joseph, 130–31

Eagle: Bald, 101, 140, 172, 210, 219, 232; Golden, 39, 101, 201, 210, 215, 218–9
Eagle, 154
Eaglet, 4
Eastmain House: climate of, 122; established, 146; furs from did not reach London, 178; Light at, 35; population, 7; swan skins from, 193; weather at, 133
Eddystone, 151–2
Edinburgh, 61–2, 70
Edinburgh Museum, 4
Edinburgh Royal Society, 30–2
Edinburgh University, 30, 136, 139
Edward and Ann, 151
Edwards, George, 3; artist, 4, 15, 17, 34–5,

38–40, 42, 44–5; and Canada Goose, 201; furlough to London, 148; and Graham, 61; new species illustrated by, 45, 52–3, 110–12; praises Isham, 54; and Sloane, 15–17; visited by Isham, 42
Effort, 155
Egg River, 89
Eider: Common, 100, 213, 221, King, 52, 100
Elk: American or Wapiti, 88, 246
Ellis, John, 139
El Niño, 113
Elton, Charles, 177, 181–3, 187
Elton quadrant, 82–3
Empson, Thomas, 66
English River (Churchill River), 195
Enlightenment, 11
Environmental deterioration, 113
Erik (first steam vessel), 158
Ermine, 244
Ernest Thompson Seton Museum, 174
Erxleben, C.P., 26
Esquimaux, 154
Ewart, William B., vii, 160; and diseases treated by HBC surgeons, 68; and Hutchins' natural history dates, 74–5

Falcon: Peregrine, 39, 101, 147, 211, 226
Falconer, William, 76
Farber, Paul, 21
Faries, Richard, 207–8

Fence Effect (Krebs Effect), 185
Fenchurch Street, 159
Fidler, Peter, 92–7, 107, 187; and channel catfish, 96; discoverer of coal, tar sands, 96; and drought, 96; meteorologist, 93–6, 123, 133; naturalist, 4, 96–7; surveyor, 11, 92–4; and ten-year cycle, 97, 177, 179
Fidler, Peter, Jr., 93
Fielding, Mark Stephen, 67
Finch: Purple, 140
Finlay, Michael, 197
Fir: Balsam, 247
First Nations: and canoe routes, 10; and childbirth, 10; dependent on weather, 123; and fur collection, 10; generosity and sharing, 10; Graham's account of, 62–3; guides and hunters, 10; nomadic existence, 9–10; oral history, 122; skills, 9; supply provisions to HBC, 8–10; transport goods inland, 55; weather observations, 122–4. *See also* Cree, Indians
Fisher, 26, 177, 243
Fisher, James, 17
Flamingo: Greater, 141
Flicker: Northern or Yellow-shafted, 58, 104, 140, 171, 209, 225
Flora, 155
Fly: Bulldog, 238
Flycatcher: Great

Crested, 141
Flying Squirrel:
Northern, 244
Forster, Johann Reinhold,
21–4; assessment of
Graham, 65; and
Canada Goose, 77; and
Cree names, 64,
208–35; describes new
species, 4, 21–3, 24, 28,
58, 64, 107, 172–3;
portrait, 22; preserves
bird skins, 110
Forster, Georg, 21–2
Fort Anderson, 178
Fort Chipewyan, 121, 192
Fort Dauphin, 93, 95, 97
Fort Edmonton, 197
Fort George: climate at,
122
Fort Gibraltar, 93
Fort Good Hope, 178
Fort Liard, 178
Fort Rae, 178
Fort Resolution, 178, 192
Fort Simpson, 86
Fort White Earth, 190
Fox: Arctic, 87, 206, 245;
Cross, 243; Grey, 240;
Red, 177, 180, 241, 243;
Swift, 240
Foxe, Luke, 174
Franklin, John, 3, 34, 152
Fraser, W.J., Jr., 136
French, Charles, 183
French Creek, 126
Frick, G.F., 139
Frog, 75, 89, 237
Furnace, 123

Gage, Thomas, 201
Gainsborough, Thomas,
26
Galileo, 114
Gallatin, Albert, 84

Garden, Alexander, 136,
139
Gardenia, 139
Global Cooling, 113
Global overpopulation,
113
Global Warming, 113
Gloucester House, 133
Glover, Richard, 55, 85,
161, 165, 172–4, 205
Glow-worm, 238
Gmelin, Johann
Friedrich, 21, 38
Godfrey, W. Earl, 59, 165
Godwit: Hudsonian, 27,
45, 80, 90, 102, 108,
206, 209, 214, 228, 233,
portrait, 50; Marbled,
27, 102, 206, 224, por-
trait, 49
Golden eagle: portrait, 39
Goldeneye: Barrow's, 172;
Common, 59, 101, 218,
220, 221
Goldeye, 209, 236
Golden-Plover: Black-
bellied and Lesser, 52,
111, 209
Goldfinch: American, 140
Goose: arrival dates, 134;
as food, 8, 134;
Barnacle, 28, 100;
"Barren," 90; Bean, 28;
Blue, 27–8, 40, 58, 171,
216; portrait, 46;
Canada, 52, 75–6, 88,
90, 100, 111, 142, 201,
220, 222; Greater
White-fronted, 52, 99;
Greylag, 28; Hutchins',
44, 66, 76–7, 111, 172,
211; Ross's, 80, 86, 90,
100, 107; Snow, 44–5,
58, 59, 64, 74, 88, 90,
171–2, 231, 233; Snow,

blue morph and white
morph, 99; White-
fronted, 214, 228
Gooseberry, 250
Gopher: Northern
Pocket, 244
Gosch, C.G.A., 173
Goshawk: Northern, 59,
101, 186
Grackle: Common, 140
Graham, Andrew, 61–5;
and anthropology and
cartography, 62–3; col-
laboration with
Hutchins, 30, 69–71,
73–8, 161–76; collector,
4, 23–4, 98, 107, 111,
134, 149; and Cree
names, 204; Edinburgh
agent of HBC, 62; and
Forster, 23–4; and fur
trade, 11, 61–2, 66; and
Hearne, 86–8; and
Isham, 53; map, 63;
and Marten, 58; and
natural history, 63–5,
86; and Pennant, 26–8;
retires to England, 149;
and Walker, 30; and
Wegg, 32
Graham, James, 67
Grant, Cuthbert, 93
Grass, 248
Grasshopper, 238
Grassquit: Black-faced,
141
Grayling, 235
Great West Life Assur-
ance Company, 160
Great Whale River: cli-
mate of, 122
Grebe: Horned, 25, 52,
99, 172, 212, 228, 229,
portrait, 26; Pied-
billed, 99, 141, 172

Greenwich House, 92
Griffier, Jan, 11; painting,
    12
Gronovius, Laurens T.,
    18, 142
Grosbeak: Blue, 140;
    Evening, 229; Pine, 52,
    59, 106, 224; Rose-
    breasted, 224
Ground squirrel: Arctic,
    86, 186
Grouse: Pinnated, 73;
    Ruffed, 58, 64, 88, 101,
    177, 204, 225; Ruffed or
    Spruce, 215; Sharp-
    tailed, 27, 58–9, 102,
    177, 204, 213, portrait,
    47; Spruce, 37, 88, 98,
    101, 170, 177, 186, 201,
    220, portrait, 36
Guillemot, 89; Black, 103,
    209, 229
Guiniad (see Whitefish
    (Tickameg)), 236; Sea,
    237
Gull: "big," 220; Bona-
    parte's, 103, 111, 211;
    Glaucous, 103, 213;
    Herring, 59, 103, 212,
    218; Laughing, 111, 141;
    unidentified, 219;
    white, 231
Gulls, 206
Gyrfalcon, 38, 59, 64, 101,
    107, 206, 216, 225, 226

Hadlow, 152
Hakluyt Society, 174
Halkett House, 93
Haller, W., 114
Hamlyn, Richard Julian,
    152
Hannah, 145, 146
Hanson, Harold, 90
Harderwijk, 18

Hare: Arctic, 64, 86,
    88–9, 242; Snowshoe,
    Graham specimen, 64;
    ten-year cycle of, 97,
    177, 179, 184, 186; Cree
    name of, 245–6
Hare, F.K., 115
Harington, C.R., 121
Harlequin, 226
Harrier: Northern, 52, 75,
    101, 108, 172, 223–4;
    portrait, 53
Harrington, W. Hague,
    174
Harris, Geraldine Alton,
    163
Harris, John, 13
Hawk: Red-tailed, 101;
    Rough-legged, 64, 75,
    101, 228; Sharp-
    shinned, 227
Hawk-Owl: Northern, 38
Hawksbee, Francis, 131
HBC. *See* Hudson's Bay
    Company
HBRS. *See* Hudson's Bay
    Record Society
Hearne, Samuel, 4, 11, 32,
    55, 57, 60–1, 79, 81–91,
    204; anthropologist, 85;
    and Cree names, 204,
    208, 211–49; explo-
    ration, 82–3, 132–4;
    founds Cumberland
    House, 55–7, narrative
    of, 32; naturalist, 26,
    85–91, 98, 107, 111, 130;
    and Pennant, 26–8;
    portrait, 82; sketch by
    Hearne, 9; surrenders
    Churchill to La
    Pérouse, 83–4; and
    swan skins, 188; under-
    standing of long-term
    weather changes, 134

Helmcken, John S., 154
Henday, Anthony, 42, 162,
    164
Henderson, J.Y., 206
Henley House: Greater
    Prairie-Chicken spec-
    imen from, 73; popula-
    tion of, 8; Ruffed
    Grouse at, 64; weather
    at, 133
Henry, Alexander the
    Elder, 179
Henry, Alexander the
    Younger, 179, 190
Herman, Landgrave IV,
    114
Heron: Black-crowned
    Night, 99; Great Blue,
    45, 99, 209, portrait,
    46; Green, 141; Little
    Blue, 141; Yellow-
    crowned Night, 141
Hewitt, Gordon, 177, 180
Hexton Manor, 159
Highland Clearances: in
    part weather-induced,
    115
Hoare, Michael, 23, 24
Hodgson, James, 13
Hood, Robert, 108; and
    Cree names, 208
Hood, Samuel, 81
Hooke, Robert, 113
Hopkins, Thomas, 67
Horse, 242
Horsefly, 258
Howse, J., 204
Hudson Bay: first in
    weather, 14, 135; name,
    109
Hudson House, 55
Hudsonian, term, 108
Hudson's Bay, 35
Hudson's Bay III, 145
Hudson's Bay IV, 146

Hudson's Bay V, 147

Hudson's Bay Company
(HBC), 3, 11, 24, 31, 34,
174, 191, 194; achieve-
ments in science, 4;
charter, 4; charter-
derived hegemony, 6;
diagram of years of
weather observations at
major posts, 120; explo-
ration, 6; first national
mapping agency, 6; fur
trade cycles and
Charles Elton, 177–82;
map of HBC posts with
over thirty years of
weather records, 119;
map-making, 6; natural
history, 6; sovereign
power, 5; transit of
Venus, 130

Hudson's Bay Company
(HBC) Archives [part of
the Provincial Archives
of Manitoba], xxiii, 3,
23, 33, 43, 111, 118, 120,
124, 128, 159–60, 161,
164, 168, 172–3, 188,
192, 208; Graham and
Hutchins journals in,
161–76; transferred to
Winnipeg, 159–60

Hudson's Bay Company
blankets, 66–8

Hudson's Bay Company
journals: prepared for
publication but not
achieved, 174; weather
information in, 116–21

Hudson's Bay Company
meteorological jour-
nals, 133

Hudson's Bay Record
Society (HBRS), 3, 62,
159–61, 208

Humboldt, Alexander
von, 112

Hummingbird, Ruby-
throated, 104, 141, 209

Hunt, Robert, 138

Hunter, William, 28

Hutchins, Thomas, 4, 12,
24, 53, 60, 66–78, 149;
collaboration with
Andrew Graham, 30–1,
107, 161–76; congela-
tion of mercury, 70–73;
Copley gold medal
awarded, 72, 98; and
Cree names, 74, 205,
208–51; medical prac-
tice, 56, 68–9; meteo-
rologist, 69–70, 131,
133; microscope, 86;
naturalist, 27–8, 58,
73–8, 98, 111; and Pen-
nant, 28; secretary of
HBC, 73; usurped
credit for Graham
specimens, 27, 169;
usurped credit for
Marten specimens, 60

Ibis: Scarlet, 138, 141;
White, 141

Idotliazee, 80

Ile-à-la-Crosse, 92, 93;
weather at, 133

Indians: Blackfoot, 42,
207; Chipewyan, 81,
85, 87, 134, 171;
Kootenay, 92; Peigan,
92. (*See also* Cree, First
Nations)

Industrial Revolution, 13

Innes, Harold A., 5, 188

Instruments, 132

Intergovernmental Panel
on Climate Change, 114

Inuit: ecological knowl-

edge of, 122

Isbister, Joseph, 126

Isham, Charles Price, 42

Isham, James, 4, 41–54,
55, 123, 146–7; col-
lector, 17, 36, 44–54,
88, 98, 110–12; and
Cree names, 43–4,
204–5, 208–51; fur-
lough to London, 148;
and fur trade, 41–2;
and Graham, 61; mete-
orologist, 126

Island Lake, 195

Isle-à-la-Crosse, 133, 192

Jack-pine: wood of, 249

Jack-rabbit: White-tailed,
242

Jacobs, Ferdinand, 62,
107, 190

Jaeger: Long-tailed, 103;
Parasitic, 52, 80, 103,
213, 225

Jaegers, 206

Jamaica, 15

James Hack Tuke Emi-
gration Committee, 174

Jameson, Robert, 31

Jardine, William, 25

Jarvis, Edward, 70, 76

Jay: Blue, 140, 230; Gray,
27, 44, 59, 65, 75, 78,
96, 105, 204, 209, 218,
231–4, caching food, 78

Jehl, Joseph R., 89

Jérémie, Nicolas, 119

Johnson, Alice, 160

Johnson, George, viii

Johnson, Samuel, 24

Jones, Cecil C., 180

Jones, J. Walter, 177, 180,
182

Jumping Mouse:
Meadow, 240

Junco: Dark-eyed or Slate-colored, 64, 106, 140, 225
Juniper: Ground, 247
Jurin, James, 114, 131

Kalm, Pehr, 19
Keeling, Clinton, 201
Keith, Lloyd B., 176–7, 185; Keith hypothesis, 185
Kelsey, Henry, 79, 119
Kendall, Edward N., 153
Kennicott, Robert, 86, 112
Kestrel: American, 140, 206, 227
Keveny, Owen, 151
Killdeer, 102, 141
Kindersley, Robert, 181
King, Richard, 153
Kingbird: Eastern, 141
Kingfisher: Belted, 52, 76, 104, 141, 172, 223
King George II, 66, 107, 148–9
King George III, 57, 92, 149–51
Kinglet: Ruby-crowned, 24, 105, 172
Kite: Swallow-tailed, 140
Kitty, 155
Kluane Project, 185–7
Knight, James, 79, 119, 125
Knot, Red, 102, 228
Koerner, Lisbet, 18, 20
Krebs, Charles J., 177, 185, 187
Krebs Effect (Fence Effect), 185
Kuckahn, T.S., 109

Labrador Tea (both plant and drink), 247–9
Lac la Pluie, 195

Lacombe, Father, 205
Lake Winnipeg, 195
Lake Winnipegosis, 96
Lampson, C.M., 180
La Pérouse, Jean-François de Galaup, Comte de, 56, 73, 83–5, 149
Lark: Horned, 58, 90, 105, 107, 140, 223
Larvae: warble–fly, 87
Latham, John, 21, 28–30, 77, 112; borrows a Graham-Hutchins manuscript, 173; deems Latin names super-fluous, 29; describes Forster's specimens, 23; describes Hudsonian and Marbled Godwits, 27; and Hutchins, 77, 173; portrait, 29; robs Graham of credit, 165, 169–70; use of Graham-Hutchins journal, 173
Leask, Isaac, 61
Leclaire, Nancy, 207
Lefroy, John Henry, 121
Lemming, 86, 185
Leopold, Aldo, 185
Levant, 152
Levere, Trevor, 85
Leveson-Gower, Richard, 181
Lichtenstein, Martin Heinrich Karl, 23
Light, Alexander, 4, 34–40; arrival, 146; col-lector, 17, 36–40, 98, 110–12; explorer, 34–5, 42; sent specimens to Sloane, 15
Lily, Wood, 247
Lindsay, Debra, 93, 95, 112
Lining, John: first Amer-

ican meteorologist, 134, 137
Linnaeus, Carolus von, 3, 4, 16–21, 24–5, 28–9, 37–9, 44–5, 52, 64, 98, 108–10, 138–42, 200–1; *Methodus*, 19; *Species Plantarum*, 19; *Systema Naturae*, 18–20, 29, 38, 110
Linnean Society of London, 21, 142, 176
Little Ice Age, 11, 85, 115, 117–18, 124, 127
Lloyd, John, 67
Lockhart, James, 112
Logan, Bari, 109
London, Jack, 194
Longspur: Lapland, 74, 106, 223, 230
Loon, 211; Arctic, 52, 99, 219, 222; Common, 99, 215; Red-throated, 99, 212
Louse: Human, 238; Mammal, 76
Lowe, A. Burnett, 95
Ludlum, David, 132
Lumsden, Harry, 188–9
Lynx: Cree name, 206, 244; "lives on rabbits," 179; ten-year cycle of, 97, 177–8, 180, 182, 184, 186

MacDonell, Miles, 93
Macduff, Robert, 37, 44, 67
MacFarlane, Roderick Ross, 112, 155, 177–8, 191
MacKay, D.K., and J.R. MacKay, 121
Mackenzie, Alexander, 11, 115, 117

Macklish, Thomas, 126, 146
MacLaren, Ian, 83
MacLulich, D.A., 177, 181
Macoun, John, 174
Made beaver: unit of currency, 7, 68
Magnol, Pierre, 15
Magpie: Black-billed, 58, 105, 108, 211, 224–5, 229
Mainwaring, 151
Mair, Charles, 178
Mallard, 100, 215
Manchester House, 92
Manitoba Centennial Corporation, 160
Manitoba Historical Society, 160
Manley, Gordon, 113
Marble Island, 79
Marischal College, Aberdeen, 139
Marsh, James, 81
Marten, 155
Marten: American Pine (mammal), 75, 78, 85, 177, 180, 245
Marten, Humphrey, 4, 23–4, 55–60; collector, 57–60, 63, 76, 98, 107, 111; and Cree names, 209–51; and fur trade, 55–6; retires to England, 149; surrenders to La Pérouse, 56
Marten, John America, 56
Martin: Purple (bird), 45, 105, 109, 228; portrait, 51
Martyn, John, 13
Mary, 34–5, 146
Mary III, 146
Mary IV, 147

Maryland, 38
Maskelyne, Neville, 130, 131
Mason, Charles, 131
Mason, Stuart, 16, 17
Matamek Conference on Biological Cycles, 182
Matthews, Vince, vii
Matonabbee, 80, 82–3, 171
Maugenest, Germain, 66, 69, 73
Mayr, Ernst, 108
McAtee, W.L., 111
McAuley, Lily, 205
McDonald, Archibald, 155
McKeevor, Thomas, 151
McTavish, John George, 152
Meadow Lake, 93
Meadowlark: Eastern, 140; Western, 227
Medieval Warm Period, 115
Men: "curious," 12
Mercury: freezing point of, 71
Merganser: Common, 101, 111, 212; Hooded, 27, 101, 141, 210; Red-breasted, 27, 59, 101, 111, 209, 212, 216
Merle, William, 114
Merlin, 101, 140, 172, 206, 227
Merry, Robert, 62
Meteorological journals, HBC, 133
Métis, 93
Meyer, David, 205
Microscope, 86
Middleton, Christopher, 41, 123; Copley gold medal, 72

Mindham, Catherine, 42
Mink: American, 157, 244
Minns, Robert, 121
Mockingbird, 141
Moncrieff, William, 67
Montcalm, 153
Moodie, D.W., 118, 159
Moor, William, 42, 123
Moose, 80, 87, 243
Moose, 35
Moose Fort (Moose Factory), 7; furs did not reach London from, 178; Hutchins left from, 73; population of, 8; re-established, 146; Ruffed Grouse at, 64; sketch, 68; sorry state of, 66; specimens from, 107; surgeons at, 36–7, 127; swans common at, 189; swan skins from, 193; view of, 68; weather at, 133
Morton, Anne, 181
Morton, W.L., 160
Mosquito, 96, 238
Moss, 246
Moultrie, John, 136
Mouse: Deer or White-footed, 239
Mullens, W.H., 17
Müller, P.L.S., 38, 52
Mushroom, 247
Muskox, 241
Muskrat, 177, 183–4, 241, 244–5
Musquash, 34
Mussel, 89, 237

Namaycush, 43
Napper, James, 34–5, 42
Nascopie, 183
National Research Council (USA), 113

Nelson, Richard K., 205

Nelson River, 195

Nesbitt, A. and W., 180

New York Zoological Society, 182

Newcastle-upon-Tyne, 198

Newton, Alfred, 28, 30

Newton, Isaac, 15, 114

Newton, John, 42

Nicholson, Mary, 177, 182

Nighthawk: Common, 59, 104, 139, 141, 205, 227

Noddy, Brown, 142

Nonsuch, 4

North West Passage, 34, 41–2, 79–80

Norton, Mary (Polly), 80

Norton, Moses, 4, 61; chooses Samuel Hearne for Coppermine exploration, 80, 82; collector, 24, 83, 107; explorer, 79

Norton, Richard, chief at Churchill, 35; explorer, 79

Norton, Sarah, 80

Norway House, 93, 195; swan skins from, 193

Nottingham House, 92

Nuthatch: Red-breasted, 105, 222

Ocean Nymph, 156

Okimâsis, Jean, 204, 206, 210

Oldsquaw. *See* Duck, Long-tailed

Orcadians, 165, 205, 213; majority of HBC employees, 56; received pay via Graham, 62; sober and tractable, 7

Oriole: Northern, 141; Orchard, 140

Orkney Islands, 3, 6–7, 11, 84, 165; South Ronaldsay, 11

Orlov, Count, 21

Os penis, 87

Osprey, 140, 215

Otter, River, 243

Owl: Barred, 104; Boreal, 104, 214; Great Gray, 64, 98, 104, 215; Great Horned, 39, 103, 167, 171, 177, 186, 205, 219, 223, 225; Long-eared, 104, 210; Northern Hawk-, 76, 80, 104, 217, 226, portrait, 38; Short-eared, 80, 104, 229–30; Snowy, 27, 37, 80, 90, 104, 166–7, 177, 231, 233

Oxford University, 181

Ozone depletion, 113

Parakeet: Carolina, 140

Parkinson, Sydney, 22

Parry, Edward, 76

Parsnip, Water, 246

Parsons, Ralph, 181

Parula, Northern, 141

Pawpitch, 56

Pelican: American White, 44, 64, 88, 99, 107, 172, 214; Brown, 28; Oriental, 64

Pemmican, 43

Pennant, Thomas, 21, 24–8, 112, 173; access to different Hutchins journal, 173; Arctic Zoology, 25; assists Forster, 172; birds given Latin names by

Gmelin, 21, 24–9; borrows Hutchins text, 171; *British Zoology* is a help to Graham and Hutchins, 53; cites Graham-Hutchins observations, 165; cites Hutchins, 73–4, 77–8; corresponds with Gilbert White, 132; corresponds with Hearne, 132; Cree names, 209, 213–51; deems Latin names superfluous, 29; describes Garden's fish and amphibians, 139, 142; describes new species, 4; glossary, 167; introduced to Graham, 32; and Isham, 53; marginal annotations [incorrectly?] ascribed to, 174; meets Hearne, 85–6; notes Blue Geese predominate to east, 58; omits mention of Marten, 60; portrait, 25; receives Graham's observations from Hutchins, 169; stimulus to Graham, 63

Perch: Yellow, 206, 236

Peregrine. *See* Falcon, Peregrine, 206

Permafrost: map, 5

Perseverance, 157

Phalarope: Red, 45, 103, portrait, 50: Red-necked, 38, 45, 103, 213; portrait, 51

Phenney, George, 138

Philosophical Transactions, 15, 22, 71, 109, 128, 131, 137

Picart, Benjamin, 67

Pickerel, 206, 236

Pigeon: White-crowned, 141; Passenger, 44, 89, 96, 103, 140, 221

Pigot's London Directory, 198

Pike: Northern, 234, 235

Pilgrim, Robert, 37

Pincherry, 250

Pintail: Northern, 100, 111; White-cheeked, 141

Plover: American Golden, 102, 111, 234; Black-bellied, 58, 102, 111; Black-bellied and Golden Plover, 230; Golden, 234; Semi-palmated, 102, 217, 218

Poland, Ernest, 178, 180

Poland, Henry, 177–180

Poland, P.R., 178, 180

Poplar: Balsam, 248; White, 74, 249

Porcupine: American, 39, 40, 89, 240

Porcupine Hills, 199

Porteous, George, 174

Port Nelson, 145

Potts, John, 67

Prairie-Chicken: Greater, 73, 102, 142, 171–2, 221

Pratt, Eleanor, 174

Preble , Edward Alexander, 111, 173, 174, 179

Prestonpans, 62

Price, John 67

Prince, Mr, 88

Prince Albert, 154

Prince George, 153

Prince of Wales, 150–3

Prince of Wales II, 155, 156

Prince of Wales's Fort (Churchill), 34

Prince Rupert II , 42, 55, 147–8

Prince Rupert III, 148

Prince Rupert IV, 62, 107, 148

Prince Rupert V, 153–4

Prince Rupert VI, 154–5

Prince Rupert VII, 156, 157

Prince Rupert VIII, 157

Princess, 15

Pronghorn, 239

Pro pelle cutem, 132

Provincial Archives of Manitoba, 159–60, 188

Ptarmigan, Rock, 25, 74, 88–9, 101, 211, 224; Willow, 8, 10, 38, 76, 87, 88–90, 101, 171, 232; portrait, 37

Public Archives of Canada, 160

Quebec, 52, 200

Queen Charlotte, 150

Queen Mary College, 116, 165

Rabbit Root, 251

Radisson, Pierre-Esprit, 4

Rae, John, 153, 154

Rafinesque, Constantine Samuel, 96

Rail: Yellow, 102, 226

Rain: days with, 124

Ramsay, Robert, 30

Raspberry, 247

Ratt, 206

Raven, C.E., 200

Raven: Common, 105, 217

Ray, John, 13, 18, 26, 200

Red Earth reserve, 205

Red River, 96, 195; Lower, 179, 195

Redpoll: Common, 59,

111; Common and Hoary, 106; Hoary, 111, 230; small winter bird, 211

Redstart: American, 105, 141, 217, 222

Reed Lake House, 133

Resources depletion, 113

Reynolds, William, 67

Rich, E.E., 41, 43, 80, 80, 83, 160

Richardson, George T., 160

Richardson, John, 21, 34, 77, 108, 121, 154, 163, 174, 178, 192, 204–5; Cree names, 208–51

River, Battle, 94; Hayes, 7; Kenogami, 73; Red Deer, 94

Roberts, T.S., 74

Roberts, William, 67

Robertson, Colin, 93

Robertson, John, 10

Robin: American, 76, 105, 140, 204, 226

Robinson, Alfred, 67, 69

Roblin, Duff, 160

Rochester, Alberta, 185

Rocky Mountains, 42, 92, 199

Roe's Welcome Sound, 34

Romantic Movement, 13

Rosamund, 151

Rose-hip, 249

Ross, Bernard Rogan, 86, 112

Rothman, Dr, 18

Rowan, William, 184–5

Royal College of Physi-cians, 16

Royal Geographical Society, 179

Royal Ontario Museum, 200

Royal Society Archives, 166–7

Royal Society fellows: Catesby, 139; Forster, 172; Pennant, 26; Wegg, 32

Royal Society Library, 121

Royal Society museum, 27

Royal Society of Edinburgh, 30–2

Royal Society of London, 4, 6; and Elsa Allen, 58; and Forster, 24, 173; and HBC, 6, 12, 24, 75; HBC meteorology journals, 128; and Hutchins and Middleton, gold medals, 72; and Hutchins manuscript, 74, 107; Jurin, secretary of, 114; and Marten, 57; and Royal College of Physicians, 16; Sloane, president of, 15; and specimens, 12; and swan skins, 75; and Wales and transit of Venus, 10, 32, 69, 130–2. See also Copley gold medal

Royal Society of Uppsala, 25

Rudbeck, Olof, 18

Ruggles, Richard, 94

Rupert, Prince, 4, 6

Rupert's Land, 108

Rupert's Land Record Society, 3

Rupert's Land Research Centre, 3, 165

Sabine, Joseph, 108

St Andrew's University, 137

Sale, Charles, 181

Salmon: as food, 8

Sanderling, 102, 220

Sandfly, 238

Sandpiper: Solitary, 213; Least, 103, 218; Pectoral, 76, 103, 227, 233; Semipalmated, 103, 214; Solitary, 102; Spotted, 102, 214

Sapsucker: Yellow-bellied, 140, 219

Saskatchewan Indian Federated College, 204

Saskatoon Berry, 248; wood, 248

Scallop, 89

Scaup: Greater and Lesser, 100, 209, 229

School: Blue Coat, 10–11; Christ's Hospital, 131; Grey Coat, 10

Schreyer, Edward, 160

Scientific Revolution, 11

Scoter: Black, 100, 216; Surf, 45, 80, 100, 220, 229, portrait, 47; White-winged, 100, 222

Screech-Owl: Eastern, 140

Scroggs, John, 79

Sculpin, 236

Scurvy, 69

Scurvy-grass, 248

Seahorse, 73, 107, 147

Seahorse II, 148, 149

Seahorse III, 149, 150

Seal, 240

Seal River, 92, 111

Seebohm, Henry, 176

Selkirk Settlers, 151

Semple, Robert, 151

Seton, Ernest Thompson, 173, 176, 177, 179

Severn: Arctic Fox rarely reached, 87; Bohemian

Waxwing specimen from, 76; Canada Goose specimen from, 77; Graham at, 61–4, 76, 98, 107, 169–70, 172; Long-eared Owl at, 27; population, 8; rebuilt by Marten, 55; Ruffed Grouse at, 64; Snow Bunting spring arrival, 24, 27; specimens from, 27, 76; swan skins from, 193, 195; type locality, 8

Severn, 84

Shaganappi, 43

Shaw, Angus, 152

Shaw, Peter, 13

Sheep: Bighorn, 241

Shelford, V.E., 183

Sherard, William, 138

Sherer, Patricia, 62

Shoveler: Northern, 100, 111, 219

Shrew: Arctic, 240

Shrike: Northern, 104, 209, 221, 231

Sifton, Clifford, 180

Sirens, 139

Sirluck, Ernest, 160

Sitwell, Sacheverell, 17

Skimmer: Black, 141

Skins, Swan, 75

Skun: Striped, 108, 244

Sloane, Hans, 4, 15, 16, 35, 39, 138; collections, 109

Smallpox, 69

Smith, Francis, 42

Smith, James Edward, 21

Smith, Shirlee Anne, 160

Smithsonian Institution, 6, 86

Snake, 237

Snipe: Common, 103, 227

Snowfall, date of first, 124

Snyder, L.L., 111

Solander, Daniel, 22

Soper, J.Dewey, 181

Sora, 45, 102, 172, 204, 220–1, 226; portrait, 49

Southall, Norman Dauncey, 67

South Branch House, 92

Sparrman, Anders, 22

Sparrow: American Tree, 106, 109, 111, 209; Savannah, 106, 213, 234; White-crowned, 58, 64, 86, 106, 216, 222–3; White-throated, 106, 216, 223

Spider, 89

Spitalfields Mathematical Society, 13

Sporer Minimum, 115

Spotwood, Andrew, 137

Spruce: White, 248

Squirrel: Northern Flying, 244–5; Ground, 186, 239; Red, 186, 239

Standard Roman Orthography, 206, 210

Staunton, Richard, 79

Stearns, R.P., 72, 139

Stephenson, William, 67

Sterling, Tom, 90

Stewart, Larry, 13

Stickleback, 235, 236

Strahan and Cadell, 84

Strait, Hudson, 6–7, 39

Strawberry, 250

Stresemann, Erwin, 23

Strickland , Hugh, 21

Strivewell, 79

Stromness, 3, 7, 178; HBC ships sailed from, 6–7

Stupart, R.F., 174

Sturgeon, 236

Sturgeon, Lake, 235

Sucker: Longnose, 24, 64, 235; White, 235

Sunspots, 96

Superior, 155

Sutherland, George, 66

Swainson, William, 29, 174

Swallow: Bank, 59, 105, 229; Cliff, 64, 105; Tree, 59, 64, 105, 228

Swan: Bewick's, 193; Black-necked, 194; feast, 170; swan quills and skins, 4, 75, 90; 188–99; Trumpeter, 4, 89, 90, 96, 100, 188–9, 217; Trumpeter or Tundra, 39, 88–90, 125, 217, 219; Tundra, 52, 89, 100, 188–9, 193, 219, 232

Swan Lake House, 92

Swann, H. Kirke, 17

Swan River: swan skins from, 195

Swan skins: uses of, 193

Swift, Chimney, 141

Swynnerton, G., 183

Tahiti, 131

Tanager, Summer, 141

Tea: Labrador, 247

Teal: Blue-winged, 141, 215; Green-winged, 100, 211–12

Tern: Arctic, 59, 80, 88, 103, 214, 217–18, 234; Black, 103

Tessin, Carl Gustav, 19

Thomas, M.K., 115

Thomas, Thomas, 67, 128

Thompson, David, 10–11, 57

Thompson, Edward, 36

Thrasher: Brown, 140

Ti pi, 43

Titmouse: Tufted, 141

Toad, 237

Tomison, William, 11, 56, 76, 162

Torricelli, 114

Tournefort, Joseph Pitton de, 15, 18

Towhee, Eastern, 140

Traders: brought disease, guns and ammunition, knives, kettles and pots, 10

Treaty of Paris, 56

Tree-line: map of, 5; moving, 85, 117, 134

Trinity Lane, 159

Trout: Lake, 235

Tullibee, 236

Turner, John, 67

Turnor, Philip, 11, 32, 66, 92

Turnstone, Ruddy, 52, 75, 102, 218, 221

Turtle, 39, 53, 237

Umfreville, Edward, 55, 170

United States National Museum, 178

University at Leyden, 18

University of Alberta, 184–5

University of British Columbia, 121, 184

University of Edinburgh, 30, 139

University of Erlangen, 29

University of London, 116, 165

University of Lund, 18

University of Manitoba, 159–60

University of Minnesota, 185

University of Orange, 15

University of Oxford, 24, 26, 138, 181–2

University of Toronto, 85, 160, 181, 200

University of Uppsala, 18–19

University of Wilna, 23

University of Winnipeg, 3

University of Wisconsin, 185

Uppsala University, 18, 20, 45

Utrecht, Treaty of, 6, 119

Vaillant, Sébastien, 18

van Kirk, Sylvia, 79

Venus: transit of, 32, 69, 130

Vireo: Philadelphia, 105, 209; Red-eyed, 141

Vole: Red-backed, 185–6

Vulture: Turkey, 230

Wales, William, 10, 23, 32, 69, 84, 130–1

Walker, John, 4, 30–1

Walrus, 156, 246

Warble-fly larvae, 87

Warbler: Blackpoll, 64, 105, 172, 209; Magnolia, 105, 217; Wilson's, 105, 222; Yellow, 59, 105, 224

Ware, William, 176

Wasp, 237

Waterhen Indian Reserve, 93

Waterstone, Menzie, 62

Watson, William, 173

Waugh, Earle, 207

Waxwing: Bohemian, 76, 105, 172, 209

Wear, 152

Weasel: Long-tailed, 242

Weather information: descriptive, instrumental, phenologic, 129; pre-instrumental, 124

Wegg, Samuel, 4, 31–3, 69, 130, 132, 172; portrait, 32

Wells, Robert, 136

West, John, 152

Westminster, 154

Weywey, 44

Whale: Beluga, 245; Bowhead, 242

Whelpley, J.D., 180

Whimbrel, 29, 59, 89, 102, 108–9, 233

Whistling-Duck: Fulvous, 28

White, Gilbert, 26, 60, 63, 132

White, John, 63

White, Thomas, 36

Whitefish, 234

Wigeon: American, 100, 212

Wilder, Laura Ingalls, 194

Williams, Glyndwr, 64, 160–1, 165, 169, 173

Williams, William, 152

Willow, 74, 249

Wills, Giles, 67

Willughby, Francis, 24, 200–1

Wilson, Cynthia, 116

Winds, north: frequency of, 118

Withers, C.W.J., 31

Wolf: Timber, 241

Wolfart, H.C., 206

Wolfe, James, 201

Wollaston Lake, 92

Wolvengrey, Arok, 203–4,

206, 210

Wolverene, 39, 240–1, 243

Wolverine. See Wolverene

Woodchuck, 246

Wood-lice, 238

Woodpecker: Downy, 58, 104, 140, 225; Hairy, 104, 141, 171, 209; Ivory-billed, 140; Pileated, 104, 140, 219, 222; Red-bellied, 140; Red-headed, 104, 140, 209; Three-toed, 31, 52, 104, 166, 225

Worm, 238

Wren, Christopher, 113

Wright, John, 67

Yellowlegs: Greater and Lesser, 58, 102, 111, 220, 228–9

York Factory, 3, 7; Arctic Fox at, 87; arrival of geese and of Snow Buntings, 134; Black Bear upstream from, 88; boxes of plants from, 44; captured by La Pérouse, 73; Fidler at, 92–3; Fidler tested alcohol strength at, 95; French occupation of, 6; furs did not reach London from, 178; Graham at, 11, 61–2, 107, 169; Hutchins at, 56, 66, 76, 107, 131, 169; Isham at, 41–54; Marten at, 55; population of, 7; Preble at, 111; sketched by Hearne, 8, 85; smallpox prevented by isolation and quarantine, 69; specimens from, 24, 74, 167; specimens of trees and shrubs from went astray, 37; swan skins from, 192–3, 195; Tomison waited at, 56; visited by colloquium, 165; weather at, 32, 70, 117–21, 123, 125–7, 133